HAROLD LARWOOD

Duncan Hamilton's *Provided You Don't Kiss Me* won the William Hill Sports Book of the Year for 2007 and a British Sports Book Award in 2008. In 2009, he was awarded the William Hill, again, for *Harold Larwood,* as well as winning the prestigious Wisden Book of the Year for 2009 and biography of the year at the 2010 British Sports Book Awards. He lives in West Yorkshire.

'It's a tour de force of research, social history and lucid prose which returns Larwood, the wronged working-class hero chosen to be England's principal strike weapon in the 1932–33 'bodyline' Ashes series, to his rightful place in history' *Independent on Sunday*

'Written with great understanding and empathy for the dangerously fast bowler who was cast adrift by his country after the Empire-threatening controversy of Bodyline . . . Many books have been written about the Bodyline series and this is one of the finest' *The Times*

'It is odd that this is the first biography of Larwood the scapegoat, a great bowler but a stubborn man. Hamilton has filled the gap magnificently' *Sunday Times*

'It's a great story, with Larwood's touching loyalty to the captain Douglas Jardine and his win-at-all-costs ruthlessness – and the disgraceful way Larwood was hung out to dry by the cricketing establishment. This book is his vindication' *Independent*

'A first-rate piece of work, [and] a fine example of superior cricket writing . . . This is a literate, sometimes elegiac look at a figure who had the rare ability to decide a whole series' *The Age*

Australian sports lovers will find this an absorbing account of how Larwood stymied the phenomenon of Bradman during the 1932–33 Bodyline series . . . [it is] well-written and fair and includes a series of magnificent photographs' *Weekend Australian*

'One of the year's best sports books . . . Hamilton's evocative biography expertly centres on the shy, working class genius struggling amid the fallout' *Metro*

'We can't write a best books of the year page and not recommend Duncan Hamilton's magnificent tome on the world's fastest bowler and his disgraceful betrayal by the MCC' *SPORT*

'He concentrates on the bittersweet romance of his career, and the result is an excellent cricket biography, one of the best of recent times. Thoroughly recommended' *All Out Cricket*

'A brilliant new biography' *Observer*

'This compelling new biography brings another age back to life – a book equally for people who don't follow cricket as those who do. Likely to be another crossover bestseller and a favourite summer holiday read' *News of the World*

'A thrilling and moving recreation of the triumph, betrayal and redemption of a working-class hero and forgotten titan of English cricket' *Yorkshire Post*

'It's a wonderful story, lyrically told and . . . beautifully produced' *Guardian*

'A fascinating marriage of sport and social history . . . Having previously written an acclaimed biography of Brian Clough, Hamilton was already acknowledged as one of Britain's finest sporting authors. This book serves to cement his position' *Northern Echo*

Chosen as a 2009 sports book of the year by *Sydney Morning Herald*, *Metro*, *The Australian*, *Observer*, *Daily Telegraph*, *Sunday Times* *Irish Times*, *Independent on Sunday*, *Wisden Cricketer*, *Independent*, *Scottish Morning Herald*, *Sunday Telegraph*, *The Age*

Harold Larwood, 1927.

HAROLD LARWOOD

DUNCAN
HAMILTON

Quercus

First published in Great Britain in 2009 by Quercus
This paperback edition published in 2010 by

Quercus
21 Bloomsbury Square
London
WC1A 2NS

A CIP catalogue record for this book is available from the British Library

ISBN 978 1 84916 207 4

Design by Balley Design Limited

Printed and bound in Great Britain by Clays Ltd. St Ives plc

To those who travelled from afar
and made a new life in Australia

CONTENTS

PART 3

Australian captain Bill Woodfull ducks to avoid a Larwood bouncer at Brisbane, February 1933, with a posse of short legs in attendance.

FOREWORD

KICKING BRADMAN UP THE ARSE

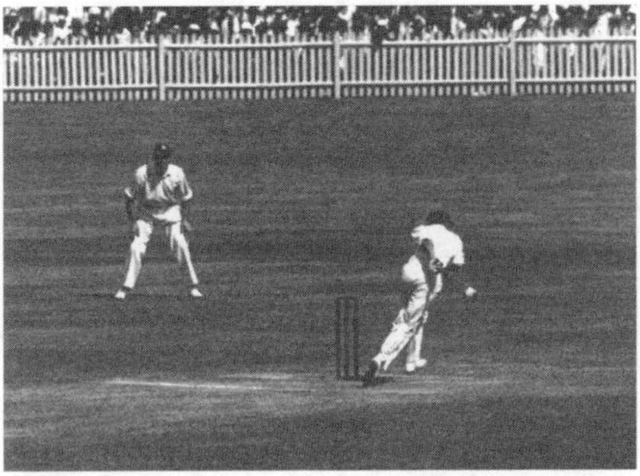

Bradman is inconvenienced by Larwood in the fifth Test at Sydney, February 1933.

Trent Bridge, July 1977

The old man laid his hand lightly on the pavilion gate. His closely cropped hair was as white as hoar frost, his caramel-coloured face lined and pinched with age. The lenses in his square, black-framed spectacles were as thick as double glazing. He wore a pale checked shirt with a gold fastener between the collars, a tightly knotted wool tie, and a dull brown jacket which looked half a size too big for him – slightly too broad across the shoulders, an inch too long in the tail and sleeves.

He carried himself with the dignity of a veteran from the Great War, his back as straight as he could make it, his chest thrust slightly forward, as if there were a row of ribboned medals fastened across his top pocket. Around him were a knot of stooped, flabby men of much the same vintage, dressed in shirtsleeves and braces, who stared at him as though revering a saint at the altar. It was early evening. The sun was still bright and the dark shadows elongated everything, like a fairground mirror. The ground was almost empty, the stands echoing to the drag of brooms which swept away the litter of a long day of cricket-watching.

A straggly crocodile line of young lads carrying bags and swinging worn, heavily taped bats walked around the boundary edge without glancing at the old man or his admirers. One of them tapped a ball on his bat. It caught the edge and rolled towards the pavilion gate. The old man stopped the ball with his foot and then picked it up. He briefly weighed the ball in his hand and rubbed his thumb on the leather before throwing it back with a careful underhand lob, the sort of soft delivery you'd get in the back garden or on the beach. 'Here you are, son,' he said. The lad reached out with his bat, knocked the ball into the air and grabbed it, like catching a falling apple from a tree. All this happened in an eye-blink; it was just a moment that passed unnoticed and without fanfare. The lad – a year or two short of his teens, I'd guess – casually tucked his bat under his arm, stuffed the ball into his trouser pocket and sauntered away without a backward glance. The old man carried on talking before shaking hands, saying his polite goodbyes, slowly climbing the pavilion steps and vanishing inside.

I was sitting a few yards away, too shy to approach the old man at first and then too slow to decide what to do when he walked past me. I missed my chance to speak to Harold Larwood, but I like to claim that I saw the last ball he ever 'bowled' at Trent Bridge.

Harold holding the ball for a swinger. ?

Harold Larwood demonstrates how to hold the ball in the improbable setting of his own back garden. He described this delivery as his 'swinger'.

I was in my first summer as a part-time junior reporter for a local news and sports agency, where it was usually my turn to make the tea or type out copy and invoices. I'd been assigned to Trent Bridge to send score updates, organize the telephones and dictate to copytakers. Extra phones for the Test – the third of a five-match Ashes series that England won 3–0 – were plugged into the long dusty corridor outside the press box and faced away from the play. I acted as gopher for the national newspaper cricket correspondents. The Trent Bridge Test was the one in which Geoffrey Boycott ground out his 98th hundred and Ian Botham took five wickets on his debut. But I remember it for Larwood. For me, the privilege of being there was to get close to him.

If you grew up in Nottingham, as I did, you knew all about Larwood. He was the local legend. You were told about him as a rite of passage. As boys we propped up an orange box as a makeshift wicket or used the lamp post in the street – floodlit cricket long before Kerry Packer thought of it or Twenty20 was a gleam in someone's inventive eye. There were men still alive back then who had bought cheap tickets to watch Larwood play, stood him a pint or queued for a sight of him at the railway station on his arrival home from Australia after the Bodyline tour of 1932–33. If you measured out a long run-up between the handful of parked cars in our cul-de-sac, naively believing that the length of your stride determined the speed at which you'd deliver the ball, there was always a voice behind you ready to chide: 'You'll never be as fast as Harold Larwood. He were quickest there's ever been, lad. Ask your grandad.'

Nearly everyone had a Larwood story, usually about batsmen too frightened to go in against him or the miles per hour he generated or how much alcohol he could sup without falling over. A besotted friend of my father's went so far as to sit a gold-framed photograph of Larwood on the sideboard, as if he was a member of the family. He always referred to him as though he and Larwood shared the same bloodline too. He called him 'Lol', the nickname Larwood was given almost as soon as he arrived at Trent Bridge in 1923. The nickname stuck to such an extent that Larwood referred to himself as 'Lol' too. He signed many of his letters with it, and men such as my father's friend would say 'Lol' naturally in conversations to create a spurious intimacy between him and themselves. It sounded to me as though 'Lol' was such a pal that he would stand everyone a beer in the pub later that evening. My father's friend kept cuttings of Larwood's career in an oversized Woolworth's scrapbook – passed on to him by his own father – and I would turn the grey pages so often that I could recite the smudgy multi-decked headlines like lines of poetry:

LARWOOD TOO QUICK FOR AUSTRALIANS
Terrific pace puts MCC in command of Test

LARWOOD ON BODYLINE
I never bowled at the man

LARWOOD'S AMAZING HOMECOMING
Mobbed by admirers at the station

Nottingham was a coal city. Skeletal mine headstocks were dotted across the county, and around each one lay the dug-out clay, the slag heaps and the messy debris of the industry. You could smell the coal that lingered everywhere; damp and musty, like one long washing day. Everything seemed to be soot-stained – the streets down which the coal cart rattled, the houses with funnels of curling smoke from the miners' allowance of free coal, the shards of coal that fell out of the bags or were shaken off the clothes of men who toted it with blackened hands and faces. The air was gritty with dust. Even the leaves on the trees were coated in smuts. Larwood had been a pitman. He knew what it was like to feel the cage jerk, and then rapidly descend from daylight into darkness. He scraped the skin off his back, his bare flesh grazing the jagged edges of the narrow tunnels which he crept along on his knees. His hands became calloused from tightly gripping a pick or a shovel. His bitten nails were rimmed black. The miners my father worked alongside – though none of them ever saw him play – regarded Larwood as one of their own and would have nothing said against him. He was working class, manifestly proud of it and made of the right stuff, which was good enough for them. When I saw him it was still difficult to connect the thinnish, short and round-shouldered old man in front of me – he was nearly 73 by then – with the raw-boned fast bowler whom I'd read about in the scrapbooks, or even the matey 'Lol' who, though he didn't know it, counted as everybody's friend. He stroked his chin, readjusted his spectacles on the bridge of his nose and occasionally ran his fingers across his bristly head. As he spoke he glanced at his hands, as if the palms were a map he could read. I focused intently on his wrinkled fingers and imagined them unblemished half a century earlier, laid down or across the thick seam of a new cherry-red ball, polished like a pearl. I wondered how many times Larwood had passed through the pavilion gate, whether or not he saw Trent Bridge as it had been rather than the way it was at that moment, and if any ghosts were there to meet him. I thought about the framed black-and-white photographs of him that hung in the Long Room. In one photograph I saw Larwood side on and at the very point of delivery. His strong neck and powerful back were arched. The eyes, just inky dots, were clearly focused on his target. The left leg was so high that the batsman must have seen the spikes, like jagged teeth, and the worn sole of his boot. His right arm was about to fire the ball in a perfect, swift arc. In another, he was standing in a team group wearing cap and piped blazer: 'Nottinghamshire: Championship Winners 1929' said the caption, without listing the names. There was no mistaking the 24-year-old Larwood: second from the left on the back row, the cap pulled tight and low over his high forehead, as if trying to hide from the camera.

The classical action. At full speed, Harold Larwood flowed like a bolt of pure silk.

However hard it was to reconcile those images with the one I saw in the flesh, I knew I was within touching distance of a 'Great Man' and of greatness itself. I reckoned then, as I do now, that Larwood was England's fastest-ever bowler and, for a period, the fastest bowler that cricket has ever seen; though, of course, most batsmen didn't see him, which is the point. He had electric pace, and delivered it in jolts of four or five overs at a time. The pros used to say Larwood had 'nip', a gentle euphemism for the frank admission that he was 'too bloody quick' for nearly all of them. In the early 1930s Larwood was timed at 96 mph. Today the indispensable Hawk-Eye uses six high-speed cameras to record a bowler's speed. Larwood was measured by a man in a bowler hat who stood halfway down the pitch with a stopwatch in his hand and then did his calculations on lined paper with a stubby pencil. An Australian mathematician with a stopwatch – but minus the bowler hat – used the same method and reached a figure of 99 mph. But with a clanking, Heath Robinson-style contraption, Larwood's bowling was electronically timed in an experiment at the White City at over 100 mph. 'I can't shout about the accuracy of any of them,' said Larwood, who supposed that he bowled at 'well over' 90 mph and 'sometimes at 100 mph'. That belief was expressed with neither smugness nor conceit. 'There were umpires who'd seen me bowl, and everyone else up till the 1970s. They said I was a yard or two faster. That's good enough for me,' he said. We can only speculate about the true figure. There isn't sufficient film of Larwood to use Hawk-Eye's sophisticated gadgetry and definitively calculate his exact speed. But it was taken for granted by the poor souls facing him that the ball would fly at them between 95 mph and 100 mph. And no one disputed the fact that Larwood was capable of both maintaining that pace and bowling with extraordinary accuracy. Against him, the distressed batsman had less than half a second to decide:

- The line and length of the ball
- The position his feet should be in to play it
- The shot he should choose

It demanded the rigorous co-ordination of brain, eye, hand and feet to survive. The batsman saw nothing but a flash of red; often not even that. The Australian Bill O'Reilly explained most eloquently of all what it was like to be on strike against him, the bat in the blockhole tapping nervously against hard, dusty earth. 'He came steaming in,' he said of Larwood, 'and I moved right across behind my bat, held perfectly straight in defence of my centre stump. Just before he delivered the ball something hit the middle of my bat with such force that it was almost dashed from my hands. It was the ball.'

I once asked John Arlott, who had watched Larwood both before and after the Bodyline series, how quick he had been. Arlott tucked his left hand into his jacket pocket, the prelude to some deep thinking. He paused for what seemed to me like an hour, but in reality lasted a minute at most. 'You cannot imagine how fast he was,' he said in that ravishing voice marinated in vats of fine wine. 'Sometimes, depending on where you were standing, you couldn't pick up the ball with the naked eye at all.' With trepidation – for to a callow, nervous teenager he looked like an angry wasp about to sting – I put the same question to Jack Fingleton, who batted against Larwood during Bodyline and became his friend. I was running Fingleton's copy for *The Sunday Times* and, after returning with one take shortly after the tea interval began, I took an exceptionally deep and fearful breath before launching into my interrogation of the formidable-looking figure hunched over his portable typewriter. At the mention of Larwood, Fingleton mellowed. A softer look appeared in his eyes, perhaps because he couldn't believe someone of my age – a boy with long hair and a scruffy grey sweater – was interested enough to ask him about the distant past. 'About twice as fast as anyone out there,' he said, jabbing his thumb, like a man hitching a lift, towards the Trent Bridge pitch. 'You needed your wits and your heart to play him.' He instinctively laid his hand over his own heart. 'He was so strong, you see.' Fingleton tugged at the peak of his flat cap, as if adjusting it out of respect for Larwood. 'You know,' he said, 'not many batsmen could play him. Those who did have still got the bruises.' Fingleton became so committed on the subject of Larwood, and I was so absorbed in what he said, that I forgot to give him back the two pages of copy, with his scribbled changes in blue ink, that I'd just telephoned on his behalf. I still have them, pressed like autumn leaves between the pages of one of his books. Fingleton talked about Stan McCabe – he'd mentioned him in his piece that afternoon – and his valiant innings against Larwood at Sydney in the opening Bodyline Test. He finished by telling me, 'I won't see a faster bowler and if you do, you'll be a lucky fella.'

The bats in Larwood's era look insubstantial compared with today's, like toothpicks next to railway sleepers. The average weight was around 2lb 4oz, the edges almost as thin as a credit card, and the bat wasn't as well sprung. The pads were flimsy too, just thin strips of poorly upholstered canvas. White cloth gloves had short rubber spikes to cushion the impact of the ball, but in reality offered scant protection to the fingers. Of course, there were no helmets and terrified batsmen stuffed bath towels down their trousers as makeshift thigh pads or into their shirts as bulky padding across the ribs. Some, especially the Australians during Bodyline (including Fingleton), wore special protection over the torso. It resembled a quilted bedjacket. But nothing stopped Larwood . . .

* * *

When generations separate them, it is almost impossible to judge one cricketer definitely against another. As Donald Bradman made clear: 'Dealing with comparisons in cricket is harder and more complex than in most other sports.' You can, he argued, assess the merits of swimmers strictly from the clock because 'the water hasn't changed' (he was talking well before swimsuits became scientifically bespoke). He went on: 'No such comparison is possible in cricket. Averages can be a guide . . . but are not conclusive because pitches and conditions have changed.' So had the cricket ball, added Bradman, and the height and width of the wickets too. The laws of the game had also been refined. If you can't trust statistics, you're obliged to rely on anecdotal evidence. Larwood emerges favourably from it. Whatever his figures, nearly everyone who played against him – and most who witnessed the pace he achieved – described him unequivocally as the finest and fastest quick bowler of his era, and any era before it.

At its meanest – which is how Larwood practised it – fast bowling is a bloody affair and the fast bowler is like the slaughterman in the abattoir. Think of Dennis Lillee, who looked angry enough to shoot you dead, and Jeff Thomson, whose slingy action made each delivery slice through the air so quickly that your eyes strained to glimpse it. Think of the West Indians: the smoothness of Michael Holding, for whom the words grace and graceful seemed to have been minted; the frenetic energy in Malcolm Marshall and Andy Roberts. Think of Joel Garner, who loomed over batsmen like a church steeple. And think of Keith Miller, John Snow, Fred Trueman, Frank Tyson, Wes Hall, Ray Lindwall, Brett Lee, *et al.* If you could put Larwood in front of them now, you'd see each one give a deferential low bow towards him.

At five foot seven and a half inches tall, and less than eleven stone in weight, Harold Larwood looked physically less formidable than his predecessors, contemporaries or successors, but he produced enough fierce heat to turn the most bellicose of batsmen into pacifists against

Harold Larwood and Bill Voce reminisce on the outfield at Trent Bridge during the third Test match against Australia, July 1977. The interviewer is the BBC's Peter West.

him. He was a devastatingly brutal and physically intimidating bowler, who routinely inflicted pain. He bruised flesh, broke bones, knocked batsmen unconscious, had them hoisted off on a stretcher and hospitalized. Some deliveries were so fast that it was impossible to duck or dance out of the way of them. If Larwood hit you, with uppercut digs into the gut or chest, or with a ball that skidded like a pebble off water onto the thigh bone, the mathematicians calculated that it was the equivalent of absorbing two tonnes.

Among the men who kept wicket to him, Les Ames used to say that he stood so far back that he was 'in another county' when he took the ball. During Larwood's first tour to Australia in 1928–29, George Duckworth laid strips of raw beef inside his gloves to protect his palms. The stench from the meat in the dry Australian heat made his slip fielders bilious. Duckworth's palms hurt all the same. Nottinghamshire's Ben Lilley strapped his fingers and hands so heavily that he looked like a burns victim. He still chipped, fractured and broke bones and accepted it as a part of a hazardous occupation. By the end of his career, the joints on Lilley's hand were badly knotted. The fingers were bent and thick and splayed, like tree branches.

A few overs of Larwood at his fastest were like a public stoning. He frightened batsmen out. Of his 1,427 first-class wickets – in an era when pitches were generally friendly for batsmen – 743 were bowled. It might be an exaggeration – but only a slight one – to say that he could turn a stump to sawdust. When Larwood bowled, the Trent Bridge groundstaff always made sure there were three sets of spare stumps: Larwood was certain to break, splinter or shave at least one of them, possibly two. He could turn a batsman to pulp too. *Wisden* provides supporting evidence of his extraordinary skill. He took one hundred wickets in a season eight times. He headed the first-class averages in five summers – 1927, 1928, 1931, 1932 and, post-Bodyline, 1936. No other bowler of the twentieth century – or after it – has equalled that feat. His sprint to the crease was so fast that he had a 'drag' of 32 inches after his final stride.

None of this seemed possible to me when I eventually saw him. He resembled my grandfather; a kindly gent who would slip you a crafty ten bob for sweets and comics, and tip his hat and stand up when a woman came into a room. It was impossible to believe that, during Bodyline, the Australians could ever have labelled this old man 'The Wrecker', 'The Murderer on Tip Toe' or 'The Killer'. Or that he'd been spat at in the face. Or that he'd been called 'a bastard' who should 'fuck off home'. Or that he'd ever been sent hate mail – unsigned letters written in red and green ink that threatened to poison or shoot him and then feed him to the dingoes.

I remember the fuss around Larwood's return to Nottingham in 1977, the frisson of anticipation for me. The homecoming headlines in the local newspapers were strung across the page like bunting. After he caught sight of something better than austerity Britain and emigrated to Australia in 1950, a decision which seemed utterly implausible at the time, Larwood had been back only once before, almost a decade earlier. He had neither the finances nor the inclination to return more often. But I'd seen a few snatched seconds of him on TV six months earlier during the Centenary Test in Melbourne. Alongside his 'mucker' Bill Voce, he was introduced, and his name put on the scoreboard. He and Voce went out to the wicket. It was as if a history book had been opened and the two of them had walked straight off the page: 44 years had passed since the pair bowled in Australia together. The difference in physique remained striking. Voce was a wide, tall, bull-muscled man, very evidently a quick bowler in his playing days. Beside him, Larwood was diffident and almost bird-like. You couldn't conceive that he had been at least five yards faster than his friend. He had the light build of a spinner, who might once have given the odd one a tweak and turned it a foot. Voce took off his jacket, handed it to Larwood and began to mark out his run theatrically with long strides. The crowd adored the make-believe. As the scene was briefly played out, it became obvious from the applause and the admiring expressions on faces all around the MCG that the Australian public regarded Larwood as a figure to be venerated. In Melbourne and at Trent Bridge, where Larwood looked so contented with his lot, and comfortably at ease with himself, I would never have detected the malevolent legacy of Bodyline. In time I came to realize that the impact of it had changed everything for him.

* * *

On the day when I saw him at Trent Bridge I was aware that Bodyline had made Larwood's name, briefly bringing him commercial benefit in a decade when the basic salary for a six-month Ashes tour was a miserly £400. I didn't know it had broken him for a long while afterwards, or begun his black disillusionment with cricket, which culminated in his desertion of the professional game and a decade spent living – as he starkly put it – as a 'recluse'. I didn't realize – because Larwood shared it with no one but his family and closest friends – the mental torment he'd been through, the grievances he had silently stored up, the anger that had settled like a stone inside him. He became unsparing with himself, and the interior monologues about Bodyline dominated his waking hours. It was grief and mourning on a grand scale. I didn't know either about the smears and whispers, the words that slid out of the side of the mouth or from behind the back of the hand about him and his bowling action: the accusations – which Donald Bradman implied in 1960 with his use of cinefilm from Bodyline – that Larwood was 'a chucker', a man who threw his fastest ball.

When I did find out, it struck me that Larwood embodied the poet Dryden's line that: 'Ev'n victors are by victories undone.' With 33 wickets, he was the undisputed victor of Bodyline. But it was a pyrrhic victory.

The series – Douglas Jardine's plot, his use of Larwood to nullify Bradman's majesty and the responses it provoked – camouflages achingly sad human consequences. History embalmed Larwood in the Bodyline series, as though he died bowling it. As a cricketer, he is preserved only in its controversy. As a man, he is hardly preserved at all except in the place in which he was born and the places where he lived.

Bodyline is so familiar that it doesn't require an elaborate description. The basic dictionary definition is enough: 'Bodyline: the policy of bowling the ball straight at the batsman so that it will strike the body.' Larwood protested that the term Bodyline was 'evil' and 'detestable' because it suggested that he bowled specifically to maim the batsman. He called it, less abrasively, 'leg theory' (its dictionary definition is notably less threatening: 'Leg theory: the policy of bowling on the striker's legs with a trap of leg-side fielders'). Whichever phrase you prefer – and Bodyline is the convenient shorthand – Larwood became inseparable from it. It attached itself to him like the hyphen in a double-barrelled name. Everything about Larwood, and everything he did, bore the memory of the thirteen weeks of that Ashes series. The complicated presence of that past always lurked in his present. Bodyline defined him to such an extent that his name was used as the way into debates about it. He died knowing what the opening line of his obituaries would be. 'It'll be Harold Larwood, the Bodyline bowler,' he'd say.

The strength of any plan depends on its timing. For Jardine, time and tide were synchronized in 1932–33. Larwood was bowling with firebrand energy. He was hardened by seven seasons in the first-class game. He knew all the tricks. Mere figures alone don't reflect the scale of the psychological advantage he gave Jardine in Australia. His softening-up of a batsman so that Voce or Gubby Allen could remove them later on; the turmoil and apprehension he created within the Australian dressing room and especially in Bradman's psyche; and the swagger and brash cockiness he displayed, a 'no bastard's going to beat me' attitude, which gave the team a belief in itself. With Larwood alongside him as both rapier and bludgeon, Jardine couldn't lose. The Australians tacitly conceded as much in the widespread adoption of the lines from a music-hall revue, which were written when Bodyline was fresh and occupying acres of newsprint. Many a true word is said in jest, and the song expressed Australian thoughts more perfectly than any contemporaneous report ever managed to achieve:

Now this new kind of cricket
Takes courage to stick it,
There's bruises and fractures galore.
After kissing their wives
And insuring their lives,
Batsmen fearfully walk out to score.
With a prayer and a curse
They prepare for the hearse,
Undertakers look on with broad grins.
Oh, they'd be a lot calmer,
In Ned Kelly's armour,
When Larwood, the wrecker, begins.

Larwood dismissed such doggerel as 'drivel'. But at his pace, and with his precision accuracy – he could hit three florins left on a length – it's debatable whether even Ned Kelly's armour would have been enough to repel him. A ball from Larwood would probably have punched a hole clean through it.

The cardinal points of Bodyline have been so well mapped that the mention of it instantly creates a jumble of moving images in the mind. The Adelaide Oval, the crucible for its ugly passions, is dipped in pure light for the third Test. There is the sweep of the overflowing Giffen Stand, its flags aflutter. There is Larwood bowling at full throttle, the ball bumped into the pitch and taken by a wicketkeeper standing in the far distance. There is Bradman backing away, mostly well outside leg stump. There is the Australian captain Bill Woodfull taking a ball over the heart from Larwood and clutching his breastbone. There is Bert Oldfield struck on the head – again from a Larwood delivery – and staggering away like a drunk thrown out of a saloon bar. There is Jardine in his Harlequin cap and white silk cravat, his stick frame like a Giacometti sculpture. There are eight pairs of clutching hands waiting for the leg-side catch. There are the mounted state police.

What came next – the fear of a feral riot, the accusations that Bodyline just wasn't cricket and the string of cables between the MCC and the Australian Cricket Board of Control, which threatened the rest of the tour and even relations between the two countries, is constantly raked over in search of any fact that might have been overlooked or any minor detail worthy of reinterpretation.

Those of us devoted to sport are frequently guilty of magnifying its importance. Sometimes we over-dramatize and hype it, judge it disproportionately and give it a status that on sober reflection is nearly always either wrong-headed or plainly unmerited. We just get carried away. But Bodyline is one of the very rare examples of a seminal sporting event, the significance of which is genuine and lasting and transcends the narrow field of the sport itself. Even people who neither cared for, nor knew anything about cricket, felt compelled to voice an opinion about it. Bodyline was the shifting of cricket's tectonic plates, which split the ground beneath its administrators. The political convulsions stretched almost to breaking the bonds of Empire and brought about a pivotal change in the game's rules.

Even today you can't be neutral on the issues that Bodyline created. Either you believe Larwood's claim that he didn't bowl specifically to injure or you condemn him for deliberately trying to cause bodily harm. Either you believe the Australian batsmen were too ready to squeal about Bodyline or you argue that its deployment was an unjustifiable case of gross intimidation, which shattered the spirit and the ethics of the game. And either you think the MCC was treacherous and cruelly pusillanimous in the way it sacrificed Larwood's Test career, having failed both to persuade and then threaten him into apologizing for bowling Bodyline, or you feel that its action was diplomatically prudent and for the long-term benefit of the game.

The repercussions that flowed from Bodyline washed away the rest of Larwood's Test career. He was the scapegoat, tarnished for obeying his captain's instructions and subjugating the world's greatest batsman. As far as the MCC was concerned, he was unclean, an outcast. Were it not for the national bowling averages in the mid-1930s, Larwood said, he might as well have been 'invisible' as far as Lord's was concerned. The MCC hurt him with silence rather than with words. But the compelling aspect of Bodyline is what Larwood suffered after it was over. His tragedy and triumph is a drama of almost Shakespearean proportions. The main strands of the plot, and the various sub-plots that grew in a tangled vine around it, embrace betrayal and injustice, sacrifice and class snobbery, loyalty and, eventually, redemption, reconciliation and peace.

Whatever your view of the MCC – and mine is that its action was callous and morally indefensible – Larwood was tossed aside for expediency's sake, as if he no longer mattered to them as either a bowler or a human being. His work was over, and he could be dismissed and forgotten. This was the period in which the demarcation between gentleman amateurs and salty professionals from working-class backgrounds was as well defined as the differences in military rank. The two camps didn't share a gate on to the outfield, let alone the same dressing room. Amateurs were given the courtesy of being addressed as Mr; professionals were written and spoken to by surname. The counties and the MCC showed a depressingly feudal attitude towards them. Most professionals were viewed as tradesman or hired hands, who did menial labouring jobs. The MCC got away with its shabby treatment of Larwood because the prevailing mood was that the pros were expendable. Devoid of duty and kindness, the MCC thought it owed Larwood nothing, and had no obligation to him. It didn't understand that for those embroiled in it, Bodyline was akin to a war, and the stresses it placed on its chief protagonists – the poor bloody infantry – induced symptoms that were related to shell-shock. There was the constant nervous tension Larwood felt at being the centre of attention. He was verbally abused inside and outside Australian grounds. Whenever he picked up a newspaper, or tuned in to the radio, his name was the prefix or suffix to a volley of criticism about unsportsmanlike behaviour. After Adelaide, there was always the prospect of personal bodily harm too. There were plenty of people prepared to pick a fight with him. At home he found that the Post Office knew where to find him. Letters, their envelopes marked with nothing more than 'H. Larwood, Fast Bowler', were soon stacked in towers in his lounge or waiting to be collected from Trent Bridge. 'My living room was like a sorting office,' he said. Larwood opened every letter and defied his wife, Lois, who wanted to 'make a bonfire' in the backyard and burn the most malicious. He was called 'dirty', a 'liar', a 'lousy cow' and a 'craven Pommie bastard', who would 'get what's coming to you'. Even Englishmen accused him of 'not being an Englishman' himself. One letter he brought back from Australia didn't even carry his name. Instead, the sender crudely drew the Devil – horns, long tail, pointy beard, three-pronged trident – running up to a set of stumps with a ball in his right hand. It was automatically delivered to Larwood's hotel room in Adelaide.

Who else could it have been for?

* * *

As well as coping with the vilification after Bodyline, Larwood faced the prospect of premature retirement. On the concrete-hard Australian pitches, which had no 'give' in them, he wrenched and jarred his joints and his feet were always sore and blistered. In the second Test at Melbourne he took off his left boot to find the socks soaked in blood. He wrung them out like a wet towel. By the time he'd finished, his hands were bloody too. In the final Test at Sydney, his body failed him. He damaged his left foot, which blackened from heel to toe, and never bowled as quickly again. He lost his gift of speed.

What Larwood needed was a tenderly supervised convalescence. Neither Nottinghamshire nor the MCC recognized it as necessary. But the agonies that Bodyline caused him were disguised behind a gutsy show of pride. The private wound is always the deepest, and Larwood suffered alone. He was confused and bitter. He felt alienated, and experienced an inconsolable emptiness that he was unable to articulate. Strength of character, and the fear of being labelled weak, wouldn't allow him to betray any of this publicly. Although his fixed ideas of fairness and faith were torn out by the root, and he was forced to re-evaluate and then re-order his entire life, Larwood survived the dark torture that used to visit him in spasms during his early middle age. Today we can stick the label of 'post-traumatic stress disorder' on what Larwood went through because of Bodyline, and offer compassion and a way of treating it. In the 1930s, it went undiagnosed. The signs were ignored, the sufferer was left to 'heal thyself'. Larwood sent out distress signals that went unanswered in the mid-to-late 1930s: loss of sleep, panic attacks, bouts of drinking and aggression born out of frustration. There was no agent to advise him, no public relations man to counsel him, no personal assistant to tidy up for him. He was on his own.

When I think about the desolation that Larwood experienced, and the way he eventually cut himself off from his former self because of it, I appreciate why the sense of recrimination took so long to leave him and was eventually overtaken by a different hurt. He regarded his treatment as unjust and dealt with it by leaving behind both cricket and his home in Nottingham. In his own mind he exaggerated – wrongly but understandably – the depth of feeling against him. When he realized his mistake, what rankled were not the original slights, real or imagined, but how much time he had wasted worrying about them. He could never claw back that lost time; he could only reconcile himself to the hard fact of the loss itself. With the clarity that hindsight brings, Larwood saw that he hadn't been damned at all. Far from it. In Australia, he discovered how much he was liked and genuinely respected. In England, as I witnessed at Trent Bridge, he was treated as a deity. The Australians still thought of Bodyline as by murder fed and by murder clothed. But no one at the end hated its perpetrator or thought him monstrous.

* * *

Brisbane, 1928: Jack Gregory lunges to take the ball at the end of his delivery stride, but loses his footing and tears his cartilage. The injury ends his cricket career. The batsman is Harold Larwood, who goes on to make 70. Patsy Hendren is the non-striker.

As Larwood admitted, Bodyline was designed and executed solely for one purpose – to 'kick' Bradman into submission. Its success is gauged in two sets of figures. Bradman's average against England in 1930 was 139.14. His average in 1932–33 was 56.57. By his own superhuman standards, The Don failed.

Larwood was a fastidious collector of his own memorabilia: cuttings, menu cards, photographs, letters. Through them he reconstructed his past. 'It's for when me memory goes,' he would say in the Nottinghamshire accent that he never shed. Larwood kept some of his ephemera in his tan-coloured MCC suitcase and tucked it underneath his bed for safe keeping. Photographs were pressed in black-paged albums. Alongside them he wrote his own captions, the writing cramped but clear, so there would be no mystery or ambiguity about who was in the photo or where and when it was taken.

In particular, he cherished two photographs. The first was of one of his heroes, the Australian fast bowler Jack Gregory, whom the camera catches straining to take a catch off Larwood's batting at Brisbane in 1928. Gregory lunges for the ball. He is sprawling forward. His mouth gapes open and his shadow falls across the pitch. His long fingers are cupped, as if he's a thirsty man trying to scoop up water. The ball is six inches from his hand. A fraction of a second later he will lose his balance and fall over in dazed pain. He will tear the ligaments in his right knee. His Test career will be over. The ball will drop beside him.

The second (and most significant) photograph was taken during the

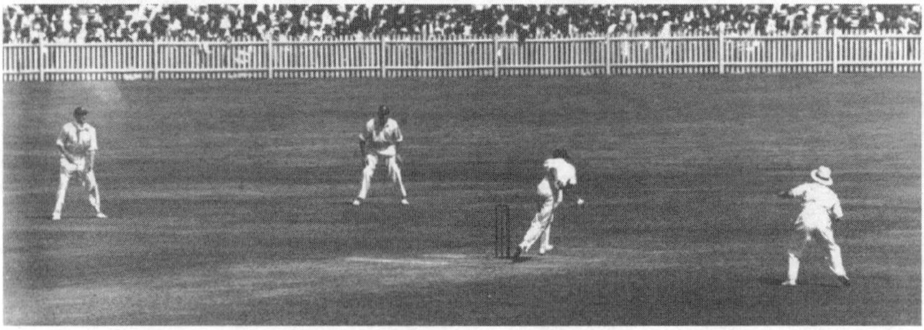

Donald Bradman misreads a Harold Larwood delivery in the first innings of the final Bodyline Test at Sydney. He turns away from the ball and it strikes him, as Larwood always made clear, 'smack on the arse'.

final Bodyline Test in 1933. It is one of a sequence of four, and Larwood has added his own commentary on a tiny square of yellow paper glued onto the page: the photograph shows Bradman struck for the only time during the series. A skidding ball hasn't climbed as high as he expected. As the shutter clicks, Bradman has his back to the camera. He is bent at the waist and has begun to fall away behind the stumps. The bat remains gripped in his left hand. Larwood has written plainly: 'Bradman, trying all sorts of shots to combat the leg-side attack.'

Newspaper reports claimed that Larwood struck him on the forearm. Not so, said Larwood. Those privileged enough to be given the photograph to examine were asked the rhetorical question: 'You know where I got Bradman?' There'd be a well-rehearsed pause before he'd lean forward and deliver his punchline: 'On the arse.' No matter how many times he recounted that story, Larwood always laughed, as though telling it for the first time. The thought of the mottled purple bruise on Bradman's backside made him smile mischievously. 'There'd never been a lot of love lost between us,' he'd admit, flatly.

He never bowled to Bradman again. But Bradman and Bodyline would still shape the rest of his life.

PART ONE

CHAPTER ONE

BLOODY HARD WORK

April 1923 – June 1925

Although Harold Larwood made his debut in 1924, he considered the following summer to be his 'first year', which is exactly what he wrote on the back of the above photograph. This emphasizes the puny frame that James Iremonger turned into a fast bowler's body. Fred Barratt stands on the left, and 'Dodge' Whysall on the right.

Trent Bridge: April 1923 – Bramall Lane: June 1925

He looked more like a waif from the pages of a Dickens novel than a fast bowler. He was 19, less than five foot four inches tall and so pitifully skinny that a thick brown leather belt held up his flannels. His sweater hung limply off him too, a flapping sail in a thin breeze. It was as if the sweater belonged to someone broader and with more muscles. Sometimes its long sleeves dropped over his hands and he had to tug them up and then fold the wool over twice in enormous cuffs so that it could grip his scrawny forearm. His feet slid around inside the pair of sprigged boots that were just too big for him, like a clown's floppy shoes. The toes were already scuffed. The skin on his face and arms was so pale as to be nearly translucent. It seemed as if most of the blood had been drained from his bony body. The parchment pallor had the effect of accentuating his dark eyes, the sockets as deep as pits, and the prominent cheekbones, which poked through the flesh. When he eventually peeled off his sweater, the outline of his ribcage was visible beneath a thin shirt. But at least he was well-scrubbed and politely spoken. He addressed everyone respectfully as either 'Sir' or 'Mr'.

Harold Larwood would always remember how intimidated he felt, and how he clipped his speech to just a few mumbled words as he got changed on the morning of his trial for Nottinghamshire at Trent Bridge. 'I must have looked a real greenhorn in my new clobber,' he said. For someone used to the rough, sloping surfaces of club cricket, the grass felt hard and as smooth as marble beneath his feet. Larwood looked around at the low wooden stands, the imposing members' pavilion behind him with its balustrade and ornately topped pillars, the spread of George Parr's tree and the dark roof-line of houses. He turned towards the Nottinghamshire committee men, who had gathered to watch him more from gentle amusement than genuine interest. A tight knot of them stood together near the nets in a corner of the Radcliffe Road end of the ground. The men were prosperous and smartly dressed: waistcoats with gold barley-twist watch chains strung between the pockets, bowler hats and wide-brimmed trilbies, high prominent collars and well-polished shoes. One of the committee had a short waxed moustache, like a music-hall villain. Another ostentatiously lit and re-lit a thick cigar that struggled to stay alight.

When he'd walked over to the nets, Larwood, nearly a foot shorter

Harold Larwood poses at Trent Bridge – circa 1926 – with, from left: Len 'Titch' Richmond, Sam Staples and Fred Barratt.

than the other players, had been hidden from view. As he carefully marked out his extravagant 20-pace run, and tried to suppress his butterfly nerves, he heard one of the committee say, 'He'll never run that far let alone bowl when he gets there.' Another dismissed him as 'too small'. The committee's reflex action was quietly to mock the puny-looking lad in ill-fitting clothes and over-sized boots. Standing beside the net, George Gunn – his hair brilliantined sleekly back, his white collar raised – waited expectantly for a fast bowler, someone tall and brawny with obviously muscled arms. He couldn't believe that Larwood might be the 'boy' he'd 'heard so much about'. Gunn asked, 'Where is he? Wheel him in.' When Larwood was pointed out to him, Gunn said disparagingly: 'Fast bowler? He looks more like a jockey to me.'

But then Larwood came on to bowl . . .

* * *

First Ben Lilley and then Arthur Staples began to clout him out of the net, the ball rising into the far distance like a golf shot. Larwood felt his shoulders sag. 'Keep going,' he said to himself, 'look after your line and length, let the ball do the rest.' With each delivery he hitched up his trousers which, despite the belt, threatened to drop around his thighs. Soon the ball was making a thudding noise as it hit the pitch, and climbing and darting away from the bat. He beat a succession of other batsmen time and again – 'good county pros', he called them – and the netting stretched and bulged as proof of his sharp pace. The committee men's cynicism vanished. Soon the men were nodding to one another in silent agreement: this boy was good.

Larwood had gone to Trent Bridge with his father, Robert, who had scraped together £9 – six weeks' wages for a senior pitman – for new kit and one shilling each for return train tickets. Father and son walked five miles from home to the nearest station, and then almost two miles from Nottingham station to the ground. Walking for hours never bothered Larwood. He walked six miles every day to work in the colliery. He walked four miles on Saturdays to watch silent movies in the afternoon 'penny rush' at the picture house. He thought nothing of walking a dozen miles or more to play local league cricket. Even when he began to establish himself in the Nottinghamshire team, Larwood often had no choice but to walk – either throwing his full cricket bag over his shoulder or swapping it from hand to hand, the leather grips making his fingers sore. The road was uneven and badly rutted, and he looked like a traveller peddling his wares.

In the winter he would walk 'for miles' around the country roads of north Nottinghamshire. There were no gyms and no sophisticated training techniques for Larwood. Walking was the only way he could keep himself fit. Well into his old age he would still talk about how important all the walking had been to build up his strength and stamina and to firm up the muscles in his legs. 'When I first started out, I'd walk for nearly half an hour to catch the train to Nottingham,' he'd say. 'I'd walk another twenty minutes or so from there to Trent Bridge and then I'd bowl me guts out all day . . . and, finally, I'd walk back home again at night to and from the station again. Whenever I see fast bowlers now, they're all driving cars everywhere. No one uses shoe leather any more.' The walking enabled him to bowl on average between 600 and 850 overs every season before the Bodyline tour and deliver 1,687 balls during it.

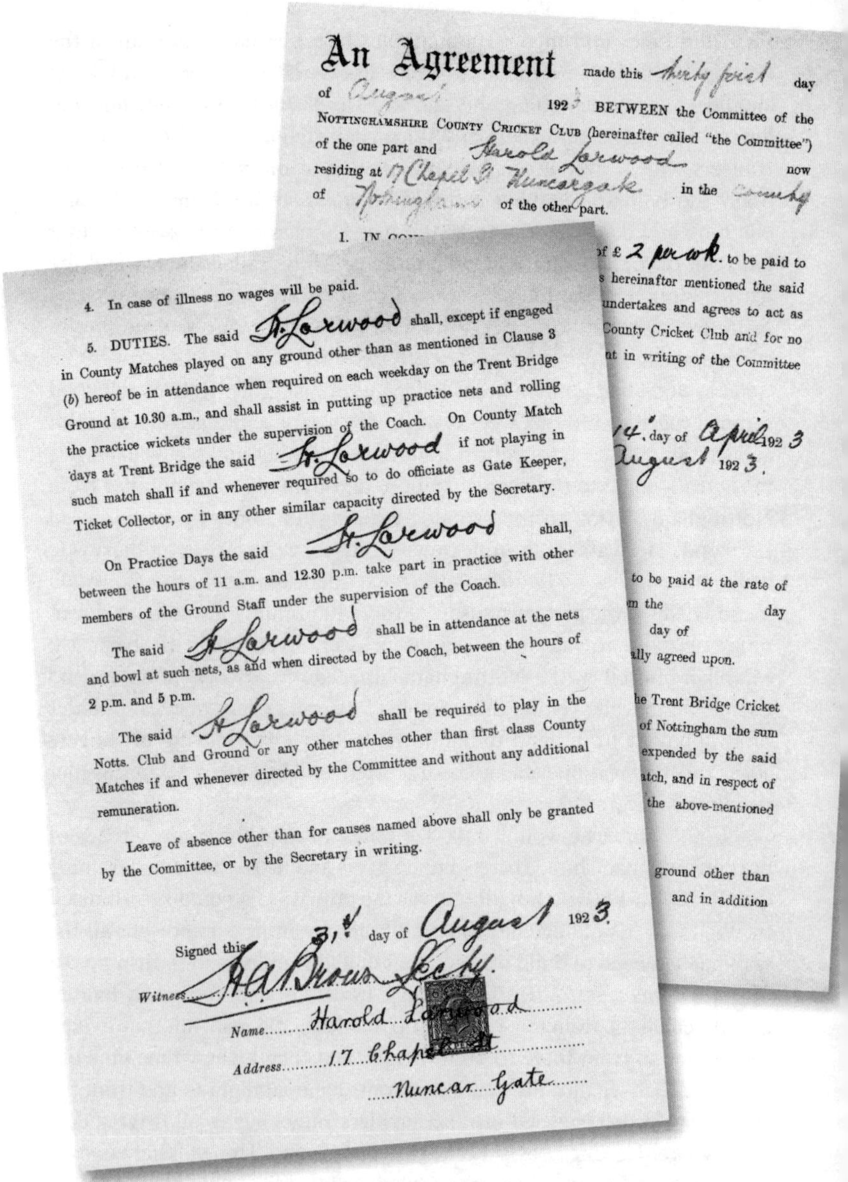

An Agreement made this thirty first day of August 1923 BETWEEN the Committee of the Nottinghamshire County Cricket Club (hereinafter called "the Committee") of the one part and Harold Larwood residing at 17 Chapel St Nuncargate now of Nottingham in the County of the other part.

1. IN CON…
…of £ 2 per wk. to be paid to
…s hereinafter mentioned the said
…undertakes and agrees to act as
…County Cricket Club and for no
…nt in writing of the Committee
…14th day of April 1923
…August 1923.
…to be paid at the rate of
…m the day
…day of
…ally agreed upon.
…he Trent Bridge Cricket
…of Nottingham the sum
…expended by the said
…atch, and in respect of
…the above-mentioned
…ground other than
…and in addition

4. In case of illness no wages will be paid.

5. DUTIES. The said H. Larwood shall, except if engaged in County Matches played on any ground other than as mentioned in Clause 3 (b) hereof be in attendance when required on each weekday on the Trent Bridge Ground at 10.30 a.m., and shall assist in putting up practice nets and rolling the practice wickets under the supervision of the Coach. On County Match days at Trent Bridge the said H. Larwood if not playing in such match shall if and whenever required so to do officiate as Gate Keeper, Ticket Collector, or in any other similar capacity directed by the Secretary.

On Practice Days the said H. Larwood shall, between the hours of 11 a.m. and 12.30 p.m. take part in practice with other members of the Ground Staff under the supervision of the Coach.

The said H. Larwood shall be in attendance at the nets and bowl at such nets, as and when directed by the Coach, between the hours of 2 p.m. and 5 p.m.

The said H. Larwood shall be required to play in the Notts. Club and Ground or any other matches other than first class County Matches if and whenever directed by the Committee and without any additional remuneration.

Leave of absence other than for causes named above shall only be granted by the Committee, or by the Secretary in writing.

Signed this 31st day of August 1923.

Witness H. A. Brown Secty.

Name Harold Larwood

Address 17 Chapel St

Nuncar Gate

Harold Larwood's first contract. He was offered as much for playing for Nottinghamshire as he received for working in the mine.

On the fresh spring day that his son's career began, Robert Larwood sat unobtrusively in the Radcliffe Road stand in his black suit and felt cap and took his old pipe out of his pocket. The faster the ball was bowled, the quicker he puffed on it. He produced enough grey smoke for a factory chimney. At the end of the session, Larwood said disconsolately to his father: 'We might as well go home. I'm not much good. Let's pack up.' Not for the first time – nor the last – Larwood was unnecessarily hard on himself. After washing and changing, he was told to report to the committee room. Larwood earned 32 shillings a week as a miner. Nottinghamshire miserably offered him the same sum for a year's contract. 'In case of illness,' the contract read, 'no wages will be paid.' The contract also stipulated that, unless he was actually playing in a match, he was expected to report daily to put up practice nets, roll the ground, collect tickets or work on the gate. 'Leave of absence,' the contract stipulated, 'shall only be granted by the Committee, or by the Secretary in writing.' He'd be paid no travel expenses.

Larwood neither hesitated nor haggled. He just wanted to escape from the mines. He'd already worked down two of them. 'In those days,' he said, 'there were so many mines that if you didn't like one of them, you could just get a job at another.' At 14, he had become a pit-pony boy, carrying an oil light and driving the pony and a train of long, high-sided tubs, each holding one hundredweight of coal. The train ran on unreliable, slippery rails and the grooved metal wheels of the heavy tubs frequently bounced free of the track. The tubs easily became detached from one another, the weight of them dragging the simple hook-and-eye coupling apart. Somehow Larwood had to heave the tubs back together again. Regularly he cut or bruised his hands, or stumbled in the futile attempt to prevent the tubs from tipping over and gashed his knee and shins. If he rode back to the coalface in the empty tubs, his knees drawn tightly into his chest and his head tucked into his belly to avoid the low roof, he ran the risk of being trapped if – and it occurred at least twice every week – one of the tubs became dislodged. Once a cart cut off a man's arm. The man, an experienced miner, was oiling the wheel-drum but hadn't put the brake on. 'I heard an awful shout and then a scream,' said Larwood. 'When I turned around his arm had come clean off.'

At 17, he moved on to the night shift at another colliery, where it was as hot as Dante's hell, and dim lamps offered the only illumination in the intense blackness. He worked in a three-foot-high tunnel, chipping away at the coal seams and then shovelling up the dirt in preparation for mining. It was so dark that he could barely see the hunched figures beside him. He noticed, as he came blinking into the daylight at the end of his shift, how mining severely aged those who worked in it, how bitter the repetitive and sweaty labour made them, and how much it took from them emotionally and physically during every dull day. Even when he left the mine, he took the consequences of it home with him. His feet, back and legs ached. His head spun. The coal dust clung to his skin and got underneath his nails. He could smell the dust even when he couldn't see a trace of it. No amount of scrubbing ever seemed to shift it satisfactorily. In the damp heat underground, where he also swallowed lungfuls of that dust, he knew that he would eventually contract the debilitating 'miner's cough': a throaty, chesty wheeze that was full of phlegm and, in time, flecks of blood.

Larwood scrubbed himself at home in front of the fire in the same cramped tin bath that his father used and which hung on a hook behind the back door. If father and son were on the same shift, Larwood waited for his turn as the water turned black and then cooled to lukewarm before his mother topped it up with china jugs of steaming water from a large kettle.

'Why didn't you ask for more?' his father asked him curtly after he'd agreed to Nottinghamshire's salaried terms. Faced with the prospect of at least one sweet summer in the fresh air, or another locked in the dark with an axe in his calloused hands, Larwood would have said 'yes' to anything. 'Why didn't you speak up?' he quickly replied. 'My father had to curb his temper,' remembered Larwood. 'Especially after the secretary turned up to remind him that I'd need at least two of everything – boots, shirts, bats, flannels. We didn't really know how we were going to afford it.'

Among the central themes of C.L.R. James's seminal book *Beyond a Boundary* is the question it asks: 'What do they know of cricket who only cricket know?' The charge implicit in that question is a valid one: that even a deep knowledge of sport never equates to profound understanding unless it is dovetailed into a much wider appreciation of life itself – social or cultural, or preferably both. Larwood came to know everything about cricket. But what motivated him to become a fast bowler was the fact that he also knew everything about hardship and the struggles of the ordinary working man. In Nuncargate, the north Nottinghamshire village where he was born in November 1904, almost every house was home to a miner or to a retired miner. The place was built on coal, survived through its dependency on coal, and the dust from the coal fell everywhere like black confetti. Coal heated the air. The miners were hopelessly trapped in an existence that was filthy and dangerous and offered no parole. Nearly every line of Larwood's family tree was coated in coal dust. The Larwoods had almost always been miners. There were few other ways of earning a living. Turn-of-the-century Ordnance Survey maps of the area reveal small clusters of villages, the modest spread of a town and around it an expanse of green fields. The landscape is dominated by pit-heads, which criss-cross it like an elaborate template for a game of join-the-dots. It was said that if you laid your ear to the ground you could hear the swing and scrape of picks hacking at the coal and the low rumble of the carts carrying it from the face. Most people never left the county; even a modest week at the seaside was prohibitively expensive. Cricket led Larwood mercifully away from a tedious and predictable life of make-do and mend. 'When I was in the mine, I thought about cricket all the time. It took you away from yourself,' he said. 'I imagined being on a pitch with the ball in my hands and the sun shining. And I imagined how I might bowl in the next match. I'd see the stumps go over, and it made me wish all the more for the weekend.'

Without exaggeration, Larwood added: 'Cricket was my early reason for living. I never wanted a holiday or to put my feet up – all I wanted to do was finish my work in time to get above ground and have a game.'

* * *

Time darkens memory and bleaches almost everything else, like the paper and ink and the strips of film with which we try to keep the past fresh and intact. The newsreel footage of Larwood during the Bodyline series preserves his bowling best of all for those of us unfortunate enough never to have seen him on a field. He's on the screen, albeit briefly, in black and white. For a second or two you glimpse what his contemporaries admired in his awesomely perfect action, the ball rising like spitting fat off the hot, hard pitches. You get an idea of the tension that wrapped itself around the Australian grounds in a clenched fist during that baking summer when the world was still lame from the Great Depression. And you sense even from such short clips that you're watching a fast bowler at his very peak; indeed, in the very moment when everything he has ever worked for and towards – the practice and the mental preparation – has come together in a perfect and white-hot conjunction, as if destiny made it so. The run in to the wicket is smooth. The final stride is measured. The delivery of the ball is sublime. You can almost hear each element of the process clicking swiftly into place, one after the other, like the mechanism of a grand clock before it strikes the hour.

Great claims were soon made for Larwood's speed: that he was appreciably faster than Charlie (C.J.) Kortright, who terrorized county batsmen in the 1890s and 1900s, or than Australia's Jack Gregory and Ted McDonald; that he was more ruthless and effective than each of them; that in his hands the ball become a precision tool; and that he made it so through an iron will and single-minded approach. All of this is true. But rhythm is never achieved effortlessly. What separated Larwood from his contemporaries, and many of the fast bowlers who came after him, was his dedication to the craft of which he became master. That dedication sprang entirely out of his impoverished background, the discipline of his upbringing and his experience in the pits. Cricket is hopelessly romanticized. Descriptions of the game always dissolve into tired phraseology – long summer afternoons, warm beer and white flannels, the scent of new-mown grass, the breathless hush in the close. From the start Larwood saw it plainly as a job of work. And the one thing he needed for cricket was the one thing the mine had given him. 'A strong back,' he said.

Nottinghamshire's coach Jimmy Iremonger saw it straight away. Watching Larwood bowl during his trial, he was struck by his upper body strength, a remarkable facet in someone with a frame like a staircase spindle. His spine was supple too. He put 'everything into every ball', said Iremonger, who realized that he needed to mould the man as much as refine the action. Larwood was courteous and disarmingly open, but also naive about the greasepaint world of first-class cricket. For Larwood, Iremonger became the equivalent of Sam Mussabini, the professional coach of the Olympic gold-medal sprinter Harold Abrahams. Like Mussabini, Iremonger was stubborn, persuasive, patient and innovative, and fanatical about the technical aspects of cricket: where the bowler placed his feet, the batsman's stance, the chess-like placing of a field. He made sure that his cricketers maintained a good diet, and he also studied the psychology of sport and the physiology of the athlete. He liked his bowlers to sleep with the bedroom window open. There was no substitute, he insisted, for fresh air at night – even in the sub-zero temperatures of winter. Iremonger was a rudimentary sports scientist before the term became common usage. He was six foot five inches tall with stringy arms and legs, a prominent nose and a moustache as thick as an unclipped privet hedge. His accent was even thicker, a cross in dialect and sound between Nottinghamshire and Yorkshire, where he was born. In cricket terms, Iremonger had been both poacher and gamekeeper. He began his career as an opening batsman who could hit the ball hard and long. He twice made four consecutive hundreds, and *Wisden* made him one of its Cricketers of the Year in 1903. He finished his career principally as a medium-pace bowler. So as well as talking to Larwood as a bona fide expert on the mechanics of bowling, he could also give him an insight into the way in which top-class batsmen thought.

Iremonger was a hardened sportsman, the football gene as prominent as the cricket one. His brother Albert was Notts County's eccentric goalkeeper; Iremonger himself played thirteen seasons for Nottingham Forest as a left back and won three England caps. With his dual sporting background, plus the fact that he'd been prominent in the 1907

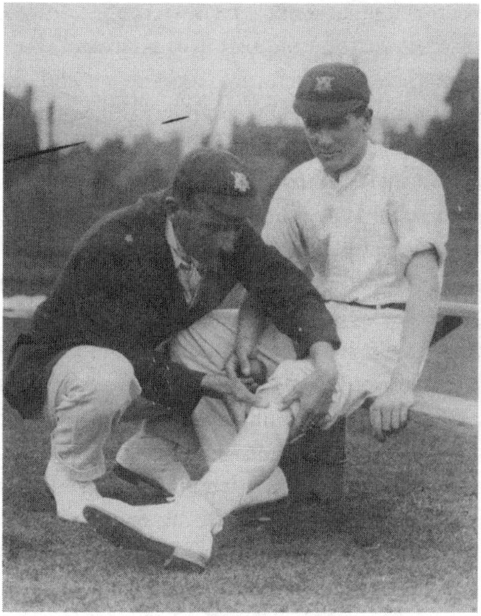

Teacher and pupil: James Iremonger taught Larwood the principles of fast bowling and discipline.

Nottinghamshire team that won the County Championship without losing a match, he didn't have to work to win Larwood's respect. The novice from the pit was already in awe of him, listening to every word as if it were scripture.

What Iremonger saw was raw talent, malleable and promising enough to be shaped into a weapon. There was still an awful lot to do. He would strip Larwood's action down, like taking a piece of varnished wood back to the grain. Larwood's run-up was askew. He was too chest-on. He gripped the ball only one way – the fingers pointing directly down the seam. He had no variation in pace or line. He didn't use the width of the crease to his advantage. He began his run with an unnecessary jerk, the shifting of his weight from foot to foot, like a man walking barefoot on hot coals. Iremonger wasn't overly concerned by any of these blemishes. He possessed scary pace: that was what mattered most of all in a new pupil. Larwood was taught that fast bowling had to be as cunning an art as spin.

Iremonger made it clear to Larwood that above everything else he valued discipline – off the field as well as on it. Without it, Iremonger said that Larwood might as well go back to the pit. Iremonger wouldn't indulge anyone who wasted time or talent. Larwood had to follow the rules, which meant being punctual, well kitted-out and committed. That implacable view never altered. Larwood and Bill Voce were established Test cricketers when Iremonger caught them splashing handfuls of water around the showers and then throwing soaking towels at one another. He wouldn't tolerate such misbehaviour, and certainly not something so juvenile. He yelled across the dressing room, ordering them to 'come here at once'. The two men instantly obeyed, like children caught red-handed. Larwood and Voce stepped out of the showers and followed the trail of Iremonger's voice, leaving wet footprints on the floor. They stood in front of him 'stark bollock naked'. Iremonger, hands on hips, turned to one and then the other. 'I was under the impression that you two lads play cricket for England,' he said. 'I hope I'm not asking too much then, if I ask you both to bloody well behave like England cricketers.' Larwood and Voce shamefacedly dropped their heads to their chests, mumbled their apologies and meekly walked away to dry themselves off. Larwood owed almost everything to Iremonger, who he believed 'taught me more than anybody else'. Iremonger was so observant that Larwood maintained: 'If anyone has got a spark of cricket in him, old Jimmy will fan it into something like a fire.'

Iremonger pressed home the significance of balance. 'If you don't have balance, you don't have anything. You'll never be a bowler.' He coached him to run almost on tiptoe and to pull his shoulders slightly back so that his weight was more evenly distributed. Larwood was cured of his habit of leaning too far forward in his approach to the wicket, which reduced his pace because it locked his shoulders in the wrong position. He'd previously strained for effect; guilty of being 'too tense' and of trying to bowl 'too fast', according to Iremonger, who insisted that speed came from rhythm and not brute force. The body, Iremonger added, wasn't built to bowl constantly at 100 mph. He wasn't sure if any human *could* bowl more than the odd few balls at such pace. The muscles, bones and their sockets wouldn't be able to withstand the pressure, and the bowler would constantly break down injured with the effort. So Iremonger drilled into Larwood the importance of a relaxed, smooth run. 'Every step of every run to the wicket must be the same,' he said. Until Larwood could achieve it without thinking, Iremonger repeated the instruction with the beady-eyed zeal of the revivalist preacher. The two of them calculated the ideal run-up for the length of his stride – roughly 14 paces covered over 20 yards, which Larwood measured in 26 ordinary steps. Eventually, Larwood said, the tracks of his boots, noticeably on wet wickets, were 'clear and distinct' because he used to 'tread each and every step in the same place for every ball'. He added: 'One of the first things Jimmy taught me was that if your run varies you lose some accuracy.'

Admiring contemporaries observed that Larwood became 'carpet-slippered'. His approach was almost soundless, as light as a ballet dancer on points. There were umpires who swore that Larwood couldn't be heard at all. To them he was a ghost who somehow spirited himself from bowling mark to crease. 'I didn't realize,' said Frank Chester, who stood in 48 Tests, 'that he was bowling at all until he was right beside me.' Another Test umpire, Frank Lee, batted against Larwood as a player. 'To watch him approach,' he said, 'gave me the kind of feeling I imagine a rabbit must get on seeing a stoat coming towards him.'

In a cricketing sense, Larwood was emerald green. 'I started to learn,' he said, 'how much I didn't know about cricket. In fact, I began to realize how much I didn't know about bowling itself.' He had extraordinarily long arms for a man of his height, and Iremonger got him to use them like pistons. 'He told me to get my hand as high as possible,' explained Larwood. He showed him how to get side-on and to develop naturally the full body swing that was necessary, as Larwood explained it, to put 'the devil' into a delivery. His arm was like a whirl of white light.

Iremonger appreciated Larwood's speed, but warned him: 'You'll have to learn to do something with the ball.' So he taught him how to shine it on one side to produce swing (though Larwood bowled so quickly that the ball didn't have much time to swing); how to disguise his slight change of pace (Larwood had two speeds: very fast and faster still); how to bowl accurately – so accurately, in fact, that he could visibly wear a specific spot on the pitch by perpetually bowling to it. Iremonger would lay down a silver coin on the pitch and challenge him to dent the edge. Eventually Larwood was able to slant the ball in so that it became impossible for batsmen to move away from it. Iremonger built up the scrawny physique with a simple programme of running and press-ups and what he regarded as wholesome food and drink for a sportsman: the fattest steak and a bottle of strong ale. Always concerned with the minutiae, Iremonger once caught Larwood with a pair of chest expanders poking out of his bag. He forced him to give them away. 'You might pull a muscle,' he explained. Larwood grew – though not very much. Iremonger told him not to worry about it. When the ball landed, his coach said, it would come off the pitch at a narrower angle. The lower trajectory meant it would lose far less pace. Larwood would actually benefit from being less than average height for a fast bowler. All this – and more – Larwood learnt from Iremonger.

Nothing excellent is ever wrought suddenly, and Larwood had to adopt the monk's habit for work during what became a three-year apprenticeship. Regarding himself as a self-made bowler rather than a natural talent, he practised for hours – a quotidian routine that he and Iremonger carried out almost robotically until it became second nature: line, length, accuracy and every step of his run-up rehearsed and honed. The more Larwood knew about bowling, the more he hungered to know, and he bowled with the fierce enjoyment of the true addict. He was told to 'think' a batsman out, and not merely beat him into submission through pace. The popular view was that only slow and medium-pace bowlers schemed and thought. Larwood dismissed that theory as a 'lie'. 'If you want to be a fast bowler,' he said, 'you have to practise and think. I practised everywhere and any time. In the streets, on rough park pitches, on waste ground and on the corner of the street. Straight from the pit to cricket. And I was always thinking about ways to get batsmen out.

People who talk and write about my "carpet-slippered" run don't know how much sweat it cost me. Or how much I worried – even when I reached the England team – about my arm action.'

As he watched matches, often seeking out Iremonger so that he could sit alongside him and hear his coach's running commentary, Larwood would file away his own mental notes about batsmen: who could hook, who played predominantly off the front foot or the back, who was visibly shaken by the short-pitched ball or susceptible to the delivery that opened like a switchblade.

The terrifying but sublime spectacle of his bowling became poetry to watch and murder to play. He was astonishingly perfect, his action like a bolt of flowing silk. Neville Cardus, who unhesitatingly made him the main strike bowler of his 'ideal team', lyrically said of Larwood: 'He ran in to bowl with a splendid stride, a gallop, and at the moment of delivery his action was absolutely classical, left side showing down the wicket before the arm swung over with a thrilling vehement rhythm.' Well, that was down to Iremonger. Douglas Jardine once said that he could judge how fast Larwood bowled – and how much he put into his bowling – because at his quickest he would scrape the knuckles of his right hand against the pitch in his follow through and then wipe the dust off on his shirt front to leave a streaky stain. His team-mate at Nottinghamshire, Joe Hardstaff junior, called him 'The Silent Killer', the 'one man who deserves to be known as The King of Speed'. He fielded at cover point to him. 'He never had a mid-off,' said Hardstaff, 'but I still had the easiest job in cricket because nobody much tried driving Larwood in front of the wicket.' He claimed to be able to detect, from the sound of Larwood's step, the speed at which he would bowl the ball. 'I used to pin my ears back and listen hard . . . If I could hear his feet tip-tapping over the turf, I knew he would be well within himself; he would still be quick, mind. But when I couldn't hear him running up, I used to look at the batsman and think "you're a split second away from trouble, son", because I knew Harold was coming in on his toes and he was going to let slip the fastest he'd got.' That was down to Iremonger too. The umpire George Hele, who stood in every Bodyline Test, was a rhapsodist on Larwood's behalf. He called his action 'copybook, classic, and utterly direct' and added that there was 'nothing loose, untidy or wasted' about it. 'I never saw a faster and more consistent bowler,' he said. Iremonger was responsible for that as well – everything done just as the coaching manual demanded. But

A fresh-faced Harold Larwood in his early days with Nottinghamshire. Beside him is 'Dodge' Whysall, who emerged as one of the county's most prominent run-makers as well as one of Larwood's closest companions. He died on Armistice Day, 1930. Larwood helped to carry his coffin.

during Bodyline the aesthetics of his action were largely lost on the Australians, who saw only the fury and violence of the end product.

Iremonger made sure there were seldom any histrionics from Larwood. He got him so fiercely focused on his bowling that his emotions were held in check. There were few demonstrations of annoyance or frustration when a catch was dropped or the ball licked the varnish of the stumps without shaking the bails loose. There was no eyeballing of the batsman, no fixed stare as grim as death in a crude attempt to unsettle him psychologically. And, if the ball was bludgeoned to the fence, there was no tell-tale grimace which might betray the agony of being, albeit momentarily, second-best in the contest. Larwood was poker-faced. 'Don't let the batsman know what you're thinking,' Iremonger told him, tapping the side of his own head to reinforce the point. As Larwood said dismissively of players in the post-Packer era, who embraced one another after claiming a wicket: 'Even when we got Bradman out we didn't go around hugging. We just rested while the next bloke came along . . . '

His eyes were also always fixed on the target. 'Some bowlers don't look at where they're bowling,' Larwood said. 'I was taught to take aim properly, and not just bowl the ball anywhere in the hope my pace would get me a wicket.'

The only thing Iremonger couldn't do was imbue lasting self-belief into Larwood, who had a tendency towards bleak introspection. What nagged at him was the illogical idea that his talent might desert him without warning: that his skill was illusory or something vaporous which would vanish over the winter. Without fail, every spring, he arrived back at the Nottinghamshire nets fearful that his run-up and timing had gone. He worried that he wouldn't be able to bowl at all, or that he wouldn't be as fast as he had been the previous summer. When he found nothing had changed and everything functioned just as before, his relief was palpable. 'Every season I was frightened that I might have lost it,' he said. However much he achieved, the dreaded feeling of insecurity, like depression's black dog, never left him. 'I never lost the shyness I felt as a boy,' he admitted. 'I am very shy . . . and always have been shy . . . Perhaps that accounts for why I didn't really believe in myself.'

He would never quite believe that the scruff of a boy from a tiny mining town grew into an England fast bowler.

* * *

With the ball in his hand, Larwood confessed that he 'loved the game but hated the batsman'. One of the reasons, as he readily admitted, was that 'cricket is a batsman's game'. The pitches were prepared to suit run-making. The laws were made to preserve the batsman's wicket. To dismiss a batsman lbw, the bowler had to pitch the ball wicket-to-wicket; batsmen could safely pad up to any delivery that strayed off line. Batsmen were considered to be top-of-the-bill entertainers and feather-bed pitches enabled them to showboat – flowing strokes through extra cover, elegant late cuts, gentle nudges around the corner. As Larwood said of the game in the 1920s and early 1930s, it 'was so biased in favour of the batsman, there was no pressure on them at all. If we got four wickets down in a day, we'd done a good day's work. If we got five we had an extra drink.' The fast bowler was the grafter, the man at the coalface, or the obedient work-horse, like Boxer in *Animal Farm,* who ploughed the same furrow over and again without complaint. The fast bowler did so without daring to think of the risk he ran, which Larwood defined as 'sprains, torn muscles, hernia and other injuries'. He would run miles and finish the day 'bone-tired and foot-sore'. In Australia, he would bowl 'till my side ached' and 'my toes bled'. He calculated that in the Bodyline Tests alone he covered 35.79 miles – roughly seven miles per match. The soles of his feet turned black with the effort, as if he'd walked without shoes or socks in the mines. The effects of so much bowling made him retch at the end of the day, and he pushed away plates of food. After he bowled a long spell, Douglas Jardine would still tell him to 'try one more, Harold'. Which is why, when asked about the secret of fast bowling, Larwood replied 'bloody hard work', and meant it. At its best, fast bowling was akin to poetry; but, like poetry also, it was always the sullen art. Iremonger taught him that truism too.

The county circle was small and word of what Larwood could do sped through it like a lit fuse. When his career took off, there were amateurs who would miss matches against Nottinghamshire at Trent Bridge because of fictitious business commitments. Even toughened pros trudged wearily to the crease with the expression of a hound on its last visit to the vet's.

But all that was to come . . .

* * *

Larwood began modestly in county cricket, a consequence not of his inexperience but of his weak physical condition. In the early spring of 1924, he contracted smallpox. The doctors counted his lesions: there were 392 of them. Larwood had been in plenty of scrapes with his health before. At two years old, he'd found a can of paraffin and drunk it. The hospital saved his life by pumping out his stomach. At 13, he'd gone to work in a grocer's shop lugging sacks of flour and cases of margarine. He was less than four feet tall and the flour sacks were larger and heavier than him. While carrying one, Larwood slipped on the cellar steps, and landed on his head. The owner found him splayed across the concrete floor, his eyes closed and his limbs limp. He carried Larwood upstairs and laid him on the counter, believing he might be dead. He was unconscious for two hours. 'I suppose it proves I had a thick skull,' Larwood said, 'and you needed one to be a fast bowler.' Even Larwood, used to making light of such things, couldn't dismiss smallpox. His own cousin had died of it mid-way through the War. The year after Larwood contracted it, there were more than 5000 cases and six deaths. He was discharged from hospital in mid-April – almost a year after signing his contract with Nottinghamshire. He'd conspicuously lost weight and had to build back his strength before finding his form. He still managed to take 36 wickets at 13.47 for the second eleven (including eight for 44 against Lancashire at Old Trafford) and at the fag-end of the season made his Championship debut.

It was a late August blighted by bad weather: unseasonal slate-grey skies, depressingly wet and cold. The match, against Northamptonshire at Trent Bridge, was a stop-start affair that the rain ruined. When play was possible, Larwood found it difficult to hold the damp ball. Streaks of red dye stained his hands and the front of his flannels. The outfield was surprisingly lush for August and the rain made the turf greasy too. Larwood found it difficult to get a firm grip with his spikes. He skated around, and the bowlers' footholds soon became churned up, the dark damp earth visible on the pale cut pitch. He didn't know where to plant his foot for the final stride without slipping. Larwood bowled 26 overs, conceded 71 runs and took his first wicket.

Vallance Jupp was a Test all-rounder, whose name sounds as if it was plucked out of the pages of a P.G. Wodehouse novel or dreamt up for the romantic leading man in a silent movie. *Wisden* described him as the 'best amateur all-rounder' in county cricket. Jupp became one of only two men to complete the double with different counties, and he was – another *Wisden* tribute – a 'brilliant' cover point. Larwood claimed Jupp in the devastating way that he'd remove scores of batsmen over the next fourteen years. He clean-bowled him. On the slow pitch, the ball kept low. With typical self-effacement, Larwood assessed his first experience of the Championship ruthlessly. Finishing with match figures of one for 71, he said gloomily: 'I wasn't ready.' Empty and dejected, he said the same thing to his coach. Rather than blaming Iremonger for his premature call-up and inauspicious start, however, Larwood apologized to him for not being more successful. His self-criticism would encourage Iremonger to drive him harder still. How soon might he expect a recall, Larwood asked Iremonger, certain that he'd let down his coach. Iremonger had taken up different vantage points around Trent Bridge so that he could study Larwood. He'd looked at him from positions at deep long-off, extra cover, third man and from high in the pavilion. Just as Mussabini, watching Abrahams once run and fail, felt he could squeeze another yard of speed out of the sprinter, so Iremonger thought Larwood hadn't begun to fulfil his potential. Fine tuning was needed; nothing extravagant, he added, just a few minor adjustments. He urged Larwood, 'You haven't started yet and you're talking as if your career's over.' Long after he spoke them, Larwood would remember Iremonger's calm words, wrapped around him like a comforting arm. 'Don't worry, lad, you'll be fine.'

* * *

Larwood waited almost another year before receiving a telegram that ordered him to report to Sheffield's Bramall Lane, a ground which the *Yorkshire Post*'s J.M. Kilburn once described as being 'synonymous with smoking skies and biting comment'. He'd be pitted against the county champions Yorkshire, and Herbert Sutcliffe. Kilburn was right: the skies were regularly smoke-filled and the wooden Grinder's Stand offered biting comment. The concrete terracing and iron crush barriers looked starkly austere and uninviting. On this day, however, the sun was intensely bright. It stung Larwood's eyes.

What happened next strikes one as apocryphal, but is true. 'As I ran up to bowl,' Larwood said, 'Sutcliffe drew away and I pulled up. Something flashing in the crowd had distracted him.' Larwood watched the umpire head towards the crowd to find out what had disturbed one of England's most accomplished and consistent run-makers. It was the clasp of Larwood's mother's handbag, which she'd set tidily on her knee like a small dog. Sutcliffe, his mouth tightly drawn around the corners, stared down the wicket at Larwood. 'I didn't dare tell him for some time that it was my mother who caused the stoppage,' he said.

When he did, Sutcliffe replied tersely: 'Youngster, don't expect your mother to help get you wickets.' Larwood never did.

CHAPTER TWO

CAPTAINS, OH MY CAPTAINS

August 1925

The unmistakable Douglas Jardine, minus his Harlequin cap.

The Oval: August 1925

All morning the shilling and sixpenny turnstiles clicked until there was no more room inside the Oval. The sign 'Ground Full' was hung onto the gates. When every seat was taken, the Bank Holiday crowd washed like a slow tide onto the outfield. Almost 35,000 people squeezed into the ground – so many that the boundary had to be shortened to accommodate them. To mark the fact that it was a day off from the office, the factory or the lathe, some men wore 'Sunday best' sun hats with bands of respectful dark ribbon instead of a trilby or flat cap. Dozens peeled off their jackets and rolled up their shirtsleeves beyond the elbow, almost willing the weather to brighten. But dark and silvery cloud hung in a sky that stubbornly refused to turn from Payne's grey to blue.

Shortly before lunch Douglas Jardine sat, padded up and pensive, on the pavilion balcony, staring over the rail at the scene below him and then raising his eyes to study Harold Larwood. During the past six weeks, since returning to the Nottinghamshire side and taking three wickets against Yorkshire at Sheffield, Larwood's bowling had inspired headlines. Reports romanticized his sudden arrival. One said that Nottinghamshire had dug into the nearest mine and emerged carrying a jewel rather than a bucketful of coal. Another claimed that Larwood had come directly out of the mine shaft, his face and hands still black, and then been schooled raw in the art of fast bowling. Almost the only truthful thing to appear in print was the shock of Larwood's pace: he was quick, and his figures provided supporting evidence – seven wickets against Worcestershire, five at Northamptonshire, six when Lancashire came to Trent Bridge, five more in a crushing win over Glamorgan. His chest had filled out over the winter. His arms and thighs and calves had more stamina in them. He still resembled a baby-faced assassin: a doe-eyed, meek-looking boy in his middle or late teens rather than someone three months away from his 21st birthday. In appearance and demeanour, he gave batsmen a false sense of security. He'd apologize if he appealed and the umpire turned him down. Off the field, he had to be taught how to book into a hotel and which knife, fork and spoon to use at dinner.

The match at the Oval was Larwood's first journey to London. He'd only ever seen its streets before in newspaper photographs. After checking into Nottinghamshire's hotel, he sat dumb and incredulous in the lobby with his black leather suitcase and cricket bag beside him. The lobby was oak-panelled, the curtains trained with a trim of gold silk and the furniture upholstered in scarlet fabric. Finely dressed women came and went. Their heavy perfume stuck to the air. Larwood's head turned to track each of them, from left to right and back again, as if watching the ball hurry over the net in a tennis match. Finally, he asked: 'Are all these women for hire?' He thought he'd been taken to a brothel.

Jardine wanted to see for himself whether Larwood was genuinely fast. He'd been told he could make the ball rise on a length so that a batsman had to hop and hurry, forcing him to change his shot at the last moment. Larwood was dangerous, the grapevine said, even on decent or half-decent batting strips. A sceptical, hard-to-please man with an arctic temperament, Jardine wouldn't believe it until he had witnessed proof of it himself. Ever since his own debut in county cricket four years earlier, he'd listened as tongues wagged about tyro bowlers or batsmen who could score runs at will, and later found them to be chimeras. Most stories were exaggerated. There was nearly always a discrepancy between the hype and the reality. Jardine supposed Larwood was no different. The fact that he'd come from nowhere that summer to take 40 wickets in 12 matches was immaterial. New bowlers, just like new batsmen, had the advantage of novelty. As barely anyone *had* played against Larwood, no one was quite sure *how* to play him yet.

Soon verbal notes would be swapped about the type of deliveries Larwood regularly bowled, comparing his strengths and weaknesses. His 'tells' would be interpreted too – the giveaway signs, such as a minor change in his run-up or grip, or a sly signal towards the wicketkeeper or his captain that would tip off an observant batsman about which ball was coming next. In time Larwood developed his own 'tells', a code for the batsmen to break. He'd thrust his right thumb into the waistband of his trousers to tug it upwards, a sign of impatience or agitation – usually the prelude to a bouncer. He'd rake the fingers of his left hand across the side of his head – a sign that he needed to concentrate. He'd thrust his neck suddenly forward as he began his run, the way a turtle pokes its head from its shell – a warning that a particularly fast delivery was on the way. Sometimes, against tail-enders, he would pretend to lose the ball – which he'd stuffed in his pocket – before brandishing it again, the way a pirate brandishes a cutlass from his belt before a sword fight. When Jardine first saw Larwood, he'd acquired none of these mannerisms or nervous tics. At the start there was no swagger or swank in Larwood that suggested he even understood his own potential. Jardine saw nothing except the obvious: Larwood was full of demonic aggression, which he demonstrated with unconscious effort.

Rain came in a short burst after lunch. As he waited for the game to re-start, Jardine edged alongside the Surrey captain Percy Fender. 'Is this chap as fast as they say he is?' he asked. Fender didn't hesitate. 'Yes,' he said, without elaborating. When play resumed, Jardine watched Larwood in silence. He claimed the wicket of Jack Hobbs, caught behind. Jardine still thought the ball wasn't moving much off the pitch. The rain had flattened it; Larwood's deliveries often went through to the wicketkeeper Ben Lilley at below waist height. 'He does not look so fast to me,' said Jardine to Fender.

Surrey were 179 for 5 when Jardine batted in the early afternoon. Larwood returned fresh from the Vauxhall End. Fender described what happened next: 'Larwood's first ball was being returned by the wicket-keeper Lilley as Douglas completed his stroke. The second ball was on its way through to Lilley when the stroke was completed. The third ball Douglas finally made contact. He immediately turned round to the pavilion and raised his cap to me.' After his gracious acknowledgement that Fender had spoken nothing but the truth, Jardine made 53 before becoming the last wicket to fall. Larwood clean-bowled him with a ball that nipped in and beat him for pace; Jardine insisted to Fender that he'd got an inside edge. *The Times* reported that his stumps were 'all over the place'. Without knowing it, Larwood had proved a point.

History never seems like history when you're living through it. Jardine's first meeting with Larwood was no more than the routine wrestle between ball and bat. Separated by 22 yards of damp turf, the two men who would plan and execute Bodyline seven years later uttered nothing meaningful to one another. When asked about the game decades later, Jardine would say that what struck him was Larwood's focus, the intense sense of purpose on his face, as if his very life depended on every ball he bowled. The eyes were as hard as flints, he said, and Larwood was able to block out anything extraneous around him. Larwood would say that Jardine was just another scalp that day. He had no bright memory of the ball he bowled to remove him. But he did remember how straight Jardine stood against anything short or brutish. If the ball poked him in the ribs, he wouldn't betray a flicker of pain. He wouldn't allow himself to rub the welt beneath his shirt in case it made him look vulnerable or 'soft', as

Larwood put it. And, he added, 'You needed a pickaxe to dislodge him from the wicket.'

* * *

Harold Larwood developed an implacable belief in Douglas Jardine's virtues. It followed a pattern of devotion to anyone he thought had 'done right by me'. He stuck by them, just as his father Robert would have done. Like so many sons who admired a father-figure, Larwood always looked for qualities in others that he'd originally seen at home. 'He was a good man,' he said of his father.

In the final analysis, four men were the axis on which Larwood's life turned. The first was Robert Larwood.

Robert Larwood was quiet, tough and disciplined, a man who tolerated no nonsense and wasn't concerned with fripperies. He put his family above everyone except God. He was staunchly Methodist, the treasurer of the United Church, a typically plain chapel with a grey slate pitched roof, a stone floor and polished oak pews that sat within 12 good paces of the Larwood home in Nuncargate. The air in the chapel smelt of old hymn and prayer books. 'For all of us,' said Larwood, who went there until he was 16, 'it was a case of having to go to church every week.' Robert was teetotal. 'I never heard him swear either,' said Larwood. His sole pleasures were cricket and smoking his pipe, usually after supper. Bringing up a family of five sons on a miner's pittance was a financial miracle. He saved £200 to buy his own house – a four-roomed red-brick terrace. After he'd done this, he saved another smaller amount to buy a second

Pride in their son's achievements is evident in the home of Larwood's parents, Robert and Mary.

house further along the street, which he rented out. Robert worked double shifts, and he and his wife Mary even went without new clothes, and often without full portions of food, to raise the children and provide a roof that, no matter how hard times became for them, could never be wrenched away.

The two-year-old Harold Larwood with his mother.

Robert captained the village cricket team. With a twist of irony, the father of one of the game's fastest-ever bowlers preferred spin to pace. Larwood remembered sitting cross-legged on the boundary as he followed the ball's dip in flight from his father's hand. He saw the pleasure that cricket gave him on those summer afternoons: the smiling satisfaction at his release from the manacles of the pit and the looser, more relaxed set of his body. It was more than a sport. Along with his dedication to God, it represented the core of his life. Watching his father, Larwood began to realize that cricket might provide the same level of fulfilment for him too.

Cricket was as much a part of the village tradition as slaving in the pit. Robert Larwood made bats for his cricket-obsessed son from off-cuts of wood and bought him ninepenny cricket balls, which, according to Larwood, 'lasted about a week because I hit them so hard and so often'; hard enough sometimes to break his neighbours' windows. Larwood also cut his own bats from whatever wood he could forage – fence posts and panels, boxes and crates. He used the point of a knife to take the splinters out of his fingers.

Robert Larwood had married his 19-year-old bride Mary in 1898. By the time his wife was 25, she already had four children, all boys: Fred (1900), Ernest (1901), Tom (1902) and Harold (1904). Her fifth son Joe was born in 1910. The house was impossibly cramped. There was a living-cum-dining room downstairs with an adjoining kitchen. Upstairs, there

The smallest boy in the class: Harold Larwood, second from right on the second row from the back, with the pupils of Kirkby Woodhouse school. Hard though it is to believe, the minuscule primary school produced five Notts and England cricketers: 'Dodge' Whysall, Sam Staples (elder brother of Arthur), Joe Hardstaff junior, Bill Voce and Larwood himself.

were two bedrooms. A brick toilet stood at the end of a small walled garden. It was reached by a thin, raised concrete path. In winter, a line of boots stretched beside the back door to avoid freezing feet in the middle of the night. There was no privacy in the house. If the neighbours rowed, it was possible to hear them clearly through the walls. And if the air was tinged blue with their bad language, Mary Larwood would cover the ears of the son closest to her and tell the others to go outside. She always insisted that all of them were in bed at 6.30 p.m. The sons all slept in the same bed; there was nowhere else to sleep.

The brothers surreptitiously played cards, a pastime which Mary Larwood considered nefarious. She saw it as the prequel to gambling and then ruinous debt. Like drinking and drunkenness, which she also abhorred, she thought anyone who indulged in it was not travelling on the righteous path. The Sabbath was strictly observed in the Larwood household as belonging to the Lord rather than to Lord's. No cricket was allowed. Larwood went to church three times every Sunday. His mother wore a steel thimble on her second finger and sat behind Larwood and his brothers, ready to rap them over the skull with it if due attention wasn't paid to the sermon. Larwood disliked the rigmarole of church: shining his shoes and dressing in a starched white collar, singing hymns he didn't like, saying prayers he didn't understand and meeting the rest of the congregation before and afterwards, which was torture for someone so horribly shy that he would leave a room at the mere mention of his name in case he was asked to speak.

Larwood's father insisted on exemplary behaviour, and advocated 'tough love'. Anyone stepping out of line risked a belting or his hand across a bare backside. 'I had a few of those – usually for being late or awkward,' said Larwood. 'It was a close community. If you stepped out of line, everybody – and particularly your mother and father – knew about it before you got back home.' When jumping on the bed sent one of the legs crashing through the ceiling, Robert Larwood couldn't find out which of his sons was responsible. 'If you don't tell me,' he warned, 'I'll have to take the belt to all of you,' which is what he did. 'We were a bit of a handful for our mother and father,' said Larwood. 'There was a lot of energy about.'

Larwood predominantly wanted to use his own energy to play sport. He kicked a ball around whenever he could find one, damaging the toes of his heavy boots. At school, where there were daily inspections of shoes and fingernails, Larwood was regularly punished by teachers for the ragged state of his footwear and then punished again on arriving home. 'There were nights when I couldn't sit down,' he said. The only academic subject that interested him was mathematics. He could add up 'my own bowling figures', he said.

The miner father wanted his sons to be different. He paid for Fred and Ernest to take music lessons (Ernest eventually became the church organist). Joe trained as a motor-mechanic. Tom went into insurance. It was obvious to his family that Harold, intelligent but not academic, had the potential to be a cricketer. Every summer his brothers would take him to the travelling fairs, the Wakes, and point him towards the coconut shy. His aim was so accurate that the stallholders, in danger of running out of coconuts, refused his money and banned him.

An austere and tough-looking Douglas Jardine – wearing an expression that the Australians came to know well.

Larwood loved his father and developed his pivotal beliefs from him, such as a sense of justice and the hushed acceptance of one's lot, however difficult it happened to be. He always responded to men who were well-mannered, strong-willed, prepared to lead and make sacrifices for others. His father was one of them. It took an inner toughness, Larwood said, to buy your own house on a miner's pay. It took a strong will to support a large family so uncomplainingly, and every day give up something for them without bitter regret.

Larwood saw the reflection of his father in three men: Jimmy Iremonger, Jardine, and his captain at Nottinghamshire, Arthur Carr. He felt comfortable around Iremonger, also from working-class stock. The two of them grew up in exactly the same way – terraced house, scrimping, coal, cricket, authoritarian fathers – and spoke an identical language. Their relationship was based on a shared understanding of what it was like to come from a mining community and what it took to escape from it. Larwood was attracted to Carr and Jardine for the opposite reason. They were 'proper gentlemen', he said.

Carr's and Jardine's backgrounds were typical for amateurs of the period: public-school men who might well have become stockbrokers or bankers and, as Harold Larwood said, 'spoke posh'; batsmen who became captains of England; ostensibly establishment figures who were anti-authoritarian (unless in charge themselves). Neither retreated from a fight, and such an implacable and uncompromising approach explains why Jardine lost the England captaincy and Carr was eventually sacked by Nottinghamshire.

The two men boiled at different temperatures. Where Jardine was cautious, Carr was rash, sometimes wantonly reckless. Where Jardine was reserved, often as formal as a dinner suit, Carr was flamboyant. Where Jardine was shy – wrongly perceived as socially remote unless the surroundings or guests were familiar to him – Carr was always garrulous and genuinely did believe that life was a cabaret (with beer, naturally). Whereas Jardine liked to smoke his pipe and read Chaucer (one of the books he took with him on the Bodyline tour was *The Canterbury Tales*), and became devoted to Izaak Walton's *The Compleat Angler*, Carr had eyes only for John Barleycorn and a packet of Player's. Whereas Jardine could sometimes slip into wintry pessimism, Carr had the attitude that his glass was always half full. Carr was, essentially, a rakish but entirely lovable and charming rogue – a toffish jack-the-lad who gave the impression of being one of those slightly disreputable characters with his elbow on the drawing-room mantelpiece, always a dry martini close by, in a Noël Coward play. The novelist Alec Waugh (elder brother of Evelyn Waugh), who had an unrequited crush on Carr, turned him into fiction. He made Carr the model for 'the tremendous' Lovelace in *The Loom of Youth*, his then controversial autobiographical novel – it openly depicted homosexuality – about his schooldays at Sherborne, which he inadequately disguised as Fernhurst. Waugh wrote in 1917: 'On a raised dais was the Sixth Form table. In the middle, haughty, self-conscious with sleepy-looking but watchful eyes, sat the captain of the House, Lovelace major, in many ways the finest athlete Fernhurst had ever produced.' Carr didn't resemble an athlete. He was heavy-set, slightly paunchy and round-shouldered. He had narrow sea-blue eyes, and very fair hair with a straight parting and a high forehead, which made it look as though he

Arthur Carr lived his life and played cricket in exactly the same way. He thought that everything should be enjoyed and savoured to the full.

was going bald. His nose was slightly crooked after he broke it and then had the bone reset without anaesthetic. 'I hardly felt a thing,' he said. Carr's stern features were set into a balloon-shaped face. When he smiled he looked like a Halloween pumpkin.

Like so much of what happened during Larwood's years at Nottinghamshire, Carr's impact on him is woefully under-appreciated. He had a far greater influence than Jardine on the way in which Larwood thought, carried himself and approached fast bowling; and also how he initially viewed Australia and Australians and the officials at Lord's. It was Carr – not Jardine – who turned him from Iremonger's prodigy into a Test match cricketer. It was Carr – not Jardine – who soon worked out the obvious and often repeated ploy to get Larwood's back up so that he would bowl with more venom. And it was Carr – certainly not Jardine – who taught the nascent fast bowler the hard practicalities of the game. At one end of the scale Carr was the antithesis of Larwood's devoutly religious and abstemious father. Carr loved cricket, gambling (especially poker), drinking, smoking, dancing and country sports – though not necessarily in that order. He embodied the spirit of the decade. For Carr, the twenties really did roar. A handsome private income – his father had been a successful stockbroker and he owned the champion racehorse Golden Millar – made him immune from the social convulsions around him: the General Strike, the Jarrow March, the Wall Street Crash and, eventually, two million unemployed. For him, the jazz age of Ellington and Armstrong and Bessie Smith, the era of the flapper in her backless evening gown who danced the Charleston and the Black Bottom, was choreographed for his entertainment alone. After the Great War, Carr was no different from the other men who experienced its muddy carnage, came home with pangs of survivor-guilt and counted themselves lucky not to have been among the Lost Generation. He ached to do nothing more than to have a good time, as if the alcohol might wash the bad memories away. Carr was 21 when the War began. Accepting that he couldn't claim back those stolen years, he decided that burning the candle at both ends would cast a lovely light on whatever he did next. It wasn't unusual for him to drink and dance until the early hours, turn up for the game in his dinner jacket and bow tie and then bat – often quite brilliantly – well before lunch. Sometimes his time-keeping went awry. He would arrive with an elephantine hangover and, because the match inconveniently clashed with a race meeting, also late.

Carr seemed to think that the answer to everything lay in a bottle. This insouciance towards alcohol began early. In 1921, after a terrible run with the bat, Carr decided to get himself drunk. He awoke the following morning with a headache and double vision. Nottinghamshire were playing Essex at Leyton in a few hours' time. He staggered into the ground and said to himself: 'What you want is a hair of the dog that bit you – that's your only hope.' He put on his whites, went into the pavilion bar and sank three double whisky-and-sodas one after another. He made a double century. 'I saw the ball perfectly,' he said, 'and I could time and make my shots as easily as kiss your hand.'

Carr was determined that his own pursuit of pleasure – he became bored very easily – would involve everyone in the dressing room. After what he described as a typical 'bender' at Eastbourne, he drove two Nottinghamshire players home in his car. One fell out; the other was too drunk to notice. The police picked up Carr and took him to the station. Long before motorists were asked to blow into a bag, the preferred way of testing whether someone had enjoyed too much of the grape or the grain was to gauge the slurring of their speech. Carr was asked to recite 'Sister Susie's sewing shirts for soldiers'. He looked wide-eyed at the officer. 'Damn it,' he said, 'I can't say that when I'm stone-cold sober.' The police let him go.

As well as the drink, he was also a three-pack-of-cigarettes-per-day smoker, who needed an ashtray the size of a dustbin lid. When Carr finally quit chain-smoking, he estimated that he saved himself £60 per year at a time when the average weekly wage was just over £2. He couldn't, however, give up alcohol, which he gluttonously supped by the vat. Carr laid down his philosophy towards life in an uncomplicated statement: 'I am the sort of person who never does things by halves. If I play cricket, I want to play the best cricket or none at all.' Another line underscored the essential Carr: 'If I have a night out, I want to have a real night out.' A real night out for him began as soon as stumps were drawn and ended with the rosy-fingered dawn. The Methodist Robert Larwood was appalled.

And yet for all Carr's breezy insouciance, there were ways in which he was so similar to Robert Larwood that the two of them might have been cut from adjoining blocks – granite blocks too. Like Robert Larwood, Carr set the bar high for himself. Whichever target he chased – a fox, a woman, another cocktail – he was steadfast and dogged. He never gave up; defeat was the word that went unspoken. Like Robert Larwood, he could be obstinate for a good cause, even if he didn't benefit from it himself. And, again like Robert Larwood, he demonstrably cared about the welfare of a certain quick bowler. As soon as Larwood came into the Nottinghamshire team, Carr made a decision: 'The best way to deal with him was as if he were my own son,' he said. In those early years at Trent Bridge, as Larwood moved swiftly from County into Test cricket, he effectively had two fathers: one for the summer months and another in the winter. Larwood much preferred Carr's decadent streak to Methodism. Introducing him to his good friends, nicotine and alcohol, Carr changed Larwood. He was soon knocking back the beer, forbidden at home, and smoking fags he cadged from Carr. An amalgam of alcohol and success loosened Larwood up, made him relax in company and brought him out of himself. If Carr led him astray off the field, at least he kept him straight on it. Robert Larwood reluctantly accepted that his son had moved into the roughhouse of professional sport, where standards of behaviour were different. Boys, he concluded, will be boys.

When Carr originally took over the team, he was warned that it didn't want any 'bastard amateurs' in charge. The players, most of them ex-miners, were a cliquey bunch and didn't take kindly to a hedonistic, highfalutin' public schoolboy in a striped blazer. Carr soon won them over. Firstly, because he was a good batsman (especially forceful off the front foot) and a shrewd, considerate captain who played the game seriously. Cricket, he maintained, 'was never intended for namby-pambies'. Secondly, because he was disarming, droll and gregarious. 'I was the biggest ass at work you ever saw,' he would tell his team. 'All my schoolwork was done by the clever boys.' He added with pride that he got sent down from Oxford after just two terms for 'not doing a single stroke of work'.

Carr's image as 'a good-time Charlie' and a 'card', as Larwood put it, cut through the class distinction between amateurs and pros. He was amiable. He bought his round of drinks. He swore and cussed. He told stories against himself. He didn't like the committee any more than the pros. When, in 1919, it cabled him to ask whether he would accept the captaincy of the Gentlemen against the Players, he cabled back: 'No, I am going to fly to China in a taxicab.' In fact, he ought to have travelled everywhere by taxicab. Carr was a terrible driver, a total terror behind the wheel. In 1925, he had three accidents in his racing-green three-wheeled Morgan. He struck a telegraph pole, drove it into a lorry and ran it off the road, nearly killing himself and five other Nottinghamshire players. He blamed the colour of the car for bringing him bad luck. He was once so desperate for a drink that he drove his car on to the steps of a pub and tried to negotiate it through the double doors. An exasperated Carr clambered inelegantly from behind the wheel, went inside and came out lugging crates of beer, which he lobbed into the seat before reversing into the early-evening traffic as if nothing had happened.

None of this mattered to the players – especially Larwood. Carr was fiercely proud of, and unbendingly loyal to, the people who played under him. He received the same level of loyalty in return. If you knew him, Larwood said, it was impossible not to like Carr or 'want to do right by him'. He had a way of drawing his team together. This, after all, is someone who received a telegram ordering him to report for war duty while he was batting against Surrey at the Oval. 'Well,' he said, softly, as if he'd just been invited to a black-tie dinner in Holland Park, 'I'll have my innings first.' Larwood heard that story about Carr, and plenty of others too, as soon as he joined Nottinghamshire. If Carr could be so phlegmatic about his call-up for war, then Larwood reckoned he had to be a 'very decent bloke' and that nothing would ever ruffle him. A crisis for Carr was running out of beer. Pressure was finishing enough drinks before the bell went for last orders and making sure that his hotel bedroom contained enough alcohol for a decent nightcap.

Larwood discovered that his captain's cavalier personal life didn't impinge on the 'tough' way he wanted to play cricket. Jardine regarded the game as a puzzle to be solved, rather like *The Times* crossword. Carr regarded it as trial of endurance and strength, rather like trench warfare. Nottinghamshire under Carr were often criticized as being just 'too competitive'. The criticism came from what Carr regarded as 'some of the more "gentlemanly" counties in the south'. The word 'gentlemanly' was transparently a euphemism for 'soft'. In reality, the charge of being over-zealous had more to do with the hostility of Larwood's bowling: batsmen would turn and head away from him, like swimmers catching sight of a shark.

Whenever Larwood saw Carr, he'd bolt to attention. There was 'something' indefinable about Carr that 'set him aside as a leader' of men, he said. 'You wanted to follow him,' was the explanation he offered. When Carr first caught sight of Larwood, he fell into the same trap as everyone else. He thought he was just a 'tiny little fellow' with a hollow chest who didn't have the physique for bowling. 'I thought he would not last in a first-class game. He was, from the very start, very quick off the ground, but he seemed to lack stamina . . . Little did I think then that he was to become the finest fast bowler in the world,' admitted Carr. When he got closer Carr was struck by the fact that Larwood had 'uncommonly big hands and strong fingers', which meant he was able to put a 'great deal on the ball'. Carr began to see 'with half an eye what there might be in him'.

The pace Carr got out of Larwood was achieved with base psychology. Larwood was self-conscious. It was terribly easy to shake his belief in himself, and yet Carr found he could just as easily restore it. If Carr thought Larwood was flagging or not properly prepared for bowling, he merely had to tell him that someone – usually one of the opposition's batsmen or captain – thought he was 'slowing up' or 'wasn't as fast as he had been'. After either whispering it in Larwood's ear or saying it aloud on the square, the 'Mr Hyde' side of Larwood's character immediately emerged. He fell for this hackneyed motivational trick every time. 'Stoking him up,' was how Carr described it. Larwood's shoulders snapped back. He looked six inches taller. His eyes were like flame. He was transformed. 'Does he believe that?' Larwood would reply to Carr. 'Well, I'll show the bastard. Give me the ball, Mr Carr . . . ' The idea that someone might think he was deficient or inferior, or just the prospect of failure itself, was enough to goad Larwood. Batsmen knew not to get clever with him or try to pretend he wasn't quick. Where his reputation was concerned, Larwood didn't have a sense of humour.

If Larwood didn't need the jump-start of the captain's words to get him going, Carr would begin a game by saying nothing more to him than: 'Now come on, young 'un,' do your best.' He always bowled him in short spurts, otherwise he feared he might splutter towards the end of a spell, like a car running out of petrol. Larwood talked gratefully about how Carr 'nursed' him along in this way and always took the bother to make sure: 'Do you really want another over?'

Carr registered from the start one aspect about Larwood that greatly amused him. He wanted to bowl batsmen out. He got more pleasure from seeing the stumps and bails fly than he did from any other form of dismissal. It was as if achieving a wicket with a catch meant that it only half-belonged to him. And trapping someone lbw, though satisfying enough, wasn't much of a spectacle for anyone in the crowd to remember and recount later on. A fast bowler's job, as Larwood saw it, was to 'knock back the timber' at least twice during an innings. 'I just loved to see the pegs flying,' he said. He was there to entertain. 'Whenever he hit the stumps,' said Carr, 'a broad smile came across his face which he tried to conceal. It would not interest him if someone was caught off his bowling.' Larwood couldn't disguise that smile when he played for the Rest of England against England – effectively a Test trial – at Lord's in 1926. A ball in the first innings zipped back and took out an unfortunate batsman's off and middle stumps. The batsman was Carr. 'He was just too fast for me – or, if you like, I was too slow for him,' he confessed. 'I very much doubt if there has ever been a faster bowler than Lol', said Carr, who added earnestly that no one could possibly conceive his true 'pace and power unless you have batted against him or fielded in the slips to him'. Carr knew because he had a ring-side seat for almost Larwood's

With more application, Harold Larwood might have developed into the Ian Botham of his era. He gradually became more assured and polished in his run-making. Here, he turns a ball from Maurice Tate to leg in the 1926 Test trial at Lord's.

entire career. 'Unless you held your bat very tight he could quite easily knock it out of your hands,' he said, 'and to catch all the catches in the slips off him you needed a collection of young men on the flying trapeze.'

The deferential master–servant relationship between gentleman amateur and tip-your-cap professional seems unimaginable today. Those ivy-clad social walls no longer exist. We're egalitarians – or at least try to be. In sport, the pecking order is rooted in skill rather than determined by which school you had the good blessing to attend or where your father came from or who he knew. Background and breeding don't rigidly fix rank on the field. Larwood's generation was different. It respected, and responded to, the officer class to which Carr's and Jardine's families belonged. In the Great War, the officers were obliterated along with their troops. Death didn't discriminate in the trenches, so the mothers and fathers in the 'big houses' mourned as deeply and as long as those in the terraces and back-to-backs. Young men like Larwood, who lived with the suffering of war around them without serving on the front line, saw nobility and fortitude in the upper classes. Larwood disliked the 'snooty amateurs who used to look down their noses at you' and 'those who wouldn't eat at the same table as pros'. He and Bill Voce used to say to one another, 'Let's go and knock the hyphens out of the amateurs.' But he really 'hated all the "them and us" nonsense'; he followed figures such as Jardine and Carr because he trusted them to lead. That's why Larwood – although his opinion might appear romantic and anachronistic now – always argued very strongly in support of retaining amateur captains. 'I was in favour of them,' he said. 'If a professional asked you to do a thing I don't think you could have answered him in the same way you would answer an amateur. He may have asked you if you wanted another bowl and you'd say you'd had enough. But if an amateur asked you – and I'm talking about real amateurs in my day, they were all moneyed men and gentlemen – you would say "Oh well, I'll try."' As Larwood also said: 'That's the way it was with Mr Carr and Mr Jardine, and I've no regrets about it.'

There was only one thing about the amateur captain that Larwood would have abolished. 'At Notts, the ten professionals had one room and the amateur captain had another, the same size, to himself. On some grounds the amateur would walk through one gate and the professionals through another and we'd meet in the middle. I wasn't in favour of that.' If you were good enough to share the same oval of grass, he argued, you were good enough to put on and 'take off your boots and fart in the same place'.

With Carr and Jardine, Larwood had a special rapport. 'We had this understanding, you see,' said Larwood. 'It was a mutual respect.' As far as Jardine was concerned, it began on that August Bank Holiday at the Oval. And as far as the Australians were concerned, it spelt trouble seven years later.

CHAPTER THREE

HIS MASTER'S VOICE

June 1926 – September 1927

Harold Larwood always thought it was important to be sartorially smart.

Lord's: June 1926 – Nottingham: September 1927

The cricketer Harold Larwood idolized wasn't a fast bowler. He was Jack Hobbs, the supreme artist of batsmanship. When he spoke of Hobbs, Larwood referred to him in hushed tones, like someone half-whispering in church. For Larwood, Hobbs was 'The Master'. He was also the 'greatest gentleman', and a 'true sportsman in every way', a man incapable of anything 'paltry or mean'. He admired Hobbs' gentle, polite demeanour and the undemonstrative way he did things. It was as if Hobbs never recognized the greatness that ran through him. 'I've never met a more modest man,' said Larwood, 'or one who is more considerate to others.' Larwood adored Hobbs' 'peerless batting' – stylish, fluent, easy on the eye. The MCC could have photographed each of his signature strokes for its coaching manual. The title of A.C. MacLaren's book captured the essential Hobbs. MacLaren called it *The Perfect Batsman,* and Hobbs consistently proved the statement true. When he retired in 1934, Hobbs had harvested more than 61,000 runs at an average of more than 50, including 199 centuries. He was the first professional cricketer to be knighted. While MacLaren's book honoured and analysed technical brilliance, the poem John Arlott wrote to commemorate his friend's 70th birthday described both the emotion and extreme devotion Hobbs inspired in Larwood and others. Arlott's fifth verse encapsulates it:

> The Master: records prove the title good:
> Yet figures fail you, for they cannot say
> How many men whose names you never knew
> Are proud to tell their sons they saw you play.

Larwood was prouder still to bowl to him. It was a bright May morning in Nottingham, just a few torn rags of cloud in a cobalt sky. There was a soft breeze, barely strong enough to disturb the pennants of the two counties, which hung limply on the flagpoles. Larwood said his original thoughts that morning were about another match, played seven years earlier, when he'd handed over money his father had given him so that he could pay like anyone else at the Trent Bridge turnstiles and watch Hobbs bat. As a boy, Larwood had cut out and kept reports of Hobbs' run-making from newspapers before the discarded copies were torn into single sheets and then screwed into spindles to light the coal fire. In his

The Master. Larwood admired Jack Hobbs more than any other cricketer.

street games, with his makeshift bat and ball, he pretended to be Hobbs. The dusty lanes and the net-curtained windows of the terraced houses became the Oval for him, and Larwood tried to stroke the ball as imperiously as he imagined Hobbs did for Surrey. When the County Championship fixture list appeared in 1919, he searched for Hobbs, and then struck the deal with his father. If Larwood could get himself to Trent Bridge, his father would pay his admission. Although Larwood was already working in the pits, he didn't save his own salary or take much 'pocket money' from it. From the start, he'd voluntarily handed over his wage packet at the end of every week to his mother to pay for board and lodging. 'That was the fair thing to do,' he explained. 'My parents grafted hard to support me, and I wanted to support them.'

With his 15th birthday still five months away, Larwood walked to

Trent Bridge – a round trip of 24 miles. 'I thought nothing of it,' he said, 'I was fit.' For the sake of his first sight of Hobbs, sore feet and worn shoe leather would be worth it. At last Hobbs would be flesh rather than just a smudgy newspaper photograph and he'd witness for himself the way Hobbs could plunder the bowling. When Larwood arrived, already half-way through the morning session, Hobbs was on 85. Larwood settled into a seat, his packed lunch wedged between his knees.

Fred Barratt was over six feet tall, with brawny shoulders as wide as a pit shaft. He rolled in to bowl to Hobbs as 'if he meant business', said Larwood. Barratt dug the ball in. Hobbs tried to turn the rising delivery off his thigh, got an inside edge instead and was caught at short leg. Larwood's long walk was rewarded with the glimpse of Hobbs batting for just one ball. Larwood didn't care. He stood up and clapped Hobbs from crease to pavilion, the palms of his hands reddening. 'I'd seen him at last,' Larwood said. 'Nothing else mattered to me on that day.'

The fact that he was now being paid to bowl at Hobbs still seemed preposterous to Larwood. He felt unworthy. He was a nobody in cricket. He hadn't even played a full season yet. Hobbs was the best batsman in the world, probably the best batsman the sport had ever seen – or would ever see. As Larwood rearranged his field for the umpteenth time, Hobbs – just as the Nottinghamshire committee men had once done – stared back at him and wondered how a bowler so wiry could bowl with such pace. He'd thought exactly the same thing the previous summer when Larwood claimed him at the Oval with a ball that moved away appreciably. For pity's sake, Hobbs thought, the scrawny lad can't weigh more than 11 stone. How does he produce so much speed and movement? 'He told me I'd surprised him at the Oval,' said Larwood, 'and that he wouldn't be surprised again.'

The ball was still fairly new at Trent Bridge; the shine hadn't been rubbed away. Hobbs, nonchalantly picking off 16 runs, was moving effortlessly into his stride, the prospect of another long innings opening up in front of him. He spun the bat gently in his hands, which he did instinctively before nearly every ball, took his stance and waited. Larwood came in to bowl. The ball caught the seam, bit into the turf, shot back six inches and 'took out the off stump', said Larwood. Hobbs stood his ground for a split second, not because of petulance or arrogance, and not because he was trying to convince the umpire that somehow he wasn't out – with the stump flattened there was nothing to debate – but because he'd been momentarily flummoxed by the quality of the delivery that had deceived him both in line and pace. He half-turned and saw the prone stump in the middle distance, replayed the shot in his mind and then looked at Larwood disbelievingly. He nodded in recognition, tucked his bat neatly under his arm and walked back to the pavilion, just as he had done when Barratt removed him under Larwood's incredulous eyes in 1919. How did it happen, Hobbs was asked afterwards? 'Oh, just a fluke, I guess,' he replied. The 'fluke' – same ball, same result, same hesitation from Hobbs and same backward glance – happened again in the second innings. The Surrey game took Larwood's tally of wickets for the season to 23. Less than a month later, before the second Test began against Australia at Lord's, it had more than doubled to 50. Improbably humbled twice in the same match by this young upstart, Hobbs could have dismissed it with a list of plausible excuses to cloak his embarrassment: he hadn't felt well, there wasn't a sightscreen at Trent Bridge, the ball struck a rough patch on the pitch. For the sake of vanity, he could have protested that Larwood had 'fluked' both dismissals. But Hobbs didn't rely on such selfish or self-serving explanations. On the contrary: he acted as Larwood's recruiting sergeant and magnanimously lobbied Lord's on his behalf. The Master's voice convinced England's selectors – including the chairman Pelham ('Plum') Warner – that Larwood ought to be called up for the Ashes Tests. Essentially on Hobbs' recommendation, and after only 35 first-class matches, Larwood became one of England's opening bowlers in June 1926.

Life turns on such chance events. Whenever Larwood looked back on it, he thought the two balls that bowled Hobbs so decisively turned the wheel of his career. Those deliveries were his short cut into the England team. 'Even though he never told me so, and I never asked him about it, I always knew Jack was responsible for me being called up for the Tests,' he'd say. 'Other people said so. He put a word in for me.'

The 1926 series seems just another random thread in the weave of Larwood's whole career. But follow the line of that specific stitch and it leads directly to Bodyline because Larwood's attitudes towards authority and the Australians were shaped by Arthur Carr; and Carr was England's captain and a serial collector of grudges.

* * *

Larwood never fell in love with his own reflection. Self-effacement was one of his virtues. When Nottinghamshire batsman Joe Hardstaff senior, who worked with Larwood's father in the mine, approached him about a trial at Trent Bridge, Larwood replied: 'Surely not, Mr Hardstaff?' Rather like Mr Jaggers' conversation with Pip in *Great Expectations*, Hardstaff explained to Larwood: 'I think you have possibilities . . . You might even become a great cricketer one of these days if you really want to.' Every summer Larwood noticed Hardstaff's bronzed figure strolling through Nuncargate for his daily pint at The Cricketers' Arms, the pub that was just a well-hit six from the village ground. He caught sight of him standing on the boundary too, always wearing a pork-pie hat. The outfield was bumpy and rutted – the chock holes so deep that children used them to play marbles – and the outfield fell into a pronounced slope. The ground itself was tiny, and Larwood's run was almost 30 paces long. The club cut a wide gap in the low hedge so that he could put down his mark in the adjoining field. Batsmen facing Larwood for the first time would watch him disappear through the hole in the shrubbery and ask: 'Where's he going?' Hardstaff knew where Larwood was going – on to the staff at Trent Bridge; Larwood didn't believe him. When Arthur Carr went to Larwood in the nets to tell him that he'd been chosen to play for England – with Hobbs' specific approval – he didn't believe him either. 'Surely, skipper,' he said, 'I'm not good enough to play for England?' Carr assured him otherwise. 'You're going to be a great bowler, Harold,' he said.

Larwood had seen Lord's only once before: he'd taken six wickets against Middlesex in 1925. Its dignity always entranced him – The Grace Gates, the Father Time weathervane twisting in the wind, the imposing rust-coloured pavilion with its smart carvings, towers and balconies. Everything was fresh and new to Larwood then, and he walked through the Long Room with its gilt-framed oils to find cricket's history staring back at him. Lord's, he said, was 'like a Cathedral' and it made 'you catch your breath whenever you entered it'. At the same time he found its stuffy formality intimidating. Even the air inside it could taste stale. He felt as if he was being watched, and had to watch his step too. 'As a professional, you didn't go where you shouldn't. Otherwise, you'd be put in your place.'

Within three years and two months, Larwood had gone from pitman to Test cricketer. At 15, he'd bowled for Nuncargate Second XI alongside tough miners already well into their twenties. He took 76 wickets at an average of 4.9. At 17, he'd moved into the first team and was bowling in his plimsolls – proper boots were too expensive for his father to buy – and doing so after a night shift. In one game he strained so much with the effort of bowling that his nose bled. His shirt became flecked with blood. He'd finished work just a few hours earlier, barely having enough time to wash and change properly. His team-mates, fearing for his health, begged him to leave the field to mop up the blood around his lips and chin. Larwood refused. He carried on, and the loss of blood became heavier. His mouth and the front of his shirt became smeared with it. He wiped the blood away with the back of his hand, leaving bloody fingermarks on his flesh and flannels. In successive balls he bowled one batsman, then another and finally a third. Even in old age, Larwood would say he could roll back his memory and remember every detail of his first hat-trick, as if it had only just happened. At 19, he'd made his Nottinghamshire debut and heard Carr say: 'I've got a fine young bowler up my sleeve.' And now, at 21, he was facing the Australians. He'd shake hands with King George V, who would come dressed in his long black coat and satin top hat as shiny as new shoes. The King, taken aback at the baby face in front of him, would ask benevolently: 'How old are you, son?'

Hobbs was given the task of shepherding Larwood through the nervous preparation and the brief practice for his debut. He urged him quietly to 'do what you can' and not to be 'overawed'. Larwood was concerned that he might let down his parents with an undistinguished performance. Learning from Carr that Larwood regarded his selection as undeserved, Hobbs used one line to reassure him: 'You're here because you're fast enough.' When it didn't work, he tried to calm Larwood by confessing the apprehension he'd experienced before his own Test debut, and the tremors he still experienced before batting. 'But you're Jack Hobbs,' said Larwood, as if the name alone protected its owner from all human frailties. Nothing Hobbs said dissuaded Larwood from thinking that another fast bowler, rather than him, ought to be sharing such exalted company at Lord's. To be suddenly on casual first-name terms with Jack Hobbs was incredible enough. To share the same dressing room as Herbert Sutcliffe, Patsy Hendren and Frank Woolley, and to be wearing an England cap as he did so, seemed supremely absurd to him, and forced this banal admission: 'I thought someone might shake me awake,' he said to Hobbs. Adding to the sense of unreality, Larwood arrived with his kit over his shoulder at the same time as Maurice Tate. Less than two years earlier Tate had 'flipped' Larwood two shillings for cleaning his boots at

Even without the ball in his hand, Harold Larwood had a penchant for speed. In his younger days, he preferred his motorbike to travelling by car.

Trent Bridge. 'You could have eaten off the soles,' said Larwood, admiring the way he'd washed and scrubbed the mud off them. 'I hugged them afterwards,' he said, 'and held them close to my chest.'

Embarrassment made him hide a secret from Hobbs. Less than 48 hours before the Test began, Larwood took a corner too sharply on his motorbike. He relished speed, and had bought the motorbike to satisfy it. The BSA machine was powerful for the era; it could reach a speed of 60 mph. Larwood steered it with outstretched arms and never wore a crash helmet. Late in the evening, after a day's play against Kent at Trent Bridge, he skidded and collided with a car at a T-junction near his home and spun over the bars and then the bonnet. He damaged the front of his bike, tore his trousers and badly scraped and cut his right thigh and knee. Larwood knew the policeman who arrived at the scene of the accident. 'Keep my name out of it,' he pleaded, aware that any publicity would prevent him from playing at Lord's. The policeman was a willing conspirator. No one – in particular the newspapers – found out about the injury or the 'intense agony' he was in because of it. He wrapped the knee and his thigh in thick crêpe bandages and clenched his teeth against the pain. Kent crushed Nottinghamshire by an innings, which fortunately for Larwood meant he didn't have to bowl again until the Test began. When he got to Lord's, he took off the bandages and quickly pulled on his flannels in a corner of the dressing room without anyone – including Hobbs – realizing that he was injured. The joint felt stiff, the muscles throbbed.

The opening Test at Trent Bridge had been washed out. Lord's at last offered the chance to assess whether England, who had miserably won only one post-war Test in 16 against Australia, might regain the Ashes. The Australians, though not exactly a decaying behemoth, were nonetheless in their twilight years: Warren Bardsley was 42; his partner Charlie Macartney was 40; Arthur Mailey and the captain Herbie Collins were both 38. But one defeat after another left England with psychological hurdles to clear, and Larwood sensed it on the opening morning of the Test when so much was expected of him. He could recall the crowds

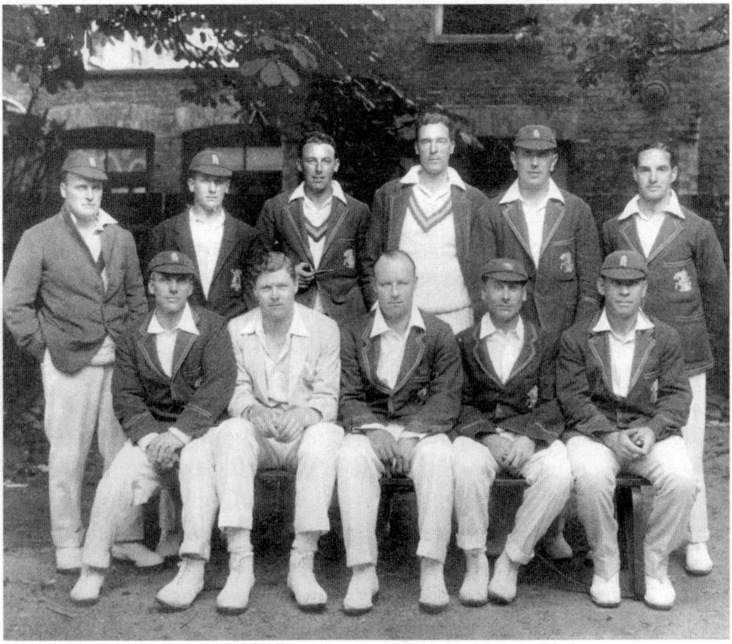

England, Lord's 1926. Back row, from left: Kilner, Larwood, Tate, Woolley, Root, Sutcliffe. Front row: Strudwick, Chapman, Carr, Hobbs, Hendren.

queuing seven or eight deep around the walls of the ground and spilling onto the pavement. He could recall the scraping noise his spikes made against the stone of the pavilion steps and then the softness of his tread across the outfield. He could recall staring into the upturned bowl of the sky and how a high sun cast shadows like smudges of ink. He could recall how Carr had walked up to him and dropped the ball in his hands, like presenting him with a wrapped gift. He could recall how he'd run his fingers across the hard, raised seam, marking out his run and glancing around him at the congested stands and taking a long deep breath, as if sucking the whole experience into his young lungs. The low hum of the crowd swept around and then past him. And then there was silence, as if a switch had been flicked, or a plug pulled, and all the sound and power in the ground had been disconnected.

Larwood began unspectacularly. His knee ached and he became over-anxious. What he described as a 'felt-like' pitch wasn't to his liking either. He struggled to make the ball 'work' for him. Bardsley, on his fourth tour of England, hooked and pulled him to the leg-side boundary and pasted him on the off. He finished with 193 not out. Larwood was forced to bowl short of a length to extract any lift, and Bardsley devoured these tame deliveries hungrily, like a crocodile opening its jaws wide to swallow lumps of meat. Larwood took two for 99 in the first innings and one for 37 in the second. The figures were 'respectable', he said, but didn't reflect either the trouble he was capable of causing batsmen or his speed, which, though nowhere near as quick as the Bodyline pace he would generate six years later, remained impressive in the conditions. 'I wasn't great,' he said. 'I wasted a lot of energy and overs.' Whenever he went into reflective or analytical mood, Larwood tended to be too hard on himself. The wicketkeeper Herbert Strudwick stood further back for him – around 25 yards – than he did for any other bowler. And Larwood's pace throughout that summer is reflected in a vignette from the tour game at Trent Bridge a few weeks after the Lord's Test. Even then, Larwood could sear a batsman with the heat of his bowling. When Johnny Taylor edged a ball from him, it bisected Sam Staples at first slip and 'Dodge' Whysall at second. Staples reached the ball a split second before Whysall, who involuntarily locked his own hand behind Staples' at the very moment of impact and felt the vibration of the catch. Within five minutes, Whysall's palm was as bruised as that of Staples.

The Lord's Test was never a true contest between batsman and

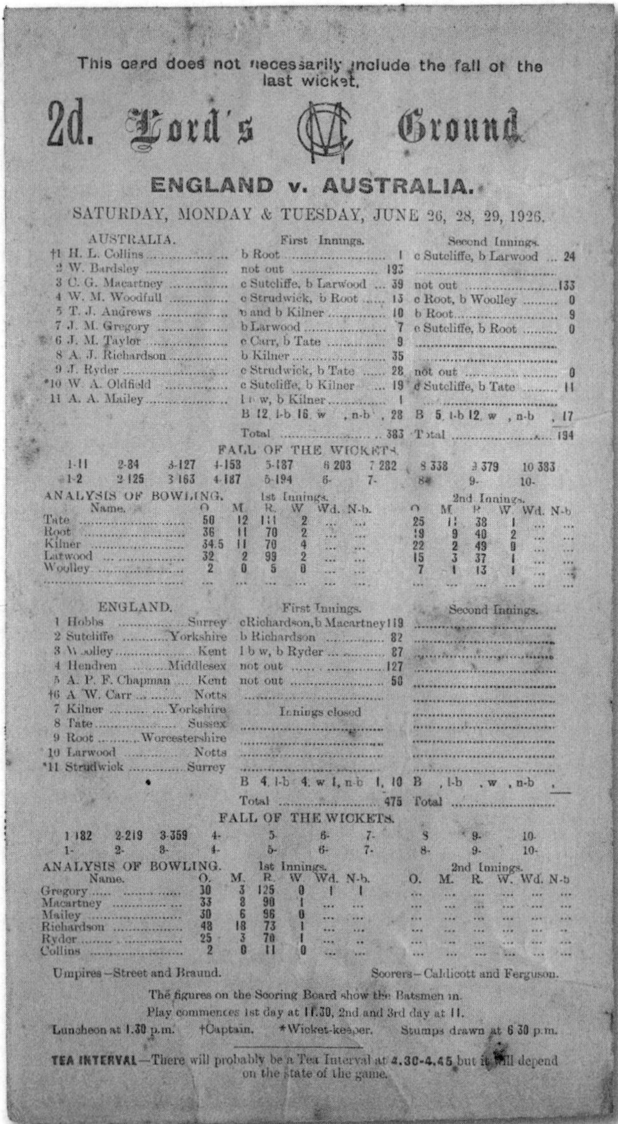

This card does not necessarily include the fall of the last wicket.

2d. Lord's Ground

ENGLAND v. AUSTRALIA.

SATURDAY, MONDAY & TUESDAY, JUNE 26, 28, 29, 1926.

AUSTRALIA.	First Innings.		Second Innings.	
†1 H. L. Collins	b Root	1	c Sutcliffe, b Larwood	24
2 W. Bardsley	not out	193		
3 C. G. Macartney	c Sutcliffe, b Larwood	39	not out	133
4 W. M. Woodfull	c Strudwick, b Root	13	c Root, b Woolley	0
5 T. J. Andrews	c and b Kilner	10	b Root	9
7 J. M. Gregory	b Larwood	7	c Sutcliffe, b Root	0
6 J. M. Taylor	c Carr, b Tate	9		
8 A. J. Richardson	b Kilner	35		
9 J. Ryder	c Strudwick, b Tate	28	not out	0
*10 W. A. Oldfield	c Sutcliffe, b Kilner	19	c Sutcliffe, b Tate	11
11 A. A. Mailey	l b w, b Kilner	1		
	B 12, l-b 16, w , n-b ,	28	B 5, l-b 12, w , n-b ,	17
	Total	383	Total	194

FALL OF THE WICKETS.

1-11	2-84	3-127	4-158	5-187	6-203	7-282	8-338	9-379	10-383
1-2	2-125	3-163	4-187	5-194	6-	7-	8-	9-	10-

ANALYSIS OF BOWLING.

Name.	1st Innings. O.	M.	R.	W.	Wd.	N-b.	2nd Innings. O.	M.	R.	W.	Wd.	N-b.
Tate	50	12	111	2	...	...	25	11	38	1	...	...
Root	36	11	70	2	...	...	19	9	40	2	...	...
Kilner	34.5	11	70	4	...	...	22	2	49	0	...	...
Larwood	32	2	99	2	...	...	15	3	37	1	...	...
Woolley	2	0	5	0	...	...	7	1	13	1	...	...

ENGLAND.		First Innings.		Second Innings.
1 Hobbs	Surrey	c Richardson, b Macartney	119	
2 Sutcliffe	Yorkshire	b Richardson	82	
3 Woolley	Kent	l b w, b Ryder	87	
4 Hendren	Middlesex	not out	127	
5 A. P. F. Chapman	Kent	not out	50	
†6 A. W. Carr	Notts			
7 Kilner	Yorkshire	Innings closed		
8 Tate	Sussex			
9 Root	Worcestershire			
10 Larwood	Notts			
*11 Strudwick	Surrey			
		B 4, l-b 4, w 1, n-b 1,	10	B , l-b , w , n-b ,
		Total	475	Total

FALL OF THE WICKETS.

1-182	2-219	3-359	4-	5-	6-	7-	8-	9-	10-
1-	2-	3-	4-	5-	6-	7-	8-	9-	10-

ANALYSIS OF BOWLING.

Name.	1st Innings. O.	M.	R.	W.	Wd.	N-b.	2nd Innings. O.	M.	R.	W.	Wd.	N-b.
Gregory	30	3	125	0	1	1	...	...	...	...	...	...
Macartney	33	8	90	1	...	...	...	...	...	...	...	...
Mailey	30	6	96	0	...	...	...	...	...	...	...	...
Richardson	48	18	73	1	...	...	...	...	...	...	...	...
Ryder	25	3	70	1	...	...	...	...	...	...	...	...
Collins	2	0	11	0	...	...	...	...	...	...	...	...

Umpires—Street and Braund. Scorers—Caldicott and Ferguson.

The figures on the Scoring Board show the Batsmen in.

Play commences 1st day at 11.30, 2nd and 3rd day at 11.

Luncheon at 1.30 p.m. †Captain. *Wicket-keeper. Stumps drawn at 6 30 p.m.

TEA INTERVAL—There will probably be a Tea Interval at **4.30-4.45** but it will depend on the state of the game.

One of Larwood's most cherished mementoes. The scorecard from his Test debut against Australia at Lord's in 1926.

bowler. The tame pitch loaded the dice for batsmen and made another draw inevitable. After Australia's 383, England heaped up 475 runs. Hobbs elegantly scored 119. Larwood was dropped – not because the selectors weren't impressed with him but because, after a summer constantly interrupted by rain, the strips for the third Test at Headingley and the fourth at Old Trafford were benign. Predictably those Tests were drawn too. The first four matches of the series were played over three days. The fifth at the Oval, designed to break the stalemate and decide the Ashes, was timeless. But the most critical event occurred before a ball was bowled there.

* * *

At the beginning of the summer Arthur Carr was made England captain for what he supposed would be the entire series. If he managed to win it, Carr knew he was certain to be chosen to defend the Ashes in 1928–29 in Australia. For two reasons, his chance never came. He bitterly referred to them as his 'undoing'. The first was a dropped catch; a catch, which as Carr lamented in a long, agonizing wail, he would normally take 'ninety-nine times in a hundred'. On the opening morning of the Headingley Test, Carr went out to inspect the wicket with Hobbs and Plum Warner. He pressed his thumb into the pitch, which was soft after more rain. The sun was blazing, and Carr expected the ball to turn wickedly as the soil dried. He won the toss and reckoned the pitch would be 'paradise for bowlers'. He misread it. The sun went in and the ball didn't turn. Tate still took Bardsley's wicket with the opening delivery of the Test. Just four balls later Macartney found himself on strike. Carr had developed a plan against him. He believed Macartney was certain to give an early chance through the slips. He planned to 'move quietly out of the gully' and join the cordon to take it. Tate got the ball to swerve away from Macartney, and he edged a catch that flew straight into Carr's hands at hip height and then spilled out again. Macartney went on to score 151, an innings described by Carr as 'just about the most wonderful century I have ever seen'. At lunch, with Macartney already past his century, Warner sat glum-faced and brooding. Carr called his expression 'like nothing on earth'. He recalled it frequently afterwards, like a bad dream. 'The whole memory of that missed catch is almost more than I can bear,' he confessed. 'I think I spent the most dreadful luncheon interval in all my experience of cricket.' Carr remembered that he could not 'think of a thing to say or eat a mouthful'.

More abject misery followed. During the rest day of the next Test at Old Trafford, Carr had dinner with Sir Home Gordon, a former Guards officer and cricket aficionado. The following morning he told the selectors he was unfit to play. Carr claimed that he woke up unable to speak. His throat was tight, and he had a temperature. 'I was ill,' he insisted. The cause of his illness was never precisely pinned down. Carr said he had tonsillitis. Sir Home Gordon insisted that Carr had contracted food poisoning from a mysterious 'something' he ate. Another story claimed that Carr had suffered a bout of fibrositis. Whichever ailment was whispered or written about, the conflicting accounts pointed suspiciously to one thing. Carr's 'tonsillitis' seemed a handy excuse for drunkenness. Given his widespread reputation as a drinker, it was the most plausible explanation. As Sherlock Holmes deduced: 'Once you eliminate the impossible, whatever remains, no matter how improbable, must be the truth.' Carr had tipped back too much alcohol and woken up with a monumental hangover.

He stayed in bed all day 'receiving constant messages about the progress of the play'. The speculation about the nature of his 'illness', and whether it was drink-related, intensified to such a pitch that Sir Home Gordon felt obliged to write to the *Manchester Guardian* to defend him. He protested that Carr had drunk just one glass of champagne on the evening of their meal together.

A week and a half later, Carr arrived at the Test selectors' meeting in London to find the temperature in the room distinctly chilly. 'I very soon sensed that something was not quite right,' he said with massive understatement. 'It was not very long before I found out what it was . . . I was to be sacked.' Hobbs and Wilfred Rhodes had been co-opted on to the committee. The two pros backed Carr. The other selectors supported Warner's assertion that Carr must be dropped to strengthen England's batting and were prepared to voice it. Agreement was reached between them well before the meeting began. In a brief speech, Warner told Carr that he was neither sufficiently in-form nor fit enough to play. For 'the sake of England', Warner added pompously, he should stand down. The incandescent Carr walked out of the meeting. 'I suppose,' he said, 'that I was dropped as some sort of punishment for having fallen sick . . . and for taking, as captain, the onus of putting the Australians in at Leeds.' Like a prime minister, the chairman of selectors has to be a good butcher.

He has to know how to wield the knife and be brave enough to use it. But the carving-up of Carr revealed traits in Warner that were to surface again during Bodyline and leave ghastly marks on Larwood, Douglas Jardine and Bill Voce.

Warner led two England teams to the Ashes: the 1903 side with Rhodes, George Hirst and Bernard Bosanquet, who devised the fiendish googly; the 1912 side with Rhodes again, plus Hobbs, Frank Foster and Johnny Douglas. In 1920, he carried Middlesex to the County Championship. He was a cricket blue blood. The bad news was Warner's character. He was pious, unctuous and duplicitous, forever using the cloak of conviviality to disguise the dagger of convenience that he would slip in – usually in the middle of the spine – either to protect himself or to advance his own causes. Put simply, Warner was a bastard.

Carr struggled with the bat in 1926. The previous summer he'd made eight centuries, including one in just 48 minutes against Sussex at Hove, and scored more than 2300 runs. But the England captaincy weighed his batting down and he scratched around hopelessly for form. This poverty of runs led him to suggest privately to the selectors that he should resign before the Headingley Test. 'I doubted I was worth my place in the side,' he admitted. Warner sent him a telegram in reply that glowed with warmth. 'Nonsense. Your captaincy and fielding are worth 100 runs an innings and you will get going soon. Love from Plum.' Warner also went so far as to write to Carr: 'You are the best captain we have had for ages . . . Cheer up, old fellow. We all have the very greatest confidence in you and I wouldn't be without you for anything.' This time Warner signed off with: 'Love from yours affectionately'.

An establishment figure from his pomaded hair to his city brogues, Warner had two more flaws: the tendency towards rank hypocrisy and self-delusion. Whether it was Carr's sacking or Larwood's Bodyline bowling, Warner tried to make it look as though his hands were clean in the matter. He was an expert in deflecting criticism away from himself; usually through syrupy prose. He couldn't stare in the eye anyone whom he'd already stabbed or was about to stab in the back. Warner was cricket's Macavity. Like Macavity, Warner always had an alibi and, when the going got tough, he was never there. Where Bodyline was concerned, he resorted to type, portraying himself as a helpless, stranded observer. During the tour he slapped Larwood on the back. He bought him drinks. He worried about his well-being. After it was over, and he was cosily back at Lord's, he condemned Bodyline as grubby and sordid, and added – perhaps even convincing himself of this – that the unsavoury business had absolutely nothing to do with him. The pattern of behaviour was already well set. After discarding Carr, he also had the brass neck to write to him: 'I cannot say how deeply I feel for you in what I know is a great disappointment . . . I believe I feel it almost as much as you do . . . There is no doubt whatever in my own mind that you are the best captain in England.' The last seven words of his letter encapsulate Warner's combination of arrogance and slipperiness. There is also a pathetic, almost childish need for self-exculpation. 'Don't be hurt or angry with me,' he pleads. Warner's cack-handed management produced embarrassing, very public and highly contradictory statements: Warner said that Carr wasn't well enough to play at the Oval – Carr said he was perfectly healthy.

One of the central factors in Carr's psychological DNA was his love of a 'jolly good argument'. He liked to clear the air, even if this meant turning it blue sometimes. On various occasions, he fell out spectacularly with Nottinghamshire, the MCC committee, and anyone who had an Australian accent. Rows were the staple diet of his life. He relished them as much as beer from the tap. 'I am not boasting . . . but I do not think that anyone big in cricket has ever had more rows than I have had,' he said before expanding on his principal philosophy, which was remarkably uncomplicated: 'If I have a row, I want to have a proper row.' The rows left scores unsettled. The devastating hurt and resentment he felt over his dismissal never left him, and the enmity between him and Warner simmered on. Carr couldn't bring himself to forgive, understand or forget what Warner did to him or his striving to defend it, and he would eventually use Larwood as a weapon to get back at his old adversary and at Australia. For as well as the England captaincy, Carr lost his sense of proportion. A wild thought burrowed itself into his mind and wouldn't shift: the perfidious Australians had somehow infiltrated the selection committee and influenced them against him.

Carr wasn't especially vain, but he did come across as a tad over-sensitive about his physical appearance when measured against the looks of blond-haired and energetically handsome Percy Chapman, who was chosen to replace him. Alongside the matinée idol Chapman, Carr was like the ugly sister in a pantomime. To prove it, and to illustrate how such a slight affected him, Carr quoted from a *Daily Express* article about Chapman, which said that his was 'the first photograph to attract any woman' and then called him 'undoubtedly the Apollo of the (England) XI – Greek perfection'. In the same piece Carr's face was summed up far less flatteringly as 'sinister'. 'Perhaps,' wondered Carr, 'there was something about my looks or my personality that the Australians did not like and the selectors were given the tip not to offend them!' The deliberately placed exclamation mark half-suggests Carr was being skittish rather than serious. It doesn't, however, disguise Carr's solid belief that the statement was true or, at the very least, contained a splinter of truth. When Carr went on to say that no one ought to be judged on his 'film star smile', he meant Chapman. Although Carr generally disliked and mistrusted Australians before his sacking – he thought them loud, gobby and uneducated – his antipathy towards them set firm after it. Larwood would be led partly astray and suffer as a consequence.

* * *

Percy Chapman was twelfth man at Old Trafford before Carr found himself 'indisposed'. Carr was unnecessarily snide about Chapman, whom – in a prime example of double standards – he frowned upon for liking a drink. Carr called him 'the always-ready-to-be-matey-and-social Percy'. While Carr was dining with Sir Home Gordon, he claimed Chapman had taken himself on a spree elsewhere. The following morning he was 'routed out' of bed and told to 'do a bit of fielding'. He got what Carr smugly said was a 'pretty nasty jar'. With perfect justification, Carr complained that Chapman was untried as a captain. He'd skippered neither Cambridge nor Kent. But in the rigid class system of 1920s cricket, the selectors were abiding by tradition and anointing the senior amateur. The selectors made two more pivotal changes for the Oval. Rhodes had first played for England in 1899, and was eight weeks away from his 49th birthday. With Rhodes sitting beside them, the other selectors turned to his slow left-arm deliveries. When Hobbs spoke, it was to urge the recall of Larwood. He had just reached 100 wickets for the season. The day afterwards he took another five against Derbyshire. 'It was Jack's word in the right ear again,' said Larwood. 'Without him, I might never have got back into the team.'

An absorbing, dramatic Test was decided by two partnerships: Hobbs and Sutcliffe with the bat; Larwood and Rhodes with ball. 'I played as if I might never get picked for England again,' said Larwood. 'You see, there were so many good players around, I thought I would never get another chance if I didn't play a part in it. I always thought there was someone better than me waiting for my place. I think it helped me get the most out of every match.'

England made a scratchy 280 in the first innings. Australia nudged just ahead of them in reply: 302. England's second innings began under bruised, ever-darkening skies, Hobbs and Sutcliffe surviving for an hour before the close of play. When it resumed the following morning Hobbs was bleakly convinced that the Ashes were already lost. A thunderstorm engulfed the Oval during the early hours. The vast queues of people, sleeping rough beside the gates to make sure of a seat, scattered for shelter. Under torrential rain, the uncovered pitch turned from lily-pale to lamp-black – the dreaded sticky dog on which the ball was certain to turn extravagantly or rear up or skid treacherously low. After Hobbs took his three-halfpenny tram ride from home to the Oval, and glimpsed the pitch again, the sun was just emerging through low cloud and the air clung damp and heavy around him. Hobbs shook his head, and said to himself that England would be fortunate to muster 80 runs on it. He went away to pad up and to smoke his pipe in mournful and monastic silence. 'He was pretty gloomy,' said Larwood.

The umpire Frank Chester assessed it in retrospect as the 'worst sticky' he had ever seen. Even after a few overs, Hobbs was confiding to Sutcliffe: 'Pity about the rain, it's rather spoilt our chances.' When the ball pitched, pieces of top soil broke away. Hobbs and Sutcliffe carefully smoothed them down with the face of their bats, like dutiful head gardeners. Larwood always claimed that the Australians were guilty of naive tactics, which tilted the scales towards England. He said Arthur Richardson, bowling off-spin at medium pace, came round the wicket – sometimes with six short legs – when he should have gone over it. Macartney bowled over the wicket when he should have gone round it on what Larwood felt was a left-hander's pitch. 'If he had bowled round the wicket and Richardson over, Australia would probably have won,' he said.

Hobbs took his guard outside leg stump and moved swiftly across as soon as the ball was delivered. Rather than allowing himself to be tied to the crease, he attacked – sweeping, cutting and pushing the ball for quick singles whenever he could. Only once was Hobbs shackled: Richardson tethered him, like the Lilliputians tying up Gulliver, for eight painstaking overs. And only once was Hobbs in danger. A googly from Arthur Mailey caught him plumb in front of the wicket. Watching from the other end,

Arthur Carr described Larwood as a first-rate fieldsman. Here he pockets a low catch from Bill Ponsford off Wilfred Rhodes at the Oval in 1926, during Australia's second-innings collapse. England won by 289 runs and regained the Ashes. The wicketkeeper is Herbert Strudwick.

Sutcliffe's head dropped like a cut flower. He judged that the ball would have taken out the middle stump. He watched Chester remove his hand from his pocket to signal Hobbs' dismissal, and he waited for the raucous appeal and then the exasperated sigh from a demoralized crowd. The appeal never came. Australia retrieved the ball and tossed it back to Mailey as if nothing had happened. The bowler and wicketkeeper, Bert Oldfield, wrongly believed the ball had pitched outside off stump (remember, at that time a bowler had to pitch the ball wicket to wicket to force an lbw). Two overs later, Hobbs casually asked Chester, 'Was it close?' and, well aware of what Chester's answer was sure to be, half smiled at the life he'd been given. Hobbs' control of the bat, the ball and the conditions was regal, his run-making as orderly as a royal procession. His century – his first in an Oval Test – arrived in three and a half hours of exemplary batsmanship. The modest and usually undemonstrative Hobbs waved his cap and bat to all parts. He made exactly 100, and Sutcliffe carried on to 161: England, 436 all out, left Australia the impossible target of 415.

* * *

When Chapman had seen the condition of the pitch after the thunderstorm, he'd immediately called for the heavy roller to force moisture to the surface and deaden it. After rain fell again, around noon on the fourth day, the Australians hesitated fatally before the same roller came out again. By the time the groundstaff heaved it across the pitch, the top soil was just flaking away. 'It felt like rough pastry in your hand,' said Larwood. For Larwood and Rhodes, the wicket was like a gourmet feast.

In the first innings one ball from Larwood marked him out as an extraordinarily fine bowler. Tommy Andrews, the Australian number five, thought the delivery was flying harmlessly wide. He lifted his bat, as politely as a gentleman gesturing to let a lady enter a room before him. The ball shot back five inches, kept low and took out his off stump. Andrews looked like a man who had just been spat at by a stranger. He lamely claimed afterwards that the ball must have been deflected by a piece of dirt on the pitch. As Larwood gruffly pointed out: 'You don't get pieces of foreign dirt on Test wickets.' Larwood said it was his 'break-back ball' – precisely the same delivery that had claimed Hobbs twice at Trent Bridge. He was striving to bowl an in-swinger. Instead, he cut his second index finger to the right of the seam and 'whipped it hard down my right thigh instead of following through in an arch to the left'. The ball swept in like an off break.

In the second innings Larwood made the ball shoot back and lift like the front hooves of a kicking horse. He still maintained – probably because he didn't have to face either himself or Rhodes – that the pitch was not 'particularly difficult' for batting. The two bowlers, from different cricketing generations, looked like father and son: Rhodes with his stony face and black pebble eyes, half covered by the peak of his cap as he bowled, edged beside Larwood conspiratorially at the end of his own overs to pass on slivers of advice. Larwood would nod respectfully, as if his own father was making a point to him. The old maestro and Larwood, who the next day's newspapers would describe as the 'demon boy' and the 'diminutive dynamic youth', ran through the Australians. Rhodes methodically wheeled away; Larwood bore down explosively on the batsmen. Larwood claimed Bill Woodfull, Macartney and Andrews again. Rhodes removed Ponsford, Collins and Bardsley. As each wicket fell, the Australians sat mute, like a group of refugees dazed and confused from the effects of a natural disaster. An innings which began at 3.30 p.m.

The demure Lois Bird, whom Harold Larwood married in September 1927.

was over in a typhoon lasting just two hours and two minutes and 53.3 overs. Australia all out 125: Larwood three for 34 and Rhodes four for 44.

The crowd crossed the fence and the ropes, covered the outfield and surged towards the pavilion, leaving heel- and scuff-marks and whole footprints as souvenirs on the earth. Larwood was chased towards the gate. Unable to run because he was so tired, he half-staggered, head down, into the sanctuary of the dressing room. He'd injected so much 'spite' into his bowling that he was physically and mentally spent. His muscles and joints ached. His head swirled with the din of the crowd, which threw him further off balance, as if he'd drunk too much. He began to weep softly with the emotion of it all and his breathing became ragged and heavy. He sat in a gently convulsing heap beside his kit and clothes. Outside, the crowd were cheering. 'It was like Armistice day,' said Larwood. Hobbs, rescued from his own thicket of admirers, eventually thrust a bottle of beer into his hand. Still quietly sobbing, Larwood took a long drink and then kept repeating, 'I don't believe what's happened.' Hobbs laid his hand on Larwood's shoulder, as lightly as a butterfly alighting on a flower. 'You can,' he said gently, 'it's real. We've won.' Larwood turned to Hobbs: 'This is the greatest day of my life,' he said. Hobbs smiled: 'There'll be more of them,' he replied.

* * *

When Ashes fame arrived, Harold Larwood had already met the love of his life. She was so petite that she barely came to his shoulder. She had a soft, gentle-looking face, like a primary-school teacher, and brown wavy hair that was always well kept. The woman Larwood picked as his wife was more shy and self-conscious than him, and she didn't care for, or much understand, cricket. But Lois Bird was an indomitable woman and her strength held her husband together. She had an inner toughness that came, like his own, from the mining household in which she grew up. He'd first seen her in 1925 on what locals called 'the Monkey Run', a Sunday promenade through the park, where the eligible men and women put on their best clothes and tried to impress one another, like peacocks parading their plumage, before the ritual flirting and courting began.

As soon as he became well-known, Larwood – handsome, muscled, square-jawed and with money in his pocket – was pursued by women; at least one of them was very well-off indeed. But Larwood had made up his mind about Lois. His parents, however, needed convincing. The Larwoods were so concerned about their son's future that the two of them began covertly investigating his new girlfriend's suitability as a possible wife. Like a pair of detectives, the Larwoods made clandestine enquiries about Lois. Who were her parents? What kind of reputation had her family carved out for itself? How had she been brought up? Was she polite? Did she go to church? How did she spend her free time? Lastly, was she good enough for dear Harold? He was a 'catch', after all.

The new Mr and Mrs Larwood at Basford, Nottingham, before embarking on their honeymoon in Blackpool.

Robert and Mary Larwood were anxious to fend off the unsuitable and the gold-diggers.

Eventually the Larwoods decided that the demure Lois passed their vetting procedure: she would, after all, make a decent match for their son. The couple were married in secret at a registry office in September, 1927. Lois was 20 years old. The new Mrs and Mrs Larwood typically wanted everything to be kept low-key. There were only three guests at the ceremony, which limited the possibility of any word of it spreading beyond the immediate family and the registrar, who was ordered not to tell the local newspapers. The modest wedding breakfast was held at Larwood's parents' cramped home. The newlyweds honeymooned at a boarding house in Blackpool, and peculiarly took Harold's parents along with them to share the coastal air.

Harold and Lois were married for nearly 68 years. They had five children – all of them girls: June (1928), Enid (1935), Mary (1938), Freda (1943) and Sylvia (1947). As a child, Enid remembered a mother who was always 'cooking, washing, sweeping, cleaning, knitting or nursing a baby'. There were always 'clothes drying inside, either round the fire or on a drying rack suspended from the ceiling'.

Larwood was devoted to his family and proud to be a father. When his and Lois' first child, June, was born just over nine months into the marriage, Larwood found out by telegram. It was handed to him on the outfield at Trent Bridge during a match against Hampshire. 'What's that?' Arthur Carr asked Larwood after jogging over from the slips to the boundary. 'You're supposed to be concentrating on the match, not reading messages.' Larwood looked up from the paper. 'I've got a baby girl,' he said. He pushed the telegram into the pocket of his flannels and punched the air. When Carr tossed him the ball, Larwood snatched at it, increased his speed by two gears and immediately took three wickets in four balls.

In the pavilion afterwards, Hampshire's batsman Philip Mead sighed: 'Thank God it wasn't twins.'

CHAPTER FOUR

BEER, FAGS AND A CHEESE SANDWICH

September 1929

A postcard specially produced to celebrate Nottinghamshire's Championship winners of 1929.

Ilkeston: September 1929

Arthur Carr claimed that the secret of Harold Larwood's success came out of a beer bottle. Carr poured gallons of it down his throat. On his instructions, a river of it, as wide and as brown as the Trent, flowed through the Nottinghamshire dressing room every day. The place reeked of alcohol, cigarette smoke, linseed oil and liniment. Carr shared his taste and enthusiasm for ale whenever possible. But he also maintained, with a poker face, that it had nothing to do with the fact that he liked to drink it himself. The beer, he explained, was only for medicinal purposes. He thought it was 'essential fuel' for fast bowlers, who were no different in his eyes from manual labourers, such as 'harvesters' or 'navvies'. According to Carr, a fast bowler burnt up 'an immense amount of physical strength in out-of-doors exercise' and as a consequence 'must have something to give him a kick'. That 'something' was always alcohol, and Carr insisted: 'Beer is best.' However passionate his argument about its recuperative effects, the theory very obviously, and most conveniently, gave him the perfect excuse to sample it well before pub opening hours. He acted as Larwood's taster – slurping but never spitting out.

Nottinghamshire had another first-class bowler, though not remotely as fast, capable of making a batsman jump – Larwood's new ball partner Bill Voce. Carr made sure that he was similarly 'well fed on ale'.

Voce was Larwood's blood brother. On the field, Larwood and Voce worked in perfect synchrony, like the blades of a pair of scissors. If Larwood didn't take a batsman's wicket, Voce usually did. One would soften up victims for the other, and vice versa. There were batsmen who actually preferred to face Larwood rather than Voce. Larwood bowled straight or the ball cut devilishly away. But Voce – with his smoothly whippy left-arm over – could make the rising delivery break back so that it struck between the ribs like a knife. It was his signature ball, and an imprint of the new hard seam would stay on the batsman's flesh. 'You needed ribs made of rock to bat against Bill,' said Larwood. Voce, though a superb bowler, was nonetheless willingly subservient to Larwood, who before each session would take out his white pocket handkerchief and hold it meretriciously above his head like a windsock before deciding from which end he wanted to bowl. He neither had to ask nor make demands; Voce always gave him the pick of the conditions. 'Look Lol,' he'd say, 'this end will suit you better than me' and then give way for the sake of his friend. Larwood and Voce were a team within a team, and the relationship between them was devoid of pernickety points-scoring or rivalry. There was never any jealousy or bickering between them over the number of wickets the other took or their status within the Nottinghamshire side because Voce always acquiesced to Larwood's needs. Voce would unselfishly toil uphill. He would run into the breeze, however stiff and nasty. He would carry on bowling when Larwood needed a rest. 'Bill was the warhorse,' said Larwood, gratefully. 'And he was just like a brother, who looked after me in every way.'

Whenever he was asked 'how things were going' by other captains, Carr used to reply, half seriously: 'Not so good financially. Most of our matches take only two days.' It was partly true. As Larwood admitted: 'When Bill and I were in fine fettle, a match *would* be over in two days. The gateman and the barmaids would joke with us: "Ease off so we get three days' pay."' C.B. Fry paid Larwood and Voce a gold-starred compliment. Among bowlers of the early 1930s, Fry said, the two of them 'jump at your eye out of the muddled morass of modern bowling with a sense of master craftsmanship'.

Off the field, Larwood and Voce watched out for one another. They travelled together. They drank together. They were usually seen together, like a husband and wife who can't stand to be apart. 'Bill made sure I went to bed early, and I watched how many beers he had,' said Larwood, tongue pressed firmly in his cheek.

Larwood and Voce were born and grew up just less than three miles apart. Their upbringing and background were almost identical, like the matching blots wet ink makes on a folded sheet of paper. They both came from large families; Voce was the eldest of six children. They both worked in the mines before breaking into cricket. They both held the same attitudes towards the game and strict opinions on the importance of family life, the good honest nobility of the working classes and the duty and the responsibility each had to the other. Larwood bowled fast and Voce aspired to match him, despite beginning his career – odd though it seems – as a finger-spinner in 1927.

Voce was five years younger than Larwood, half a foot taller, and impressively barrel-chested. He carried himself like a military man given a solid middle rank. His shoulders eventually grew so wide that Larwood used to kid him: 'You'll have to walk through the door side-on, Bill.' His hands, with long, spatula-like fingers, were large enough to make the ball look like a child's marble in his palm. When the two bowlers walked on to the field, it seemed obvious to anyone who didn't know them that Voce, not Larwood, was sure to be the quicker and nastier.

Just as Jimmy Iremonger had steadily built up Larwood, thickening out his upper body and legs with his drill-sergeant ways, so he did the same for Voce. Early photographs reveal Voce as implausibly thin for a bowler and long-legged too. It looks as if he's been squeezed in a press before being stretched on a rack.

With Fred Barratt to call on as well, Carr had the luxury of being able to rotate his front-line attack. At the captain's pleasure, Nottinghamshire could rely on pace for most of a full day's play. Carr ordered buckets of beer for his bowlers. The liquid take-aways were booked from the Trent Bridge Inn on the far side of the ground and carried into the dressing room as surreptitiously as possible by groundstaff. The buckets were placed on a table in the dressing room alongside dimpled pint-pot glasses, which were used as ladles. The main beneficiary was Larwood. When questioned about it, Carr would say calmly, as if his way of thinking ought to seem perfectly logical to everyone else: 'When I have particularly wanted Lol's tail up in order to get a quick wicket or two . . . I have seen to it that he has not wanted for a drop of beer.' Carr's 'drop' would have satisfied most drinkers on a Saturday-night pub crawl. Larwood consumed what became known as the 'fast bowlers' lunch' or a 'Nottingham sandwich'. It comprised a few pints of ale – the Surrey batsman Andrew Sandham calculated that it might be as high as four – plus a couple of cigarettes and a cheese sandwich. Who cared if it left Larwood tipsy afterwards? What did it matter if the ale slightly blurred his vision in the first half-hour of the afternoon session? Larwood would sweat the beer out through bowling. Carr even swore that half a yard of ale made Larwood half a yard quicker. 'A pint too much might make him slightly tiddly for a while – but only for a little while,' he said, casually dismissing this strange regime, before adding, as if to reassure himself, 'he very quickly perspires it out of his system.'

The habit defied common sense. In the present sporting era, when nutrition, physical fitness, moderation and self-control are obligatory (at least during matches), it seems perverse and self-destructive that the simple cuisine for England's number one fast bowler was as much beer as he could stomach and a slice of Red Leicester. Carr was adamant. 'I made it my business to make sure he took to beer,' he said of Larwood, who had been a reluctant, half-a-pint-of-shandy man before arriving at Trent

The premier, front-line bowling attack. Harold Larwood with Bill Voce, who became his 'fifth brother'.

Bridge. 'You cannot be a fast bowler on a bottle of ginger pop or a nice glass of cold water.' When Carr once poured him wine instead, it went to Larwood's head to such a dizzying extent that he didn't realize he'd claimed the wicket of Sussex batsman K.S. Duleepsinhji. Watching Duleepsinhji walk off, Larwood asked the umpire: 'What's happening?' The incredulous umpire replied: 'You've just got him caught behind.' Larwood then tried to bowl the next ball before the new batsman had reached the crease. 'Hold on!' Carr told him. 'Give the next fellow a chance to get in.' Larwood admitted: 'I couldn't remember a thing about what had just happened. The skipper came to me and said: "You'd better take more wine, Lol, it's obviously good for you."'

Voce often found himself acting as Larwood's protector. One evening he commandeered a wheelbarrow from a pub landlord to take Larwood back to Nottinghamshire's hotel. The two men had again drunk 'a drop or two' too much. He tipped his friend into the barrow, like pushing a noisy baby into a pram, and set off down the street. Larwood's head rocked back and his legs dangled over the front, the heels of his shoes sometimes scraping the pavement. Everything went according to plan until Voce found a policeman blocking his way. 'Don't worry,' he told the officer, 'I'm Voce.' The policeman looked at Voce cynically and then at the drunk man slouched in the wheelbarrow. 'And I suppose your friend here is Larwood,' he said. Voce eventually convinced him that England's premier front-line bowlers were wheeling along a deserted pavement well after closing time. The policeman went back to the hotel with them for a nightcap.

* * *

Arthur Carr vehemently believed two things: what happened inside the dressing room ought to stay inside it. No one should gossip. And he thought the team that drank together stayed together, which is why he established a drinking culture. So much so that Larwood came to parrot the line Carr fed him. 'Beer gives you strength . . . and you've got something to sweat out', he said. The first thing Larwood asked new recruits at Nottinghamshire was: 'Do you like ale?' If the youngster gave the correct answer, he'd reply: 'Good.'

Larwood's 'nip' of beer became as indispensable to him as Popeye's spinach. Even during the Bodyline tour, he took ale breaks. 'When they brought the drinks out, Mr Jardine said to me: "Lol, why don't you take one?" I told him I couldn't drink that orange juice muck. I wanted my half-pint. "Oh," he said, "you can't drink beer on a cricket field. What would Lord's say to that?" Anyway, all I can tell you is that the next drinks break there's a glass of beer hidden amongst the orange juice. And Lord's never did get to hear about it.' Jardine made sure the beer was placed in the middle of the tray, well camouflaged by the other glasses, and Larwood drank it down quickly in two gulps. 'Squash blows your stomach up,' he'd say. 'Beer just gives you a bit of momentum.'

On the boat to Australia in 1932–33, Larwood and Voce ended Eddie Paynter's lifetime of abstinence. Paynter was a 30-year-old teetotaller. He said he had never 'touched, tasted or handled' anything alcoholic until the 'expert guidance' of Larwood and Voce steered him towards drink during a fancy-dress party. 'I took my first shandy . . . and have never looked back,' he admitted much later. The beer binges began an established and accepted ritual of playing – even during the Bodyline series.

Before the opening Test at Sydney, Jardine said quietly to Les Ames: 'Leslie, you know as well as I do that our chance of winning this series depends on Larwood and Voce and that they're both very fond of their beer. Well, I want you to see that they go quietly before and during the Tests.' Ames nodded convincingly, but was unsure about how he could curtail the drinking of two men capable of draining a lake dry. Ames tagged along with Larwood and Voce in the hope of slowing down their alcoholic consumption. But he merely got drunk himself. 'The trouble was,' he said, 'that what was nothing to them was too much for me.'

Shortly before the second Test in Melbourne, Larwood and his friend, the Derbyshire spinner Tommy Mitchell, decided to 'go on the town'. The two of them ran into actors from a pantomime. Larwood and Mitchell drank during most of the afternoon and wobbled back to the hotel in the early evening like a pair of buckled bicycle wheels. Larwood began slapping guests on the back: 'How are you, you old bastard?' he'd ask, obviously very drunk. Jardine had Larwood tailed the next night. When Larwood reached the theatre again, he was called to the phone and heard Jardine's voice at the other end. On his captain's orders he returned immediately to the hotel. 'Harold went,' said Mitchell, 'and he said: "I'll be back at half past ten, or eleven o'clock." No Harold Larwood came at half past ten, or eleven o'clock. That were [sic] the end of being a naughty boy.' From then on Jardine detailed at least two players to follow Larwood, like secret policemen, and make sure he returned early and (mostly) sober to his room. On the eve of the third Test in Adelaide, Larwood, Mitchell and Voce still absconded for another drinking session to drown 'the nerves' inside them. This clandestine escapade unravelled when Mitchell returned to the hotel and decided to serenade Jardine from the landing directly outside the captain's room. While he sang 'Sweet Adeline', 'at the top of his voice', Larwood and Voce ran off like burglars caught carrying swag. Jardine diplomatically said nothing. In fact, he patiently turned a blind eye to most of the indiscretions.

Carr actively organized parties. On Saturday nights, his private income meant he could generously open his wallet, scatter white five-pound notes like wedding confetti and take the whole Nottinghamshire team for a prolonged drinking session. With no such irritating beast as competitive Sunday cricket, there was an entire 24 hours to sleep off any hangover. The idea was not just to get drunk, Carr said, but to thrash out tactics, find out any concerns among the players and cement personal relationships. The way to bond, said Carr, was to drink. 'Now the gloves are off,' he'd say, clapping his hands after getting in the first round. He'd rearrange pub tables, often dragging them from one end of the room to the other, so the team could sit together before he'd demand: 'Let's hear what's on your mind.' Occasionally what was on the mind of the Nottinghamshire pros led to rows and recriminations, and verbal fisticuffs, which Carr would try to resolve with another visit to the pub on the next available lunchtime or evening. He was garrulous but entertaining. You could say of him exactly what Hazlitt said of Coleridge: 'He talked on for ever; and you wished him to talk on for ever.' Larwood said: 'He always had a new story to tell you.'

Carr made a habit of taking Larwood and Voce out alone every Monday on another 'boy's night'. Voce said: 'When we were thirsty it cost him a bob or two.' While it is true that very few cricketers in the 1920s and 1930s rattled a tambourine for the temperance movement, Nottinghamshire under Carr acted like an advertisement for the brewery industry. All of them were 'hail-fellow-well-met' types, who liked a night out, which is exactly what Carr wanted. If the County Championship had ever been decided through alcohol consumption rather than cricket, there is no doubt which side would have easily taken the title – and almost every season too. Nottinghamshire might occasionally be forced to follow on. No opposition, however, could force them under the table. Carr turned pub drinking into a creative art, and it led to one problem. However much Carr found title-tattle traitorous, Nottinghamshire's weekly exploits in saloon bars across the country, and especially within the county itself, invariably became the subject of discussion. There was no shortage of anecdotes, most of which were played down rather than spiced up. When George Gunn celebrated his 50th birthday, during a match at Worcester, the team went to the nearest music hall and were caught toasting him furiously past midnight. 'Dodge' Whysall, due to bat with Gunn the following morning, announced that he'd 'got some music' and said to Gunn: 'Shall we start the concert now?' The players gathered around a piano and Gunn played excerpts from *Iolanthe* and the song 'Watchman, What of the Night'. Gunn admitted that 'the sun was out like billy-oh' by the time he climbed between the sheets. A few hours later he was walking out with Whysall at New Road. 'Are you all right, Dodge?' asked Gunn, realizing that his friend looked as if he needed to lie down rather than bat. 'Yes,' lied Whysall. 'Are you?' Gunn looked across at him. Whysall only had one eye open. The other eye was squeezed shut against the light. He still managed to score 70. Gunn piled up a double century.

Whatever the occasion, Larwood and Voce were never slow to have a pint. In 1932, the night before Nottinghamshire met Glamorgan at Cardiff, there was a mix-up over their hotel accommodation. Larwood and Voce were the last to arrive, at 2 a.m., after a tortuous journey from Nottingham. They repeatedly got lost along mostly narrow, bumpy roads and in bone-shaking transport. There were no rooms left in the hotel. The two fast bowlers had no option but to sleep on the floor of the draughty billiards room. At first Larwood tried sleeping on the table itself, rolling up his jacket as a pillow. He found it as hard as stone.

The following morning, stiff and achy, the bowlers prayed for Carr to win the toss, which would allow them to have another soothing bath and catch some rest before bowling. Carr did them a favour; he called correctly and Notts batted. But worse was to come. The Glamorgan groundsman had prepared the pitch specifically to counter Larwood. It was like a duvet, and produced a low, docile bounce, which came off the track so gently that the batsmen virtually sighted the ball in super-slow motion. Glamorgan later took savage advantage of the feathery conditions, the fact that Larwood and Voce, still fatigued, began the innings like arthritic, disgruntled and rather drowsy old men and tested 'leg theory' in preparation for the Bodyline tour. Only a late collapse enabled Larwood to take a decent five for 78. The last six Glamorgan wickets – through sheer boredom and a dash to top up the total beyond 500 – went for just 66. Larwood and Voce still didn't stop grumbling about the doctored pitch, the unappealing journey across country and the prospect of heading back to Nottingham.

With just a day to go, the match was nailed on as a draw. A mixture of disgust and frustration overwhelmed Larwood and Voce and the rest of the Nottinghamshire team who, typically, on Carr's orders, spent the entire evening singing songs in the dressing room with lots of beer for company. One bucket rapidly followed another (during matches the team avoided pubs as much as possible in case anyone saw them drunk). When it was eventually time to head back to the hotel, Larwood, Voce and a few members of the team decided there was only one way to register their dissatisfaction with the pitch. The team came out of the pavilion, zigzagged across the outfield to the placid strip, unbuttoned their flies and pissed all over it. The following morning, the groundsman found dark yellow stains on the grass. The pissing contest was hushed up. The Glamorgan captain didn't want to jeopardize the future of Nottinghamshire's pros by complaining to Lord's.

Even the opposition had to beware of Nottinghamshire's extreme social activities. Middlesex's Jack Hearne, a batsman and googly bowler, once stayed up all night playing cards with Carr, Larwood and a handful of their Nottinghamshire team-mates. Hearne tried to match them drink for drink, an act as pointless as trying to match Larwood for pace. When he woke up a few hours later, his head throbbing and his face as white as parchment, he vomited twice. He struggled to get to the ground and struggled again to put his kit on properly. He went out to bat with what the Middlesex spinner Ian Peebles, watching from the balcony, recalled as a 'rigid zombie-like step'. The pitch had been cut wide of the pavilion gate. With Hearne's eyes shut, his batting partner Patsy Hendren gradually edged him further away from the stumps. When Hearne opened his eyes, and noticed there wasn't a fielder within 40 yards of him, he turned wearily to Hendren and complained: 'We're too early. They're not out yet.' The Nottinghamshire players – and Hendren – fell about at the practical joke, and Hearne turned round to the sound of laugher and to find them 'doubled up' over it. Hearne told Larwood how dreadfully ill the previous night's excesses had made him. Would Larwood be kind enough to take it easy? he asked. 'Keep the ball well up,' he pleaded in a small voice. Larwood nodded and took pity on him, cutting his delivery stride and turning his arm over at no more than decent medium pace, as if he were taking part in a light net session. Hearne was bowled with the first straight delivery, and made his grateful way back to the pavilion to sleep off the beer.

The Nottinghamshire committee were a puritan lot who distrusted Carr, complained among themselves about his high-society living and didn't believe his psycho-prattle about the importance of beer. Carr regarded them as dullards and prudes. As early as 1926 the fed-up committee was trying, unsuccessfully, to 'chuck' Carr out of the captaincy . . . 'because, so they said, I was not exactly tee-total and rather too fond of sitting up too late at night'. The question is: how did it take them so long to notice? The committee tried again in 1930. Carr's stubborn streak emerged early that season. Hampshire required a single run to win in the County Championship at Southampton. Carr – wanting another night in the hotel and no doubt thinking that an early finish would disrupt the

Larwood in a model's pose, as if about to set out on a relaxing trip to the countryside.

hours he was about to dedicate to drinking – refused to let them have one more over to seal the win: Hampshire had already taken the permitted extra half hour. Carr improbably claimed that rain might arrive overnight, turn the outfield into a lake and give Nottinghamshire the chance of salvaging a draw. The forecast didn't suggest so.

The following morning Hampshire returned to an empty ground to find every Nottinghamshire player on the field wearing his lounge suit; Barratt and Voce wore overcoats too. Carr put himself on to bowl in what one newspaper report described as a 'well tailored dark suit', and ambled up off two paces. The winning run came off the second ball. It was 'bad form' in a game which prided itself on manners, and became another reason, among a long list of others, for the committee to frown on Carr. He was quietly tipped off much later in the summer that the committee

Sam Staples (left) and his younger brother Arthur (right): Sam scored more than 6,000 runs and took over 1,200 wickets for Nottinghamshire. Arthur scored over 5,000 runs and took 500 wickets for the county.

regarded him as a 'bad lad', which was hardly breaking news. The informant added that the committee was on the brink of sacking him because he 'drank too many cocktails and didn't set a good example to the younger players', such as Larwood and Voce. Carr counter-attacked, adopting the gung-ho policy that he followed on the field. He rang his friend Percy Fender, who as well as being Douglas Jardine's captain at Surrey also doubled as a journalist. Fender wrote about Carr's predicament and claimed that he might resign as a consequence – exactly the angle that Carr had asked him to take when planting the story. Fearing a player revolt – with Larwood and Voce prominent in it – the committee capitulated. At least it gave Carr a valid reason for yet another of his beery celebrations.

The best came after Nottinghamshire won the County Championship in 1929 – a moment Larwood considered to be one of his finest. The title ought to have been theirs in 1927. But without the injured Larwood for the final match, Nottinghamshire inexplicably lost – beaten by an innings and eight runs – to Glamorgan, who were bottom of the table. The team commiserated with one another over a vat of beer and consoled themselves with the idea that, if Larwood stayed fit, the pole over the Trent Bridge pavilion would soon be flying the Championship pennant anyway. Just two summers separated them from defeat and that title – and the pungent, hoppy smell of more ale.

Willis Walker: he scored more than 1,000 runs in Nottinghamshire's Championship-winning season.

* * *

In Larwood's era, batsmen scored mountainous heaps of runs. The pitches were the equivalent of an 'as-much-as-you-can-eat' buffet for run-makers. Trent Bridge was flat and bare and true, and Larwood had to sweat hard to make sure the ball didn't come off at a friendly height and pace.

In 1929 the game between Sussex and Kent at Hastings produced 1451 runs, with Duleepsinhji scoring 115 and then 246. The usual suspects were wedged at the top of the batting averages: Hobbs with 2,263 runs at 66.55; Hammond with 2,456 runs at 64.63; Woolley – outscoring his rivals – with 2,804 at 56.08. Even allowing for the number of first-class fixtures (28 in the County Championship) this gorging on runs is almost unimaginable today. So is the number of wickets taken and overs bowled, which resemble the figures on a billionaire's bank statement. In the same summer, Middlesex's 'Gubby' Allen took all 10 wickets against Lancashire at Lord's; 'Tich' Freeman did the same for Kent against Lancashire at Maidstone and went on to claim 267 victims. In total, 28 bowlers broke three figures. Larwood had been England's leading strike bowler in 1927 (100 at 16.95) and 1928 (138 at 14.51). In the title-winning season, drained by a demanding winter in Australia and called away for representative games, he finished, disappointingly for him, with 117 wickets – 61 of them bowled – at 21.66. He took 11 in a single game against Glamorgan at Trent Bridge.

What contemporary bowlers would regard as a remarkable achievement, Larwood viewed as nothing more than an ordinary performance; the very least he could do. Nottinghamshire nonetheless clicked as a team – a chain without a weak or sensitive link. Voce, Barratt and Sam Staples each took over 100 wickets: Carr, Gunn, Whysall, Wilf Payton and Willis Walker scored more than 1000 runs. 'We were the best team,' said Larwood. 'You know if you've won something by default or because someone else isn't very good. But we were good – the very best that year.' So good, in fact, that when the final round of fixtures arrived, the mathematics made Nottinghamshire overwhelming favourites. Yorkshire, the county Larwood most admired and constantly tried to imitate, had to win at Worcestershire. For Nottinghamshire, sent to Ilkeston for a border dispute against neighbours and rivals Derbyshire, who had dogged them throughout the summer, it was enough merely to avoid defeat.

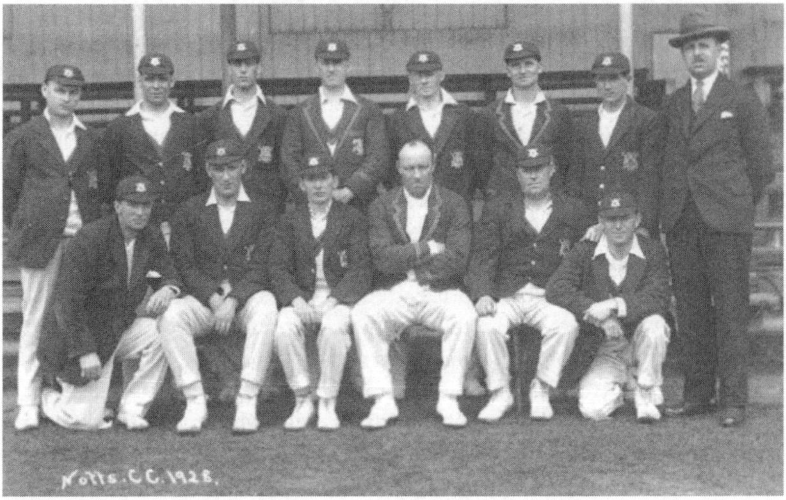

Arthur Carr's Nottinghamshire in 1928, the season before they won the County Championship. Harold Larwood is second from the right in the back row, with Sam Staples on his left.

The Derbyshire skies were so low and heavy that it seemed that the clouds might slowly sink, like a grey and purple blanket, into the earth. The foul weather came as a blessing and made the outcome a foregone conclusion well before the match was over. Rain swept in, and then stayed, so Nottinghamshire became Champions without much of a final effort: only one hour and 20 minutes' play was possible on the last day. There was no thrilling run chase, no desperate grasp for a last wicket, no climax at all. There were hardly any spectators to witness the end either. The wooden benches were wet and virtually deserted. Carr went round to each player, offering congratulations and the promise of a 'pint or three' later on, when buckets of beer were already being drunk. At a reception, arranged immediately afterwards at the Council House, Carr spoke from the Council House steps with a funnel megaphone clutched between both hands. He was framed by a pair of Ionic columns. A crowd of more than 500, mostly men who took off their caps and swung them in the air like football rattles, and sons perched on the shoulders of fathers, listened to him. Larwood instinctively took half a step back. For one thing, he didn't like fuss or flummery. For another, he thought he hadn't quite played his full part in the Championship win, which was nonsense.

The substantial Len 'Tich' Richmond: leg-break and googly bowler.

In a more formal speech, Arthur Carr would later playfully describe Nottinghamshire as 'a team of comedians', qualifying it with the thought that one day it was capable of scoring 653 for three and the next of being out for 130. It was a clannish side, as tight as a family, and its members were fiercely protective of one another. Like Larwood, the players were bred in the coalfields. Essentially the team were Victorian: Carr was born in 1893; Gunn in 1879; Payton in 1882; Walker and Sam Staples in 1892, and Staples's brother Arthur in 1899; Barratt and the wicketkeeper Ben

Lilley in 1894; Whysall in 1887, and Len 'Tich' Richmond in 1890. (Richmond became so bulky and awkward-looking that his body seemed wholly inappropriate for any sport played outside a saloon bar. His head was so large that he seemed to be wearing a cap four sizes too small for him. He put on so much weight that he was forced off the staff in 1928, but remained a 'drinking member'.) Only Larwood and Voce were born in the twentieth century. The dates on the birth certificates meant one thing: Nottinghamshire's County Championship was the equivalent of the politician's last hurrah. From then on, age was always against them.

There was Gunn, the oldest player in the County Championship and still one of its most prolific run-makers, a batsman whom the cricket writer Dudley Carew said could 'walk away from a fast bowler and cut him past point with the action of a man decapitating a dandelion with a walking stick'. He would come down the wicket at a bowler, however fast, and viciously hook the ball too. He also had an obstinate streak. He once removed the bails at one o'clock, thinking it was lunch, and handed them to the umpire. The umpire said: 'We're taking lunch at one-thirty

Wilf Payton: he made his Notts debut in 1906 and played for the next 25 years.

George Gunn: a batsman who relished coming down the pitch – even to fast bowling.

today, George.' Gunn took the next ball, stood back from a straight delivery and let it hit his stumps. Walking off, he said to the umpire: 'I take my lunch at one o'clock.'

There was the prematurely bald Barratt, fattish and with blanched skin and a maladroit run to the wicket. He came at the batsman chest-on like a lorry carrying a particularly wide load.

There was the flamboyant Whysall, who collected the most merit money in the Championship season – £40 – and would die just 14 months later after he slipped on a dance floor, cut his elbow and contracted blood poisoning from his suede jacket. Larwood carried his coffin and wept at his grave, which was edged in green and yellow, the club's colours.

And there was Lilley, who, after taking the ball from Larwood's bowling for five and a half months, said: 'My fingers ache so much that I have to boil 'em in water to move the joints.'

This disparate band partied on after the official reception, taking advantage of a pub 'lock-in' that lasted until the beer and most of the spirits ran out. Larwood left a bag with some of his kit in it, but it was returned to Trent Bridge a few days later. He couldn't remember losing it.

* * *

Harold Larwood used to look back and recall the camaraderie among 'a grand set of men . . . who'd do anything for you at any time. That's what made winning the Championship so important . . . you did your part for the team.' He'd tell anyone: 'With them you were never on your own. We were mates who just happened to play cricket and we were always looking out for one another. In the winter months – even if I was away with the MCC – I couldn't wait to get back among them to catch up and talk. Most

Fred Barratt: he claimed the wicket of Jack Hobbs before Harold Larwood could see his hero properly.

had been in the War, so a bit of fast bowling didn't bother them. They'd seen things I could only imagine. And, of course, we were pros together. Our livelihoods depended on how well we played. When you know someone needs a wage from cricket to eat, you give them a hand, don't you?'

Above all, Harold Larwood acknowledged how much he owed Arthur Carr, and how much he paid him in return. Carr schooled him, and Larwood delivered. 'He did all right by me – and I did all right by him,' he'd say. 'He was a good captain and a good companion on the road.' If Carr was thinking deeply on the field, Larwood said, his shoulders would droop and his head would tilt towards his chest, as if he were drawing an imaginary battle plan on the turf on which he stood. And if the game was going his way, he would rub the underside of his chin with the back of his right hand or fold his arms behind his back and stare at the sky. From the slips, where Carr usually fielded, he would purse his lips and nod his head in appreciation of Larwood's bowling. Larwood was able to rate his own performance strictly from Carr's reactions. He would look for simple gestures of approval and be grateful for them,

'Dodge' Whysall: he scored more than 2,000 runs in each of his final five summers.

Ben Lilley: his fingers were always swollen and bent after 'keeping to Larwood and Voce.

like a pupil proud to receive a large tick from his teacher.

There was much for Carr to admire. Larwood was lethal. The men who faced him wrote and spoke about it as if the experience was like being sent to the Front. When Frank Lee made his first appearance for Middlesex at Trent Bridge, Larwood bowled him a delivery so quick that it struck the outside edge before the bat left the blockhole. Lee saw the ball squirt down to third man and set off in a panic, not for the sake of a run, but primarily to escape to the safety of the non-striker's end. When he got there, the umpire Alf Street said to him quietly: 'Harold's a nice boy. He always gets you new boys off the mark with his slower one.'

Lee was fortunate. Larwood generated so much pace that he flicked the peak of West Indian Freddie Martin's cap and turned it around on his head before the batsman's feet moved. To prove it wasn't luck, or just a party trick, he 'creased' the cap of Martin's partner George Challenor and spun it towards the slips like a plate. Martin and Challenor were fortunate too. Middlesex's Dick Twining – later to become President of the MCC – was knocked almost unconscious at Lord's in 1927; Patsy Hendren was hospitalized in 1929 and South African wicketkeeper Jock Cameron was stretchered off in 1931, his eyes swimming like ornamental fish in a bowl. When Gloucestershire's Reg Sinfield was struck on the skull, it took an hour and a half and a jar of smelling salts before he came round. Lancashire's Ernest Tyldesley took a ball in the face and was carried away, a fist-sized mark beneath his cheek. Warren Bardsley had the bat ripped out of his hands and the shock of it pushed him backwards, as if he'd taken a blow from a heavyweight boxer. He trod on his wicket. Wilfred Rhodes was rapped on the right instep. He flung his bat away and began to hop around holding his foot. Grimacing and groaning, Rhodes took off his pad, his boot and then finally his sock. He began to rub his foot, a bruise already visible on the flesh. The umpire strolled towards Rhodes, now lying on the ground. 'Can you walk?' he asked him politely. Rhodes looked up with watery eyes and said that he thought so. 'Then walk right back to the pavilion, you're out lbw.'

With pints of ale inside him, Larwood accepted bets during lunch. 'A shilling says you can't knock so and so out,' he'd be told, or 'half a crown says you can't belt a batsman in the ribs and break one.' Larwood always accepted the challenge. 'Other players around the counties knew what we did,' he said. 'You'd see some of them relax a bit after I got someone because my bet would be won.' Sam Staples bet Larwood a 'packet of smokes' that he couldn't dislodge the turban of Indian batsman Joginder Singh. When Singh missed the inevitable bouncer, the ball lifted his turban towards the slips. A few overs later, Singh was holding a cloth to his left cheek to mop up the blood after missing another short-pitched delivery from Larwood. Shaky on his feet, he was shepherded off the field.

Larwood was far more compassionate when Surrey's Alf Gover was yanked out of the bath at the end of a day's bowling to become night-watchman. 'I was in no state really,' he said. Larwood immediately struck him in the box. 'I went up the wicket and told him: "Easy Harold, they've dragged me out of the bath."' Larwood apologized and made sure Gover didn't need to play the next few balls.

A few batsmen developed the dangerous technique of playing forward to Larwood, which was rather like the matador rushing the bull. If the ball got up it would go over their heads. If it didn't, it would hit them. Hampshire's George Brown deliberately took two bouncers from Larwood on the chest, standing impassively at the crease like a sentry on duty. 'When are you going to bowl really fast, Harold?' he said – a second or two before the impact of the previous deliveries forced him to his knees, like a man hit with a hammer. Brown was soon coming out at Trent Bridge wearing a 'crash helmet' in the form of a padded woman's cloche hat.

Surrey's Erroll Holmes had particularly strong wrists, became a fierce driver of the ball and thought there was no point in playing cricket unless you relished every moment. But he didn't relish the inside edge he got on a ball from Larwood that cut back sharply. It hit him flush on the inside of his right knee. He went down 'like a shot rabbit,' he said. Holmes staggered to his feet, and took guard for the next ball. His knee was so painful that he couldn't put any weight on it. Holmes decided to lean on his bat instead, which he gripped as desperately as a drunk clings on to a lamp post, and slightly raised his right leg off the ground. There was only one flaw in his plan. When he came to play the next delivery – quick and full – he lifted the bat, lost his balance and fell over. The ball uprooted his stumps. 'I must have looked pretty foolish,' he admitted, hobbling off and using his bat as a walking stick. In the dressing room, Holmes discovered his knee was so swollen that he couldn't roll his trousers over it. The bruise extended from groin to ankle.

Even his drinking pals weren't immune from the Larwood treatment. When he bowled, the fizz of Tommy Mitchell's leg spin sounded like an angry wasp as it cut through the air. By every season's end, there were blood blisters on the inside of his right thumb. But when Mitchell batted, he usually poked and prodded around like the archetypal tail-ender. And when – just the once, mind you – he came down the pitch to rap Larwood audaciously to the boundary, he found the next ball coming at him like a Force Nine. The delivery lifted his cap clean off his head after striking the peak. It was as easy as taking the top off a bottle. Larwood followed through, soon staring Mitchell down from a few yards away as he tried to find his cap on the floor. 'You shouldn't make me look silly,' he told him, as if Mitchell's aggressive hitting was a sign of insolence. If he thought a batsman affronted his dignity, Larwood never forgot it. Retribution might follow weeks, months or even several summers later.

During the Bodyline tour, a stone found its way into Larwood's boot and he bowled a few tame, wayward balls. At the end of the over Les Ames said to him: 'What ever is up with you then . . . if you're going to go on bowling lollipops I better come and stand up to the wicket.' Larwood was furious; he interpreted Ames' rebuke as a slur. 'Leslie,' he said, 'when you next come to Trent Bridge, you are going to get one round your ears – don't forget it.' When Kent did come to Trent Bridge, Ames stayed, as he always did, with Larwood. The two of them travelled to the match together. Ames found himself batting in the last over before lunch on what he called a 'very fast pitch'. Larwood had the wind at his back too. The first delivery was on a good length; Ames pushed it towards Larwood, who collected the ball, stared down the wicket and said: 'Leslie, Adelaide 1933 – you are going to get one . . . so watch out.' Ames thought it might be the 'three card trick': Larwood would a bowl a yorker rather than a bouncer. He didn't. Larwood dropped the delivery short and Ames flung his arms at the ball as it soared past his shoulder. The ball hit the middle of the bat and climbed into the highest wooden row of seats for six – the only time, Larwood claimed, that he was ever hit for six in England. 'Great shot, Leslie,' he said, clapping and then wrapping his arm around his friend as the two of them walked off for lunch together.

* * *

Carr, Jardine, Voce (and most others who played with him) always said that Larwood never bowled to hit anyone deliberately. Frank Woolley disagreed. After being 'roughed up' in a representative game at Folkestone – both Larwood and Voce were bowling leg theory before the Bodyline

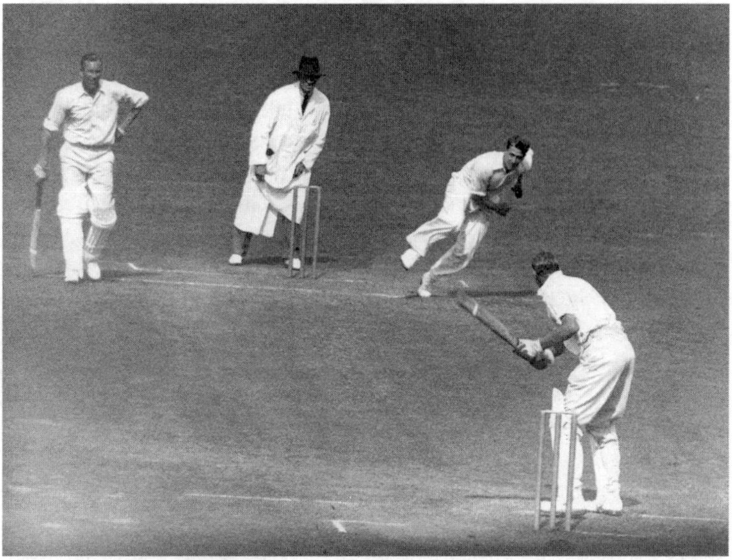

The perfect follow-through: eyes still on the target, and a full shoulder turn.

tour – Woolley asked Larwood: 'Are you trying to hurt me, Harold?' Larwood half turned towards Woolley and then slightly dipped his head in apology, like a dog caught chewing the carpet.

He would certainly goad incoming batsmen. 'That was the fast bowler's job,' he'd say. When Somerset's Bill Andrews, a tail-ender, wore a chest protector against him, Larwood turned to Voce and said: 'Look at that, Bill, let's both see if we can try to hit it.' Andrews felt the colour ebb from his face; Larwood just winked at him. In another game at Trent Bridge, Andrews was so scared of facing Larwood that he developed stomach pains. He was sitting on the toilet when he heard the shout: 'Bill, you're in.' He asked: 'Who's out?' The reply was: 'Frank Lee. They're bringing him back on a stretcher.' Andrews said: 'I was really in a state, and it took some time to adjust my clothing. As I passed the umpire, I said – hopefully – that I must have broken the two-minute rule.'

Andrews could recall Larwood's venom as late as 1935. Although nowhere near as fast as he had once been, he still petrified batsmen. The

Somerset bowler made the mistake of striking him in the box, which meant he couldn't open the Nottinghamshire attack on the second morning. All day Larwood lay on the masseur's table. And all day whispers circulated the field. 'He's after Bill and is going to give him all he's got.' On the third morning, Larwood was marking out his run to finish off the stragglers. Dickie Burrough was struck on the face, his blood staining the pitch, and retired hurt. He'd tried to fend off the short delivery with his glove. The ball flattened his thumb and turned it 90 degrees. Next man in, Wally Luckes, was 'pale and intent on getting a quick touch for a catch behind'. He went swiftly, the relief all too apparent. The number eleven Horace Hazell came in humming 'Nearer My God to Thee'. 'In all my career,' said Andrews, 'I had never seen such bowling. Larwood would make the ball swing into the batsman and then when it hit the pitch, it would hurtle away at 90 miles an hour.' Andrews meekly surrendered his own wicket. In 4.3 overs, Larwood took four wickets for one run.

Harold Larwood checks and re-checks his luggage before the 1928–29 Ashes series in Australia.

For Larwood, anyone from Somerset seemed easy meat. Arthur Wellard never forgot his first meeting with him. 'Who's this Larwood?' he asked. 'Supposed to be a bit pacey, is he?' Wellard soon found out. 'I got four balls . . . and I didn't see any of them. The fifth ball knocked my hob over and I didn't see that one either,' he said.

The first prize for stupidity went to Haydon Smith, a Leicestershire fast bowler. Smith, who had a bad stammer, liked the look of the Grace Road wicket before a match against Nottinghamshire. 'I'll tell you what, s-s-skip,' said Smith, 'I think I'll b-b-bounce one or two.' The skipper looked worried. 'Wait a minute', he said, 'you know who they've got on the other side? They've got Larwood and Voce.' Smith was unrepentant. He did bounce them, and Nottinghamshire took offence. Larwood and Voce tore through Leicestershire, and Smith suddenly found himself at the wicket. The Notts fielders began to yell. 'Here he is. Let him have one, Lol.'

Larwood's opening ball reared past Smith's face. He didn't see it, but felt the cold air as it rushed past him. The second took the edge as Smith backed off towards square leg. The ball shot towards gully, where Sam Staples caught it on the bounce. Smith began to pull off his gloves and walk off. 'Wait a minute,' Staples shouted. 'It was a bump ball. I didn't catch it.' 'Yes, you f-f-f-fucking-well did,' said Smith, not daring to look back.

According to Voce, Smith escaped lightly for his impudence. 'You know,' he said, 'the thing that people forget about Lol is that no one in England saw or faced him at his fastest. He was quicker in Australia in '32 than anywhere else. Goodness, he was fast there.' The Australians – and specifically Donald Bradman – didn't realize how fast until Larwood began to bowl.

PART TWO

CHAPTER FIVE

THE LITTLE BASTARD

August 1932 – September 1932

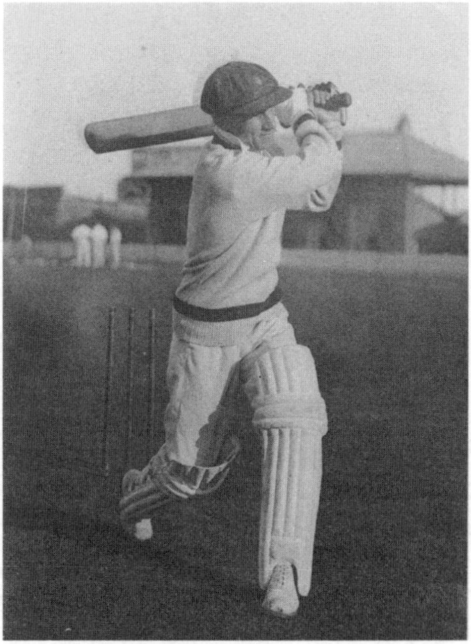

Donald Bradman, the most complete batsman in the history of cricket.

The Piccadilly Hotel, London: August 1932 – Lord's: September 1932

With his usual combination of self-deprecation and professional pessimism, Harold Larwood didn't expect to go on the 1932–33 tour to Australia. He thought he'd spend the winter mournfully reading about it in the newspapers or listening to the radio broadcasts. At least the cold months at home wouldn't be spent trudging to the pit, and the intense blackness and dour, back-breaking labour of hewing coal. Larwood had invested in a smallholding, where he grew vegetables and flowers and kept poultry, and worked beside his father and his brother Ernest. Money would be tight. As usual, he'd comb the lining of his jacket to make sure a stray coin hadn't dropped through a worn hole. He'd make familiar economies. During the summer, he could afford to smoke Player's cigarettes. In the winter, he'd buy Woodbines, which were nearly sixpence cheaper. For an impecunious professional cricketer, every penny counted. 'A man couldn't expect too much,' he said, which was always Larwood's stoical view of hardship. He would have £400 or so, saved from county matches and Tests, to tide him over until the following spring.

Thinking of home? Harold Larwood stares across the sea on the voyage to Australia in 1928.

The averages in the summer of 1932 reveal a bowler nearing the summit of his career – fit, fearsome, in control of line and length and with the 'nous' to read pitches and batsmen. Larwood claimed 162 wickets at 12.86 from fewer than 900 overs. On figures alone, he was on the boat to Australia from midsummer. He just didn't believe it himself. 'I thought others were equally as fast as me,' he said. 'There was Bill Voce, Nobby Clark, Morris Nichols and Gubby Allen –

all good bowlers and all capable of leading an attack. I didn't fancy my chances against them.'

The root of Larwood's gloomy mood lay in what happened to him in Australia in 1928–29. It hadn't been love at first sight. Larwood frankly didn't like the country. He hated the thick heat, which made him sweat and choke and run for the nearest shade. He burnt the back of his neck so badly, between his hair-line and collar, that the skin resembled a strip of tenderized meat. He hated the flies, which he flicked away from his face and hurried indoors to avoid. He hated the fact that, aside from the sun and cobalt skies, Australia looked so much like home without actually being home. 'Everyone spoke the same way,' he said, 'and the food was the same . . . but it wasn't like being in England.' Larwood was only 23 when he set off for that tour, adrift from his family for the first time and constantly occupied with home thoughts from abroad. 'I was a bit homesick,' he said. 'I missed my family and I missed my friends.'

The month-long sail seemed interminable, like a jail sentence with good food. When he got there, the barrackers unsettled him. 'It was a bit too thick at times,' he said of the abuse. 'I got called every name you can imagine and every four-letter word you can think of was used against me.' He took 18 Test wickets with an average of 40.22. Often the ball felt like a torn rag in his hand. 'After a few overs, the thing wouldn't swing,' he said. 'The shine had gone on the hard pitches out there. It was different back home. You didn't get the wear and tear on the ball. All I could do was try to bowl as straight as possible.' Larwood was sufficiently desperate in the Adelaide Test to bowl 'rising balls on the leg stump' – though without the posse of tendril-like hands in the batsman's pocket. 'No one complained about it,' he noted wryly after his leg theory of 1928–29 became the cursed Bodyline of 1932–33. Larwood had been the only fast bowler picked in that tour. Why, he asked himself, would the MCC alter its tactics this time? Surely there'd be only one quick bowler in the party, and it wasn't likely to be him. And, of course, there was Donald Bradman, who seemed to loom over him malignly.

Larwood faced Bradman in 1928–29. He bowled to him at Brisbane, where Bradman made his modest Test debut batting at number seven and scored 18 and 1, and then at Melbourne, Adelaide and Melbourne again. Bradman finished the series with two centuries. By the time the 1930 Ashes came and went, Larwood had done more than enough leather-chasing. Larwood watched the ball fizz past him like a fire-cracker at

England players emerge from the pavilion at Sydney to face New South Wales in November 1928. From the left: White, Jardine, Hendren, Tate (partly hidden), Hobbs, Sutcliffe (hidden), Geary, Duckworth (hidden), Mead and Larwood.

Trent Bridge, where Bradman hit 131. He struck 254 at Lord's and then surpassed it at Headingley thirteen days later, making 334 – then the world-record score in Tests. At the Oval, Bradman – almost playing for fun now – caressed 232.

Larwood had bowled to Bradman in seven Tests. He'd taken his wicket just once – after Bradman had already scored a double century. His track record against him was so meagre that he scarcely seemed – at least to Larwood himself – to be the bowler to interrupt Bradman's imperious progress. 'He was cruel in the way he flogged you,' said Larwood. 'He made me very, very tired.' But Bradman also made him 'very, very angry'. For there were professional and personal scores to be settled.

* * *

Larwood nursed a sense of injustice. He thought Bradman had been dishonest. 'He was out at Headingley in 1930 even before he'd scored,' he always maintained. 'The first ball I gave him was a bouncer, and he snicked it . . . you could hear the snick all over the ground. George Duckworth caught it, and you could hear his appeal in Manchester. We all went up. I knew he'd snicked it, and everyone who was close to it will tell you the same. Even Jack Hobbs – who would never appeal unless he thought a man had a good chance of being out – shouted with us. I didn't complain at the time . . . the umpire just gave him the benefit of the doubt.' As far as Larwood was concerned, Bradman hadn't done the decent thing and walked – something he could never have imagined Hobbs doing, for example. 'I expected a man to leave the crease when he was out,' he'd say.

It was also Larwood's belief, humbly encouraged by his father, that all men from whatever background or circumstances were created equal and that you treated everyone the same way irrespective of class or creed or achievement. Larwood liked Australians. He considered them to be matily earthy, and always willing to split a round of drinks. On the field, he admired their competitiveness and resilience. Off it, he liked the fact that once the tough combat of the day's play was out of the way, the average Australian didn't hold grudges or try to score points, and became instead 'just one of the blokes'. Bradman was different. Larwood found him unsociable, over-mannered and icily detached, as if he didn't belong with either of the two teams. As Jack Fingleton would later say of Bradman: 'Those who knew him best did not know whether to like him or dislike him.' Fingleton – who admittedly had his own reasons for disliking Bradman – thought he had a 'jealous streak', craved 'the limelight' and didn't like it cast on anyone else. He talked about Bradman brushing 'brusquely past autograph hunters who had waited in the rain for hours to get his signature' and dismissing reporters with a 'gesture of contempt'. He was 'still a great hero but in many ways was a little churlish man,' added Fingleton. When an admirer gave Bradman £1,000 to commemorate his 334 at Headingley – a sum equivalent today to almost £50,000 – Bradman didn't buy a drink for the team out of it. 'Many would not have had one,' said Fingleton, who argued that 'to Don Bradman the world revolves around him alone.' Larwood could never have imagined keeping the whole sum. He'd have divided at least part of it among the dressing room. Larwood would nod in agreement when Fingleton spoke about Bradman's driven attitude towards his financial affairs. Larwood felt Bradman 'was out to make money. No mistake about that. Everybody knew it and he made it.'

Larwood never strayed from his working-class roots. He identified with the ordinary man, especially the miners, to such an extent that it embarrassed him to drive past his friends or former workmates from the pit, who were heading to the colliery as he set off or returned from Trent Bridge. A car Larwood once bought with wages earned from his Test appearances was soon left on the kerbside. He felt that driving it, or being showy with his money, distanced him from the men around him who were less fortunate. He couldn't understand why anyone from a poor background, such as Bradman's, could be so haughty and aloof from others, especially his colleagues. In the beginning, Larwood's attitude was greatly influenced by Arthur Carr's 'enmity' towards Bradman – and, it has to be said, Australia and Australians in general. Carr said he wouldn't entertain most Australians in his home, and dismissed Bradman as 'conceited'. He advised Larwood to have nothing to do with him. Later, as Larwood settled on his own opinions, he agreed with Carr. He diagnosed Bradman's frostiness as arrogance rather than shyness. He also believed Bradman was purposefully distant because he regarded himself as better than anyone – both as a player and a person. He disliked his self-absorption, the cold intent to tick off his big scores in a calculating, machine-like manner. It was Larwood's view that Bradman became so intense in his hunt for runs that he found it impossible to loosen up without the bat in his hand.

But, while mediocrity knows nothing higher than itself, one genius instantly recognizes another. Larwood always honoured the Bradman of the record book rather than the Bradman he knew in the flesh. 'He was a genius in the middle,' he said.

* * *

You could say that Bradman was a glorious fluke, not just because of the phenomenal heap of runs he scored, but also in the way that he accumulated them. The author and cricket historian David Frith put it best of all. Bradman was not 'one in a million', said Frith. 'He was much rarer than that.' Once asked his opinion on the 'best ball' to bowl at Bradman, Bill Voce was unequivocal: 'There's no bloody best ball,' he said.

Bradman was not a copybook batsman. Abraham Lincoln had his log cabin. George Washington had his axe and the cherry tree. The seminal tools of Bradman's boyhood in Bowral – and an integral part of his legend – were a golf ball and a cricket stump. He used the stump as the bat for a game he devised on an eight-foot strip of concrete between an 800 gallon water tank and his mother's laundry door. He hurled the golf ball against the circular brick base of the water tank and played a stroke as it rebounded to him at speed, frequently at sharp, difficult angles. Whenever he was asked to give advice about how to become a fast bowler, Larwood reached for his stock reply, drenched in common sense. 'Practise,' he said, 'and then practise again . . . too many cricketers don't practise hard or long enough.' Bradman practised until his hands ached. Like Larwood bowling on the narrow streets of Nuncargate, entire 'Test matches' were fought out in Bradman's head as the golf ball reared towards him and he dispatched it towards a boundary that only he could see. Also like Larwood, Bradman needed a colourful imagination. He didn't read a cricketer's autobiography, or see a first-class match, until he played for New South Wales. He was the architect of his own unconventional methods and always forcefully maintained that it was wrong to 'fog a boy's mind' with complicated instructions or analysis. Bradman found his own way; a certain something which worked for him.

Larwood studied him hard, as if swotting for an exam. He took notice of the fact that Bradman always walked very slowly to the wicket, so his eyes became accustomed to the light. He saw that the bat was placed with the face closed between the feet rather than behind the right toe. He didn't rap it into the hole dug by his guard, sending up dust, or against the rim of his boot. The life-size bronze cast of his right hand, on display in the Bradman Collection housed in Adelaide, is small and delicate, like a woman's. The artist Bill Leak, who painted two three-quarter-length portraits of him, thought his hands were 'very strong, quite solid, sort of sculptured'. These hands were close together on the bat handle – the thumb and first finger of each hand forming an inverted V. As a result the pick-up, rather than straight, could be anywhere between point and second slip. For Bradman, the philosophy of batting had to be based around the straightforward premise of getting into a 'comfortable and natural' position, which gave him the option of more 'versatile stroke-play'. He wasn't a stylist in the classical sense. Percy Fender called him 'one of the most curious mixtures of good and bad batting that I have

Donald Bradman batting at Trent Bridge in 1930. He made 131 in Australia's second innings. The wicketkeeper is George Duckworth, with Hammond in the gully and Woolley at slip.

ever seen'. And as R.C. Robertson-Glasgow observed: 'There was no style for style's sake' in Bradman. 'The charm in his batting', he added, was 'for the spectator to find or miss'.

What also defined Bradman was his temperament. Until Larwood scrambled his mind a little, his concentration was impeccable. He slipped easily into what contemporary sportsmen and women almost mystically call 'the zone', the ability to block out the extraneous and to concentrate exclusively on the task in hand. He was rigidly still at the crease – as if cryogenically frozen – until the very point at which the co-ordination of hawkishly sharp eyes, quick brain and muscle slipped into gear and he decided how and where to play the ball at will. Bradman had the nimble feet of Fred Astaire. In an eye-blink he was able to work himself into the best position. He did it with such nonchalance, as though gathering runs was as natural as breathing and walking. The Australian opener Bill Ponsford grasped the reason for it. Bradman, he always maintained, saw a delivery 'two or three yards quicker than the rest of us'. His bat was light too – between 2lb 2oz and 2lb 4oz – which also meant he could swish it whippishly, like a willow wand, in the smooth flow of his strokes. He was more forceful off the back foot rather than the front, and the power came from his hips and wrists. Most importantly of all, what Bradman became mirrored the criteria C.B. Fry laid down as necessary to perfect the art of batsmanship – 'an unconscious and subconscious habit'. To achieve it, Bradman was singleminded to the extent that he felt unreachable to most of those around him in the dressing room. He was never famished for runs; he was often bereft of understanding.

In the 1920s, after the War and the rip and tear of lives during the Great Depression, Australia craved a hero and tried to establish its own culture and identity separate from Britain's. Its size counted for nothing. On the vast scale of Empire, it remained, in the opinion of most Englishmen who mattered, an insignificant smudge on the map. Jobs were almost impossible to come by – in 1932 almost 29 per cent of the Australian workforce was unemployed – and the act of just eking out a drab living imposed an unbearable strain upon the ordinary working man and woman there. Without a bat in his hands, Bradman seemed to the Australian public ordinary too – suited and unassuming – and so he quickly came to embody the hope, the promise and the prayer that tomorrow might be better for them as well as for himself. He also brought relief from their own huge miseries. As rudimentary radio broadcasts began to spread, and cinema newsreels recorded the flickering highlights of Test matches, Bradman bore the weight of an entire country's longing for more promising times. He became to Australia what Charles Lindbergh was to America; Bradman flew higher and further than any other Australian, and the country began to see itself through his successes and feed off them. What Bradman received in return was instant, back-slapping recognition and a personal fortune, which afforded him a level of fame that would have been disabling to anyone lacking the mental strength and self-conviction necessary to withstand the demands it constantly made on him. Foremost among them was that Bradman wasn't allowed to fail. The acclaim for him – and the expectation it inspired – was never diluted. He didn't let Australia or Australians down. Bradman became so lucid in the language of run-making that alongside him everyone else seemed ungrammatical. The basic statistics of his career are so stunning that each one is worth recording in illuminated script. He only ever dealt in high numbers:

- 99.94 – his final Test average
- 452 – his highest-ever first-class score
- 334 – that record Test innings at Headingley
- 974 at an average of 139.14 – seven innings in the 1930 Ashes series in England

'One does not go seeking records,' said Bradman almost casually. 'They simply just happen.'

Douglas Jardine used to call him 'the little bastard', which should be interpreted as a compliment rather than an insult or taunt. If this seems a perversely ludicrous way of conveying admiration, it has to be judged against what Jardine's sore eyes had witnessed in 1930. Like everyone who watched Bradman club England to death with his bat, during a summer in which he nearly tore the stitching off the ball with the savagery of his strokes, Jardine absorbed one lesson from such a damaging experience. If the Ashes were ever to be regained, Bradman had to be badly broken and beaten first. His pride needed to be stripped away. Someone had to deprive Bradman of his sense of invincibility. By 1932, Jardine was convinced that he knew who could do it.

* * *

The Grill Room of the Piccadilly Hotel had a white, high ceiling, ornate coving, Corinthian columns inlaid with gold, chandeliers that cast a tallow light and white tablecloths laid with silver and cut glass. Waiters in starched collars and black jackets padded discreetly around the table, serving food and refilling glasses for four men who didn't want to be overheard: Larwood, Bill Voce, Arthur Carr and Douglas Jardine.

'One or two of us are going out,' Carr had told Larwood without much elaboration during the preparation for Nottinghamshire's County Championship match against Surrey at the Oval. Almost as an aside, he added that Voce would be 'coming along too'. Larwood saw nothing significant in it. 'We were always going out with the skipper,' he said. 'I thought it was just another get-together over a pint or two.'

In the Test trial at the end of July, Larwood had found himself in the Rest of England side rather than England's. Carr thought the decision was a gross insult to his bowler. 'He said to me: "Don't play, Lol,"' remembered Larwood. 'And then he offered to pay me the fee for the match out of his own pocket. But I decided to play anyway. I couldn't say no.' Rain swept into Cardiff and spoilt the game; Larwood bowled a mere 15 overs and took a solitary wicket. On the penultimate day of the match, however, he and Voce were given places on the Australian tour. *The Times* wasn't enamoured with Larwood's inclusion. It endorsed him half-heartedly with the line: 'He is not to be compared to the great men of the past . . . but he has his moments.' Some man. Some moments. 'I still didn't know how effective I'd be when the shine went off the ball in Australia,' said Larwood. 'I did know I'd have to do things a bit differently.' At the restaurant, he found out how differently.

Jardine was already waiting. In profile – with his aquiline face and blade nose – the MCC captain looked like Basil Rathbone, minus the deerstalker and pipe that would eventually turn the actor into Sherlock Holmes. The analogy is apt, for in the two months since his appointment as captain for the Ashes tour, Jardine had examined the problem of Donald Bradman with the calm rationality and incisive intelligence of Conan Doyle's fictional detective. In the privacy of his home, Jardine sat hunched over charts which revealed where Bradman scored his runs. He studied Bradman's dismissals on the scorecard, counting up the occasions when he'd been caught or bowled or out lbw. He spoke to bowlers and other captains, and trusted friends such as Percy Fender, who gave him letters from his own Australian contacts. The letters suggested that fast bowling should shape England's attack because the Australian batsmen were sure to move across the stumps to pull, hook or flick deliveries to the on-side. Jardine knew that his tactics against Bradman needed to be unconventional to succeed. And then, as Holmes often did, he experienced his Eureka moment. It came after he'd watched a short clip of film of Bradman – no more than a couple of minutes long – batting against Larwood at the Oval in 1930. A reel-to-reel projector was set up in a room at Lord's. The curtains and blinds were drawn. A strong rectangle of light fell on to the screen, illuminating the dust in the air, and the low whirl and rattle of the film as it moved through the spools broke the silence of the room. Showers had freshened up the Oval pitch. 'A spot of rain had fallen,' was how Larwood remembered it. As the sun began to dry the soil, the odd delivery reared; Larwood called it 'popping'. Jardine found what he thought was Bradman's previously undiscovered Achilles heel. He unmistakably flinched and backed to the leg side to fend off Larwood, who struck him on the chest. Bradman dropped his bat. He stood bent almost double with his gloved hands resting on the rolls of his pads. 'I've got it,' said Jardine. 'He's yellow.'

The meal began awkwardly. The men had taken drinks in the bar before sitting down for dinner in an effort to make the occasion less formal. When the food was served, Larwood and Voce stared shyly at their plates of steak and potatoes. Larwood fiddled with the knot of his tie and pulled at his cuffs, and looked at his knuckles, which he wished he'd scrubbed cleaner. At the start, there'd been polite handshakes, and well-mannered coughs, as if everyone had to clear their throats before the conversation could begin properly. The cricketers were apprehensive of one another, like would-be suitors on a blind date. 'It took some time to warm up,' admitted Carr, because Jardine was 'not exactly hail-fellow-well-met'. Jardine's voice was reedy. It rose in scale when he was nervous or ill at ease. His pale nails were always bitten down too – another sign of nerves, which he concealed. To outsiders, he didn't inspire an easy affection. He was unfairly labelled as high-minded and overbearing, and often came across – especially to Australians – as a man made up entirely of sharp edges: conceited, seldom conciliatory and with a tongue like the lash of a bull-whip. Larwood thought differently: 'He wasn't a snob,' he said, 'and he had a very dry sense of humour. With some of the things he said, you couldn't tell if he was joking or not. Some people just took him the wrong way . . . but I don't pretend that he was an easy man to understand. Like others, I was inclined to be suspicious of him at first . . . but I soon found he was a good man with a good heart.'

Neville Cardus likened Jardine's batting to the man himself: calm, well bred, not given to rhetoric, common-sensed and imperturbable. Cardus also got the crux of him by observing that he wasn't interested in whether the 'best team won' but merely in becoming the best team. That ethos defined the Bodyline series.

Jardine nevertheless had to be coaxed into accepting the England captaincy. In Sydney, in 1928, he'd been barracked by the Hill as much as Larwood. The decibel level was almost high enough to perforate his ear-drums. Jardine tried to take no notice. He half turned his head, spat on the ground and walked away. When Patsy Hendren said to him: 'They don't seem to like you over here, Mr Jardine', his reply was curt. 'It's fucking mutual,' he said. Jardine's difficulty with Australia began at Oxford in 1921 when he was denied a century against them. Warwick Armstrong cut a three-day tour game down to two to give the Australians a rest before the Test. The scoreboard did not show a batsman's running total. As there was nothing to alert him to the closeness of his century, Jardine found himself stranded on 96 at the close, as downcast as someone who had just missed the last tram home.

Jardine told Larwood and Voce to prepare body, mind and heart for the tour. He spoke about Bradman's weakness on leg stump. Larwood, clearly remembering the Oval Test two years earlier, vigorously agreed. Larwood thought Bradman 'held the straightest bat I've ever seen', but yet instantly recognized the solitary flaw that Jardine highlighted, like a small chip in an otherwise immaculate Meissen figurine. Larwood had seen Bradman stumble backwards against both Walter Hammond and Allen. 'If that bugger can do it, then so can I,' he said of Allen. Jardine also recounted the anecdote about the aboriginal bowler Eddie Gilbert, who in one over had flicked Bradman's cap, lifted the bat out of his hands and dismissed him for nought.

Jardine asked two questions of Larwood: 'Can you keep a good length? Can you keep on Bradman's leg stump?' Larwood didn't have time to catch his breath and shape an answer before Jardine demanded: 'Of course, you've got to be accurate . . . do you think you'll manage it?' So that there could be no misunderstandings, Jardine went through the justification for his approach and firmly laid down what he required of Larwood:

- Restricting stroke play to one half of the field meant the opportunity for scoring would be drastically reduced
- The control necessary to achieve it was vital
- The mental application required in pressurized situations would be murderous
- The crowd would be hostile in its opposition

Larwood reminded Jardine of an incident in the Melbourne Test of 1928. He'd watched Alan Kippax hook every short ball he bowled at him. 'Can I have another man on the fence?' he'd asked his captain, Percy Chapman. Chapman had asked why. 'Even if I give away 20 or 30 runs, I reckon I can get him caught on the boundary. The wicket's slow here. It's my best chance to get a wicket,' replied Larwood. Chapman nodded his head and sent Jardine to the fence. Kippax kept pulling and hooking. At one stage he cleared the boundary, the ball arching over Jardine, who craned his neck and watched it drop into the belly of the crowd. Larwood had to persuade Chapman to persevere with Jardine at long leg; Jardine was already grumbling about the futility of it. 'Please keep him there,' Larwood said to Chapman. In the next over, Larwood sent down a short delivery on the line of Kippax's body. He moved inside it and top-edged the ball, which flew skywards before dropping into Jardine's hands. He only had to move half a pace to his right to get directly under the catch. 'Time was always on the batsman's side,' said Larwood, justifying his thinking that day. 'Every match was played to a finish. The batsman would lift his bat and let the ball go through and try to tire you out as a bowler. I thought: If you won't play me, I'll make you play me.'

Larwood was convinced he could meet the moment again. As Jardine expanded on his plan, and tongues loosened as more alcohol was poured, it became clear to Larwood that, while other captains had only a nebulous idea of how to hold Bradman in check, Jardine had made conquering him his sole, impassioned purpose. It greatly impressed him, and his admiration for Jardine began. One thing drew them together as solidly as dovetail joints: the desire to beat Bradman. 'Accuracy is the key to it,' Larwood told Jardine. 'If you give him anything loose, he'll murder us.'

Larwood reckoned from the start that Jardine was determined to do more than scrape the glaze off Bradman. He was going to worm his way into his head and heart. But the application of his strategy, Larwood knew, was wholly dependent on whether he could bowl a satisfactory line and length, and the pace he was able to generate. Bodyline, he freely admitted, 'was a gamble'. He would be both the expression of Jardine's idea, and a willing prisoner of it.

Jardine and Larwood appreciated between them that if you strike at a king, you have to kill him. In cricket terms, Bradman would have to be 'killed'. 'He could murder you,' Larwood said of Bradman. 'Anything loose and he'd send you to the fence. We had to find a way of stopping him. He was the sort of player who got one hundred and then set himself to get another.'

Jardine preached a policy of competitive 'hate'. You had to hate the Australians on the field to beat them. So the Australians would see him as he wanted to be seen – remote and stony. For his part, Larwood would never waver from his belief that he was of use to his captain, but never used by him. 'You know,' he said, 'I think Mr Jardine would have made a famous soldier.'

Even though he wasn't going on the tour, Carr had an almost carnivorous appetite for trying to humiliate the Australians and grinding them, and especially Bradman, into the dirt. At the Grill Room, he enthusiastically volunteered to give 'leg theory' a dry run in the County Championship – even if it was detrimental to Nottinghamshire's own prospects of winning it. Country would have to come before club; it was a higher calling and Carr saw fulfilling it as a sense of duty, like an officer sent out on a mission.

Larwood and Voce began bowling a mild form of Bodyline at Jardine's own team. *The Times* innocently reported that Larwood and Voce bowled to 'many short legs', and that Surrey's wicketkeeper Edward Brooks was 'hit on almost every part of his body'. Afterwards, over the ritual beer in the pavilion of a game truncated by the weather, Surrey's Alf Gover wanted to know why batsmen who could hook well had been 'fed' shortish deliveries on the leg stump. It defied logic. 'Why did you bowl so badly?' he asked Larwood. 'We're trying something out,' countered Larwood. That special 'something' was served up again at Essex two days later. Six fieldsmen were packed around the stumps on the leg side like white tombstones; two more lay predatorily behind them. Carr moved into one of the leg slip positions, his eyes like a startled owl's. There was only one man on the off-side – as alone as a desert island castaway. Jack O'Connor had his protector knocked inside out. He retired hurt and took no further part in the match. The opener Dudley Pope took deliveries on the chest and back and the ball broke his skin. The welts stayed with him for two weeks.

At Cardiff at the end of the month – two days before Bradman celebrated his 24th birthday – Larwood and Voce bowled it once more. Glamorgan hammered more than 500 runs off them. In the crowd against both Essex and Glamorgan sat a bewildered, 18-year-old John Arlott, who had taken a 'cricket holiday' with his best friend and saw these micro rehearsals for Bodyline. 'We couldn't understand this,' said Arlott. 'We came back so baffled that we didn't even mention it to anybody.' Neither did Larwood and Voce. The pair didn't widely gossip about Jardine's strategy outside the Nottinghamshire dressing room, and no newspaper made the link between Larwood's place in the tour party and his ostensibly peculiar decision to regularly bowl to a leg-side field.

Accompanying him on the tour were Voce, Bill Bowes and Gubby Allen. Bowes' short-pitched bowling had shaken Jack Hobbs at the Oval

Harold Larwood holds his daughter June at Nottingham railway station before setting off for Australia on the 1932–33 MCC tour. To the left of Larwood are his wife Lois, his father Robert and his mother Mary. Bill Voce and his wife Elsie stand to his right.

in front of Jardine earlier that summer. He bounced him to such an extent that Hobbs resorted to patting the pitch near the bowler's footmarks to make his gentlemanly point about the over-reliance on such aggression. 'No, not there, Jack, but back here,' said Bowes, gesturing towards the middle of his run-up. Hobbs walked behind the stumps to flatten down imaginary divots with exaggerated care. 'Bowes must alter his tactics,' complained the indignant cricket correspondent of the *Morning Post,* appalled at the rapid succession of bouncers and the sight of five men on the on-side. 'That is not bowling,' he went on, 'indeed, it is not cricket . . . These things lead to reprisals, and when they begin, goodness knows where they will end.' The *Morning Post* writer was Plum Warner. Jardine conveniently ignored his tour manager's condemnation.

After taking seven wickets for Yorkshire against the Rest of England,

Bowes was called up so hastily, like a guest invited at the eleventh hour to fill an empty seat at a dinner party, that he had just three days to pack and prepare. Jardine's pace attack was now complete.

* * *

On an overcast morning in mid-September, as the previous summer's suntans were already beginning to fade, Jardine marshalled his tour party together for an official photograph in flannels and blazers near the old Tavern at Lord's. Twenty faces, arranged in three tiers, stared obediently at the camera. Front and centre, Jardine sits with eyes as dark as lead, his mouth arranged in a semi-smile. A white silk scarf is tied like a cravat around his thin neck; Allen is to his left with an immaculate prep-school parting; Warner stands in a grey double-breasted suit, the jacket just a little too tight for him across the chest, and holds himself like the headmaster of a particularly fine public school; the Nawab of Pataudi, his hair the colour of liquorice, lightly lays his hand on Hedley Verity's left shoulder, as though reassuring him about something. Almost inconspicuous, Larwood lurks in the back row, sandwiched between Maurice Leyland and Eddie Paynter. The resigned look on his face suggests that he can't wait for the picture to be taken and for the fuss to be over. The collar of his shirt has collapsed beneath his lapels. His hair is shaved at the back and on the sides and cut across on the top. It resembles a neatly trimmed box hedge. 'I had my orders and I was going to carry them out,' he'd say of Bodyline, briefly slipping into the vocabulary of the military, which was appropriate. For under Jardine, Larwood was about to change the strategy of cricket the way the tank changed the strategy of warfare.

* * *

Need, circumstance and the inexplicabilities of fate drew captain and bowler together for what became known as the Bodyline series. And although the two of them came together only briefly – in the time it took to board a liner, cross the world and win the Test series – Harold Larwood believed he had a privileged understanding of Douglas Jardine and the high standards he demanded of himself and everyone around him. He got closer to him than any other professional. 'We didn't mix on the 1928–29

The MCC touring team to Australia, 1932–33. Back row, from left: Duckworth, Mitchell, Pataudi, Leyland, Larwood, Paynter, Ferguson (scorer and baggage). Middle row: Warner (manager), Ames, Verity, Voce, Bowes, Brown, Tate, Palairet (assistant manager). Front row: Sutcliffe, Wyatt, Jardine (captain), Allen, Hammond.

tour,' said Larwood. 'That was normal. The pros went one way, the amateurs went another. We didn't get together off the field often and we were too busy on it to chat. I don't think we had any more than half a dozen brief conversations on the boat and in Australia. But I got to know him well in '32, and he was an interesting, intelligent man. He trusted me.'

On the boat to Australia, Jardine again discussed with Larwood the letters Fender had given him. He relayed the useful facts of his discussions with Frank Foster, who alongside Sydney Barnes on the 1911–12 tour made Australia wither to 38 for six on a perfect Melbourne wicket. Usually Foster bowled to the 'death trap' of six fieldsmen on the leg side, and inflicted damage with cut and vicious swing off a short run. The batsmen frequently received bruising blows to the thigh and chest. Foster's 'leg theory' rewarded him with 32 wickets on that tour; Barnes claimed 34. Jardine explained to Larwood that he would use what Foster had told him as his own template. Larwood listened and absorbed the message.

He became accustomed to Jardine's fussy quirks, his argumentative

A relaxed Douglas Jardine prepares to smoke his pipe after strolling on the deck of the Orontes *on the way to Australia in 1932.*

streak and his attention to what seemed to most of those around him as pernickety inconsequential detail: checking that Larwood had been to the dentist for an extraction and fillings before leaving for Australia; the way he restricted the amount of time the players were allowed to sunbathe on the ship; his refusal of a bottle of Scotch for every man in the party in case it gave them a taste for it; his confiscation of golf clubs; his daily checking up on his team – as if the players were locked in a military compound rather than on a cruise ship – to find out what time each of them went to sleep and woke again; the space he deliberately put between himself and most of the players so that he wouldn't become over-familiar; his tetchiness and impatient dismissal of the press; and his warnings to everyone – especially to Larwood and Voce – not to fraternize with them. 'You didn't want to be seen talking to a pressman before a Test in case you got caught,' said Larwood.

Jardine nonetheless cut Larwood yards of slack. 'I could talk to him,' Larwood maintained. 'I was able to ask him to explain things to me like tactics. I think I understood the way he acted. He wanted to win so badly, and so did I, and I'm sure he saw that in me from the start. And he appreciated what I needed to do my work as a fast bowler.' In the early days at sea, as the rest of the bowlers were running gently around the rolling deck, Jardine found Larwood and Voce lounging in chairs, staring out to sea, with cigarettes burning in their hands. 'Why aren't you exercising with the others?' he asked. 'We're relaxing after a hard season to get ready for the tour, Mr Jardine. We need our rest,' replied Larwood. Jardine nodded, moved on and made no demands on either of them.

For without Larwood, the Bodyline plan would have been still-born. All through the tour those who saw Larwood thought of him as more force of nature than mere fast bowler. The series represented what he described as his 'peak'. He had never been fitter or faster. 'I could bowl

Harold Larwood wanted to do nothing but rest his aching bones before embarking on the 1932–33 Ashes series. Here, he writes a letter home beside Tommy Mitchell, left, and Eddie Paynter.

as quickly at six o'clock at night as I could first thing in the morning,' he said. He had never been more confident about what he could achieve, or had such mastery over the ball as it left his hand. 'It was as if I could put any delivery anywhere.' He had never been so bullishly destructive, knocking over a batsman's stumps in one long swing of his right arm, like a wrecking ball. And he'd never felt before as though every cog and wheel of his action had been so smoothly synchronized – his run to the wicket, the plunge and then the firm unshakeable grip of his front foot on hard pitch, the swiftness of his shoulder, arm and wrist movements and muscular follow-through. The crowds gawped slackjawed at his pace, the first bouncer always like an eviction notice to the batsman. Les Ames said that he 'couldn't remember Larwood bowling a wild ball'. He was amazingly consistent, and 'every ball was fast'. It was the closest Larwood ever came to perfection, and the experience felt 'exhilarating'.

But the series that made Larwood – 33 wickets at 19.51 – would also break him.

CHAPTER SIX

WE CONDUCT CRICKETERS' FUNERALS

December 1932 – January 1933

The MCC tourists of 1932–33 during a stop-off in Ceylon.

Sydney: December 1932 – Adelaide: January 1933

Bodyline is no more than a spot in time. No one survives who played in it. Very few survive who saw it. But the smoke from it is still rising, the shouting about it has never really died, the arguments over it remain . . .

In advanced old age, Harold Larwood would tell any stranger who visited his bungalow in Sydney not to ask him about the series. 'I'm elderly and I've forgotten everything. I won't talk about Bodyline – and you'll be out of here if you ask me questions.' He'd say it rather gruffly, as if he truly meant it. But he hadn't forgotten, and he would talk about it. A name, a place or a sound would transport him back to 1932–33. The reminiscing would begin, his right index finger crooked, like a butcher's meat hook, as he stabbed the air to make a vigorous point. Larwood was no rhetorician. He could, however, date and then forge an emotional attachment to every stored memory from the tour. Those who heard him were impressed by his power of recall. He could remember what had been said, what had happened to him and how he had responded to it. He could hear the noise of the crowds swirling around him like a rush of water.

At the two Centenary Tests in 1977 and 1980, Larwood met foes and friends alike and saw how age had slackened skin on bone, made handshakes less firm and steps bowed and uncertain, just like his own. The veterans of Bodyline looked at one another through rheumy, tired eyes. But when the images of Bodyline returned to Larwood, the faces he glimpsed weren't sagged or tangled with wrinkles, but young and lithe. And every ground in which Bodyline was played out like stage drama – the first and final Tests at Sydney, the second at Melbourne, the third and most pivotal at Adelaide and the fourth under the unrelenting Brisbane sun – remained as he had seen them more than half a century earlier. The Hill still swarmed with its barrackers, the stands at Brisbane were aglow again in the high heat of the day, Melbourne and Adelaide remained in their Spartan finery. He was 28 years old again.

In one sense, Larwood would always stay that age, like a stopped clock. For no one would let him forget Bodyline. He was constantly pitched back into it and so saw himself as he had once been. His complexion was smooth and tanned, like the colour of strong tea. Warm sweat soaked his shirt and ran in tiny rivers across his forehead, down his back and neck and spread into butterfly shapes underneath the arms of his shirt. He had the ball in his hand and his spikes dug into soil. His feet were sore with all the bowling he'd done. He could feel them ache the way an amputee feels a stab of pain from a limb that's no longer there. Spread in front of Larwood, as though his living room had become one of the Bodyline grounds, he could see – and tell whoever was listening – which player was fielding where: who Douglas Jardine had moved further back or forward on the leg side; how the captain had done so with just a sharp nod of his head and a barked surname. He could hear the tap-tap-tap of the bat against the rim of the batsman's big boots. Larwood could replay it all, ball by ball, in his head and in vivid colour: a 4–1 series win that changed his life.

When Larwood spoke about individuals, he saw his friend Jack Fingleton twist his expression into a narrow-mouthed grimace as the ball struck him. He saw Bill Woodfull try to walk off the pounding he gave him with short-pitched deliveries. He saw Donald Bradman, the Baggy Green tight on his head, his gaze full of apprehension. He saw Stan McCabe in majestic flow at Sydney thrashing the ball to the fence. He saw the near-fatal misjudgement Bert Oldfield made as the ball struck him on the head on a hot Monday afternoon at the Adelaide Oval. We have the privilege of knowing what happened on Jardine's voyage of the damned because of that one ball to Oldfield: the snap and crack of bone; the riot it came close to causing; the accusatory cables, thrown like poisoned darts, between the Australian Board of Control and the MCC and back again; the charge of unsportsmanlike behaviour; the political manoeuvrings that threatened to cleave the Empire clean open; the debate Bodyline caused – and which is still on-going – about ethics, fairness and the virtuous spirit of the game; and, finally, the personal cost to Larwood. After another five summers, he would fall into premature and disillusioned retirement, his heart for the first-class game burnt out. All because of Bodyline.

* * *

It happened like this:

England took the first Test at Sydney by 10 wickets, which Bradman missed through exhaustion after being ruled out on doctor's orders on the afternoon before the opening day. He was described as 'seriously run down'. Douglas Jardine always maintained that Bradman actually suffered

Harold Larwood, extreme left, and members of the MCC tour party during a visit to the Ballarat gold mines in Victoria in 1932–33. Douglas Jardine, third from the right, bears a striking resemblance to one of the Flowerpot Men.

a minor breakdown through stress: the accumulation of Australia's high expectations, a dispute with the Australian Board of Control over his newspaper work and, of course, the prospect of Larwood bowling at him. Bradman and the Australians certainly knew what to expect in the series. The evidence of Jardine's reliance on speed was perfectly visible, scattered like clues at a crime scene, well before the journey out. And, after arriving, the Australian vice-captain Vic Richardson directly asked Bill Voce: 'What sort of team have you brought?' Voce replied candidly: 'Not a bad one . . . and if we don't beat you, we'll knock your bloody heads off.'

The proof of it arrived as early as mid-November. Jardine's brand of leg theory was unveiled against an Australian XI at Melbourne, where Larwood struck Bill Woodfull on the heart for the first time. Bradman was so jittery that he made only 49 runs in two innings. The effectiveness of the ploy ensured it would be used in the Tests. Jardine excused himself from the match. He went fishing, and his vice-captain Bob Wyatt carried out his orders *in loco parentis*.

With or without Bradman in Sydney, Jardine adhered to his plan rigidly. On his instructions, a deliberately solemn tone was set in the middle. As uncooperative as ever towards the press, whom he regarded as rapacious and reptilian, Jardine refused to name his team in advance. His attitude was the dismissive: 'We're here to win the Ashes – not provide stories to the newspapers.' It also demonstrated his paranoia about 'dirty tricks', which contributed to the cloak-and-dagger secrecy. 'All of us had to be in our whites before the Test started, as if any of us might play,' said Larwood. 'You can imagine that the lads who got dressed and didn't play weren't too pleased about it.' The edgy Jardine was constantly on the lookout for any Australian impropriety, which he imagined was constantly being practised, such as tampering with the pitch. He sent whoever was twelfth man into the Australian dressing room with a clutch of autograph books for them to sign. 'Find out what they're saying in there,' he ordered. The books never disguised the true motive of the mission. 'We could see the purpose of it a mile off,' Fingleton told Larwood.

Jardine brought his players onto the SCG in a church-like silence. There were to be no favours for the enemy, no fraternization and no pleasantries of any kind, however innocuous, for the opening session. He demanded that no one spoke to the umpires or the Australian batsmen. And then the sixth ball Larwood bowled almost decapitated Woodfull. Roughing up the Australians had begun.

Without 187 from McCabe – one of the most coruscating examples of hooking and pulling and sheer bloody bravery ever seen – Australia would have been rolled over in three days. McCabe, just 22 years old, came in at 82 for three in the first innings. 'If I get hit,' McCabe told his father before batting, 'don't let mum jump the fence.' Larwood struck him frequently on the thigh; McCabe took the bruising and batted on imperviously, and his mother didn't budge from her seat. The ball came off the middle of McCabe's bat like a pistol shot. His innings was so awe-inspiring that Larwood called it the 'best I've ever seen'. Voce never forgot it either. 'I gave him everything I'd got in that Test and he hit me around the ground as if I was bowling a tennis ball at him. Why couldn't Bradman have batted like that?' he said. 'McCabe spared no one. It was the finest innings I ever saw.'

McCabe contributed more than half of Australia's total of 360, which England comfortably overtook with 524, chiefly comprising Herbert Sutcliffe's 194, Walter Hammond's 112 and the Nawab of Pataudi's 102 – a century so slow that it took almost six hours to compile. Larwood remembered laughing when he heard what Yabba, the well-known barracker on the Hill, had shouted at the umpire George Hele as Pataudi

A solitary spectator sits on the Hill at Sydney to watch Herbert Sutcliffe complete England's win in the first Test.

made his ponderous but precious contribution. Hele's day job was to read gas meters. 'Put another penny in him, George,' barked Yabba, 'he's stopped registering.'

In the first innings Larwood took five for 96 from 31 overs without, he insisted, the need of a blanket leg trap. In the second, with full-blown Bodyline tactics, he took five for 28 as the Australians were tamely bowled out for 164. He antagonized the Hill in doing so. Whenever Larwood appealed, the Hill tried to provoke him. He responded by flicking the V-sign at them or thumbing his nose very slowly, which set off another hail of abuse that fell around him like spears. 'I enjoyed it,' said Larwood. 'It was a bit of fun.'

Whenever Jardine introduced the leg-side field, Larwood said: 'I could feel the tension of the crowd pressing in on me all the time.' He questioned Australia's tactics. 'We'd probably have dropped leg theory if the batsmen had attacked us in that match,' he said. 'I expected to get hooked . . . in fact, we set the field to encourage it. I thought the batsmen would hit me. Most of them just ducked.'

On the fifth day England required a solitary run to win the Test. Larwood kept a photograph of the one spectator who sat in front of the scoreboard on the Hill to witness the last rites for Australia. 'I never forgot him sitting there,' said Larwood. 'He looked so alone.'

* * *

The term 'Bodyline' was soon slipping off the tongue of most Australians like a curse. The search for a convenient shorthand phrase to describe the devastation that Larwood's speed caused was a tortured one. There was 'Header Bowling', 'The Shock Attack', 'Torso Bowling', 'Body Bowling', 'Body Theory' and 'Direct Attack'. The Australian dressing room had its own sobriquet for it. Larwood's bowling was called 'scone theory' and his bouncers were referred to as 'sconers', a slang word for the head. 'When they started having a ping at us, we'd say "Hullo, the scone's on",' said Bill O'Reilly.

The Australians always watched Larwood without saying much to one another. 'We all sat around the windows looking out,' said O'Reilly, 'and the only time anyone would break the silence would be when one went extra close, and then you'd hear "Oh 'struth, look at that one."' When the 'scone theory' was being meted out no place was 'more quiet than the Australian dressing room'. O'Reilly also confessed: 'When a man would go out to bat you'd wish him the best and give him a smack on the back, almost with the feeling that you mightn't see him again on his feet – he might come back on a stretcher.' Larwood would eye up incoming batsmen as if he was an undertaker measuring them for a coffin. A display advert, mocked up in the Australian *Smith's Weekly*, expressed this droll sense of black humour:

We conduct
CRICKETERS' FUNERALS
With Neatness and Dispatch
Only Australian Materials Used
Under Direct Patronage of the Board of Control
JARDINE, LARWOOD & CO.

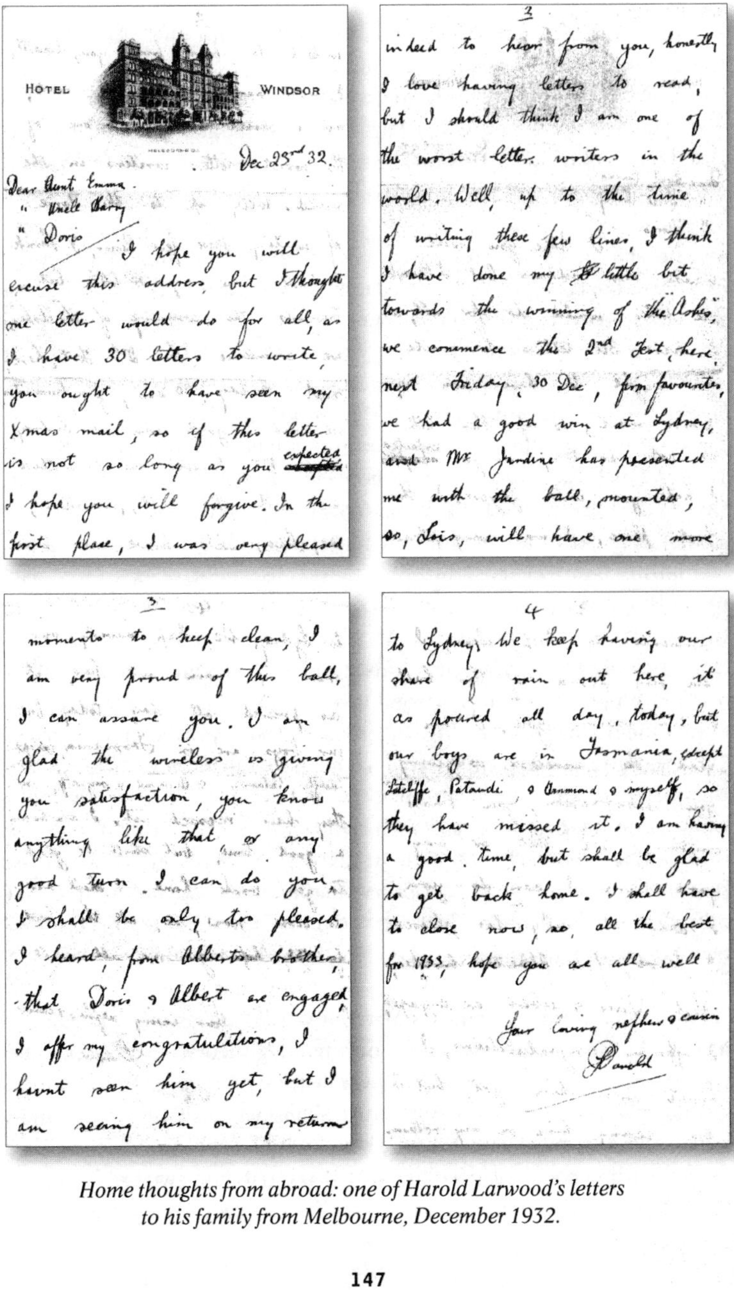

HOTEL WINDSOR

Dec 23rd 32.

Dear Aunt Emma
" Uncle Harry
" Doris

I hope you will excuse this address, but I thought one letter would do for all, as I have 30 letters to write, you ought to have seen my Xmas mail, so if this letter is not so long as you ~~expected~~ expected I hope you will forgive. In the first place, I was very pleased

2

indeed to hear from you, honestly I love having letters to read, but I should think I am one of the worst letter writers in the world. Well, up to the time of writing these few lines, I think I have done my little bit towards the winning of the "Ashes", we commence the 2nd Test, here, next Friday, 30 Dec, from favourites, we had a good win at Sydney, and Mr Jardine has presented me with the ball, mounted, so, Lois, will have one more

3

momento to keep clean, I am very proud of this ball, I can assure you. I am glad the wireless is giving you satisfaction, you know anything like that, or any good turn I can do you, I shall be only too pleased. I heard, from Alberts brother, that Doris & Albert are engaged, I offer my congratulations, I havnt seen him yet, but I am seeing him on my return

4

to Sydney. We keep having our share of rain out here, it as poured all day, today, but our boys are in Tasmania, except Sutcliffe, Pataudi, & Hammond & myself, so they have missed it, I am having a good time, but shall be glad to get back home. I shall have to close now, so, all the best for 1933, hope you are all well

Your loving nephew & cousin
Harold

Home thoughts from abroad: one of Harold Larwood's letters to his family from Melbourne, December 1932.

The Australians perfectly understood the truth of it. Alan Kippax came back after being trapped statuesquely on the crease in the first Test, laid down his bat, shook his head and admitted: 'He's too bloody fast for me.' Kippax took the view that Jardine's anti-Bradman scheme began as a slightly revised and buffed-up adaptation of 'leg theory' before evolving into a cricketing version of Frankenstein. Like the monster, Kippax suggested, it dominated its creator Jardine, got calamitously out of hand and became impossible to control. The theory is plausible, but wrong. From its concept, Jardine knew exactly how he would deploy his high-voltage attack in Tests, which were 'timeless' and therefore sure to produce a definite result. 'You're my weapon,' he told Larwood. Failure is an orphan; success has many parents. With hindsight, several figures claimed to have been involved in the architectural design of Bodyline: Larwood himself after his 'spot of rain had fallen' moment at the Oval; George Duckworth, who said he noticed Bradman flinching there too. Eventually Larwood called Jardine the 'sole instigator' and dismissed the idea of Bodyline as a prefabricated construction that grew 'bit by bit'.

Jardine appreciated how the Australians might react to it – particularly the crowds – and he steeled himself for it. What he didn't foresee was the depth of the feeling against him, the political convulsions these caused or the MCC's weaselly obfuscation and then abandonment of its original support for him, Larwood and the tactic. Jardine's family have always maintained that the MCC 'discussed and approved' it in advance.

The descriptive term 'Bodyline' has several 'fathers' also. In the *Australasian*, the sportsman-turned-writer John Worrall wrote about 'slingers on the body line' and then removed the space in his account of the opening Test. R.W.E. Wilmot crafted the sentence 'on the line of the body'. Hugh Buggy of the *Melbourne Herald* used 'bodyline' on the first day of the first Sydney Test. Ray Robinson, a sub-editor on that newspaper before becoming his country's most respected cricket writer, used 'body-line' in the text and removed the hyphen in headlines. The genesis of the word was immaterial to Larwood. Like Jardine, he deplored it. For him, the strategy was no more than leg theory – albeit operated with a speed and a consistency never witnessed before. If a common language divided England and the Australians over a suitable description of it . . . well, Larwood maintained, it was an ignorance for which neither he nor Jardine could ever be blamed. 'If the ball had swung,' he'd add, 'I might never have used leg theory at all.' Larwood thought the hand-made cricket balls of the period, on which the stitching was smaller, smoother and trimmer, produced far less swing.

* * *

The second Test at Melbourne belonged to Australia, who won it by 111 runs after England batted abysmally. The bowling attack was handicapped because Larwood's boots weren't strong enough to withstand the frenzy of work he put them through. The sole of his left boot split from the ball of the big toe to the heel. Much to Jardine's exasperation and the crowd's hooting derision, he had to leave the field four times during the first innings and went through three different pairs of boots: his own, which he had repaired within hours, a new pair and a pair belonging to the wicketkeeper George Duckworth, who was also a size seven. Larwood's leather boots, with their functional iron spikes, were bulky and unattractive things. The boots were nearly eight inches high and Larwood strapped them to his feet through 20 lace-holes, as if he was pulling on a pair of ice skates. The crowd, believing Larwood was resting or soaking in the bath, tore into him. When he tried to explain the trouble with his boots, the raucous chorus of booing and jeering became worse. He refused to go off again in case of physical assault. The new boots, which weren't broken in, lifted the skin off his toes and he limped across the outfield like a wounded animal. 'The harder I bowled, the more it hurt,' he said. He was in no fit state to walk, let alone bowl.

The Test was emphatically Bradman's – even when he failed. He always came to the wicket with an abiding sense of entitlement, as if his presence alone was, like cricket's version of a banker's draft, the absolute guarantee of runs. Bob Wyatt, fielding in the deep, heard nothing but the bullying taunt of: 'Wait until our Don comes in.' When he did, the acclaim was enough to carry him to the crease. Bradman took a semi-circular route to the wicket to accustom himself to the light and conditions. With every step, the noise grew louder; so loud that the fielders could only communicate by yelling to one another. 'Good reception, Don,' said Herbert Sutcliffe laconically when Bradman reached the crease. Bradman acknowledged it, and then replied: 'Yes, but will it be so good when I'm coming back?'

The field was set: Hammond, Voce and Sutcliffe at leg slip; Jardine at leg gully; Wyatt in his captain's pocket, but squarer; Pataudi at fine leg;

Shock and awe: Bill Bowes claims the wicket of Donald Bradman first ball with a long hop that Bradman drags on to his stumps.

Allen at suicide square leg; Leyland at mid-on. The ball was in the hands of Bill Bowes: gawky wire glasses, wheat-coloured hair and doughy, comedian's face, and a body so elongated that he had to fold himself like an anglepoise lamp to climb inside a car.

As Bowes began his run towards Bradman, the din grew so loud that it seemed as if the stands might fracture. Bowes took two strides before pulling up abruptly. He couldn't hear himself think. Purely to waste a few seconds, and to regain his composure rather than make any attempt to distract Bradman, he asked Leyland to switch to silly mid-on. He flicked the ball from hand to hand before leaning into his run for the second time. The cacophony disturbed Bowes again and he stopped after another two strides. In an effort to mute the crowd, he made more adjustments to the field; Pataudi was waved onto the boundary rope. As he did so, he saw Bradman glance at the field with the cautiousness of a man looking both ways before crossing a busy road. A thought struck Bowes. 'He expects a bouncer,' he said to himself. 'Can I fool him?'

He screwed his face into a grimace; what he believed was the most murderous expression he could muster. Even before the delivery, Bradman was moving across his wicket to take care of the short ball. What came instead was a shocking long hop that half slipped out of Bowes' hand. 'It deserved to be clouted to the fence,' said Larwood. The ball kept low. Bradman could have dispatched it anywhere he wished through the off side – probably for four. Instead, already committed to the shot he'd visualized in his mind, he got the faintest of bottom edges and then heard the awful click and clatter the ball made against the stumps. Bowes put his hands on his hips, turned to the umpire and said in his Yorkshire accent: 'Well, I'll be fucked.' Bradman, red-faced and cold in the stomach, tugged at the peak of his cap, bowed his head and walked back to the pavilion. The normally undemonstrative Jardine, who saw displays of emotion almost as a betrayal of etiquette, threw his arms in the air and began hopping on the spot, like a North American Indian in a war dance. A mortuary silence fell across the ground. All that could be heard was the stately rattle of nearby trams. A woman in the crowd broke the silence with a solitary handclap and, as Bowes put it, 'there was suddenly bedlam'. A few overs later Wyatt, posted on the boundary again, was mischievously asking the crowd: 'When's your Don coming in?' Bradman was so rankled by his mistake that he was still asking Bowes about the dismissal in 1954. On a flight from Sydney to Adelaide, Bowes said that Bradman 'asked me to confirm that I bowled a bouncer which he pulled into his stumps from shoulder height'.

The Australians struggled to a first-innings 228, propped up by 83 from Fingleton. 'A brave knock,' was how Larwood described it. England shrivelled to just 169 in reply; only five batsmen reached double figures. Bradman then made England pay for the embarrassment of being dismissed first ball by Bowes. He spun his gold with an unbeaten 103 in a second-innings total of just 191. Larwood's toes were still raw, as if each one had been rubbed down with thick sandpaper. He struggled through 15 overs and claimed only two wickets. As England collapsed to a pathetic 139, the Ashes series was perfectly balanced again.

And so to Adelaide . . .

* * *

Jack Hobbs described Adelaide – 'the City of Churches', where Donald Bradman eventually made his home – as the most handsome cricket ground in the world: 'Not a discordant note anywhere.' From the members' stand, you saw the trees of sap and emerald-green and soft light browns, which stretched elegantly into rolling blue hills. The roofs of the houses were green and brown too, as if camouflaging themselves for privacy. The spires of St Peter's Cathedral elegantly pricked the sky. It was hardly the place where you'd expect the braying that practically declared war on both Larwood and the Harlequin-capped Jardine, who advised people to listen to recordings of the Test 'armed with two wads of cotton wool' jammed in their ears.

The crowd was edgy and unsettled on the first morning. For one thing, there had been scuffles and fights near some of the gates because the queues were so long and progress through them was slow in the heat. For another, it was furious with Jardine, who had ordered that net practices before the Test should be closed to the public. During the first of them, as several thousand Australians eagerly clustered around to watch Larwood bowl, he and Jardine had been barracked viciously. The lexicon of abuse may have been predictable and limited, but it was constant, like the monotonous thud of a drum. When Bowes knocked over Jardine's stumps, the crowd ridiculed the captain. Jardine wouldn't tolerate it again. He made sure that police guarded each of the entrances to the ground so that his team could prepare in private. To the average Australian, it was much more than a snub. It was another indication – if anything further was needed – that Jardine was a snob and disdainful of them, as though he looked down on Australians and regarded them as nothing more than an uncouth, grubby rabble. Jardine wasn't worried about more bad publicity; criticism bounced off him like rain off a roof. As well as protecting himself against the jeering, he wanted to protect Larwood too. He'd begun to realize the strain his fast bowler was under. Condemnation of his bowling followed Larwood everywhere – on the street, in hotels, across the pages of newspapers. 'There was hardly anywhere to go where you wouldn't hear someone talking about the Tests,' said Larwood. 'I was soon fed up with it.' He also knew he'd let down his captain at Melbourne. If he did so again at Adelaide, he worried about his place.

In the break between the second and third Tests, the team had gone to Bendigo for a country match. Larwood expected to rest, bathe and

Gubby Allen, who found Bodyline repellent, neatly takes Donald Bradman off Harold Larwood in the first innings of the third and most controversial Bodyline Test at Adelaide.

bandage his skinned toes from Melbourne. He'd also arranged to drive out to the country just so 'I could escape for a while.' Instead, he found himself marked down as drinks-carrier for the insignificant friendly – an unlikely twelfth man, who would be compelled to fetch refreshments and towels, run baths and fuss over everyone else. He went into a rage. He took a pencil and scrubbed his name off the team sheet. And then he took the team sheet in his hand and screwed it into a tight ball, as if he might bowl it at someone. Finally, he sought out journalists to tell them that he wouldn't play under 'any circumstances'.

Jardine, who had taken himself and the amateurs off to an official function, had to calm Larwood down on his return. Larwood swore and paced his room. A cack-handed compromise was reached: the MCC would field twelve players rather than eleven. Larwood, who wanted nothing more than to put his feet up, would have to pull his boots on again. 'I didn't think it was fair,' he said. He bowled at quarter-pace, and didn't speak to Jardine for two days. 'I could barely look at him, let alone talk to him,' he said. When he broke his silence, it was to make a threat. Jardine arranged fielding practice before the Test. The team were spread like the spokes of a wheel across the outfield, and Jardine randomly struck the ball to them. It had to be returned smartly and accurately to George Duckworth behind a single stump. Bill Voce lost his patience. He was tired and hot, begging for shade. He began throwing the ball deliberately high over Duckworth's head, making it impossible for him to take it. Jardine warned Voce that if he did so again, he would be sent home. 'If Bill goes home,' said Larwood, 'then so do I.' The captain backed down.

Larwood saw Adelaide as the most critical few days of the series. If England lost, he reckoned morale would fall and momentum might swing irrevocably towards the Australians. If England won, there was no doubt in his mind that the advantage it gave them would be forced home in the final two Tests – and the Ashes won. The pitch had been cut and prepared for speed. It was almost as if the strip was bespoke for him. After a cold spring, it was almost bare of grass, the meagre growth fine and tight. Jardine called tails, won the toss for the only time in the series and decided to bat. At one stage on the cliff-edge of collapse at 30 for four, England lurched back on course to make a decent fist of it with 341 in four and a half sessions: Maurice Leyland stroked 83, Wyatt 78 and Eddie Paynter 77. Even Hedley Verity, batting at number nine, added 45.

And then came Larwood . . .

His routine before bowling was always the same. He reached into his left trouser pocket and lifted out a pinch of snuff between his fingers; his favourite brand called Top Mill. 'I did it throughout my career,' he explained. 'I'd take a good sniff and my head would clear. It was just something to give me a bit of bite.'

The flags atop the Giffen Stand were blowing away from the city, and the branches of the fig trees swayed with them. Larwood had the breeze at his back. The scoreboard laid out the story of the match so far, and the Australian batting order. Larwood's own name was spelt in thick white capital letters. A total of 174,351 people would watch this Test: men in summer suits crammed in so tightly shoulder-to-shoulder around the concrete track, which ran beyond the white wooden picket fences and the first few rows of seats, that it was almost impossible for them to reach into their jackets for a handkerchief. The sun poked through a sky billowing with clouds, piled up like a Constable painting, and dwarf shadows fell across the field. The temperature was in the eighties – more than warm enough for Larwood. There was silence when he shaped to bowl from the Torrens end. Despite the size of the crowd, the shuffling

A Larwood thunderbolt sends Woodfull's bat spinning out of his hands at Adelaide, January 1933.

of feet and the rustling in the members' areas, it was as if time had slipped out of joint and only the figures on the neat oval of grass were moving. The crowd was rigid with expectation. The only sounds were the pounding of Larwood's boots on the ground, the tapping of Bill Woodfull's bat in the crease, the deadening thump of Ames' gloves as he brought them together and crouched down. In the slips, Herbert Sutcliffe said it was so quiet that the fieldsmen could hear one another breathe.

There's an awful irony in what came next. Larwood's name was blackened for something he emphatically didn't do. The evidence exists in film of the Test, which has been played and replayed and is now available on *YouTube* with just a click of a computer mouse. The ball that hit the slow-moving Woodfull wasn't bowled to a Bodyline field. The sixth delivery of Larwood's second over caught him on the back foot. Larwood insisted the ball was straight. Jardine claimed that Woodfull had stepped outside his off stump to play it. The umpire George Hele said Larwood bowled it on leg stump. Wherever it started, the ball took Woodfull near the heart and tore the skin. He dropped his bat and pressed both of his gloved hands against his chest, half-stooping as if he'd taken a bullet. He unbuttoned his shirt to inspect the damage. The mark was already red, like a port-wine stain. The booing lasted for three minutes.

What appalled Woodfull – and critically dictated his own response to events over the next 48 hours – was the reaction to his discomfort. Jardine folded his arms, walked past the groggy Woodfull and slapped Larwood on the back. 'Well bowled, Harold,' he said loudly. The stagey congratulations were no more than base psychology – designed not so much to heap more misery on Woodfull, but to unnerve Bradman, who was at the non-striker's end and so heard what Jardine said. As Larwood ran up to bowl his next ball at Woodfull, Jardine stopped him theatrically in mid-stride for exactly the same reason. He clapped his hands, gestured to the fielders to move into the leg trap and then waved Larwood towards him like a film director arranging his actors on set. The only thing he didn't do was shout 'Action!' Larwood promptly sent the bat spinning out of Woodfull's hands again. Jardine knew – and didn't care – that he would provoke both Woodfull and Bradman, who made a meagre eight runs before Larwood claimed him. His were deliberate acts with a specific purpose, of which Pelham Warner was unaware. If he had been, the defining moment of the series – when the best possible intentions led to the worst possible consequences – might have been avoided.

After Woodfull was out, bowled by Gubby Allen, Warner's Victorian attitudes towards fair play and the Corinthian spirit obliged him as a matter of duty to commiserate about the ball from Larwood which belted him in the chest. The tour manager was naive, incapable of anticipating Woodfull's mood.

The exchange between them in the dressing room lasted less than a minute. But 25 words of it became imprinted not just onto the series, but onto the whole cricketing world too; 25 words chased Warner away; 25 words raced around Australia and then England before exploding like a box of detonated nails. Wrapped in a white towel, and slowly recovering after Larwood had felled him, Woodfull saw Warner come through the door in his pale suit and Panama hat. He listened to him offer a tame expression of concern and sympathy. As ever Warner was playing the diplomat; Woodfull was in no mood to be diplomatic in return. His reply was terse, spat out:

I don't want to see you, Mr Warner. There are two teams out there. One is trying to play cricket and the other is not.

Warner was used to being spoken to as if he were a Lord in ermine rather than dismissed like a mere footman. He was so jolted that he was found sobbing, shaking and wailing in his bedroom much later. The charge of 'not playing cricket' would always dog Larwood. Warner couldn't grasp why Woodfull had responded to him with such brusqueness. He believed in the fantasy that a gentleman's handshake could solve everything. If Warner had waited for an hour or so before attempting to talk to Woodfull, rather than knocking almost immediately on the dressing-room door, those terse three sentences probably wouldn't have been spoken. After time had taken the edge off Woodfull's aggression, the conversation would have been less sparky, couched in a more emollient language. Larwood certainly thought so. The Bodyline furore, he always maintained, was caused by Woodfull's 'temper' and Warner's 'need to say sorry'.

The combination of insult and humiliation, and Warner's dismay, soon reached those 'in the know' – the players, the officials and administrators. Jardine locked the dressing-room door to tell his own team personally, and ordered them not to discuss it, especially with anyone holding a pencil and paper. When the extent of Woodfull's snub to Warner was spread across the newspapers, it broke the last, already frayed threads of the relationship between the two teams. As Larwood put it, with a high degree of understatement: 'The players on both sides were perhaps not quite as friendly as some of us would have liked . . . ' Even if some of the Australians didn't complain on the field, he added, some wilfully 'played to the gallery'. He was specifically talking about Woodfull and Bradman.

While the matter stayed within the walls of the dressing room, and any deep grievances about Bodyline weren't openly talked about by anyone taking part in it, the pretence that this was just another rough Ashes series could be maintained. But the news soon seeped out, and was scribbled in notebooks and battered out on typewriters. With Woodfull's searing opinion set in hard type across the front pages, it became impossible to hold that line. He'd set in motion a chain reaction of accusation and recrimination that was unstoppable.

The bumptious Warner, seriously accident-prone, compounded his original error by suggesting that Woodfull had apologized to him for his rashness. 'We are now the best of friends,' he added sanctimoniously. Woodfull was enraged. Warner's thinking was flawed again when he assumed that Jack Fingleton, as a working journalist, was responsible for splashing the story of Woodfull's wrath. He offered Larwood £1 if he got Fingleton out; Larwood, who never needed the incentive of hard cash to remove anyone, bowled him for nought in the second innings. Fingleton maintained that Bradman was the source of the story, and was still insisting the same thing to Larwood after piloting his emigration to Australia. Bradman understood that Woodfull's response was incendiary, and that he could use it as a weapon to fight Bodyline – something he'd been unable to do consistently with his bat. Whether Bradman did so for cricket's sake, or for the sake of his own skin, is a moot point. Fingleton thought the case of mistaken identity cost him a place on the 1934 tour to England. In 1946, he wrote to Woodfull to clear his name, and received in response his former captain's assurance that: 'I did not connect your name with the passing on of that conversation . . . I seem to recall that you told me, on the day it was published, that you had nothing to do with it. I still do not know who was responsible for the leakage . . . '

Woodfull's admission about what he really thought about Bodyline provoked the crowd, who awoke to the incendiary headlines and crammed into the ground restless and vindictive. It may not have been spoiling for a fight, but the prospect of one – especially when Larwood had the ball in his hands – was a distinct possibility. The Australian Board of Control approached Warner and asked him to ensure that there were no more predominantly leg-side fields. Warner could only reply, with as much firmness as his depleted spirit could muster, that he had no jurisdiction over Jardine on the field. The Board of Control, peeved at Warner's refusal to support it, went off to begin composing the first of its highly publicized cables.

And then, of course, came Larwood again . . .

CHAPTER SEVEN

IT WASN'T YOUR FAULT, HAROLD

January 1933 – February 1933

Leg-side attack.
Larwood bowling to McCabe

Stan McCabe, the genius of the Sydney Test with an unbeaten 187, faces Harold Larwood at Adelaide. In the leg trap are, from left: Leyland, Allen, Jardine, Hammond and Sutcliffe.

Adelaide: January 1933 – Sydney: February 1933

The tipping point of the Bodyline series – the ball that felled Bert Oldfield – wasn't bowled to a Bodyline field either. But it didn't matter. The climate was so fevered that Bill Woodfull, the Australian Board of Control and even those who paid to watch were blind to, and unable to discriminate between, genuine fast bowling and Bodyline – even when Jardine, the auteur of it, didn't deploy a leg-side field. It became impossible for them to distinguish legitimate aggression from the tactic itself. Whatever the strength of the evidence – and however clear that evidence might be – the accused was always going to be Harold Larwood, exposed to a spillage of hate, and the verdict against him was always going to be guilty.

Larwood noticed on his first trip to Australia that one of every three or four balls skimmed off the surface of pitches and that the bounce was unpredictable. 'There was no real need to dig it in,' he said. 'The bounce occurred naturally – especially with the new ball. You never really knew how high it might be.'

Oldfield was on strike when Jardine took the new ball, which he lobbed to Larwood. Oldfield had made 41 impressive runs, frequently pulling Larwood through mid-wicket. The delivery that struck him was short and dropped a foot outside off stump. He decided to step across to hook or pull again, lost sight of it because of the low sightscreen and mistimed his shot. He played blindly and too soon, and got an edge that flew into the right side of his forehead – just below the hairline. The ground began to slide away from him. Oldfield knew immediately that if the ball had struck him on the temple 'it would have been the end for me'. He moved in rapid, short jerky steps from the crease. His legs collapsed beneath him, everything spun – the picket fence, the ground, the faces in the far distance. In confusion and pain, he tried to take his cap off, and then he put it on again. After he had hit Woodfull, Larwood did nothing more than kick the turf at the bowler's end, bringing up a small divot, and then turned his back on the scene, as if he didn't care. This time he dashed up the pitch, his face as white as alabaster. A clammy terror went through him; he feared Oldfield was dead. If the peak of his cap hadn't broken the trajectory of the ball, he might have been. Oldfield was lucky. He suffered a linear fracture of the right frontal bone. 'I'm sorry, Bertie,' said Larwood in blind terror. Oldfield's eyes were flat and blank, like dark windows. 'It's not your fault, Harold,' said Oldfield eventually in a low moan. 'I was trying to hook you for four.' If only Oldfield's reply could have been broadcast at the moment; or if only the crowd could have heard his view that 'criticism of Larwood is unjustified'.

As Oldfield went down under the force of the blow, the Oval swelled with anger, and that anger rolled down and across the pitch as a visceral, shrieking roar that 'frightened' Larwood. The atmosphere turned sulphurous. Crimson faces, with eyes on stalks like cartoon characters, came to the fence and seemed to press against Larwood's own face – even though he was more than 30 yards away from most of them. He could feel the crowd's loathing prickling his skin. There was screaming, and he could see fists clenched into tight balls of hate. 'I felt,' he said, 'as if one false move would bring the crowd down on me.' If one 'idiot' lunged over the fence, he was convinced that thousands would follow and he'd be buried beneath them. He turned to Les Ames, who was equally distressed: 'If they come,' he said, his voice breaking, 'you can take the leg stump for protection. I'll take the middle.'

Oldfield hit on the head

The defining moment of the Bodyline series. Harold Larwood has just struck Bill Oldfield, who drops his bat and staggers away. 'It wasn't your fault, Harold,' Oldfield tells him.

The suited Bill Woodfull, arms pumping like pistons, strides out to tend to his wounded colleague Bert Oldfield as the England team cluster around him. Larwood, third from the left, eyes the approaching Australian captain with apprehension.

The police deployed mounted troopers to ensure order. Contemporary reports talked about the threat of riot and physical violence, and all his life Larwood was convinced that view was valid. On the field, he prayed quietly to himself that it wouldn't happen. A jug of water and a towel were brought to bathe Oldfield's bloody, broken head. Woodfull emerged from the picket pavilion gate in a dark suit – his face grim, his stride long, purposeful and bristling, his legs and arms working furiously to get him to his stricken colleague. There's no question that Woodfull's sole concern was the welfare of his wicketkeeper. He was a loyal, principled man, and he would have seen it as his duty as captain to be alongside the wounded Oldfield. But the sight of him in such sensitive circumstances – solid and slightly aggressive, like a marching soldier heading for the front line – was inflammatory. Here was Woodfull, who everyone now knew abhorred Bodyline and was sickened by it, emerging as the gallant focus of the opposition to the tourists' tactics; white knight to Jardine's black.

Larwood lay on his side near his bowling mark, tossing the ball up in the air with his right hand, as if casually flicking a coin on a street corner. Waiting for his panicky heart to slow, he began picking at dry stalks of grass and tried to give the impression that the noise – so extreme he could barely think – and the stream of insults didn't worry him. But his stomach was churning, and there was a rough, dry taste in his mouth as he watched Woodfull slowly guide Oldfield off the field.

Larwood got to his feet gradually, as if any sudden movement might provoke the crowd, and the England fieldsmen returned to the same positions for the new batsman, Bill O'Reilly. 'I reckon it took me ten minutes to get in and to shape to the first ball,' remembered O'Reilly. 'I wouldn't have minded if it had taken me twenty minutes.'

Jardine displayed what Larwood called 'cold courage'. He looked unflappable, as if just waiting for a lightning storm to pass. 'I don't know what was going through his mind,' said Larwood, 'but he seemed so calm.' Jardine gestured with a nod of his head to check whether Larwood was composed enough to bowl. As he began his run, the crowd started to count him out in a ghastly shout of 'one, two, three' which ended after ten with the cry 'out, you bastard!' Their words couldn't hurt him. England bowled out the shaken Australians for 222.

On the field, Larwood was so commanding that he created an illusion. His wide shoulders and stocky build gave the impression of height. Off the field, he could wander into an Australian bar in his suit and tie rather than his whites and no one recognized him. 'I'd go in for a quiet drink and hear them say all of sorts things about me. People who'd just seen me play had no idea that I was standing next to them eavesdropping on their conversation. Most Australians thought I was six foot six.' It explains why at the end of that day's play the flustered policeman who came into the dressing room to escort him out of the ground had to ask: 'Which one is Larwood?' Bill Voce pointed out his friend. 'What have I done wrong?' asked Larwood innocently.

Larwood had been called a 'bastard' so many times that the word had lost its meaning to him. He came out into the jostling knot of swearing, spitting men in suits, who looked ready to string him from a gibbet. The policeman stood close to his shoulder; Voce followed behind to ward off anyone who might lurch at Larwood from behind. 'Bastard . . . bastard . . . bastard' was all he could hear. Larwood went back to the hotel and stayed in his room.

As the crow flies, just three miles separate the terraced house where Larwood was born and grew up from Lord Byron's ancestral home, Newstead Abbey. Setting aside the geography of Nottinghamshire, the poet and the fast bowler have nothing else in common – except for this: Byron awoke one morning to find that his poetry had made him famous. Larwood awoke, the day after striking Oldfield, to find that his bowling had made him infamous. He sat in the lobby and hid behind his newspaper.

* * *

Soon the cables began. The Australian Board of Control was thoughtlessly knee-jerk in its approach and intemperate in its language. It didn't possess sufficient guile to frame an appropriate and subtle policy against Bodyline. It also lacked the cleverness to condemn Jardine strongly without insulting the MCC and the farsightedness to draft a diplomatic plan that might have curtailed the tactics. Rather than resolve the problem, its accusations made it worse. Its first cable to the MCC – sent on 18 January, the penultimate day of the Adelaide Test – fell into the easy trap of relying on the term Bodyline, a word created in the world of journalism rather than cricket, and then of adopting a mildly threatening tone:

> Body-line bowling has assumed such proportions as to menace the best interests of the game, making protection of the body by the batsmen the main consideration. This is causing intensely bitter feeling between the players as well as injury. In our opinion it is unsportsmanlike. Unless stopped at once it is likely to upset the friendly relations existing between Australia and England.

The Board of Control made another crass mistake in releasing the telegram as a curt statement to the newspapers at the same time as dispatching it in a huff to Lord's. It appeared in the Stop Press columns in London before arriving at Lord's. The subsequent headlines raised the stakes still higher, and pricked the egos of the MCC committee. In its rush simultaneously to reclaim its dignity, communicate its anger and lash out, the Board of Control failed to grasp two fundamentally important things: from half a world away, the MCC's view of Bodyline was based on accounts in English newspapers, which had been generally positive. If Bodyline was used today, the Test would be live on satellite television. The wickets and major incidents would be seen on an endless loop on news programmes, and played and re-played in slow motion in front of pundits – grizzled ex-pros gathered around a microphone pontificating about it. The newspapers would provide sophisticated graphics of field-placings. The TV cameras would be waiting outside the hospital where Oldfield was taken and the hotel where England were staying. The average-man-in-the-street – in England and Australia – would be canvassed for his views. And Larwood would be pursued for an interview even before leaving the field. He and Bodyline would be in the swirl of 'instant news'.

In 1932–33, newsreel footage could take up to six weeks to arrive from Australia. Bodyline for the MCC was read about rather than viewed. Also, the phrases in the Board's cable, such as 'menace the best interests of the game' – and certainly the use of the word 'unsportsmanlike' – were provocative. At that stage, the MCC saw its duty as supporting its captain and manager. It wasn't fully aware of the sensitivities Bodyline had pricked, the growing resentment among the Australian public, or the passion that had spurred the Board to write the cable in the first place. The MCC slapped the Australians straight across both cheeks. The opening two lines of its cable, which followed after five days of thinking carefully about what to say, were deliberately wounding:

> We, the Marylebone Cricket Club, deplore your cable. We deprecate your opinion that there has been unsportsmanlike play.

The last, very long, line was an exercise in gauntlet-throwing:

> We hope the situation is not now as serious as your cable would seem to indicate, but if it is such as to jeopardize the good relations between England and Australian cricketers and you consider it desirable to cancel remainder of programme we would consent, but with great reluctance.

A week later the rattled and disunited Board of Control sent its reply. The truth came to them belatedly, rather like the descending apple that struck Newton. The Board realized that the MCC's opinion was prejudiced by the fact that it hadn't seen 'the actual play'. It could easily shelter behind the irrefutable point that Bodyline did not contravene cricket's sacred laws; any tawny-coloured copy of *Wisden* proved that too.

The Board finally understood that it needed to act positively rather than negatively. The Australians appointed a committee to report on how Bodyline bowling could be scrubbed cleanly out of the game and added, rather sheepishly, that 'we do not consider it necessary to cancel the remainder of the programme'. For one thing, it would have been financial insanity to have done so. As Larwood made clear: 'Bodyline drew back the crowds.' The Australians did reiterate that Bodyline was 'opposed to the spirit of cricket' – another euphemistic dig at England's supposed lack of sportsmanship – and said that it had become 'unnecessarily dangerous to the players'. The Board missed a trick. It ought to have withdrawn the allegation of 'unsportsmanlike' behaviour, instead of sharpening it. On 2 February, the MCC was able to bite them again – albeit very politely – when it asked: 'May we accept . . . that the good sportsmanship of our team is not in question?' Unless it was prepared for the sight of the England players packing their bags and walking up the gangplank on the next boat home, the Board had no option but to concede that Bodyline hadn't been unsporting after all. 'We do not regard the sportsmanship of your team to be in question,' its next cable assured the MCC. It had just performed a Tour de France of back-pedalling.

The accusation of unsportsmanlike play – the worst possible insult because it implied cheating – couldn't be allowed to stand. To have been boneheaded enough to level it in the first place was one thing. To repeat it was more than a slur; it was like the white glove across the face that summoned the recipient to a duel to protect his honour and reputation. The MCC committee was cricket's high society: titled, ennobled through birthright or distinction, mostly educated at Eton or Harrow and Oxbridge, and politically Conservative. If the MCC committee had been a building, then Gaudi would have built it and given it a modernist twist. It was a grand, elaborate, complex-looking construction which included three Viscounts, one Duke, two Earls, four Lords and three Knights. The President was Viscount Lewisham, a former Tory MP and previously Lord Great Chamberlain of England. His father and grandfather were both past

The Daily Mail *cartoonist Tom Webster envisages how the Australians might bat against Larwood in the Brisbane Test, following the 'battle of Adelaide'.*

Presidents of the MCC; Lord Hawke dominated English and particularly Yorkshire cricket for half a century and served as President during the First World War; Viscount Bridgeman had been Home Secretary and First Lord of the Admiralty during the 1920s; Sir Stanley Jackson was, like Hawke, a distinguished former Yorkshire cricketer – more than 10,000 runs and 500 wickets – as well as an MP, Chairman of the Conservative Party and Governor of Bengal. And so it went on . . .

This aristocracy, the *Debrett's* of cricket, saw itself as the infallible arbiter of what was and was not cricket. It upheld the values of sporting prowess taught on the lush playing fields of the public schools and had its own clear-eyed view of the proper and correct way to 'play up and play the game'. Even if it hadn't, the players, seething against the term 'unsportsmanlike', would have rebelled unless the Board withdrew its charge

Seldom has England witnessed a braver innings. Eddie Paynter left his hospital bed to make 83 in the fourth Test at Brisbane. England won the match – and secured the series too.

against them. As Larwood recalled: 'We felt we were in a false position in having to take the field with the stigma of the Board's term still on us.' Larwood remembered Jardine's anxiety both before and after the cables began. The Australian press whipped up several stories about dissent and squabbling among the England camp, dramatically described as 'being at war with itself'. Maurice Tate was said to have flung beer over Jardine, which Larwood said was untrue. There was supposed to be open hostility towards Jardine's disciplinarian approach, which was only partly true. As Larwood made clear, any 'grievances . . . were not nearly as serious as was made out' and stemmed not from Bodyline but from the frustration of players unable to force a way into the team. 'There were players who were unhappy,' he said, 'but it was because they couldn't get into the Tests. Australia's an awfully long way to go if you don't get a game.'

At the end of the fifth day of the Adelaide Test, Jardine called a meeting in a private room of the team hotel. There were only two points on the agenda. Should Bodyline/leg theory be abandoned? Should Jardine continue as captain? When Warner was the first to speak, Tommy Mitchell told him to sit down and shut up: 'It's got nowt to do with you,' he said. Everyone, however, finally had a say. The players liked the direction and purpose Jardine brought to the series, and the thought of winning the Ashes too. Jardine won his vote of confidence unanimously; 'a vote for England' is how Larwood put it. Bodyline would stay. For him, the ends justified the means. His captain's stiff-upper-lip, win-at-any-cost, grind-the-bastards-down attitude convinced Larwood and others that the Ashes could only be won with Jardine. He was as different as it is possible to be in approach and temperament from the circumspect Woodfull. 'Jardine might have been unpopular with a few of the players,' said Larwood, 'but everybody respected and admired him and many of us liked him.' Asked to define his qualities, Larwood replied simply: 'He was ruthless.'

England made 412 in their second innings and smartly removed the Australians – with Oldfield 'absent hurt' on the scorecard – for 193. In a win by 338 runs, Larwood finished with match figures of seven for 126. 'I was quick there,' he said. 'People just forget it because of what else happened.'

* * *

Almost a month later at Brisbane, during a heatwave so intense that metal girders at the Gabba almost melted, England regained the Ashes. Larwood was given half a dozen sips of champagne for lunch because he couldn't force down a scrap of food. It was too hot to eat. So hot, in fact, that he would strip naked in the dressing room and lie on the massage table. Bill Voce fetched vast cubes of ice and Larwood held them against his forehead, the melting water showering his dry skin. There were no energy drinks or vitamin supplements for the players of the Bodyline series. There was no carefully controlled diet either. 'I'd never eat much during a match,' said Larwood. 'I'd have a sip of beer and a cigarette at breakfast, lunch and tea. Mind you, I'd always tuck into a big dinner. That kept me going.'

The Brisbane match was Eddie Paynter's hour. Suffering from tonsillitis, and lying in hospital with a temperature of 102°, Paynter left his sick bed against the opposition of the ward sister, who convinced herself

Page 22 THE DAILY MIRROR Friday, February 17, 1933

ENGLAND TRIUMPH IN FIGHT FOR ASHES

DASTUR AGAIN FOR EPSOM?

Famous Horses in Big Spring Events

By BOUVERIE

The names of famous horses are freely sprinkled along with those accepted as mere handicappers in the second series of entries for the spring events.

Dastur, who found only April the Fifth too good for him in the greatest of all races at Epsom, can make another attempt on the "switchback" in the City and Suburban.

Other well-known horses entered for the Epsom race are Nitsichin and Pricket, and of course a number of those that will be concerned earlier with the Lincoln.

But, as usual it is the Jubilee that gets the cream. In addition to Dastur, the Aga Khan has entered the St. Leger winner, Firdaussi. The Beckhampton nominations include Bru- ... a brilliant Oaks winner, who afterwards

D. R. Jardine.

Pluck, Skill and the Will to Win Defeat Australia

BRAVO, JARDINE!

BY OUR CRICKET CORRESPONDENT

England's cricket quest has been triumphantly successful. The climax has been reached, and the Ashes are ours—"Let us now praise famous men."

Pluck, all-round team work and the will to win have brought our men out on top even more than their cricket ability, and for this triumph of temperament over matter Jardine, the captain, deserves the highest praise.

Often unfairly attacked, and even more often unkindly barracked, he has shown a firm front to every criticism, and has led his team magnificently.

Whatever may be felt about our plan of campaign—which was obviously carefully thought out before the team sailed—everybody must admire the wholehearted way in which this plan was carried through to the very end.

Convinced that their methods were in accordance with the true dictates of sportsmanship, our players allowed no outside influence to disturb them individually or as a team.

The team spirit—fostered by Jardine—was splendid, and every man pulled his weight. Some may have had a bigger influence than

Larwood, our greatest bowler.

that he was condemning himself to certain death. 'Where are you going?' she demanded. He was off to save England, who were in danger of falling far short of Australia's first innings of 340. Paynter climbed into a taxi while still wearing his pyjamas and dressing gown, changed into his kit at the ground, wedged a Panama hat on his head and made 24 not out in 75 minutes against the new ball. He went back to hospital that evening, slept comfortably and returned with pills and throat mixture the following morning to reach 83. He shared in a stand of 92 with Hedley Verity as England reached 356. Some of the Australian newspapers had the temerity to claim that Paynter didn't have tonsillitis at all. He was actually in hospital, the reports said, because of a fight with Larwood. The headlines confirmed Jardine's opinion that the press were more interested in sales figures than facts and gave him another excuse to treat them disparagingly.

Australia made only 175 in the second innings, leaving England to seal a six-wicket win by coasting to 162 for four. Larwood took another seven wickets – this time for 150. His figures were gilt-edged for one reason: Larwood claimed Bradman in both innings. In the first, he bowled him despite supping too much beer the night before. Worried about Bradman's form, Jardine pulled Voce to one side in the dressing room. 'Make sure your friend is in bed early tonight. We need him to take care of Bradman tomorrow,' he told him. Larwood was in his room at 9 p.m. when the phone rang. A casual acquaintance was on the line. Would he care to come to a party? Larwood rallied Voce, Ames and Maurice Leyland.

'I'll go with you if you only stay for an hour – and there are no drinks,' Voce said to Larwood, who reluctantly agreed. The small band slunk out of the hotel without Jardine's knowledge and jammed themselves into a taxi. For an hour, Larwood and his companions only drank orange juice. But a cask of beer propped in a corner finally proved too tempting. The inevitable followed. All four cricketers were 'blotto' by one o'clock in the morning. When Leyland began singing loudly in the hotel foyer, Voce stuffed a handkerchief in his mouth to avoid waking up Jardine. Larwood had already fallen over some journalists in the lobby. 'I bet them ten shillings each that I'd get Bradman the next day – and do it inside three overs too,' he said.

Larwood awoke with an upset stomach and a thick head. Ames was struggling to see through blurry eyes. Leyland felt bilious. Voce had the task of getting his friends dressed and ready. He wondered how each of them would manage a full day's cricket. Larwood won his bet nonetheless. He clipped Bradman's bails. As Bradman walked off, Jardine went across to Voce. 'Well done,' he said. 'Thanks for taking such good care of him last night.'

* * *

Larwood pleaded to be left out of the final Test at Sydney. With the series won, he reckoned he deserved a rest after 'bowling my insides out'. If Jardine's vindictiveness towards Bradman and Australia hadn't overtaken common sense, darkly misting over his rational judgement, the rest of Larwood's career – and perhaps even his life – would have unfolded differently. He would have been able to bowl during the 1933 season. He wouldn't have undergone an operation. His playing career wouldn't have been cut short. What is more, his searing pace would have survived for a few more seasons. He would have claimed so many wickets that England could not have ignored him for the 1934 Ashes series – irrespective of the politics involved in such a decision and the loss of face among the hegemonic powers in the MCC committee.

Jardine listened to Larwood's arguments. He was dog-tired. He'd never watched a Test and would like to see one in Sydney instead of playing in it. It wasn't a question of ducking out or wanting to avoid the grit and stink of another fight. He was just about all but spent and needed to freshen himself mentally and physically. Jardine thought about it for

Harold Larwood falls two short of a century in the fifth and final Test at Sydney. He was caught by Bert Ironmonger – one of the worst Australian fielders of his generation.

half a minute. Larwood had an idea that he'd convinced his captain to give him a brief holiday. But Jardine shook his head. 'I'm sorry, Harold. I can't grant you the favour,' he said. Larwood watched him press his thumb against a tabletop and twist it into the wood. 'We've got the bastards down there, and we'll keep them there,' he said. What he really meant was this: Bradman was reeling and he didn't want to give that particular 'bastard' the chance of recovering. Jardine's determination to humiliate Bradman over-rode any consideration of what Larwood wanted. The result was Larwood's injury, which cost him his speed.

The Test was Larwood's 'Dickens moment': it was the best of times; it was the worst of times. In old age, Larwood would describe what he did with the bat rather than the ball as his 'greatest moment in Test cricket'. England had bowled out Australia for 435, and the footsore Larwood wanted nothing more than to soak his weary bones in the bath. Jardine ordered him to put on his pads and go in as nightwatchman. 'I couldn't understand it,' said Larwood. 'I'd bowled my guts out . . . I was angry.

I didn't want to go in. If it was necessary, I was determined to get out.'

When in later years visiting members of the England tour party called at his home in Australia, Larwood talked them through his innings at the SCG as if he had just returned from the crease: how he'd batted shortly before the close and wanted to throw away his wicket in protest at Jardine's decision; how Bradman ought to have run him out, but wildly missed the stumps because he tried to hit them directly, the ball skidding off to the boundary; and how the crowd rose to a man and gave him a standing ovation at its end.

The reluctant nightwatchman was still fuming with indignation at Jardine's decision the following morning and decided to attack wholly 'on spleen'. He didn't care where the ball went. As the Australian bowler 'Bull' Alexander – as fast as Voce but inaccurate – tried to bounce him out, the Hill yelled at him to 'knock the bastard's head off'. Larwood, with five runs overnight, stood straight and hooked and pulled without fear. The scoreboard ticked on like a taxi meter. Larwood cut and drove and thought about his coach Jimmy Iremonger. 'A lot of the runs were his,' he said. 'I remembered how he taught me to bat.' Moving beyond 50, his stroke-play became more cavalier, like a man in a sword fight. His partner Maurice Leyland walked up the pitch to calm him down. 'You're 98,' he said to Larwood, who had no idea his century was so close that he could reach out and touch it. He had been playing instinctively, striking the ball freely and blocking out the jeers and crowd noise. But Leyland's well-meaning intervention broke his concentration. Telling Larwood to look at the scoreboard was rather like a hypnotist suddenly snapping someone awake from a trance with a click of his fingers. The startled Larwood looked around him and realized what he was so near to achieving – the Grail of a Test century – and it unnerved him. For the first time in the innings, he began to think about his shot selection. He planned to on-drive the next ball to the picket fence. The prospect of the hundred caused him to delay the stroke fatally, checking it instead of attacking. He said: 'The ball hit the bat rather than the other way around for the only occasion in my innings.' It dollied towards Bert Ironmonger, a fielder so maladroit with his hands that he usually needed a clothes basket to catch the ball. To Ironmonger's utter astonishment, and everyone else's, he didn't drop it. A sponsor had agreed to give a pound for every catch taken. 'He went around whooping "I've won a quid", and I went back to the dressing room,' said Larwood.

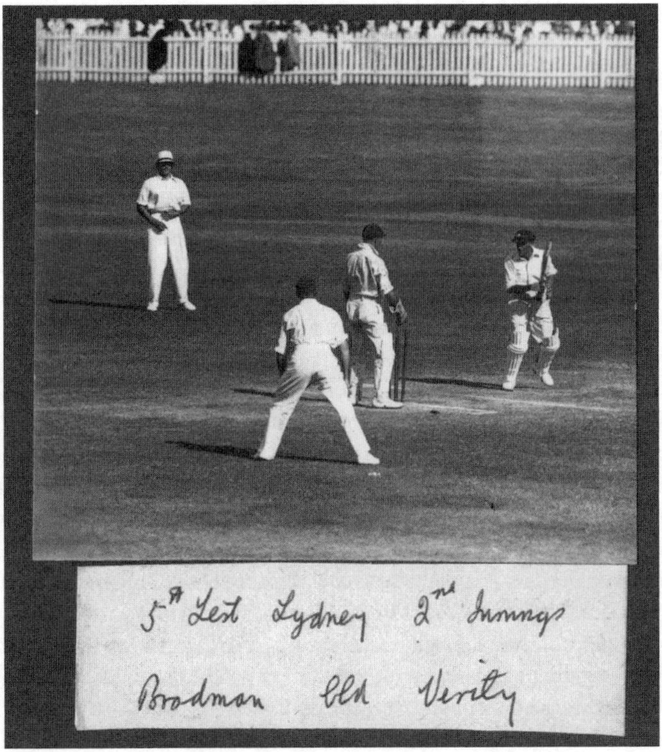

Clean-bowled: Hedley Verity's guile brings an end to Donald Bradman's second-innings 71 at Sydney.

After his improbable cameo he peeled off his gloves and waved his bat in the air in gratitude. The cheering for an innings lasting two hours and twenty minutes, and which included one six, one five and nine fours, still hadn't died away by the time Larwood unbuckled his pads and flopped on the bench next to his kit. 'I went to sleep that night with the roar in my ears,' he said.

England made 454, bowled out Australia for 182 and finished on 168 for two in reply to win by eight wickets. Larwood, however, wasn't celebrating.

With every ball he'd bowled on tour, he felt the vibration on impact at the end of his stride. It ran through his left boot to his knee, on to his hips and then on along his spine. The accumulated wear and tear of the series, the day-after-day job of pounding his foot against stone-hard pitches – especially without cushioned protection – took its inevitable toll. England lost a fast bowler for ever. Even when Larwood knew he was lame in Australia's second innings, and he dragged himself to the wicket as if his leg had withered, Jardine's intransigence reached preposterous proportions purely because Bradman was batting. 'What's wrong?' Jardine asked Larwood, who had first slowed his pace and then stopped, before collapsing and writhing around on the grass. 'I've done something to my foot, skipper. I can't walk,' he told him. 'You'll have to walk,' said Jardine. 'You'll have to finish the over.'

He was no more than an invalid, able to do nothing but 'stand against the crease and swing my arm over'. Bill Woodfull graciously pushed five deliveries back to him with a dead bat, as if it were a father-and-son's game in the back garden. Given the state of the series, the trouble Larwood had brought on Australia and the mental torment that Woodfull had experienced as captain, anyone else would have taken sadistic pleasure in causing humiliation in that moment and felt justified about taking his revenge. Larwood assumed he'd be flogged to the far corners of the boundary. This was Woodfull's chance to pillage runs. In acute agony, Larwood saw the ball disappearing into the distance and pictured himself standing uselessly beside the wicket waiting for it to be returned. He wanted to rush through the rest of the over so that the ritual mauling wouldn't be prolonged. He never forgot the kindness that Woodfull demonstrated instead. The Australian captain proved himself incapable of malice, performing one of the most generous and noble acts in cricket.

Even when the over ended, Jardine still wouldn't let him hobble away. 'I can't run. I'm useless. I'll have to go off,' said Larwood. Irritable and angry, Jardine waved him towards short cover point after whispering in his ear: 'You can't go off until this little bastard's gone. Let him think you can come back for another spell at any time. I want you to stand there and just stare at him.'

Bradman survived for a few more overs before Hedley Verity bowled him. Jardine clapped his hands, as if dismissing a servant. 'Right, Harold, you can go now,' he said peremptorily. 'I had died with my boots on,' is how Larwood saw his exit in hindsight. He went to the pavilion a few limping steps behind Bradman. His slow pace and sad slouch, his head partly bowed most of the way, made it look as though Larwood was walking behind a hearse. These two men – the batsman who was the cause of Bodyline, the bowler who perpetrated it – neither looked at one another nor spoke.

* * *

The statistics of the Tests seem inconsequential against the wider issue of whether Bodyline was unscrupulous or a piece of lateral thinking that stretched the rules, and what the Australians might have done more smartly to counter it.

Archie Jackson, who had withstood Harold Larwood's attack on the rain-affected pitch at the Oval in 1930, called him 'The Red Devil' and a 'devastating whirlwind'. It is one of cricket's imponderables: if the 23-year-old Jackson hadn't been dying of pulmonary tuberculosis in a Brisbane hospital during the series, could the outcome of the Bodyline Tests have been different? Jackson, called the 'greatest master batsman since Victor Trumper', was sure that quick footwork was the key to countering it. He bemoaned the squealing of the Australian batsmen and maintained that Larwood would 'not intentionally hurt a fly'. Larwood put Archie Jackson on a higher pedestal than Donald Bradman. 'I never knew him to flinch or complain at any time . . . he did not seem to hit the ball, he caressed it. He wasn't like some of the grumblers,' he said, making a sly dig at Bradman.

There were several options available for a batsman to quieten Harold Larwood. He could duck and sway and wait for the bad ball – if it ever arrived – or for Larwood to weaken through exhaustion. He could hook or pull – as McCabe did in the first Test at Sydney and, according to Larwood, as Jackson

The Australian captain Bill Woodfull: he deplored Bodyline and refused to employ it himself in retaliation.

would have done. 'I can't understand why I didn't get hooked more often,' said Larwood, underplaying his speed. He could absorb the deliveries on his flesh – as Bill Woodfull and Bill Ponsford frequently did, but not necessarily from choice. 'If I'd wanted to, I'm sure I could have hit Woodfull with each ball I bowled,' said Larwood, as if the Australian captain was a stuffed sack who could be bayoneted at any time. Or he could move away from leg stump and try to slash or manoeuvre the ball to the leg side – as Bradman did with reasonable but inconsistent success. But each of these possible remedies to Bodyline offered a palliative rather than a cure.

Larwood was accurate. He bowled very few loose deliveries, and so a batsman had to score against him whenever the chance came or become bogged down and impatient as a result. The hook or pull might get him caught in the deep. As the flesh is weak and bones are breakable, choosing to let the ball hit you was about as sensible as diving into an empty swimming pool. Bradman's voluntary movement towards the leg side brought him 396 runs, but didn't prevent Larwood from getting him out four times in eight Test innings. Only Jackson, he insisted, could have tamed him.

Larwood always kept the telegram that Jackson sent from his hospital bed two days before he died on 16 February 1933 – the final day of the Brisbane Test:

CONGRATULATIONS MAGNIFICENT BOWLING.
GOOD LUCK IN ALL MATCHES.

The words are so faded as to be barely visible now. The print, wholly in capitals and once inky black, is as pale as a shadow. You strain your eyes to read it. The creases have turned brown and the thin strip of paper is torn and worn. The postmark, which falls off the page, is nonetheless clear, as if it was only recently stamped. Larwood folded it into a tight square and tucked it into his pocket. Jackson's batting would have altered the Bodyline series, perhaps decisively: Larwood was convinced of it to his own dying day. He was sure Jackson would have hooked, pulled and improvised against him. The contest would have been keener, far sharper. Larwood remembered Jackson cover-driving him for four in that Oval Test – a shot so perfect that he wanted it framed and hung on his wall. 'The delivery I've just bowled would have knocked out any other batsman,' he said to his disbelieving team-mates. He stood and applauded it.

But Australia didn't have Jackson. It had a captain in Woodfull who responded too passively to Bodyline. If the easiest way to end a war is to lose it, then that's what Australia effectively did under Woodfull's captaincy. He was a practical, patient and self-effacing man with Christian attitudes. His motto was the rousing 'Boots an' all', and his orders came in short sentences or asides. He commanded an iron trust. His principles nonetheless got in the way of effective tactics that might have blunted Bodyline or prompted Jardine to change tack. With the pacey days of Jack Gregory and Ted McDonald long behind them, Australia couldn't generate the speed that Larwood did. There was nonetheless enough ammunition available to Woodfull to unsettle England seriously for an hour. Herbert Sutcliffe and Walter Hammond – though probably Jardine was the exception – didn't want to contemplate a Bodyline trap against them, and the injuries and discomfort it would bring, any more than Woodfull or Bradman did. A session or two of it, and a few blows into the ribs or thigh, and Jardine might well have found that his batsmen were calling for a truce rather than for extra padding.

Woodfull refused to match Jardine flame for flame. He found Bodyline repugnant and would never countenance employing it – even for a solitary ball. He didn't want to be 'dragged' to Jardine's level because he thought it would jeopardize the future of cricket: a 1930s twist on the contemporary phrase 'mutually assured destruction'. Bodyline might have ended almost as soon as it began if Woodfull had attacked rather than endured it. He was too tolerant of the intimidation. Woodfull's scrupulous behaviour, his abiding need to do the 'right thing', was demonstrated when the sick Eddie Paynter batted in Brisbane, barely holding himself together, let alone gripping a bat, after leaving hospital. Woodfull never sought to do anything other than bowl to him. There was no sledging, and no attempt to unsettle Paynter, whom Larwood said looked 'white and ill'. Woodfull's concern was always for Paynter's health above the price of his wicket. It was demonstrated again in the dead bat he dropped after Larwood broke down in the final Test.

Australia would still have been better served during the series with a captain like Vic Richardson. After the Bodyline series, Jardine insisted that he'd faced leg theory against South Australia in 1928 and he couldn't understand why Bradman, Woodfull or anyone else was making such a huge drama out of a reasonably commonplace occurrence. There were 'only two, or sometimes three men, on the offside', he recalled. Richardson was the South Australian skipper responsible for it. Richardson believed that Bodyline – or 'Headline' as he preferred to call it – didn't infringe the laws of the game, but violated its ethics. He was as opposed to it as Woodfull, but would have done more than just voice that opposition. Far more uncompromising than Woodfull, Richardson would have retaliated with missiles of his own. When Jardine rapped on the Australian dressing-room door to make a complaint, Richardson opened it. 'I would like to speak to Woodfull,' Jardine told him. 'One of your men called Larwood a bastard and I demand an immediate apology.' Richardson was a tall, straight-backed man with a little zip of a moustache. He blocked Jardine like a sentry at a checkpoint. A cartoon hanging at the Adelaide Oval depicts the exchange. Richardson is in a towel. Jardine stands at the door, his nose drawn extravagantly large. The shirt collar is high above his piped lapels. Richardson is turning towards the dressing room, where the other Australians are gathered. He says: 'Hey, which of you bastards called Larwood a bastard instead of Jardine?'

When Larwood nearly hit him with a short ball,+ Richardson gave as good as he almost got. 'If it happens again,' he said, 'I'll knock your bloody block off.' Richardson shortened his arm-swing to fight Bodyline and swayed out of the way. He was seldom hit. 'I would have thrown it right back at them straight away,' he said. 'I'm Australian. If you hit me, I'll hit you.' Richardson thought that retribution would have killed Bodyline almost as soon as it began. 'I doubt that Bodyline would have lasted. In fact, I know it wouldn't have. Herbert Sutcliffe and Walter Hammond both told me there is no way they would have played under those conditions. They said they wouldn't have lasted ten minutes.'

Richardson stressed that he saw 'more bruises to square feet of flesh on a batsman' during Bodyline than he did 'during the remainder of my career'. He likened Larwood to a heavyweight boxer 'going in for the kill' and thought that 'the power' he wielded during the series proved to be a 'great temptation' to him. 'Power,' he added, 'corrupts.'

Years later, Larwood found himself in conversation with Richardson and said to him that he only bowled Bodyline against 'the good players'. He went on: 'It was a compliment, really.'

Richardson replied wryly: 'If you lived to appreciate it . . . '

* * *

Harold Larwood used to tell the story of a child who caught sight of him in a cinema during the Bodyline series and turned to his mother to say: 'But mummy, he doesn't look like a murderer.' And, with relish, he would talk about the young Australian who handed him a piece of toilet paper to sign. 'What are you going to do with this?' asked Larwood incredulously. 'What do you think?' the boy replied, before adding: 'Thanks, mate. I'm going to wipe my arse on it.' Larwood signed the paper anyway.

Was Bodyline worth the anguish that followed it? When he was almost 90, Larwood was asked – once more – whether he wanted to repudiate it and to criticize Douglas Jardine. Was there anything he regretted about the tour? Was there anything he wanted to recant? Was there anything he would have done differently? Larwood shook his head. 'Not a thing,' he said. 'I didn't think Bodyline was unfair at the time . . . and I don't think so now.'

CHAPTER EIGHT

WHY DIDN'T YOU BOWL UNDERARM?

April 1933

Douglas Jardine presents a cheque to Harold Larwood and Bill Voce on the balcony at Trent Bridge in June 1933. The money was donated by the Nottingham public in recognition of their performances in the Bodyline series.

Nottingham: April 1933

The crowds choked the platforms, the booking area, the great hall and even the wide, dimly lit streets to wait for the hero to come home. More than 20,000 people were trapped in the crush around the dark red-brick of Nottingham station as the hands of its illuminated clock nudged towards midnight. They had waited for hours just to glimpse Harold Larwood. The whole of Nottingham, it seemed, wanted to welcome him back. He had neither asked for, nor wanted, this fame, and he accepted it reluctantly – and only then because he could not escape it. Suddenly Larwood was a celebrity in an age when you had to achieve something to become one; fame wasn't ubiquitous or cheap. Some of his admirers stood shakily on top of cars and taxis, or perched on whitewashed windowsills and looked down, without suffering vertigo, at the vast swarm of people a few floors below them. Others shinned up poles and lamp posts and clung to them like a ship's mast. It was a clear, bright night. The moon was almost full, hanging in the sky like a Christmas bauble. The Gothic station was like a stately galleon and the heaving, swaying movement of the crowd around it resembled the roll and toss of the sea. The air was thick with cigarette smoke, which drifted like an ocean mist.

Larwood expected a bus full of friends and family. He thought a few hundred well-wishers might sacrifice an early Saturday night to say 'well done'. He sat in a private carriage of the *Scotch Express* from St Pancras, the windows shut tight against the darkness and the smuts that the steam carried. His trilby and suitcase lay in the rack above his head. His skin was so deeply tanned that he seemed to have been cast in bronze. As the train pulled clear of London, and before the early evening spring light began to fade to dusk, Larwood was relieved to see the greenery of England again after the biscuit-coloured earth of Australia, where the soil was parched and dead, and looked to him to be in need of a month's water to bring it alive again. He saw homes in the far distance, smoke curling from squat chimneys, and clumps of trees that were clothing themselves in nascent green leaves. He thought about the state of his own garden, and the smallholding and poultry farm he'd created to make his living during the winter in case cricket ever let him down. He was wedged between his wife Lois and his Nottinghamshire captain, Arthur Carr. Carr had been with him since the boat carrying the injured Larwood home alone – Jardine and the rest of his team had gone on to New Zealand – docked at

Port Said. Everybody wanted a piece of Larwood and his story. 'I was surrounded,' he said, 'and everyone was asking me questions or taking pictures.' Larwood's contract with the MCC prevented him from talking to the newspapers. Its secretary William Findlay had wired him a clumsily phrased telegram:

> Confidential communicate the following from Findlay to Larwood: Am sure you will regard matter connected with tour strictly private and not give any information to friends including Mr Carr or Press who may meet you at Port Said or elsewhere stop telegraph us Lords saying you will be on your guard

The 'matter' in question was Bodyline, and the specific reference to Carr emphasized the MCC's nervousness about the rogue gene in his personality. Carr wasn't representing Nottinghamshire, or trailing exhaustedly across land and sea merely to shake the hand that had tamed Donald Bradman. He was doing so as a Gentleman of His Majesty's Press in pursuit of an exclusive. The *Daily Sketch* had paid for his passage and the curious messages he'd sent to Larwood, which were written in dark pencil. The first, in the confused, chopped and unpunctuated language of wires, read: 'Important meet alone Suez please don't come ashore and rejoin boat Port Said letter wife. Carr.' The second said: 'Meeting you Suez don't talk to anybody until I see you.' The last few words of the third managed to sound simultaneously pleading and like a captain's order: 'Travelling with you from Suez no mystery wife's letter crowd journalists boarding . . . see me first. Carr.'

Carr tried to soft-soap his fast bowler. He claimed he'd already told the *Daily Sketch* that Larwood wouldn't be able to talk because of his agreement with the MCC. He'd added that he knew his friend was a man of duty who would adhere to the wording of his contract. He'd assured the newspaper that nothing – certainly not money – would induce Larwood to say anything indiscreet. It wouldn't, however, prevent Carr from trying to wheedle out any fragments of information from him that would make a decent headline. He hadn't spent almost a week on board ship to meet Larwood – and then another five days on the return – for the benefit of his own health or Larwood's. Nor did he see his mission as entirely humanitarian. Carr wasn't the good shepherd escorting Larwood home. He was a working journalist, who had initially tried to pretend that he wasn't planning to see Larwood at all. 'He may see Larwood if he arrives in time,' his wife defensively told newspapers.

Carr found Larwood fending off questions from newspapermen, each one starving for a line and all asking the same things at once. Did he think Bodyline infringed the spirit of the game? Did he continue to support it and Douglas Jardine? What did he think about Donald Bradman? For Larwood the task of stone-walling proved difficult. He couldn't bring himself to be impolite and tell them where to shove the sharp end of their pencils. When Carr arrived, he thrust a slip of paper into Larwood's hand, as though he was tipping him with a gold coin. Larwood broke off to read it. The note urged him not to say anything, except of course to Carr himself. Larwood was so trusting that he gave Carr the benefit of the doubt. 'He was there to help, and to protect me,' he always maintained. What Carr actually did was fulfil his contractual obligations to his newspaper, which earned him his fee and expenses. A story, designed to sensationalize, was cobbled together. It claimed that Bodyline would be used during the coming summer. 'Nothing but legislative action by the MCC will stop the leg theory tactics from being employed,' said Carr emphatically. The reader was left in no doubt about what he meant: Larwood, under Carr's direction, would not be restrained from bowling Bodyline for Nottinghamshire. The cavalier Carr added that leg theory would make cricket 'more exciting'. The accompanying headline naturally used Larwood's name as bait to spark the readers' attention: 'Leg Theory bowling this season. Larwood and Carr get their heads together on trip on liner.'

Larwood neither asked for – nor received – any money in return from his captain, who was blatantly cashing in on his relationship with him. Given his friendship with Larwood, Carr was perceived as his front. It was assumed he'd act as Larwood's megaphone until the MCC lifted its gagging order. 'Talks of anything but Leg-Theory', ran one of the headlines in the *Nottingham Evening Post* the day after his return. As usual, the loquacious Carr was available to fill in the blanks. 'If Larwood ever tells the full story,' he said, like a fairground barker yelling up an audience, 'it will be amazing . . . You will never know how this boy has been pestered, worried and maligned.' The quote was deliberately enticing, and cranked up the price of the book Larwood quickly wrote. The *London Evening Standard* was soon waving white five-pound notes at him too. It offered £100 for just 300 words of Bodyline gossip;

Larwood declined. The ban on speaking publicly about Bodyline – he'd found the nervous Findlay waiting for him at St Pancras to reiterate the point yet again – had the obvious effect of increasing rather than sating the appetite for full disclosure. Like the MCC itself, anyone following the Tests in Australia had seen only a few grainy minutes of Larwood's bowling in newsreels at the local cinema, which was like squinting at the action through a keyhole; you only got a narrow picture of what was actually happening. Newspapers fed on Bodyline like ravenous crows. Rows and recriminations sold copies, and the circulation wars between them were a bitter business.

The exorbitant cost of sending a correspondent away for eight months meant that most newspapers were solely reliant on agency, freelance or syndicated copy from Australia. The public neither noticed nor cared. Even those with only a passing interest in cricket, or who had virtually no interest in it at all, were galvanized into reading about Bodyline because of the strength of the characters involved in this faraway soap opera: the former miner, the incomparable 'Boy Wonder' Bradman, the spat between the cradle of Empire and a jumped-up, presumptuous Dominion. The MCC was so concerned about Anglo-Australian relations that it mistakenly thought that not talking about Bodyline would make the beastly thing go away. It didn't anticipate the craving for news and opinion about it. Douglas Jardine labelled the gag it imposed on Larwood as 'a failure of policy'.

As the *Scotch Express* pulled on to Platform Four at Nottingham station, Larwood gauged the impact of Bodyline properly for the first time. No sooner had he motioned to open his carriage door than a thicket of thrust-out, eager hands almost pulled it off its hinges. The cheering and shouting rippled back from the platform, reverberated around the station's great hall and echoed out into the city streets, where it was loud enough to have blown off the Council House's stately blue dome. The dozens of policemen sent to guard Larwood were swept aside, and the crowd attempted to lift him across the platform and along the staircase. Grasping hands tugged at his long beige-coloured coat. Women tried to kiss him. Men tried to take his hand or pat him on the shoulder or back. Flowers were thrown, the heads and petals crushed and trampled by thousands of feet. The scene was eerily illuminated, like a Reynolds canvas, by the phosphorescent flashes of the photographers' bulbs. It cast Larwood and those around him in bright light. Half-blinded and blinking furiously, Larwood thrust out his right arm to protect his wife. The police and a few porters regrouped and managed to push them both into a luggage lift and slam the iron gate. Larwood was given ten seconds of peace before the gates opened again, and he fought his way through a long snaking line of faces, and hands which yanked at the front of his jacket, visible beneath his open coat. A man grabbed Larwood's trilby and began waving it above his head. There were shouts of 'Good old Harold,' and 'Speech, speech', and a wag yelled, loud enough for him to hear: 'Why didn't you bowl underarm to them?' In the push and struggle it seemed as if Larwood might be sucked back into the crowd. It took him almost an hour to escape into the coach, its engine revving, which would take him home.

In the wee small hours Larwood slept fitfully. There was too much going through his mind, and he couldn't settle. The following morning he dragged open the curtains to find hundreds of pairs of eyes staring at the house from above the top of his front hedge. When he wanted nothing but to be left quietly alone, there was yet another crowd, which had come along for a voyeuristic peek at him. Sightseers filled the pavement and spread along the gentle curve in the road. Cyclists propped bikes against walls. Motorists parked indiscriminately. Newspapermen and photographers stood together in long coats and hats waiting for any quote, however trivial, to be fed to them. Larwood didn't want to let anyone down. He always felt obliged to overcome his shyness and play a role, no matter how much his stomach turned with nerves at the thought of promenading. He pulled on a V-neck sweater and a pair of black trousers, and went for a walk through the poultry farm with his wife and parents. He chatted amiably to people who had 'taken the time and trouble' to come to see him. 'It's being polite,' he said. He deflected questions about Bodyline with a 'Thank you for coming. I'm very grateful,' which he wasn't. His left foot ached and he wanted to go back to bed and sleep and then spend time alone with his family.

If you're a sporting hero today, you sign a fashion contract, you're photographed with a model or two draped over your bare torso, you promote watches and cars and TVs. Your face stares out from billboards and glossy magazines. Your image and signature become attached to the equipment of your trade – a pair of boots or a ball. Larwood only ever endorsed one product: Green's Lawn Mowers. His photograph appeared in newspaper adverts under the slogan 'Triumphs of the Turf'. But then

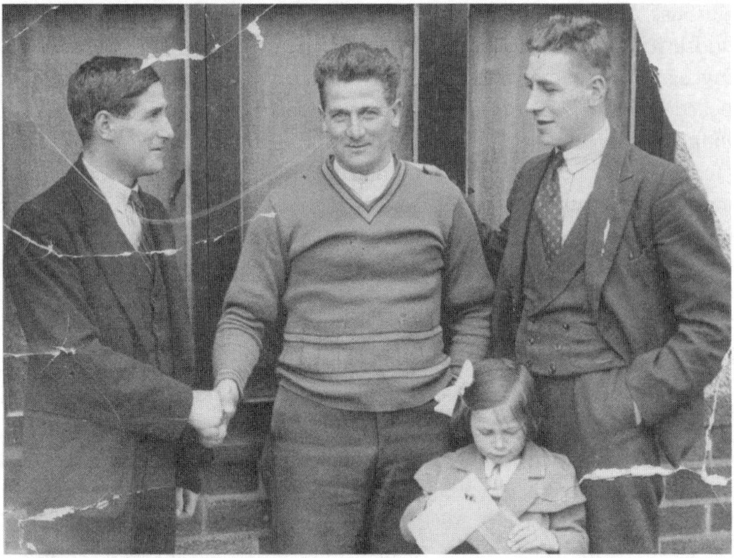

Harold Larwood is welcomed home by two of his brothers, Joe and Fred. His daughter June is more interested in other things.

Larwood never had much interest in money and consequently no shrewd knack of making it either. On the boat he had accepted an unlikely invitation: a week's work at Gamages, the London department store, for 100 guineas. The enterprising owners booked him to demonstrate Bodyline. It cleared space near its 'sporting goods' department and set up a makeshift pitch – a strip of polished wood for a wicket and a set of stumps. Netting was draped around it to protect the public. Twice a day, Larwood took a two-pace run-up and bowled gently on the line of leg stump. Whoever faced him would fend the ball directly into an invisible leg trap. Larwood, who didn't enjoy public speaking, talked through Douglas Jardine's tactics and told shoppers who came to see him what 'the skipper' had wanted. He coached too. Schoolboys in short trousers and long socks, wearing ties and hooped caps, would strap on a pair of pads and learn the basics of cricket from him.

For the time being Larwood was financially comfortable. Nottinghamshire were bank-rolled by Sir Julien Cahn, an eccentric but efficient and philanthropic multi-millionaire who adored the arts and worshipped cricket. Cahn was a dapper-looking man with a high forehead and scraped-back, brilliantined hair – dark enough to suggest he might have dyed it. He had a trim but bushy moustache, hooded eyes and a bulbous nose.

He was a furniture dealer with a chain of more than 200 stores, and made his fortune as one of the first entrepreneurs to introduce hire purchase for his customers: shopping on the 'never, never' proved seductive and affordable. Cahn used the resources of the furniture shops to diversify. With more money than he could ever spend, he bought a 150-year-old estate at Stanford Hall – 35 bedrooms, nine reception rooms, a total of 3,000 acres – and spent £100,000 to turn it into a palace. His wife had a suite with French-made floor-to-ceiling silk panels. He had a sunken marble bath and enough wardrobe space to accommodate 120 suits. He spent another £73,000 on a private theatre with a Wurlitzer organ. Cahn hired the leading British stars of the day to perform on the stage, and took to it himself to satisfy his passion for performing magic tricks.

Apart from his business – which turned Cahn into a workaholic – cricket became his obsession. Between 1926, just as Larwood was breaking into the England team, and 1939, Cahn lavished £30,000 a year on Nottinghamshire and the fabric of Trent Bridge. He maintained his own ground for country-house Sunday matches at Stanford Hall, developed another one less than a ten-minute walk from Trent Bridge, arranged and paid for winter tours (with Fortnum and Mason hampers for the players) and always captained his own team. The visiting tourists would be invited to play his own XI, and Cahn had ten nubile 'ladies' waiting for them. There were only ten because 'the bugger' who got Cahn out wasn't to be included in the pleasures of the bedroom. Cahn wore inflatable pads, which were pumped up by his general factotum-cum-butler. Deliveries flew off the pads like a tennis ball thrown against a brick wall, but no umpire ever dared give a leg bye against Cahn when he was batting. He really was the man who had everything. At one stage his wife, knowing he didn't want or need paintings or cars or clothes, bought him a pair of performing sea lions, which she kept in the swimming pool.

Cahn would quietly 'donate' money to key players such as Larwood so that neither the taxman nor anyone else knew about it. Cahn partly paid to have Larwood's house built on two and a half acres of land, which provided him with the space to create his smallholding. He was always available to 'make a loan' if necessary. Larwood was nevertheless scared that the injury he sustained in Australia might shorten – perhaps even prematurely end – his career. He needed money in the bank to protect him and his family. The only way to make it was to sell his story.

Without an agent to advise him or an accountant to tell him how to manage his finances, Larwood made a series of awful decisions. As soon as he believed the 'silent night' clause in his MCC tour contract had expired, he spoke to the *Sunday Express* for an amount he described dejectedly as 'only' £50. He had also agreed to write a book entitled *Bodyline?* (the question mark deliberately provocative) which would be serialized in the *Sunday Dispatch*. Larwood didn't appreciate the intense competition between the newspapers. In the finest traditions of Fleet Street pugilism – the newspapers were scrapping for the same readers, after all – the *Dispatch* tried to get him to pull the piece in the *Express* to protect its own exclusive. Nottinghamshire made a token attempt to force Larwood to withdraw the column too. Larwood soon realized – far too late – that expressing his thoughts so candidly wouldn't merely reopen Bodyline's wounds. The force of the accusations he levelled against the average Australian cricket fan, his questioning of the Australian Board of Control's competency and specific charges about Bradman's courage – or the lack of it – and Bill Woodfull's technical frailties would create more of them. Larwood made a belated attempt to extricate himself from his deal with the *Sunday Express.* At one stage he even returned the cheque. But after the newspaper published his story anyway, and sent him the payment again, he showed no remorse for being so blunt. 'I was never sorry for that. It's the way I felt and I wanted to say it.'

* * *

'Now I can speak,' he said with a hint of drama in the article, as if the MCC had held him captive, like some cricketing version of the Lady of Shalott, and now he was free. Repressed anger poured out onto the page. Each of his points was thrust in like a dagger.

He talked about the 'temper and venom' of the Australian crowds, which he had suffered 'in silence'. He spoke about the press in Australia who had tried to 'wreck us'. He criticized the Australian Board of Control, which he thought could not 'even control its own crowds, and half of its members could not tell you the weight of a cricket ball'. He rebuked the 'mob' of Australians and their 'cheap wit and abuse'. He defended 'leg theory' and described the controversy shrouding it as 'a lot of hot air' and 'rubbish'. He insulted Bradman and Woodfull. Bradman, he insisted, was 'too frightened' of him; Woodfull was 'too slow'. He called them both 'failures'. To anyone who knew him, Larwood was a softly spoken, painfully reserved and cautious man. To anyone reading the cold text, he was a bellicose loudmouth and an insufferable braggart. These were no pearls of polished thought. From opening paragraph to last, the article reeked of revenge. 'My feelings are too deep to forgive or forget,' he said. 'Never can I forget the treatment I received in Australia, and as long as I have those memories I simply could not and will not play against them. Nothing can move me.'

When the Australian newspapers reprinted lengthy quotations from the *Sunday Express*, including the criticisms of their own conduct in spinning and stirring up bile, the response to Larwood's assault was predictably one of unfettered fury. 'Deplorable' was the mildest of the admonishments from one of the Australian selectors. Another said, far more emotively, that 'the bruised bodies of Woodfull and others provided a sorry answer to Larwood and the team's 'win at any price' tactics. Bradman responded in the only way he possibly could. He claimed not to have been scared of Larwood and added sneeringly: 'Larwood's statements were apparently a financial success . . . Probably when Larwood visits Australia in 1936 the crowd will express its opinion of his remarks.' Vic Richardson was more adroit. In a few crisp sentences he avoided making a direct attack on Larwood, defended the honour of the average Australian and firmly condemned Bodyline. 'If Bodyline bowling is continued, it will kill cricket,' he said in a tone that implied regret rather than either crimson-faced anger or disdain for Larwood. 'No crowd could remain quiet when the bowling was continuously causing injury and anxiety to its players.' He made one more valid comment: 'If Marylebone Cricket Club could have witnessed the bodyline bowling in Australia I am convinced that they would have been entirely in agreement with 99 per cent of the Australian public.'

It had never occurred to Larwood to hold anything back or to sweeten what he had to say. Plain speaking was a virtue in his eyes; that's the way his father, Robert, had raised him; that's the way he'd told his story of the tour to Jimmy Iremonger and to Arthur Carr and Sir Julien Cahn. He'd also spoken about it with what he called his 'brother' professionals. Not to have done so candidly to everyone else would have been dishonest, he said. He was being idealistic. Larwood believed if you did the 'right thing' yourself, then the 'right thing' would be done to you in return. He misunderstood the way in which a newspaper article – especially when someone else has written it for you – can be read by others.

Under pressure from the MCC, worried that Larwood would upset Australia again, the flustered Nottinghamshire President A.W. Shelton flung out a garbled statement. It partly repudiated the views Larwood expressed. Shelton claimed Larwood had written it without 'sufficient thought'. At least that line was true. Larwood hadn't bothered to think through the possible repercussions of his words. He'd merely said what was on his mind, like a patient unburdening himself on the psychiatrist's couch. Shelton added that Larwood regretted what he'd said and had tried to back out of the agreement. Larwood didn't appreciate that his frankness – raw, unambiguous and without clever nuance – would have consequences.

He appalled the Australian Board of Control, convincing it more than ever that only a rule change, pushed swiftly through, could possibly end his bond with Bodyline. His outburst and the subsequent book, in which he expanded on his thoughts about the tour and turned his fire on the usual suspects, severely rattled the MCC, already concerned about whether the following summer's Ashes series would go ahead. If it emerged – as the MCC imagined it might – that the issue of Bodyline persuaded the Australians not to sail, it would be compelled to take a large brush, lift the carpet at Lord's and sweep the dust of the dispute beneath it. If the stubborn Larwood was among the debris, so be it. As it turned out, the MCC used every word Larwood wrote to build its case against him and Bodyline. There was no shortage of evidence. Larwood had constructed the prosecution's argument for them, and it was all the more potent because it grew out of resentment rather than rational calculation.

The contents of his book *Bodyline?*, which was published just six weeks after his return to England, put together the most forceful and implacable defence of his bowling, and insulted Australia and Australians. If Larwood had read it himself before publication, the content might have been amended or toned down. But he was so trusting and callow that he had a habit of telling journalists to write articles on his behalf, 'which I will sign'. Edward (E.H.D.) Sewell, a former Essex batsman as well as a journalist, arranged for the book contract and complained that Larwood had put in no more than 'three hours' work for which he received '£800'. He implied that Larwood hadn't glanced at the proof.

Larwood said the phrase Bodyline was 'evil', 'unfair' and 'detestable'. It had been 'maliciously coined by a cute Australian journalist for the express purpose of misleading and for obscuring the issue . . . If certain critics had not made such an effeminate outcry about it during and after the third Test the whole bother would be too childishly ludicrous to merit further consideration by grown-up men.' Larwood continued to attack. 'If I was asked to put the whole trouble in a nutshell, I would say that the average Australian is a thin-skinned bad loser,' he added. As for the newspapers in Australia, Larwood had nothing but contempt for them: 'There is no doubt whatever that most of those who write about cricket in the Australian Press have no pluck at all. They are content to sneer and jeer . . . from their snug shelter behind the screen of a nom-de-plume, or that valuable title "our special correspondent".'

He was equally scathing about the Australian players who gave radio interviews after each day's play (Bradman was among the regular broadcasters). He contrasted them with previous Test cricketers, who 'did not dash to the microphone . . . to sell their souls and damage the name and fame of the game'.

And so it went on: 'A cricket tour of Australia would be a most delightful period if one was deaf'; the 'howling' and 'disgusting behaviour' of the barracker was tiresome; 'the cricket ground is not a bear garden (for the barracker) . . . if he really wants to howl out loud there are plenty of wide open spaces in Australia'; 'if amateur cricketers had to put up with what Jardine heard, no one would go there'; there were two Australians – one 'inside the cricket grounds' and the other 'outside it'; the barracker had 'secured for Australia a most evil reputation as the home of bad sports . . . ' If Bodyline was outlawed, Larwood said, he would quit cricket. 'It is my resolute determination that if anything is done with the purpose of preventing it or which in practice will have the effect of diminishing my destructiveness as a bowler of Fast Leg Theory, then, to use an American term, I quit. I shall retire from first-class county cricket as soon as my contract permits . . . ' He thought it unlikely because he felt no county would 'show the white feather in such a way'.

His opinions stung Australia, which thought Larwood self-regarding and indulgent. Who was he rudely to question the fibre of their batsmen, the honour of their crowds, the moral right of daring to protest against

Bodyline? One letter he received from an incandescent, ordinary Australian accused him of 'slandering Bradman from beginning to end' and ended with the lines: 'What else can be expected from a village Bonehead like you? The Hangman's name is Larwood.' He never forgot the phrase. The book sold more than 30,000 copies. But 'The Hangman' became enmeshed as a result in something far bigger than himself; something, moreover, that he now couldn't control or manage.

* * *

Returning from Australia, Larwood thought it sufficient to say that he'd been following his captain's strict instructions. He had 'done nothing wrong'. He had bowled at the line of leg stump – or, if the batsman moved, at where leg stump would have been. He had 'done my job'. Larwood expected the unfailing support of his country and his club. 'Mr Jardine backed me,' he'd say, 'so will Lord's and Notts.' He had a clutch of 'well bowled' cables from the MCC to support him. 'I asked Bill (Voce) whether he wanted to keep them,' said Larwood. 'He said he didn't. But I did. They were proof of what the MCC thought about it at the time.' The MCC's annual report also 'warmly congratulated' Jardine and his team, and the 'able and determined' captain in particular.

Larwood made the wrong assumptions about the attitude at Lord's towards both himself and the legitimacy of Bodyline. He made the wrong assumptions, too, about powerful voices that existed against it – and to an extent himself and Voce – from within the tour party. In adversity, the individuals Jardine had taken to Australia ostensibly became more like a tribe than a team. Even those who vehemently disagreed with Jardine's tactics – Gubby Allen and Bob Wyatt – refrained from saying so publicly for the sake of the spirit and harmonious weave of the tour. Allen's selection was an improbable one. As an amateur, his business commitments had restricted him to just five games for Middlesex during the 1932 summer. He'd bowled only 1,472 balls in all matches, taken 25 wickets at 25.36 and finished a lowly 102nd in the first-class averages. It was essentially dear old Plum Warner who picked his friend. After Allen refused to bowl Bodyline, regarding it as an insult to cricket, and verbally scrapped with Jardine because of it, Warner confessed to him: 'Oh, you can't have a row with Douglas. We really picked you because we thought you'd be the one person who'd get on with him.'

Larwood was aware of just two conspicuous rebellions in the camp over Bodyline. The Nawab of Pataudi disobeyed an order to field in the leg trap at Sydney. 'I see His Highness is a conscientious objector,' said Jardine. Larwood heard of Pataudi's refusal because he was on the field. Off it, he didn't fraternize much with amateurs such as Allen and Wyatt, who never discussed the tactic with him. He did, nonetheless, hear Allen politely turn down Jardine's request to adopt a leg-side field and bounce Stan McCabe in the same Test. 'If you want me to do that you'll have to take me off,' said Allen. As a professional, Larwood said nothing. Allen's reply would have made more sense to him if he'd known about the succinct conversation between Jardine and Allen, which took place on the opening morning of that first Test:

Jardine: I was talking to the boys last night.
Allen: What boys?
Jardine: Oh, Larwood and Voce and one or two others. They all say it's because you're worried about your popularity with the crowd that you won't bowl bouncers to a leg-side field . . .
Allen: I've never bowled like that, and I don't think it's the way cricket should be played.
Jardine: Well, you've got to now.
Allen: I'm sorry, but I'm not going to.
Jardine: But you must.
Allen: Douglas, you've got twenty minutes to make up your mind whether you want me to play or not. But I'm telling you that if you leave me out every word you've just said will be made public when I get back to England.

Allen was principled in his opposition, but spiteful about his companions. In letters sent from Australia in 1932–33, the contents of which were not disclosed for half a century, he claimed that Jardine was 'loathed', and had acted like a 'perfect swine'. He called him 'stupid' and 'difficult'. He accused him of whining 'if he doesn't have everything he wants'. 'Some days,' Allen said, 'I feel I should like to kill him . . .' Allen wrote off Larwood and Voce as 'swollen-headed, gutless, uneducated miners'. If either of the 'uneducated miners' had known about it, Allen would have been picking himself up from the floor. No one could ever have described Larwood as 'swollen-headed' – he was modest

Gubby Allen: so opposed to Bodyline on principle that he refused to bowl it.

in the extreme – and he was certainly not 'gutless'.

While blissfully ignorant of Allen's scathing verdict on him, Larwood was soon aware of vociferous anti-Bodyline sentiment in England. Waiting for him were boxes of letters from home and abroad. The hate mail was largely unsigned (or was signed with a pseudonym or sobriquet), but none of it went unread. Larwood methodically went through the letters, slitting them open himself and reading pages of dense, tight handwriting. He replied briefly but with restraint to everyone who included an address. 'If someone bothers to write to you, it's the least you can do to write back,' he'd say, waving aside any idea that he shouldn't waste ink on people who disliked him. 'I was brought up to be mannered,' he said. He absorbed the name-calling with indifference; it wasn't any worse than the barracking in Australia. In the letters he was called 'a dirty swine', a 'damned liar' and 'Jardine's puppet'. He should be 'tarred and feathered', said one, or 'hung and drawn', claimed another. He was a 'disgrace to cricket' and shouldn't 'be allowed to taint it' again. Larwood didn't care. He believed he was in the right. He also thought the MCC, embodied by the patrician 'Mr Warner', would protect him.

But he didn't really know 'Mr Warner' at all.

Warner emerged in *The Cricketer,* which he edited, piously to announce in the 20 May issue that: 'It would be improper, both on public and private grounds to discuss, at the present moment, the controversies, which arose in Australia . . .' In the months, years and decades that followed, Warner would say unequivocally what he thought about Bodyline: that it 'breeds anger, hatred and malice, with consequent reprisals'; that he 'objected to it'; that it was 'wrong ethically and also tactically'; that it was against 'the best interests of cricket' and 'akin to intimidation'; that Larwood had been more 'sinned against than sinning' but had been too loyal to Jardine; that 'it is not unfair to say that Jardine was occasionally "difficult" and did not always recognize who were his best friends'; that he was 'not sure I would trust' Jardine, who 'rose to his present position on my shoulders'; and that the MCC had treated Larwood and Jardine with 'great loyalty and generosity'.

Each article, every letter, and all his statements about Bodyline were designed to exonerate him from what had happened during it. The hypocritical Warner, who had been among the first to wildly celebrate the series win in 1933, unfurling a tattered MCC flag he'd carried on previous Ashes tours and flying it at Brisbane, began to distance himself from the series. In his article for *The Cricketer*, Warner claimed that Jardine was 'one of the best captains England has had for many a long day'; his 'management of the bowling and placing of the field were admirable'. Larwood, he went on, 'may well claim comparison with any fast bowler of any age'. The following month, as accounts about the tour were selling heavily as 'instant history', Warner had the nerve – again demonstrating his penchant for double standards – to criticize Larwood and Jardine for writing books. This, after all, was the ex-cricketer turned editor and journalist who made a decent slice of his living from his pen. None of it would have

The older 'Plum': the 79-year-old Sir Pelham Warner arrives at Lord's for Eton v Harrow, July 1952.

mattered – certainly not to Larwood – if Warner, whom he counted as one of his supporters, hadn't been so determined to bury Bodyline. And he didn't intend to mark its grave with a smart headstone. When Larwood learnt of Warner's opposition to Bodyline, his hurt response was: 'He never said a thing about that on tour.' He would never forgive him for it.

As a devotee of Chaucer, Jardine recognized Warner as the 'Smyler with the Knife'. In Larwood's plainer terms, Warner was simply two-faced. In Australia, Warner didn't question him, or seem to care about whether Larwood had been beastly, ungentlemanly or unsporting. He merely looked pleased to have won the Ashes. In England, Larwood found himself condemned by Warner through association with Jardine. Throughout the summer of 1933 Larwood heard that Warner was covertly triangulating efforts to separate himself from Jardine, ensure Bodyline would perish and – foremost in this cleaning-up operation – purify his own name in the process.

While reassuring Jardine and Larwood of his personal support, Warner took part in an elaborate dance with politicians, the MCC and the Australian Board of Control. His objective was to clear the littered path for the Australians' 1934 tour to England. Nothing else, apart from his own standing as a gentleman, mattered to him. When the MCC investigated the Bodyline tour, Larwood insisted that he wasn't invited to talk formally to them. 'In my case,' he maintained, 'British justice was not applied . . . The star witness was not asked to attend.' The MCC, however, insisted that both Larwood and Bill Voce *were* interviewed. Larwood met Sir Stanley Jackson five days after returning home. Jackson came to Trent Bridge to perform the ceremonial opening of Nottinghamshire's new gates. But the evidence of these meetings – and the MCC's inquiry – vanished in a magician-like act of smoke and mirrors. Nothing, not even a scribbled note, exists of the accounts of the tour that Warner, Jardine, Larwood, Voce or the assistant manager Dick Palairet gave to the MCC. Nor does the report that a seven-man sub-committee put together after investigating the fairness or otherwise of Bodyline. To lose one official report of the Bodyline tour is unfortunate. To lose everything – even the minutes of the meeting held to discuss them – looked to Larwood like a deliberate cover-up rather than carelessness. The main beneficiary was Warner. Larwood felt that the documents didn't drop between a crack in the Lord's floorboards. He knew Warner needed to clean up after himself. The logical explanation is that he 'hid' or tidily disposed of them. Larwood thought that this piece of housekeeping took place during the War when Warner 'ran' Lord's. Posterity was important to Warner, and so his explicit feelings about Bodyline and the participants in it were conveniently concealed. We don't have to think too hard about the line he took. He confessed – albeit privately – to criticizing Bodyline 'in every way'. When Warner gave his evidence at Lord's, journalists peering through the window witnessed him 'bobbing and weaving' as if he were facing Bodyline deliveries himself. If only, thought Larwood later.

Perhaps the man at the railway station had been right. Larwood should have bowled underarm.

* * *

Harold Larwood was always perplexed about one thing: why did Bodyline continue to cause so much controversy? At the Centenary Test in 1977, he sat alongside Bill Bowes and studied Dennis Lillee. Larwood, who particularly admired Lillee, took a mental note of how often the Australian fast bowler peppered England with short-pitched deliveries. He began to count the bouncers Lillee bowled. One ball from Lillee struck Derek Randall, ironically from Nottinghamshire, on the head, making him stagger a few paces sideways and fall to the floor rather like Bert Oldfield had done at Adelaide 44 years earlier. The Australian Rick McCosker was hit in the face by Bob Willis.

A quizzical look crossed Larwood's face, and he began to shake his head. 'You know, Bill,' said Larwood, turning towards Bowes, 'these fellers have bowled more bouncers in this match than I ever bowled in a season.' From his armchair at home, he'd seen Jeff Thomson tame England on the 1974–75 Ashes tour of Australia, the ball often dropping short or whipped in with alarming speed. He'd seen Lillee crack a delivery against John Edrich's ribs. He would switch on his TV during the 1970s and early 1980s and study the battalions of West Indian quick bowlers, who came out of the islands with the regularity that, in the 1920s and 1930s, English fast men like himself had emerged from pit shafts around the East Midlands and Yorkshire. He totted up the number of bouncers, the number of times batsmen were hit in the ribs, struck on the arm or shoulder or had to back away for dear life, the number of occasions when the bat was used purely for protection rather than to score runs or the ball was taken at head height by the wicketkeeper.

He'd seen photographs of Brian Close, his flesh like a painter's palette – the bright mauve and bottle-blue of ugly bruising – after Michael Holding had dug the ball in at Old Trafford in 1976. He'd seen one quick bowler after another throughout his lifetime make batsmen flinch and curse: Jack Gregory, Ted McDonald, Ray Lindwall, Frank Tyson, Keith Miller, Fred Trueman. He knew enough about cricket's past to be able to point to other leg-theory bowlers, such as Derbyshire's Fred Root, Frank Foster, Hampshire's Arthur Jaques and Worcestershire's W.B. Burns. And hadn't Gregory and McDonald in particular reduced England's batting to old scrap when Warwick Armstrong's Australians toured in 1921? Larwood could never understand why his bowling on the Bodyline tour was any different from the intimidation his predecessors and successors regularly meted out. 'Fred Root bowled to exactly the same field as I did in Australia. I was faster. I was more accurate. Perhaps, I had more men on the leg side. But it was roughly the same.'

Why, Larwood would continually ask, had Bodyline been singled out and stigmatized when other fast bowlers had also seriously threatened the bones and limbs of batsmen well before he'd started bowling, and then long after his career had finished? Surely, he'd add, there was a pronounced difference between bowling at leg stump, as he had done, and bowling at someone's head. Ergo, it was grossly unfair to brand him as unsporting and dangerous. He argued that every new, commanding fast-bowling attack was criticized for being too bloodthirsty in the hunt for wickets. He'd witnessed on TV sustained bursts of bowling that had made him physically recoil. Larwood maintained that they had been more likely to cause harm than anything he did during the Bodyline tour. His opponents felt he was being a little disingenuous. He was, after all, bowling short and at high pace – too fast for a batsman merely to whip him to leg. In his eighties, Larwood continued to protest. 'I used to hear the commentators praise the West Indian fast bowlers for bowling waist high – or higher. For me, that was Bodyline – or worse than Bodyline.'

His bafflement over Bodyline was far more pronounced in the 18 months after his return from Australia. It explains why Larwood was so vehement in defending himself; and also why that defence partly proved to be his undoing.

CHAPTER NINE

I'M AFRAID YOU'LL HAVE TO APOLOGIZE

May 1933 – November 1934

After his winter in Australia, Harold Larwood inspects blooms in his market garden.

Nottingham: May 1933 – November 1934

Like the sailor who fell out of love with the sea, Harold Larwood became the cricketer who fell out of love with cricket. And he had every justification for doing so.

Just 13 months after returning from Australia, his Test career was over. By the end of 1938, he had slipped away from the County Championship like a memory lost. When Larwood was talked about, which wasn't often in the bleak years that followed, Bodyline dominated the conversation, as if everything he'd ever achieved had been squeezed into that single series. 'Oh,' he used to say restlessly, 'you don't know how sick I am of the whole business.' Some people forgot his name. He heard himself referred to and written about as 'The Bodyline Bowler', just as Dr Crippen was 'The Wife Murderer'. The public perceived Bodyline as the full stop that ended his cricketing life. Very few could recall that Larwood cut down his run and turned himself into a prolific wicket-taker after it. Or that he had headed the national bowling averages in 1936 as England prepared to tour Australia for the first time since the Bodyline series. Or that his form sent such cold panic through the MCC during the summer that Sir Stanley Jackson responded to questions about whether Larwood would go to Australia with the nervy confession: 'This is a matter of some difficulty. I must be excused from discussing it.'

For more than a decade, from the end of the 1930s until he sailed away from England in 1950, there was little peace of mind for Larwood. Almost everything he stood for or held dear – cricket, generosity of spirit, loyalty and trust – fell to pieces around him. Every aspect of his life was either changed in some way, or completely stripped away, because he refused to bow the knee to what he disdainfully called 'the Establishment' at Lord's. Events rushed by, as if he was viewing them from the window of a very fast train. 'The MCC turned against me,' he concluded flatly. He was disturbed by what he saw happen around him: Douglas Jardine soon manoeuvred out of the England captaincy until he had no option but to resign before being sacked; Arthur Carr eventually dismissed as Nottinghamshire's skipper; Bill Voce forced to feign injury to appease the Australians; and his own abandonment.

'Well,' he'd say, 'the MCC wanted someone to sacrifice, and I was the obvious choice.'

* * *

Even before 'the obvious choice' arrived back from Australia, the scent of betrayal hung in the air, like noxious gas. The first betrayal was over his injury. A fast bowler who couldn't bowl was like a miner who couldn't hold a pick at the coalface; and Larwood couldn't bowl during the summer of 1933. He managed 10 paltry overs in extreme discomfort. His left foot was so swollen that he found it difficult to pull on his boot, let alone walk or run, without pain. After an X-ray, the early diagnosis was that Larwood had fractured the sesamoid bone in his left big toe. The joint itself, and the flesh around it, had thickened. An assumption was made: Larwood had chronic arthritis too. The first doctor who examined him in London concluded bleakly in his letter to the MCC that 'Larwood will not be likely to function as a fast bowler very much longer.' As newspapers constantly badgered him about his fitness, he admitted in June that year: 'The pain (in the foot) is almost continuous. It is something like a toothache . . . I feel it most after a lot of walking.' To another journalist, he added forlornly: 'You ask what I feel. I will tell you the truth. At this moment I could not run a yard, and every morning when I wake the pain in my foot is terrible. I am doubtful about my future.'

But Larwood hadn't fractured the bones in his toe at all. By August, the swelling had gone down. There were no signs of arthritis either. When he finally underwent an exploratory operation, there was 'little or nothing' to explain the problem, said his surgeon. As the diagnosis of sports injuries has developed, we now know that Larwood probably suffered chronic inflammation of the joint or avascular necrosis, a condition in which the blood supply to the sesamoid bones is temporarily cut. Today it would be picked up in an MRI scan. Larwood would have been told to rest and been given a surgical boot to wear. Instead, he suffered both from the medical ignorance of the age and from Nottinghamshire's desire to cash in on him. Well aware that Larwood was the main box-office draw in domestic cricket, the club's committee conveniently ignored its duty of care towards him. Everyone wanted to know what he thought and felt about Bodyline; but everyone wanted to see him bowl Bodyline too. Larwood was pressed to open the bowling in the County Championship, however hopeless the end result might be. As trusting as ever, and with his usual damned sense of duty, Larwood complied without complaint, as if not wanting to believe the prognosis of his injury, which he seemed to think he could shake off like a bad cold. The effort was futile. He bowled in rain-affected matches against Worcestershire and Glamorgan at Trent Bridge in early May. Even at half pace, and on the much softer pitches, Larwood exacerbated his condition. He wouldn't bowl again until the following season.

Rather than rest him, Nottinghamshire decided to play Larwood purely as a batsman. The decision was taken on the basis of his 98 in the final Bodyline Test at Sydney, which would remain the highest score by an England nightwatchman until Alex Tudor scored 99 against New Zealand in 1999. When he originally arrived at Trent Bridge, he 'had no idea at all of handling a bat'. His grip was poor, he found wearing a box and a pair of pads cumbersome, moving with the exaggerated step of a diver underwater, and he didn't know how to stand properly at the crease. His feet were too far apart, his stance ridiculously open. 'I went in last man. If anyone had ever told me that I'd get a century, I'd have laughed at them.' His first 100 came against Gloucestershire in 1928, a sign that Larwood might become a genuine all-rounder – an Ian Botham-like figure in that era. He was already a first-rate close-in fielder. His quick reactions and diving persuaded Carr that his fast bowler was capable of 'catching flies in a farmer's field'.

Nottinghamshire convinced themselves that Larwood could repeat the heroics of Sydney. The odd experiment produced limited results: just two half-centuries in 11 matches. By early July, still in extreme pain, his season ended prematurely.

Larwood had been under the MCC's jurisdiction in Australia. When necessary, Lord's never missed the chance to preach about the sense of obligation it was owed – by players who appeared under its colours and by teams that were bound to the laws and spirit of the game it administrated. Surely it had a sense of responsibility to Larwood? Altruism, alas, wasn't high on the MCC's agenda. Lord's loftily responded to Nottinghamshire's enquiry about compensation. In its reply, the MCC said that 'Larwood' – it didn't have the courtesy to use his Christian name – might find it beneficial to examine the Workmen's Compensation Act Policy, which covered workplace injuries. Statutory compensation was available, the MCC explained, and it 'might be possible' for him to claim it and add the sum to his pay. Although the money was grudgingly given, the insurers couldn't resist pointing out that: 'Of course some doubt exists as to whether the condition of his foot was caused by a gradual process of vigorous wear or by a sudden definite injury which would constitute an "accident".' He waited until October before being admitted to a London clinic. After handing out either slovenly advice or no advice at all to Larwood, the MCC at least paid the bill of £222.

While Larwood nursed his injury and his grievances, the MCC continued to mould a face-saving form of words that would pacify the Australians and enable them to tour in 1934. Like spouses squabbling over marital possessions during a divorce – and displaying such commonly shared emotions as anger, suspicion and mutual remorse – the MCC and the Australian Board of Control moved towards compromise. The telegraph industry continued to be overworked. In cables between them the term Bodyline was replaced with the mealy phrase 'that type of bowling in Australia to which exception was taken'. The correspondence reeked of sham diplomacy, but was purposefully woolly enough to just about hold together the competing egos and agendas of the senders. In September 1933, the Board of Control pointed out that 'the continued practice' of leg theory as demonstrated in Australia 'would not be in the best interests of the game', and asked whether the MCC concurred. The MCC held its nose for three weeks before replying: 'Your team can certainly take the field with the knowledge and with the full assurance that cricket will be played here in the same spirit as in the past and with the single desire to promote the best interests of the game in both countries.' Larwood clung to the diminishing hope that England might recall him unconditionally – a case of self-delusion. 'The thought kept me going through the winter,' he said, 'but I think, deep down, I knew what was going to happen.'

* * *

Bodyline bowling infiltrated the bloodstream of the English summer in 1933. Bill Bowes struck both Lancashire's Frank Watson and Nottinghamshire's Walter Keeton. He was cat-called at Cardiff after repeatedly bouncing Glamorgan's front-line batsmen. In the Varsity Match, Ken Farnes hit one of the Oxford openers on the neck, the number 11 on the jaw and pounded the ribs, chest and arms of most of the others. Arthur Carr was forced into a truce against Leicestershire at Trent Bridge, agreeing to end what he called 'head-high deliveries' when there was a danger of being battered himself. Somewhat sheepishly, Carr insisted: 'I don't call it Bodyline . . . [but]

somebody is going to be killed if this sort of bowling continues.' Even games on the village green weren't immune from the spread of Bodyline. A coroner in Leicester, carrying out an inquest into a batsman who died after being struck in the stomach, asked: 'Was there any Bodyline bowling?' Witnesses said no, and the coroner recorded a verdict of accidental death.

Douglas Jardine had to conquer his own theory in one of its most blatant examples during the second Test against the West Indies at Old Trafford. He made 127, albeit on a far less pacey pitch than anything Australia prepared and against two bowlers who couldn't match Larwood's laser-like accuracy or speed. Jardine faced down Learie Constantine and Manny Martindale and emerged from the scrap with his only Test century. When the ball hit him on the body, he took it like a boxer absorbing a blow, neither backing away nor complaining. He stared back at the bowlers impassively. Constantine claimed that the decision to bowl leg theory came directly from the MCC; Lord's wanted to see it deployed in a Test match and the West Indies complied. Neither Jardine's bravery nor wins against the West Indies at home and in India during the winter were sufficient to save him as captain the following summer. Although he'd lost just one Test match since 1931 (against Australia at Melbourne), the MCC pushed Jardine aside. In a letter written in January 1934 to Sir Alexander Hore-Ruthven, then the Governor of South Australia, Pelham Warner wrote acidly about the forthcoming Ashes series: 'The real trouble is Jardine. Is he to be captain? At present, I say No unless he makes a most generous public gesture of friendliness and then I am not sure that I would trust him.' Warner ended his correspondence by covering his back. 'But, please,' he said, 'keep my own opinion on DRJ to yourself.' Sensing the fate the MCC had in store for him, Jardine voluntarily walked the plank, half relieved to be free of the strain. 'I have neither the intention nor the desire to play cricket against Australia this summer,' he declared in a telegram to the *Evening Standard* in March 1934.

Jardine was 33, already comfortably off, and had a lucrative career in the city waiting for him. He could afford to resign. Larwood was 29, uncertain of whether he would bowl again – and, if so, at what pace – and lived by selling his potatoes and flowers during the winter. Jardine wore his smart business suit. Larwood wore an old jacket, a pair of thick boots and a wide-brimmed hat. Jardine had sent him a Christmas card from India in 1933 – a black-and-white photograph of the Taj Mahal on stiff chocolate-brown paper. Jardine helpfully identified the scene in a scribbled note, as if Larwood might not recognize it. Otherwise, the two men hadn't spoken or written to one another for more than six months. When Larwood found out about Jardine's resignation from the newspapers, he had an inkling what the MCC's next move would be.

* * *

The two decisive conversations in Harold Larwood's career were both about Bodyline. The first was Jardine's careful laying-out of the plan at the Piccadilly Hotel. The second was on Sir Julien Cahn's private ground near Trent Bridge in mid-May 1934. Still unsure about whether his foot would stand up to the number of overs Nottinghamshire and England expected him to bowl, Larwood had gone to watch a friendly match against Cahn's XI. Cahn's chauffeur arrived at the wheel of a chocolate-and-cream Rolls Royce with hampers of food large enough to have fed the Larwood family for a year during Harold's boyhood. At lunch, Cahn sent a message asking whether 'dear Harold' could spare him a moment or two of his precious time. Larwood was escorted into the pavilion and found Cahn sitting alone in a wicker chair with a piece of paper beside him. Smiling and benign, as though the two of them were old friends unexpectedly reacquainted in the bar of a gentleman's club, Cahn said how pleased he was to see him. He was over-friendly, gesturing for Larwood to sit down. Players usually stood in his presence. Cahn lifted a cigar from his top pocket. He offered it to Larwood, who refused. Cahn began to question him about what he'd done during the winter; about the surgical aspects of the operation on his foot; about Nottinghamshire's prospects for the coming summer and, finally, about the Australian tour. Was Donald Bradman still potent? How quick were the Australian bowlers? Was Bill Woodfull a shrewd captain? Realistically, what were England's chances of holding on to the Ashes? It was rather like the conversation nervous fathers used to have with their sons before obscurely relying on the birds and bees to spell out the facts of life.

Larwood waited patiently for the purpose of the meeting to become clear. After the Bodyline tour, Cahn defended him, making clear he would having nothing said against a member of 'his club'. So where was all this talk and oily flattery leading? However much financial aid he gave to Larwood, Cahn didn't seek him out or solicit his opinion. He'd never called him 'Harold' before either. At last, having run out of small talk,

Sir Julien Cahn's XI, c. 1938. Cahn (front row, third from right) cut no corners when it came to providing members of his team with the best of everything.

Cahn came to the point. He drew Larwood closer. There was a pause, as if he was still rehearsing lines he must have spoken to himself that morning. 'Harold,' he said, 'I'm afraid you'll have to apologize to the MCC. There's a letter here, and I want you to read it.' Larwood sensed immediately that the letter Cahn was about to hand him was linked to the Bodyline series. He asked nonetheless what 'sir' expected him to apologize for. 'For your bowling, Harold,' came the predictable reply. Cahn gave him the piece of paper, which had been neatly typed and carried Larwood's name at the bottom in preparation for his signature. 'You want me to sign this?' asked Larwood, knowing the answer but prolonging the conversation while he thought about how to frame his response appropriately and without losing his temper. 'Yes, please,' said Cahn. Larwood thrust his shoulders back, as if on parade. 'I've nothing to apologize for, sir,' said Larwood, folding his arms like a barrier against Cahn. 'You must, Harold,' implored Cahn, 'you must apologize to the MCC for your bowling and you must agree to bowl legitimately in future. If you don't, you will not be picked in the Tests against Australia.' Cahn drove home the message with a marked change in his tone of voice. It was low and bitter. 'Unless I have your word, I am afraid you won't be considered at all,' he said scoldingly, as if the stern approach might make a difference.

Larwood recognized that the MCC was using Cahn the way a ventriloquist uses a dummy. He didn't know that Cahn had acquiesced to the role because he saw himself as a future administrator of the game and wanted a seat at the MCC's high table. Cahn believed that persuading Larwood to apologize for Bodyline would put the MCC in his debt. He expected the favour to be repaid with generous interest. The MCC thought differently. Cahn was no more than a messenger to them – useful but, like Larwood, disposable. The MCC looked disparagingly at Cahn because he was Jewish, and a man of common 'trade', who had made 'new' money; certainly 'not one of us'. Well after Cahn's death in 1944, as demand for membership of the MCC was rising, the President of the club wrote to its Treasurer to caution him: 'If we apply too stringent an economic sanction, we will find the place full of Sir Julien Cahns.'

Larwood was disgusted with the proposal. He'd made himself ill with the effort of bowling in Australia; sometimes vomiting phlegm at the end of a day's play in the sun. He'd been so tired that he could barely chew his food, which felt like cobblestones in his mouth every evening. He'd undergone an operation which might end, or at best truncate, his livelihood as a cricketer. He'd done it for King and Country and the MCC, and had been proud to do so. Now here was a toff, who hadn't been in Australia, who really knew nothing about professional cricket or cricketers, and who was only a significant figure at Nottinghamshire because he paid to be so and the county consequently indulged him like a child with a toy train set. Larwood was angry with Cahn. He was angry with the MCC for recruiting another member of 'the Establishment' (he had no idea of the MCC's low opinion of Cahn) to deputize for it and carry out what he saw as the 'dirty work' that Lord's didn't have the backbone to do itself. He was angry with the Nottinghamshire committee, who must have been aware – but said nothing in advance to him – of what Cahn was now asking him to do.

The truth settled on him like a chill. The MCC was prepared to jettison the one man who had done most to win the Ashes, purely for the sake of defending them harmoniously again. In Larwood's mind, the image he had of 'the MCC' was principally Plum Warner and William Findlay and Sir Stanley Jackson. Beyond them, the picture lost its focus and melted into an anonymous group of faces: florid and crusty, privileged, titled upper-class men with double-barrelled names and silver-tipped canes, who spoke with smooth vowels, as if their words had been polished like glass. The sort of men who drank fine wine and sat in grand, chauffeured cars and rang a gilt handbell to summon a valet. He didn't speak to them. He didn't know their names. These were men who seldom acknowledged he existed until it suited them, and who would flick him aside when it didn't as casually as flicking ash off their finely tailored jackets. Apart from Warner, and now Cahn, he had no one on whom specifically to hang his resentment. There was no one he could specifically accuse, like picking out a thief in an identity parade. For him, the MCC was amorphous – the committee were simply 'posh rich bastards' who were 'out to get me'.

When provoked, Larwood could be an implacably stubborn man. He made up his mind about things – and people – quickly, and hardly ever changed it. If he thought someone was trying to exploit his good nature, or force his hand in any way, he set a stony face against them. He chained himself to his principles and refused to budge. Probably only the King could have persuaded Larwood to sign the letter Cahn gave him. But even the King would have needed to explain why it was necessary and coerce him far more skilfully than Cahn could ever manage. Cahn's crude approach – the false bonhomie followed by the request to read and sign a letter he'd only just seen and had no part in drafting – revealed how little he knew of Larwood or his character. He underestimated Larwood's independent streak, his allegiance to his family and his class. Cahn thought Larwood would be easily led. He was the titled entrepreneur; Larwood was just a professional cricketer. He'd spell out what needed to be done in a calm and kindly way, and Larwood would surely doff his cap respectfully, rather like one of his gardeners after being asked to trim the hedges.

Larwood knew immediately that an apology – however it was couched or packaged for the newspapers – would erode his self-respect and credibility. He'd be demeaned in the eyes of his family, his team-mates and the public. He wouldn't be able to walk down his own street or into Trent Bridge without bowing his head in abject shame. He wouldn't be able to face anyone: his mother and father, Bill Voce and Douglas Jardine, or even his own reflection in the bathroom mirror each morning. And he wouldn't be able to rid himself of the stigma. He'd be remembered as the bowler who was unsporting – and had confessed to being so. 'I couldn't do it,' he said. An apology would catch in his throat, like a fishbone, and stay lodged there. Eventually he would choke on it. To apologize so that Cahn could tell the MCC that his mission had been neatly accomplished was repellent to Larwood. Cahn and the MCC had insulted him, and there was no pride anyway in playing in another Test series when you'd dishonoured yourself to do so. And, after all, he had nothing to apologize for. Larwood wished he could brandish his tour contract in front of Cahn and point to clause two:

> Harold Larwood shall . . . conform to the directions of the said Captain or said Deputy-Captain . . .

His captain and his 'deputy-captain' had ordered him to bowl Bodyline. He *had* conformed. 'I won't sign this,' he said to Cahn, giving him back the letter. 'I am an Englishman. I will never apologize.' Cahn's high brow furrowed into pleats, like a strip of corduroy. He asked, almost out of desperation: 'Would you take it home and show it to your mother and father?' Larwood shot back his reply: 'I will . . . but I know what both of them will say.' The meeting ended awkwardly, a block of silence forming around the two men.

Larwood found his mother Mary sitting in her chair at home. She was reading the newspaper, her glasses high on her nose. He told her about Cahn and the letter. She settled the newspaper in her lap, dropped her head, pushed her glasses down and peered over the silver rims. Larwood was emphatically his mother's son. She was defiant, proud and hard. Barely five feet tall, with grey hair scraped back from her forehead and a square jaw, she stared at her son with flinty eyes as he laid out the details of his conversation with Cahn in chronological order. When he'd finished, she said: 'If you apologize, you'll never see me alive again.' And then she went on reading her newspaper.

* * *

A fortnight later Larwood blatantly lied to cover the fact that he didn't think he'd be chosen for the opening Test match against Australia – coincidentally staged at Trent Bridge – and to hide his genuine fear that 'Bradman might murder me.' He said he wasn't 'one hundred per cent fit', a statement which was revealed as nonsense when he took nine for 84 at Leicestershire, five for 66 against Sussex and then finished with match figures of nine for 113 at Essex in back-to-back fixtures over the next ten days. At county level, he was as lethal as ever. The pitches were appreciably slower than the Australian wickets, and so was Larwood. If Bradman got hold of him, Larwood knew he would flog him 'to all parts', a prospect that filled him with terror. It became another reason to abandon Test cricket. 'I didn't want to be embarrassed in front of my own people,' he said.

Australia won the Trent Bridge Test by 238 runs. The talk afterwards was whether Larwood would be picked for the next one. Still hurt and incandescent with the MCC and Nottinghamshire, and seriously worried what Bradman and his raging thirst for runs might do against his bowling now that the 'bite' had gone from it, Larwood made the speculation superfluous. A wiser course would have been to remain silent. Larwood instead wrote a ghosted article for the *Sunday Dispatch*, which it spread across its front page with a photograph of him staring meanly down the wicket. The multi-deck headlines told the story before the reader reached the copy itself:

LARWOOD: I REFUSE TO PLAY IN ANY MORE TESTS
POLITICIANS TRYING TO HOUND ME OUT OF TEST CRICKET
I WAS FIT FOR THE LAST TEST
THEY FEARED I WOULD BURST THE EMPIRE
SHILLY-SHALLY MCC
AUSTRALIANS SQUEALED . . . BATSMEN WHO CAN'T FACE MY BOWLING

The following year's editorial in *Wisden* complained about his 'dash into print', which it claimed put Larwood 'beyond the Pale of being selected for England'. Of course, it missed the point. Larwood didn't want to be chosen – not on the MCC's terms; and certainly not after his pace had slackened. The article was his raging not so much against the dying of the light, but in response to the extreme pressure he felt. The MCC's casual cruelty towards him made Larwood contemplate retirement. Only his contract with Nottinghamshire, and his obligations to his family, prevented it. Neither the Bodyline tour nor his book and newspaper articles made him financially self-sufficient. He needed his wage packet. Add the fact that his long service would bring him a fairly lucrative benefit season, and Larwood knew it was impossible to turn his back on cricket.

The MCC didn't like being rejected; certainly not by a professional. While the amateur was given latitude to express his dissent, the professional was expected to conform. Larwood grew increasingly certain that, having slapped them with his refusal to apologize, the MCC was biding its time before exacting suitable retribution. It added to the extreme stress he felt.

Larwood found it impossible to relax. He was constantly nervy, pacing rooms and drinking more than usual in the evenings. He had difficulty sleeping. His mind was like a fairground wheel, constantly whirling. Larwood talked incessantly about the difficulties he now found himself in, ploughing and re-ploughing the same furrow with Bill Voce and Arthur Carr without reaching any satisfactory conclusion or strategy – except the rank injustice of it all, which rubbed his fragile nerves rawer still. And then the whole depressing cycle would begin again. Nothing anyone said could soothe him. Nothing he did could soothe him either. If he was on his allotments, he wanted to be at Trent Bridge. If he was at Trent Bridge, he wanted to be on his allotments. The pressure was terrible and never-ending. His every move and utterance was scrutinized. The previous winter he admitted the press 'hounded the life' out of him; now newspapermen 'chased me everywhere'. There was hardly a moment when he wasn't being asked about Bradman and Bodyline and the Australians. Voce often had to 'persuade' journalists not to talk to Larwood by giving them a menacing glare.

Larwood's constant self-examination, which led nowhere, made him prickly and sensitive. He was like a walking argument. Everything was a provocation, and he wore the chips on his shoulders like epaulettes. Even if you said hello to him, said his colleagues, he might bite your head off if you did it in the wrong way. Larwood claimed – only half in jest at the end of 1933 – that even the roosters on his poultry farm used to wake up with the chorus of: 'Body-line'ul do'. He couldn't break free from that tour. Larwood's newspaper article was a simultaneous cry for help and his way of letting out the anger inside him. Larwood said he wanted the public to 'know the truth' and outlined his own conspiracy theories.

In August 1933 he'd read a report in the *Daily Mirror* of the farewell lunch at Claridge's for a team which Cahn was taking on a long overseas tour to Canada and the United States. With typical Cahn extravagance, the room was laid out like a cricket field: imitation grass on the floor, pitch markings and two sets of stumps. The tables were arranged in fielding positions, the waiters dressed as cricketers, and the menu was

Jimmy Thomas, a politician who relished the scent of smoke-filled rooms in which to cut deals.

printed like a scorecard. The food was described as 'body lining'. The chief speaker was the Secretary of State for the Dominions, J.H. (Jimmy) Thomas, a canny, calculating and efficient politician, a Welshman and former trade unionist who had already spent more than 20 years in the House of Commons and previously served as Lord Privy Seal. 'Sparks of controversy were apt to fly from everything he touched,' wrote Thomas's biographer. What he'd touched earlier in the year was Bodyline. His fingerprints were all over the diplomatic bag and baggage of it.

Thomas had an avuncular look about him: a neatly trimmed grey moustache, a pair of round, black-framed spectacles, a pipe and waistcoat. He was the archetypal fixer, a backroom politician who cut deals and greased palms. When Bodyline briefly threatened to trail political as well as sporting consequences behind it, he was the conduit between the British and Australian governments, and always self-deprecating about his efforts.

'Any idea that I am intervening in the dispute is more in the nature of a leg-pull than of leg-bowling,' he said after the MCC's senior members met him at the Dominions Office for what Thomas described as 'a friendly chat' to pick through the wreckage of the Adelaide Test. But at the Claridge's dinner, with the dust still settling from the previous winter, he admitted that: 'No politics ever introduced in the British Empire have caused me so much trouble as body-line bowling' and added, turning to Cahn, who was sitting alongside him on the top table: 'All I can say is, don't take Larwood with you to Canada.' The throwaway remark was meant to match the spirit of the lunch – convivial and light-hearted. Larwood took it literally. The politicians, as well as the MCC, were the dunces in confederacy against him.

After Cahn's failure with the MCC's pre-prepared letter, Larwood saw himself as a helpless spider caught in the centre of a very convoluted web. Carr fuelled his paranoia. Carr relayed a conversation he'd had with Cahn: Thomas, he claimed, wanted Larwood out of the team. Even the historian A.J.P. Taylor was convinced of it, writing in his *English History 1914–1945* that Larwood 'was dropped from future Test teams on the insistence of J.H. Thomas . . . the only occasion on which a cabinet minister has chosen a cricket eleven, even negatively'.

In the *Sunday Dispatch* article, Larwood declared that there was a 'big hush-hush campaign to bury leg theory' and to 'brand me a dangerous and unfair bowler'. He said he'd been 'badly let down by those in authority', some of whom had 'conveniently short memories'. Pulling Thomas directly into the argument, he added: 'The MCC has given way to political or other influences which are determined at all costs to placate Australia.' According to Larwood, 'the conspirators' were 'spreading poison everywhere'. He expressed 'disgust' at what he saw as 'so many of my fellow countrymen turning yellow like certain of the Australians'. He cut loose still further by criticizing Bill Woodfull for the slander against him and the rest of the England side. 'I have not forgotten that two years ago in Australia, Woodfull said: "There are two teams playing and one of them is not playing cricket." He has never taken back that statement, which was a direct thrust at Mr Jardine and myself . . . I have no intention of playing against an Australian captain who regards me as an unfair player.' He would 'not play against the Australians in this or any of the Tests' and he 'doubted whether he would ever play' against Australia again.

However fanciful Larwood's ideas about a 'hush-hush' campaign looked in print – especially after Thomas flatly denied them – he could point to compelling evidence of it during the very weekend that his piece appeared. Nottinghamshire were playing Lancashire at Trent Bridge. The match fell into sour comedy. Before a ball was bowled, Carr drew Larwood and Voce aside. 'There's going to be a protest,' he said, turning to Larwood and referring directly to his bowling. 'It's going to be about you and Bill.'

After hearing what his captain had to say, Larwood initially refused to play. Carr ordered him to get changed and, as ever, he obeyed his captain meekly. The pitch was easy-paced and Larwood, wary of what might be said about leg theory, cut his speed and didn't bowl it. In one spell he took six wickets in 29 balls and conceded a solitary run (his figures ought to have been even better: the slips dropped five catches). Voce used leg theory and struck the flesh, including the thigh and ribs of his and Larwood's friend, George Duckworth. Larwood seethed over the headlines it created. Lancashire *had* protested about his bowling. There were photographs of Duckworth, presented like an accident victim, showing off his bruises. Copies were subsequently posted to the MCC. 'What the hell have you been up to?' Larwood demanded of Duckworth. 'Nothing,' said Duckworth. 'I just protested about your bowling.' It was a blatant and clumsy campaign. Tom Higson, a selector for the 1932–33 tour and the Lancashire chairman, tried to use Duckworth as go-between with Larwood. 'He'd like to see you, Lol,' said Duckworth, carrying the message like a dog carrying a newspaper in its mouth. 'If he wants to see me, let him come and ask me and not send a little shit like you to tell me,' replied Larwood. For the rest of his life, Larwood would maintain that Higson was the 'chief culprit' behind the protest.

A week and a half later, Neville Cardus, who covered the game for the *Manchester Guardian,* took the trouble to send a handwritten letter to the Nottinghamshire President A.W. Shelton on his newspaper's headed notepaper. Cardus told Shelton that he 'saw nothing to take exception to' in Larwood's bowling. 'Every fast bowler I have seen has exploited the short rising ball.' Cardus asked pertinently: 'Must a fast bowler pitch the length the batsman likes?' One of the umpires, 'Tiger' Smith, also said that Larwood had bowled 'at the stumps' and added: 'If I thought the batsman was being intimidated, I'd have had a word with the skipper.' Lancashire refused to play Nottinghamshire the following season. When

George Duckworth, who found himself at the centre of another 'Bodyline-like' dispute in 1934.

Warner wrote his book *Cricket Between Two Wars* in 1942, he used Duckworth's story to paint Larwood, Voce and Bodyline lamp-black. Arriving at Old Trafford for the third Test, Warner claimed that people asked him: 'Have you seen young Duck? You must see him, Mr Warner.' He said that he found Duckworth 'lame', his arm in a sling. He then wrote a scene that would comfortably sit in one of those novels, so popular of the period, in which characters of breeding like Warner are benevolent towards – and ready to mend the rough and misguided ways of – the working class after a straightforward piece of catechism:

Duckworth: Haven't you heard about that match with Notts at Trent Bridge?
Warner: I heard there was a bit of a fuss; tell me about it.
Duckworth: It was tough, I can tell you. They bowled Bodyline at us.
Warner: What, your old friends Larwood and Voce?
Duckworth: Aye, they nearly knocked out Mr Lister and our skipper, and I got a few. The worst was here (he pointed to his neck, which was bandaged).
Warner: But you used to lecture when you returned from Australia, defending Bodyline and saying it was all right.
Duckworth: Maybe. But it's too tough and makes trouble. I am not for it now.

The gap between the end of the Nottinghamshire–Lancashire match and the third Test was 17 days. Warner would already have been well aware of the intimate details and the 'bit of a fuss' of which he feigns almost total ignorance. In portraying Duckworth as a sap, Warner's purpose is transparent. Here was another handy stick with which retrospectively to beat the Bodyline triumvirate and advance his own standing. He didn't mention that the 'lame' Duckworth – not lame and minus his sling – was fit enough to face Hampshire at Old Trafford 72 hours after Larwood and Voce supposedly roughed him up like thugs in a back alley.

Larwood made two predictions in the *Sunday Dispatch,* both of which came true. The first was: 'People in high places, at Lord's and elsewhere, will probably wash their hands of me.' The second was: 'I am burning my boats.' He was; and you could see the flames for miles.

He didn't know that he had one aristocratic friend: Lord Hawke believed Larwood was committed to play against the Australians in the second Test – until he began acting like a weathervane caught in a changing wind and spun in a different direction. He was suspicious. Hawke thought the highly impressionable Larwood had been deliberately stoked up to make his outburst. 'Who got at him to make him so suddenly change his mind – was it Jardine or your captain?' he asked Nottinghamshire. 'The MCC has been blamed for his omission and why, I cannot see . . . There must have been some very important devilment in all this business and it is high time the truth was known.' Hawke saw Carr's Machiavellian brain at work. 'I detest even to suggest that your Captain (and many, many folk think he is responsible) is at the bottom of it all.' Hawke regretted

Larwood's absence, calling him 'a very nice fellow'. Even if Larwood had been aware of Hawke's concern for his well-being – or the tribute he gave him as a 'nice fellow' – it was scarcely career-changing. Larwood had exiled himself.

* * *

As the summer wore on, Larwood's fitness deteriorated. He didn't play in the tour match against the Australians at Trent Bridge, which began the string of unfortunate events and confirmed what he already knew: 'the Establishment' truly was out to 'get us' – Voce and Carr included. Voce took eight wickets for 66 on the opening day against the Australians – minus Bradman – and then bowled two overs late in the evening that Bill Woodfull regarded as 'Bodyline'. Carr, recuperating after a mid-season heart attack, watched from the pavilion. Within an hour he was told of a formal Australian complaint. The team would walk off the field if Voce attempted Bodyline again.

The following morning Carr arrived at Trent Bridge to find Voce still dressed in his suit. 'What's this, Bill,' he said, 'not changed yet?' Voce told him: 'I'm not playing today.' Nottinghamshire concocted the fairytale that Voce had 'sore shins'. When his wife arrived at the gate, she asked how many wickets her husband had taken. 'He isn't playing, he's got sore shins,' the gateman told her. 'Well, it's the first I've heard of it,' she said, giving the game away. The match was slipping around on the black ice of farce. The crowd began to shout for Voce, who said he was 'fit and willing to play'. Voce's shins did ache, but 'not badly enough to leave me out'. He blamed Woodfull entirely: 'When Woodfull came in to bat, his object was – no matter where I bowled – to duck into the ball. I appealed time after time for lbw. I only hit him when he was crouched. But then he threatened to withdraw his team. When the committee called me in, and told me I'd better rest, I knew what was wanted before I spoke to them,' he said.

The Australians were booed returning to their hotel and then again after leaving it the following morning. Carr made his position clear. 'If I was captain in this match, Voce would be in the field and bowling.' That statement was the beginning of the end for him. Outspokenness cost Carr the captaincy of the club. Rather than inform Carr of its decision to his face, the craven Nottinghamshire committee wrote him a letter during the winter, the contents of which had already been leaked to the newspapers in advance. A messy, fractious period followed, in which the committee lost a vote of no confidence at a Special General Meeting and then had it rescinded at the Annual General Meeting. Even though Carr was elected to the committee, Larwood felt as though he had lost another ally. In November 1934, he'd lost the final argument too. The MCC's pacifying resolution declared that 'any form of bowling which is obviously a direct attack by the bowler upon the batsman would be an offence against the spirit of the game'. The umpires would be the arbiters.

Larwood didn't have to think about what 'direct attack' actually meant, or how it would be interpreted to dilute his bowling. Did the MCC really mean bouncers? What would happen if he bowled a ball that cracked a batsman in the ribs or the head or dislodged the bat from his hand? Didn't any of those possibilities constitute a 'direct attack?' In fact, didn't he contravene the rule merely by taking the ball in his hand? He was always directly attacking batsmen. That's what Nottinghamshire and the MCC paid him to do. That's why Lord's appointed Jardine as captain in the first place. And that's why the MCC had been so ecstatic – and uncritical – when Jardine told it he not only had a plan to pummel the Australians but also the instrument in Larwood to carry it out.

But the MCC didn't care any more about Larwood, or what he thought. The disapproval of one fast bowler, who because of his injury might not bowl fast again anyway, didn't matter to them. Larwood was suddenly in a very dark place indeed; certainly darker than any mine he'd ever worked in.

CHAPTER TEN

NO BUGGER CAN DRIVE ME

August 1936

Harold Larwood and Sam Staples prepare for yet another summer with Nottinghamshire.

Trent Bridge: August 1936

Harold Larwood had only one splintering row with Bill Voce, and the friendship nearly perished because of it. As a cricketer, Voce recognized without rancour that he was junior partner to Larwood. 'It is all Larwood, Larwood, Larwood,' he said matter-of-factly. 'Why? Because Larwood is a better bowler than I am.' Voce phlegmatically accepted that he would never be as fast as Larwood. He would never generate the queues that made the turnstiles spin. He would never attract the same devoted following. Larwood returned the compliments Voce routinely paid him. 'You couldn't have a better friend than Bill,' he said. 'He knew what I was thinking before I did. He's what I'd call a man's man – loyal, dependable and trustworthy. And we liked a pint together. He could confide in me, and I could confide in him.'

When a shilling fund, organized by Nottingham's newspapers in 1933, raised almost £800 for the Bodyline pair, two thirds of it was supposed to go to Larwood. He insisted the sum be shared equally with Voce. 'I owed him so much,' he said. 'We spoke the same language, and we liked the same things because we were the same. Exactly the same in most ways.' But one significant difference existed between Larwood and Voce and it manifested itself in the turbulent aftermath of Bodyline.

When Voce was 13 his father died of tuberculosis. He watched him die slowly, the muscles melting on the bone, and heard him coughing from diseased lungs as he lay in his bed. The premature loss dictated his attitude to everything that followed in his life. Voce had no time to mourn. He was immediately sent to work in the pits, where he earned the family's only wage packet. Like Larwood, he tipped out his salary into his mother's hands every week. Like Larwood, he would walk five miles or more to play cricket, and then walk home again before his next shift. And, also like Larwood, he practised his bowling with an unshakeable devotion because it represented his only chance to escape the mines and provide better care for his family. Voce would draw chalk stumps on the nearest wall or stick a pole on rough ground and put a tin can on top of it. If he didn't hit the target, he would practise harder. The light would fade, or Voce would see the men who lived around him heading for the pit, before he would reluctantly drop the ball and change his clothes for work. He did it hoping to earn more money for his family.

The responsibilities he took on after his father's death made Voce

Before the storm: Harold Larwood and Bill Voce play up to the camera in Ceylon on the way to Australia in 1932. The touring party docked in Colombo and played a one-day game against an All Ceylon XI.

mature well beyond his years. Circumstance gave him an unwanted appreciation of the fickleness of life, and what it took to survive whatever the circumstances. That knowledge didn't inure him against misfortune; it did enable him to put a setback or slight into sobering perspective. Nothing – losing form, being injured, coping with the aftershocks of Bodyline – could possibly be as bad as bringing up a family of five brothers and sisters, and financially supporting your own mother, before your voice had broken and you had barely begun your teens. Voce adopted Kipling's sanguine philosophy of treating triumph and disaster just the same. He was stronger in the broken places – far less innocent too, more adaptable and mentally tougher than Larwood.

Voce was clearer, and more self-assured, about his own worth. He was also prepared to say no – even to authority. Voce originally refused the professional terms Nottinghamshire offered him. Larwood had been overawed by the committee room, and the men in it. Three years later, Voce stood in exactly the same place and rejected the salary offered in his first contract as insufficient. 'I can't go home and tell my mother that I've accepted the same amount of money as I'm earning in the pit,' he explained with a conviction that caught the committee helplessly off guard. 'My family depends on me for food.' He said thank you, put his cap firmly on his head and marched out of the room. The committee, still able to hear the tread of his boots retreating across the wooden floor, called him back to strike a compromise. Voce spoke few words. But the resolve of the quiet man was demonstrated that day, and would be again – much to Larwood's displeasure.

The torment of Bodyline wore Larwood down. He was indivisible from the tactic, as if it belonged solely to him. Voce stood on the periphery of the row, four-square beside his friend but without the need constantly to explain his part in it or to defend himself. He still received his share of hate mail in 1933. The worst letter claimed that acid would be flung into his face. But Voce didn't have to cope with the suffocating amount of stress Bodyline created for Larwood. After the tour was over, he wasn't the chief concern of Australia's Board of Control, the MCC or even his own county. When he opened the newspapers each morning, he read derogatory or accusatory headlines about Larwood rather than himself. Every tongue brought in a tale, and nearly every tale condemned Larwood as a villain. Voce's distance from Douglas Jardine – he was never personally as close to his captain as Larwood – shielded him from an identical fate. Voce admired Jardine, and yet principally saw him as another captain to be honoured and obeyed, which was the essential role of the professional. 'I always did,' Voce explained, 'exactly what my captain told me – whoever that captain happened to be.' A word or two of praise from Jardine or Arthur Carr acted like an adrenalin shot for Larwood. He ran in harder, bowled faster. Voce was less susceptible to the blandishments of his captains. He didn't have to be stoked up or micro-managed. He just got on with the heavy lifting. 'Anyone can lead me,' he once said, 'but no bugger can drive me.'

Voce didn't want to be photographed or gossiped about like Larwood unless it was because he'd taken a basketful of wickets. He and Larwood took plenty of them in 1936 – Larwood's benefit season – and it constantly stoked newspaper speculation about whether the two of them would go to Australia again during the coming winter and face down

Donald Bradman and the barrackers who would be waiting for them with memories of Bodyline. Larwood's figures – despite predictable problems with his foot and also a back injury – reveal prolifically consistent performances: five for 56 against Gloucestershire; six for 55 and five for 40 against Middlesex at Lord's; four for 47 and five for 30 against Essex. The wickets came in a torrent: 10 apiece against Lancashire and Kent and 12 – for just 80 – against Surrey.

In 1934, he'd taken only 82 wickets. The following summer he took 102. His testimonial year of 1936, however, galvanized Larwood. He felt in reasonable physical shape. His rhythm was back. His action looked smooth and well-grooved again. Form dictated that Larwood ought to go to Australia. He claimed 119 wickets at just 12.97 and headed the national averages. He was unquestionably the most successful bowler in England, and arguably the best too. But for the MCC, the biggest sin was to shout the loudest. Larwood's lashing out at Australia in 1933 and 1934 – and at anyone who opposed Bodyline – locked him into a position from which he found it impossible to escape. Larwood could neither wash away those words nor abandon his principles. That would have made him appear weak and foolish, and given the Australians the moral high ground from where, Larwood feared, his detractors would tip buckets of bile all over him. He couldn't even modify or clarify his stance; that would have reflected damagingly on himself and Douglas Jardine. No, he wouldn't recant. He had reached a stage at which he didn't trust the MCC as a body or almost any individual on it. There were 'back channel' discussions about him between Lord's and Nottinghamshire in 1934. Lord Hawke made overtures to A.W. Shelton. The selector Peter Perrin and Sir Stanley Jackson approached Larwood discreetly but directly. If only Larwood would apologize and give specific guarantees about Bodyline, the MCC would embrace him again. Larwood thought the damage done to him was irreparable. He regarded himself as spurned and humiliated, and had lost his belief and faith in the MCC. He saw nothing – apart from the MCC's capitulation to him – that could ever restore it.

Even though Larwood wasn't remotely quick enough to revert effectively to Bodyline again, and despite the fact that the change in the laws neutralized the possibility of anyone bowling it in its purest form, the MCC played a safe, perfectly straight bat in 1936. Lord's made sure that the most effective man with the ball in English cricket during that season wouldn't be given another chance to apologize or explain his past.

Although the possibility of Larwood doing either of those things was non-existent – he'd have to face his fierce mother Mary, for a start – the MCC wasn't prepared to take the risk. To include Larwood in the touring party would require not just a soothing explanation to the Board of Control, but also the assurance that Larwood wouldn't try to bully the Australians or resort to any tactic that might cause them alarm. The publicity generated by one or both statements would have scarred the tour before the ship pulled anchor. Larwood waited for another approach from Lord's, a nudge or wink to let him know he was being considered. It never came.

Having already extricated themselves once from the consequences of Larwood's bowling, the MCC didn't want to trade reassuring cables again with the Australian Board of Control over his selection unless it could send them a letter from Larwood containing his apology for 1932–33. The MCC used the excuse that Larwood's injured foot wouldn't withstand the Australian pitches. The excuse didn't conceal the fact that the MCC simply didn't want Larwood. It did, however, want Voce.

* * *

If the roles had been reversed, Bill Voce would have handled the fall-out from Bodyline more phlegmatically, and with appreciably more guile, than the highly-strung Harold Larwood. Larwood's reactions were usually governed by the gut. He made a statement, and then counted to 10 afterwards. Voce was different. He'd learnt that occasionally compromise was preferable to confrontation. He said that you had to be firm to get what you wanted in life, but it was also sensible to circumnavigate problems rather than tearing directly through them all the time. Voce hadn't written a book about Bodyline. He hadn't put his name to a plethora of newspaper articles about it. He'd largely confined his views about Bodyline to snippets of a few paragraphs, which were solidly based around the fact that, as a professional, he always followed his captain's orders. When longer pieces appeared, Voce was also careful to extract the emotion from his language. In 1934, he'd backed Larwood: 'If fit,' he said, 'England can't go onto the field without Larwood.' He warned, however: 'If Larwood plays, I am sure the Australians will object.' He expressed the reasonable opinion that Australia shouldn't be allowed to influence the composition of the England team. His view of Bodyline was succinct.

'Bodyline has been bowled from the day round arm bowling started,' he said. His pragmatic approach served him well. The tour captain for 1936–37 was Gubby Allen, who earlier in the season had read and heard about Larwood taking 11 wickets against his county, Middlesex, at Lord's, and seen him claim another six at Trent Bridge. But it was Voce that the MCC needed to buttress its attack.

A year earlier, Larwood and Voce had made it privately clear to the MCC that the two of them shared 'no desire to play in first-class cricket except for (the) county'. It was a classic example of dig-your-heels-in solidarity, the friends living out the musketeers' philosophy of 'all for one and one for all'. That seemed to be the end of the matter until Sir Stanley Jackson told Allen that England's bowling was so 'weak . . . we must try to strengthen it' through the recall of Voce for Australia. Allen subsequently changed Voce's mind, and did so in a way that created a sense of *déjà vu*. In the opening week of August, Nottinghamshire were at Surrey, where four years earlier Douglas Jardine had invited Arthur Carr and his fast bowlers for the 'Bodyline' meal at the Piccadilly Hotel. Now Allen, feigning injury so that he avoided playing in a match against Sussex, approached Voce at the Oval to persuade him that the door to Australia was ajar; all he had to do was gently push his way through it.

Voce was sceptical. He wouldn't bend at the knee over Bodyline. And he wouldn't condemn Jardine, and especially not Larwood, for introducing it. 'But you'll always obey your captain, won't you?' asked Allen. 'Of course,' replied Voce. The obvious but clever diplomatic deal was eventually struck with a handshake: Voce didn't have to give a guarantee not to bowl leg theory, but he also knew that Allen – implacably opposed to Jardine's tactics – wouldn't ask him to do so anyway. He would merely do whatever his captain demanded of him. A few days later, Voce prepared the way. He announced that he'd be willing to tour 'if picked', which he knew was a foregone conclusion, and wrote to the MCC to confirm it. The MCC was soon broadcasting that Voce had given it 'an entirely satisfactory statement', deeply regretted any trouble from the past and had 'placed himself unreservedly' at their disposal. Voce was coy, refusing to comment until he 'got the official invitation' to tour. Larwood heard of Voce's selection on the radio and within an hour found reporters clustered on his doorstep. Asked about his own possible chances for the tour, he said irritably that he had 'heard nothing' and he would say 'nothing more'. The newspapers reported that he lit a cigarette and smiled. It was a show of bravado. Larwood was furious with Voce, and resentful too.

The morning after Voce had taken the MCC's shilling, the two men, dressed in suits, walked off to a corner of Trent Bridge – ironically close to the place where the Larwood and Voce Tavern now stands. Larwood looked volcanic, as if he might lash out. His mouth was set into a hard line, the eyes had narrowed and the index finger of his right hand was soon pointing towards the bottom of Voce's breast bone. Voce was very calm. Allen, whom Larwood regarded as a prejudiced and snobbish amateur, had divided him from his friend. Larwood demanded to know what Voce was 'playing at' in agreeing to tour when both of them had made a pact. He felt betrayed and cheated, he said. He felt isolated again. As the row boiled on, Voce spoke sensibly in response to Larwood's angry questioning. Larwood had a business to sustain him during the winter, he explained. Voce earned his off-season salary through playing semi-professional football. He needed the money that the Australian tour would bring him. He had just turned 27, he was perfectly fit and might figure in Test matches for at least another decade (if war hadn't rearranged the fixture list, Voce would probably have played well over 50 Tests rather than 27). He outlined more home truths. It was ridiculous to cling intransigently to a point of principle when it damaged you so ruinously, affected your career prospects and your family's well-being. In certain circumstances family had to come before friendship; common sense had to come before blinkered self-interest. 'We had words,' was the only thing Larwood said about his verbal fisticuffs with Voce, refusing to elaborate and deleting the expletives. The language between them was as colourful as a spat on a building site. But Larwood didn't want to give either the Australians or the MCC the satisfaction of knowing that Voce's place in the team – and his friend's swift agreement to accept it – had shaken him so badly. He publicly pretended not to care, when he actually cared very much.

There was a period of silence between Larwood and Voce. Seniority in the Nottinghamshire dressing room was determined by the position of the coat pegs. The pegs nearest the door were given to the players expected to be exiting through it before long. Larwood and Voce sat beside one another. The temperature between them was almost sub-zero. The friends only spoke to one another when it was absolutely necessary, and barely cast a chilly glance in each other's direction. Even the usual pints of beer were drunk without conversation. The other players,

Harold Larwood and Bill Voce walk purposefully together to a net session at Trent Bridge.

embarrassed about the fractured relationship and uncertain about how to tippy-toe around it without favouring or angering either Larwood or Voce, found themselves in an invidious position. Some tried to ignore it. Others tried to draw them together.

The quarrel passed before the season ended. Larwood and Voce liked and respected one another too much for the rift to be permanent. Larwood was able to forgive his friend in a way he could never forgive the MCC. He also, reluctantly, accepted that Voce's principal argument was true: you couldn't hold a grudge for ever. If you did, it would corrode your life to rust. His wife Lois told him not to be so hard-hearted about Voce. 'Don't lose your friends,' she told her husband. 'It isn't worth it.' He knew she was right.

* * *

Hindsight is twenty-twenty vision. Long after he'd pulled off his heavy boots for the final time, Harold Larwood saw clearly that what happened in August 1936 constituted the end of his career as a professional cricketer. In truth, it inflicted a death of the heart on him. As he walked away from Trent Bridge at the end of that summer, he felt more dejected than ever. Anyone with doubts about his ability to bowl and get wickets – and there had been plenty of critics – had at least been forced to shed them. He'd proved himself again, and the irrefutable proof was in the black and white of the averages. Nothing he'd achieved was sufficient to bring the MCC cap-in-hand to him and secure him a place on the tour to Australia – unless he'd been willing to grovel for it. He'd pushed himself to the absolute limit and been rebuffed. What, he asked himself, was the point of doing all that again next season? Where was the sense of inflicting more punishment on his weak body? What more could he achieve? And where was his motivation?

Larwood would watch his friends pack kit and cases, just the way he'd done to go to Australia in 1928 and 1932. He'd read about the ship setting sail without him, and think about the black smoke, like a veil spread across the sky as it fanned out from its funnels. He'd think about the chop of a sea so intensely blue that it hurt your eyes to look at it, and the way in which the sun prickled your skin and regenerated your spirits so much that you soon forgot about the rain in England, the drabness of your own country and all the tiring overs you'd bowled during the previous six months. Most of all, he'd think about the camaraderie on deck: the dances and singing, and Voce conducting the choir the way he'd done in 1932, and the port calls and the rest of the travelling that lay ahead to jewelled, sun-bright cities such as Sydney and Adelaide and Melbourne.

Larwood could have gone to Australia to write about the tour. A contract with the *Sunday Dispatch* waited for his signature and a ghost-writer had already been assigned to him. But Larwood didn't want to be a journalist. He thought about how awkward he might feel as part of the touring party, but not among its intimate inner circle. The players might think he was an inky-fingered snoop, always eavesdropping for stories. An Italian proverb encapsulates his dilemma. 'In life, you meet everyone twice.' Larwood wasn't anxious to meet the Australian press again – at least not so soon – after insulting them in his book *Bodyline?* What could he possibly say to pacify them? He also calculated, probably correctly, that his reception in Australia might be rough anyway because the rawness of the Bodyline series was still so evident. If he went as a writer, rather than as a fast bowler, the MCC would be under no obligation to protect him. Indeed, it wanted a peaceful and gentlemanly tour as balm for Bodyline. It didn't need Larwood intimidating the locals merely by being there with a pen in his pocket.

He'd banked more than £2,000 from his testimonial. At least the Nottingham public still adored him. The cash gave him and his growing family a financial cushion. He also had his smallholding, and he remained – in cricket terms anyway – a celebrity. None of it in his confused eyes offered much consolation. Larwood didn't really care whether or not he played again for Nottinghamshire; and he wasn't convinced that his left foot, his back or his knee joints would withstand another 600-plus overs anyway. The game had curdled on him. He looked tired and drained, like a man who hadn't slept.

At least he had Lois, a wife who loved him. After his abandonment by England, Larwood wouldn't have coped without Lois's support – especially in 1933 and 1934 in the aftermath of Bodyline; and then again during and after 1936 as his life darkened. Lois may have been the silent type, but she was formidably steadfast and strong, and tolerant of the stresses her husband had to endure when his cricketing life collapsed. When he doubted whether he wanted to play cricket for very much longer, or whether his foot would stand up to a county season, she was there to reassure him. When he came home, sometimes in a black mood, he found order and stability and a good meal waiting for him.

In the first two summers after Bodyline Larwood was one of the most famous sportsmen in the country, recognized and pestered wherever he went, gawped at like a rare animal in a cage. There were plenty of newspapers willing to hype his hero worship. The copy almost read like a love letter. When he arrived home from Australia, one of them reported that Larwood had 'clear shining eyes, blue as the Mediterranean Sea'. It noted the 'sheen of health on his suntanned cheeks, and the increased sturdiness of his frame'. He 'looked like a living model of physical strength and fitness'. The tan soon went, and gradually so did the living model of strength and fitness. His features were drawn. In team photographs of 1934 and 1935, he seems to have aged a decade in three summers. The crow's feet are more pronounced around his eyes, his shoulders are slightly slouched, his mouth is turned down at its edges.

When friends saw him, especially during the winter months, he looked distant and alone. People still wanted to ask him about Bodyline and the Australians, about whether he would play for England again; and about the outlawing of leg theory as a direct consequence of his own bowling. Larwood didn't want to discuss any of it. He didn't even want to think about it – though, of course, he couldn't stop. His mind focused on almost nothing else. He didn't want to see anyone. If a journalist approached him in search of a juicy quote, Larwood would turn pale and sweaty and rush off in the opposite direction. If he got caught unexpectedly in a crowd, or in a small room that might become congested, he would turn panicky and back his way out of it. If he went out of the house to do anything but play cricket, he wanted to remain as inconspicuous as possible, pulling down his hat and lifting up the collar of his coat, which merely made him look highly suspicious. There were only two places where he felt comfortable – on a cricket field, where no one could get at him, and at home with Lois.

* * *

In the early autumn of 1936, Larwood was two months away from his 32nd birthday, and yet it seemed to him that the worthwhile part of his career was already over. There was nothing more to achieve, nothing more he could win. He'd only play another 28 County Championship matches and take just a further 76 wickets in two seasons. What remained for England's fastest-ever bowler was the downhill slither to retirement – and a chain of poor decisions that compounded the misery he felt.

The first of a series of mistakes was to take a coaching job in India. He could eat nothing on a three-day train ride across the country, which seemed to him to last 'forever', like purgatory. The stench of cooking food and inadequate sanitation made him retch. The carriages were impossibly crowded, as if the whole of Delhi had jammed itself beside him. The chatter and shouting never stopped. It was like playing in front of the Hill at Sydney again. Larwood gazed dejectedly at the barren, flat land from his carriage window, the heat pressing down on him, and knew his judgement had been flawed. His employer, the Maharaja of Patiala, ignored him. Larwood sat in his tiled palace like a flunkey waiting for an audience that never came. He was so awfully homesick that he eventually absconded, like a prisoner jumping over a jail wall, when he thought no one was looking. He sailed back to England out of pocket and utterly disillusioned. The Maharaja briefly threatened to sue him. 'I wish I'd gone to Australia,' lamented Larwood. 'At least my testimonial money kept us going.' The souvenir he brought back from India was a smuggled tiger skin. He knew how the once-proud tiger must have felt after the hunters captured him.

He felt cursed in the summer of 1937. His form was so patchy that his name almost vanished from the averages; he took just 70 wickets at 24.57. In early June he cut his head and badly bruised his neck as a passenger in a car which, moving across a road in Northamptonshire to avoid a bus on a bend, double-somersaulted and landed in a steep-sided, deep ditch. When Larwood recovered after missing four matches, he immediately contracted fluid on the knee and couldn't bowl. The combination of his abject winter, his loss of form, his motor accident and then his injury pushed Larwood into a pit of despair, from which there seemed no possible means of escape.

Pelham Warner wrote to A.W. Shelton. Might there still be a way to break Larwood's intransigence over Bodyline? As the correspondence came from Warner, perhaps looking to salve his own conscience, Larwood was angrily dismissive. In that same year, Warner was at last given what his whole life was arranged to achieve – a knighthood for his services to cricket. 'Services to himself more like,' said the disgusted Larwood.

A sequence of unfortunate events drove him further away from cricket. He didn't want to see a cricket ball, let alone hold and bowl one. In late August 1937, he ran away for the second time in nine months. Instead of reporting to Trent Bridge for practice, Larwood took Lois for a short holiday by the sea. Their destination was convenient rather than exotic. Larwood chose a cheap, brightly painted boarding house in Skegness, where he and Lois shared the seafront with workers on annual leave from the mines and the factories, who flopped into deckchairs, rode on donkeys, ate fish and chips out of newspaper and got gloriously drunk in the pubs. His mind lost its linear train of thought. Confusing and competing issues sparked away: the need for a holiday, the reluctance to return from it, the question about what to do next and whether cricket should be part of it. Larwood was past caring. He gave no thought to what Nottinghamshire would think about his unauthorized absence, or what action the committee might take in response to such insouciance. He arrived home, shaking the sand out of his shoes, to find himself summoned to a committee meeting, like an errant schoolboy caught playing truant. Nottinghamshire suspended him for the final two matches of the season. Larwood offered a lame defence. 'I've never been asked to go to practice before,' he said. 'I keep myself very fit. I could have played again.'

Larwood was still fighting this private war when he wrote to Shelton shortly before signing a fresh contract in November. He hesitated before committing himself to Notts for £124, a sum for the summer unchanged since 1925. He felt guilty about making a paper promise that he might not fulfil. And he didn't want the members at Trent Bridge to think he was taking money and giving little in return. He was also still sore with the committee. 'I have not got over the shock of my suspension . . . why didn't they caution me or let someone off the committee warn me?' he asked Shelton. The wailing continued: 'I have not been cared for since the trouble in Aussie, so I have come to the conclusion Notts don't want me, only they are finding trouble as to how to get rid of me.' He said that he knew 'where the pressure came from' to discipline him: the Nottinghamshire captain George Heane. After the liberal, beery management of Carr, he found it difficult to adjust to Heane's strait-laced captaincy. He was a sombre man who took things too seriously for Larwood's liking and lacked Carr's inspirational *joie de vivre*. What's more, Heane didn't drink. 'You couldn't have much fun with him,' said Larwood. 'You had to make your own entertainment.'

In his old age, Larwood admitted he'd been 'a naughty boy' over his Skegness escapade. He accepted the fact that the committee did him a favour by rebuking him. He was in no fit state to bowl – either mentally or physically. With its rebuke, the committee gave Larwood time in which to recuperate as best a tormented figure could under the circumstances. Lois now sensibly counselled her husband to take his punishment in silence and think about his long-term future. Her husband did both.

PART THREE

CHAPTER ELEVEN

A LONELY AND DESOLATE CHAP

June 1948

Behind the counter of his sweet shop in Blackpool, Harold Larwood wanted to be known as a shopkeeper rather than a businessman.

June 1948

No passer-by ever pointed him out, or even bothered to cast a second glance towards the middle-aged man in his dark suit and black round-framed glasses. He was just another anonymous figure on the beach.

He was still neat and trim, and his face remained remarkably lean and uncreased. But his hair was much shorter now, shaved severely on the sides and taken off across the crown. His eyes were slightly sunken, more from tiredness than age. He'd ease off his jacket and fold it neatly on the sand, as if laying down a bowler's mark. Sometimes he'd roll up his sleeves and then fake a monster's stare, as if he was about to deliver one of those snorting, short-pitched deliveries that used to terrify batsmen. And then he'd lob a white tennis ball benevolently towards his young daughters, who took turns to swipe at it with a makeshift bat cut from boxwood. The full tosses and long hops were dispatched towards the Irish Sea.

To anyone who didn't know him, Harold Larwood was like any other holidaymaker enjoying himself in the sun. He didn't look as if he'd once been the fastest bowler on God's earth.

Instead of Adelaide's Giffen Stand or Sydney's Hill, Larwood played his cricket in front of Blackpool Tower and its rows of penny-slot amusement arcades that ran in a ribbon of neon lights along the seafront. The air was heavy with the wafting scent of salt and fish. White-coated men sold whelks from stalls that resembled the booths of Punch and Judy shows. The skeletal frame of the Tower dominated the front, drawing tourists towards it like a beckoning finger. Blackpool was always full of people passing through for a week or a fortnight. Larwood knew this type of visitor well: the average working man and his wife surviving on a peppercorn salary, who travelled by coach or train and carried suitcases used only once a year. The couples lodged in regimentally run boarding houses that pushed them out on to the streets every morning, irrespective of the weather, and had a set meal waiting for them at a specific time in the evening. After the factory hooter or the pit cage, the seaside with its variety shows and fortune-tellers felt faintly exotic, a kind of garish Shangri-la. Larwood felt lucky to live in Blackpool, and grateful that most of the people in it were sightseers. It was easier to get lost in a place where no one could get to know you for long.

In summer, Larwood would snatch an hour's break from The Victory

Sweet Shop, a confectionery-cum-tobacconist's corner shop he'd bought for almost £5,000 in 1946 to replace his smallholding and market garden in Nottinghamshire. The shop was a 10-minute walk from the sea. He could see the neck and head of the Tower from his backyard. Its high-ceilinged shelves were choked with glass jars of sweets in shiny wrappers. He sold Capstan and Woodbines cigarettes, tins of Gold Flake tobacco, soft drinks and greetings cards. Sometimes Larwood served behind the wooden counter in his shirt and tie. Mostly, he preferred to organize the stock. He'd had enough of being centre stage – even on a modest shop floor. He didn't want customers staring at him like a seafront attraction. But customers stared anyway. Men who'd seen him play came in with a child in tow and bought a bag of sweets for the sake of it. Too shy to ask him about cricket, they'd exchange a few words about the weather or the briskness of trade. Outside on the pavement, they'd turn to their child and ask: 'Do you know who that was?' Or say instead: 'That man in the shop . . . he used to be Harold Larwood.'

He still *was* Harold Larwood; but he was different now. The shop, and the six-room apartment above it, was his refuge from a world that had worn him down and which he'd been uncomfortable living in since his retirement from cricket. His decision to uproot his family and take them to Blackpool cut the umbilical cord to his home town, where he'd grown up, become famous, married and begun to raise his daughters. He had reached the point where he hoped to vanish effortlessly into a crowd rather than attract one. He needed to escape somewhere, start again. Everyone knew him by sight or reputation in Nottinghamshire, and it was impossible to go anywhere without being bothered by, or constantly reminded of, his past. Well-wishers, who wanted nothing more than to meet him, began testing his patience and politeness. Often if an outstretched hand came towards him, he would hurry away from it.

Larwood had tried to preserve his privacy by seeing almost no one, refusing to stray far from his house and the allotments. After the Bodyline tour, the Duchess of Portland had visited to ask about his foot injury. As nobility, part of a land-owning dynasty as highly respected locally as the royal family, Larwood was always solicitous towards her; she also sent her staff to him to buy vegetables. Her husband, the Duke, became President of Nottinghamshire. On this occasion, Larwood said: 'At her request I pulled off my boot and sock and showed her where the damage was.' But at the start of war, when she came to his smallholding to purchase a dog

Harold Larwood briefly found contentment on his small holdings, which became a refuge from the prying eyes of the newspapers.

from a recently born litter, he retreated on to the roof of one of his red-brick outbuildings and stayed there pretending to repair tiles until her chauffeured car had vanished from the drive. He'd experienced far more than 15 minutes of fame, and the price he'd paid had been too high: the rows and rifts, the journalists knocking on his door or approaching him in his garden for quotes, the speculation about his fitness. He wanted to pick up a newspaper and not find his name in a headline. But even failure was newsworthy and guaranteed him column inches.

Odd though it seems, the war brought with it a particular calm for Larwood. No one spoke very much about cricket. With two and a half acres of fertile soil to farm – plus five greenhouses, two double brick outhouses and four large wooden sheds – he had the benefit of a reserved occupation, which was just as well: his knee and foot injuries made him unfit for active service. He answered the call on the posters to 'Dig for Victory' and 'Grow More Food'. The sole of his right foot was always on the shoulder of a spade. He worked 'every daylight hour'; but at least that work kept Larwood busy, leaving him no time to dwell on the end of his cricketing career. It was exhausting to earn his living this way. The allotment wasn't always profitable, and Larwood couldn't see a way of making it so after war ended. He'd also had enough of the land in which he'd grown up. The wallpaper of his life hadn't changed since the day he was born and, like wallpaper, the pattern of it repeated. It was time to move on.

Like everyone else who had experienced war, Larwood didn't want things to stay the same after it was over. He wanted something different as a reward for six years of sacrifice. In Blackpool he thought he could convert himself from well-known cricketer into unknown shopkeeper, just plain Harold Larwood. He didn't want a shop on the main parade: that would have invited the attention he'd gone to Blackpool to avoid. For the same reason, he didn't change the shop sign to incorporate his name. Larwood had it painted instead in a small gold font above the lintel of the door, where it might go unnoticed.

Of course, it was impossible for Larwood to slip into the resort without publicity. The newspapers came out of curiosity to interview him. Photographers snapped him among the sweet jars – barley sugar twirls, treacle mint drops and blackcurrant chews – and then levering the stubborn top off a bottle of fizzy drink. He went through the motions for them, talking amiably and uncontroversially about Bodyline. He had learnt precisely what, and exactly how much, to say without stirring up any old unpleasantness that could be picked up and used against him in Australia. Larwood expected the interest in him to be shortlived. There'd be enough coverage to get the shop talked about and persuade a few customers through the door, not enough to trample all over his privacy again. He'd be able to stroll around the streets without people nudging one another or stopping to chat about cricket, which no longer interested him.

With an endearing slip of the tongue, he recalled in a chat with Bill Bowes in 1980 that his three and a half years in Blackpool were his period of 'solitary refinement'. He fell gratefully into domesticity, not watching or talking about cricket and hardly bothering to read the County Championship or Test scores in the morning newspapers. Larwood saw few people he'd either played with or against, and he had neither the desire nor the inclination to seek them out. 'I'm a football fan now,' he'd say, taking himself off on winter Saturday afternoons to watch Stanley

Matthews at Bloomfield Road. 'If it wasn't for the football,' Lois said, 'I don't think he would have left the shop.'

* * *

The closing acts of Larwood's County Championship career in 1938 were pitiful to watch. As it became physically impossible for him to bowl, because of the condition of his left foot and the recurrence of a cartilage injury in his left knee, Larwood lost the will to push for a place in the team. The specialist advice that he received sounds ridiculous now. He might, said a doctor, pull an elastic bandage over his knee joint to support it. A doleful Larwood thought it pointless. 'I was on the way down,' he said.

George Heane, Carr's successor as Nottinghamshire captain. Heane disliked the 'social aspects' of cricket, according to Larwood.

His final years with the county were also blighted by friction with the committee, which he resented. The Nottinghamshire secretary rebuked him for excessive drinking after an anonymous complaint from one of his own team-mates. Larwood called it 'a few quiet beers in an out-of-the-way pub after finishing a match'. He and Bill Voce were summoned into the committee room. 'We have received a complaint,' Larwood was told. Larwood asked about the identity of the complainant, whom he assumed was a 'non-drinker'. The secretary wouldn't tell him. 'Being professionals,' said Larwood, 'neither of us could say anything.' The fact that Larwood liked a drink was hardly classified information. 'It was ridiculous,' he said. 'Here I was, a grown man of more than 30, who had put up with so much flak from Bodyline, being lectured like a schoolboy.' Larwood never found out who ratted on him and Voce. He visited retribution on each of the chief suspects. He dug the ball into them while bowling in the nets. One batsman was hit directly in the box, another on the shoulder, a third in the chest. Net practice was truncated that day. 'I let a few fly at those I thought might be responsible for my dressing-down,' he admitted. Again, he mainly blamed George Heane – 'the non-drinker'.

He played in only nine matches that summer and didn't bowl in the last three. He took four County Championship wickets at 84.75. His final appearance – like his first 14 years earlier – came against Northamptonshire at Trent Bridge. He bowed out with a six over mid-wicket, his last scoring shot. At 33 years old, Larwood walked off the ground in late June. He'd go back there only four times in the next 39 years.

There had already been reports that Larwood was heading into League cricket, where he would earn as much as £700 per season, plus expenses – far more than Nottinghamshire were paying him. The move, which seemed sensible and obvious, had been pre-planned. Although his knee might collapse under the rigours of the three-day game, it could withstand one prolonged bowling spell each week. In October 1938, Larwood asked Nottinghamshire to release him from the remaining two years of his contract, and claimed to be facing an 'uncertain future'. A fortnight later, he signed for Blackpool. Nottinghamshire's committee shed tears for the benefit of public relations, but were relieved to let Larwood drift away. He had turned unpredictably spiky in his dealings with them, and he couldn't be relied upon to bowl any more. Larwood was relieved to be free of them too. The grudge he nursed over his treatment after Bodyline, plus the firing-squad dismissal of Arthur Carr and the ingratitude the committee demonstrated for his efforts, made it impossible to establish a working relationship with them. The ticking-off over his drinking proved it.

The offer from Blackpool was astutely timed. It coincided with Larwood's final, if reluctant, acceptance of his parlous position – he had to leave Nottinghamshire, however disruptive the upheaval – and the committee's realization that he was no longer useful to them. After the things Larwood had achieved for them with his pace, and the crowds he had drawn around the boundary ropes to witness it, this was an abrupt and inadequate way to part. But as neither Larwood nor the committee had much to say to one another apart from goodbye, it was far better to say it quickly. 'Things were not happy there,' he said, 'and they were not keen to keep me.'

He worked on his smallholding from Monday to Friday, and

travelled to Lancashire on Saturday. There was no direct train from Nottingham. His brother Joe drove him to and from Derby station. He was coy about his salary. 'They're treating me generously,' he said. Blackpool were a baleful outfit, lacking talent. The smart tree-lined ground, with its neat pavilion and stacks of wooden bench seats, didn't draw much of a crowd. The membership struggled to rise above 700. The club wanted Larwood as much for his name as his bowling. He would give them some stardust. It hadn't hired a professional after the death of its Australian pace bowler Ted McDonald, who was killed in a motorcycle accident in 1937. In an awful piece of symmetry McDonald died on the same day that Larwood was found upside-down in a ditch after his own car crash in Northamptonshire.

Blackpool finished near the bottom of the Ribblesdale League in 1938. Even at half- or three-quarter pace, Larwood would make a difference to them. He'd also act informally as a coach to coax along the more promising players. Larwood liked Blackpool, and Blackpool liked him. He and the town fitted together because there was something companionably earthy about both of them. As he'd honeymooned there, the locals instantly took to him and Larwood found he could talk to them. The crowds who came to watch him play were amiable and honest workers, like his father and brothers, who cared about him and cricket, and spoke the same unpretentious language. There was no discernible class distinction between Larwood and the Blackpool committee, who were grateful to have him in the team and treated him like a favourite son. The introverted Larwood had never been skilled at convivial chat with people he didn't know. He learnt it wasn't necessary at Blackpool. He was welcomed and accepted on his own terms.

Larwood began to relish his cricket again. He felt young, the grounds and opposition were new, and each delivery obediently did his bidding. Whatever he attempted came off. He barely had to break sweat to claim 68 wickets at 10.57 – 41 of them bowled. He was too canny for League batsmen. He possessed tricks most of them hadn't seen before. The batsmen were incapable of dealing not only with the extra yard of pace he could muster at will, and the clever ball that seamed extravagantly and came back to take the off stump, but also with Larwood's wily ways, as if there was a unique geometry to his bowling. In the Ribblesdale League, Larwood was like a hawk in a cornfield, contentedly swooping down and devouring pliant batsmen. He spent his summer weekends with a smile on his face. At the end of the 1939 season, he optimistically left his kit in the pavilion for another summer that never came. 'See you next year,' he said, aware, like everyone else, that some of them would never meet again: the shells and bullets and bombs of war would make certain of that. In 1946, when he had neither the spirit nor stamina to play again – 'I'm tired of the game,' he said – Larwood sent one of his daughters to the ground to retrieve his whites, his pads and his bat. When she got there, she found that someone else was already wearing them. The unfortunate player had to be dragged off the field to take off and return Larwood's things.

* * *

As he'd played there before the war, Blackpool seemed to Larwood to be his obvious destination after it. 'It has always been my desire to reside in Blackpool,' he confessed in 1945. But he wasn't a businessman. If he had been, he wouldn't have bought a sweet shop.

Along with almost everything else, sweets were rationed in an exhausted country so bleak that Larwood remembered it as being uniformly monochrome. He hoped the Government would succumb to public pressure and take sweets off ration quickly. There wasn't much else to lift the spirits during cold snowy winters, and amid the rubble of bombed-out towns and cities. Customers could buy only three ounces per week, which were mostly bought on Sunday night on the way to the cinema. Larwood couldn't make a wage from his shop; in fact, he could barely make a wage at all. 'We worked seven days a week every week,' he admitted, 'and it didn't really give us a living, or at least not much of one. We always had to be careful. The shop became a bit of a burden.' He took in coppers, but spent silver to keep the business ticking over and his family in food and clothes. The accounts read like a misery memoir.

The work became dull and back-breaking – worse, he concluded, than sowing and selling vegetables had been. The responsibilities of tending a shop were painstaking, and he felt trapped there. Nothing, it seemed, worked satisfactorily for him, and every path led him into a cul-de-sac of despair. He'd abandoned cricket for a life on the land, and abandoned life on the land for a shop counter. On each occasion he was convinced he'd done the right thing, that prosperity was waiting with outstretched arms around the next corner. With the failure of the shop he gloomily realized that he could change the landscape of his life as much as he liked without necessarily changing the life itself. He didn't know what to do or where to go next. As he'd deliberately turned himself into a 'recluse' in Blackpool, locking the door on his cricketing past, he felt embarrassed about contacting his old friends. Where would he start? What would he say? How would others respond to him? As usual, Larwood saw dragons where none existed and underestimated the warmth and respect that he generated among the old cricket pros. He was unable to accept that people liked him enormously.

Pride was the first obstacle. Irrational thinking was the second. Larwood always thought he'd be 'a bother' or 'there'd be too much fuss' or someone would think badly of him for contacting them. This combination of reticence and fear isolated him unnecessarily. Even when he did go to cricket matches, he refused to ask for favours. It was as if Larwood believed he owed a debt to the game rather than the other way around. 'How did you get in?' asked the incredulous secretary of Lancashire after Larwood went alone on a rare visit to Old Trafford to watch Lancashire against an Australian Infantry Forces team. 'I paid,' he said, having passed unrecognized through the turnstiles and queued to buy his scorecard like everyone else. Wally Hammond caught sight of Larwood looking up towards the players' balcony and waved him towards the dressing room. He shook his head. George Duckworth almost had to drag him into it. 'If you come back,' the Lancashire secretary insisted, 'you don't pay.' Larwood never went to the ground again.

* * *

Larwood was still counting sweet coupons and pennies in the summer of 1948. Donald Bradman was on his long, valedictory tour of England, and acclaimed everywhere like a king for whom every waking hour was a coronation. He occupied the crease regally, dispatched the ball with a flick of his wrists beyond the ropes at Lord's and Headingley and the Oval. 'The Invincibles' were a team imperious and knowingly self-assured. Australia swept through the Tests like a scythe, convincingly winning four of them, drawing the other and making England – without much of a pace attack to counter Bradman or the rest of the batting – a bedraggled, well-beaten team. For the first half of that mostly wet grey season, Larwood was purposely distant from the tour. He read about the Australians in the newspapers and occasionally caught the reports or commentary on the radio: 721 runs totted up in an unforgettable day against Essex, and 187 of those runs to Bradman in just two hours and thirty-five minutes; an innings and 158-run win over the MCC in which Bradman scored 98. Bradman finished the Test series with 508 runs – his top score an unbeaten 173 at Headingley – at an average of 72.57. If Eric Hollies hadn't implausibly bowled him second ball with a perfect-length googly at the Oval, grazing the inside of the bat and clipping the off bail, Bradman would have taken home on the boat a Test average of more than 100. ('But,' as Larwood pointed out, 'if we hadn't bowled leg theory at him in '32–'33, he'd probably have finished with an average of 150.')

Harold Larwood had not met or spoken to an Australian since 1934. Having gone to pick up his new bat from the Gunn and Moore factory at Nottingham, he found Bert Oldfield collecting a spare pair of wicket-keeping gloves and some other items of kit. Neither man had expected to see the other:

> 'Hello, Harold,' said Oldfield, the surprise apparent in his voice.
> 'Hello, Bertie,' came the reply.
> 'I am happy to see you again,' said Oldfield reassuringly.
> 'How are the boys?' asked Larwood.

Oldfield reassured him about the Australians' health and well-being. Larwood, clutching his bat, shook him by the hand and headed off to Trent Bridge. Although Oldfield bore no malice towards him, Larwood didn't want to prolong the conversation in case it drifted into the difficult terrain of Bodyline.

Even in his last summer in the County Championship, he'd taken drastic steps to avoid Australia in case the series was mentioned. He'd written to the Nottinghamshire committee and asked not to be picked for the tour match. The committee reluctantly agreed, no doubt fretting over the loss of gate receipts, but stressed to Larwood in a tightly worded reply that: 'It would redound to your credit if you did play.' Larwood ignored the chiding remark. He didn't want to be hammered around the ground at half pace, and he didn't want to gaze into the eyes of any Australian who'd been connected with Bodyline. It would have been too traumatic for him. If he'd played, buckling under pressure from the committee, the newspapers would have made the dry bones of history dance again. He'd have been forced to relive every ball, and go through the tiresome process of defending it and himself once more. Far better to let it lie undisturbed, he said to Bill Voce.

In 1948, the Australians wouldn't be visiting Blackpool, and Larwood wouldn't be calling on them at Old Trafford, Headingley or Trent Bridge. He was so far removed from cricket, especially Test matches, that he blithely expected the months to drift by uneventfully. And then one bright morning in July, after the Australians had drawn the third Test at Manchester, the door of his shop clanged open, two men in grey suits and trilby hats sauntered to the counter and asked for Larwood by name. Within a few hours, the course of his entire life changed after one conversation and a few pints of beer in the pub across the road.

* * *

Harold Larwood remembered Jack Fingleton as one of the bravest and most gutsy of the Bodyline batsmen. Fingleton took the ball on his ribs and arm without flinching or grumbling 'like an old maid' about it afterwards. He stood up to Larwood, gave him a cold hard stare and tried to tough out the torture. 'He was brave,' Larwood acknowledged. 'He took it and tried to give it back to you. I admired him for it. I gave him a few bruises but he didn't hold any grudges.' Fingleton never forgot Larwood. 'I had this interesting experience from batting against him,' he wrote. 'The first dorsal interasseous muscle, between the thumb and the index finger, ached for a week . . . so severe was the concussion of the ball hitting the bat.' All his life he relived one delivery Larwood sent down to him at Adelaide, which pitched leg stump and 'knocked my off stump flying'. He called it 'the best ever bowled to me'. Fingleton recalled his own audacity – or was it stupidity? – at Melbourne. After a Larwood bouncer he strolled down the pitch to ostentatiously pat the spot where the ball had landed. Larwood took it as an act of cocky defiance for which there was one penalty: Fingleton got more bouncers for his cheek.

After his cricket career ended, Fingleton turned himself into a journalist who expressed his views cogently, like jabbing a finger into your chest. He demanded to be read for his tactical insights and anecdotes, and the wisdom of being able to compare and contrast the cricketing generations. He contended that 'Larwood was so fast and so skilful in the 1932–33 season that his figures would still have set a standard in history' – even if he had bowled to an orthodox field. He questioned whether retaliation would have 'been the best and quickest way out of the mess' of Bodyline and declared it to be a 'moot point'. He didn't subscribe to the theory that the Australians were too ponderous on their feet to fight Larwood. 'One would have needed feet of quicksilver to get out of trouble,' he said, and added that Bodyline forcibly 'prostituted the art of batting'. Fingleton said that the job of ensuring your own physical safety came well ahead of shot selection, which came an ungracious second on a batsman's list of priorities. He also maintained that 'Trumper, Hobbs, Macartney and the other luminaries' wouldn't have countered Larwood any more successfully than Bradman or Stan McCabe, who were 'brilliant when fortune favoured them; dishevelled and negative when it didn't'.

Despite the bruising he took, and the fact that he was dropped after Larwood removed him in the second innings at Adelaide to seal a pair, Fingleton felt privileged to have faced a bowler at his fastest. Nor was he resentful about his physical assault. He held nothing against Larwood. Indeed, he was more interested in the mechanics of his action, the pounding his body took to muster such pace and how he withstood it. He was interested in Larwood as a person too; especially when his friend George Duckworth, also working as a journalist, told him about the way in which Larwood had cast himself adrift from cricket and was now serving sweets in his struggling shop. 'It's a neat little mixed shop,' said Duckworth. The human interest of Larwood's story fascinated Fingleton. Even more so when Duckworth told him: 'He is a lonely, desolate chap and would love to see you.'

Fingleton had published his classic inside account of the Bodyline series, *Cricket Crisis*, two years earlier. He said in it that the tactic was 'nothing more or less than a revolution against Bradman'. He began with a confession, as if he was digging up and robbing graves by putting his thoughts between hard covers. 'It has not been easy to write this book,' he wrote. 'It is easy to imagine many cricket devotees will express the opinion that it would have been better for the game had it not been written.' He was covering the 1948 tour, and would produce another book from it: *Brightly Fades the Don.* As soon as he found out about Larwood's predicament, Fingleton didn't hesitate. He set off for the seaside with Duckworth as his guide. Larwood didn't own a telephone and there wasn't time to write him a letter to pre-announce their arrival or wait for an invitation. Larwood's eldest daughter, June, was tending the shop. Her father was upstairs, she explained. Fingleton found him in

Harold Larwood with Jack Fingleton in later life. Fingleton (left) was responsible for persuading Larwood to emigrate to Australia and did much to smooth his passage.

a 'homely room', which was 'festooned with photographs of some of the most stirring times known to the game of cricket'. Larwood gave Fingleton a 'quiet but warm' welcome.

'He knew I was a journalist,' said Fingleton, aware that Larwood might be cagey in front of a reporter who had space to fill in his newspaper. Fingleton reassured him that he wasn't chasing a scoop. He had no angle, and no axe to grind. He wouldn't be grilling him about his views on Bradman or the Australians, or whipping up the business of Bodyline again. He knew how Larwood must feel about it. He'd merely heard that Larwood might want to see a face or two from the past.

'He thought, not unnaturally,' said Fingleton, 'that I was on the scent of a story.' That suspicion was only removed, Fingleton added, when 'we had a sup of ale at the local'. The conversation, which began stiffly, broadened as alcohol lubricated it. Names were swapped, stories passed around and a lot of catching-up was done as the rounds of beer came and were drunk to the last draught. Larwood took copious pinches of snuff out of his pocket and expertly laid the tobacco on the back of his hand before drawing it into his nostrils. Duckworth accepted a pinch, and breathed it in so deeply that his eyes began to water like a dripping tap. 'It's much better for you than cigarettes,' Larwood told him.

Fingleton discovered that Larwood was appreciably 'thinner' than when he'd last seen him. Most of the muscle he'd used to bowl quickly had vanished. 'Walking behind him, one would never guess that here was the great fast bowler,' he observed. He found him reluctant to talk about Bodyline. Fingleton reported: 'He wanted to bury the dead, and had no wish to recapture the past. He wanted only to forget it, and so his business, to all appearances, was no different from thousands of similar businesses throughout England that were run by the Joneses, the Browns, the Williamses and the Smiths.'

Registering that the anger about his treatment over Bodyline still rolled around inside Larwood – he said in a mild voice that he was 'pretty bitter' – Fingleton listened to him sympathetically. 'I don't think,' he said of Larwood's grievance, 'it is with the Australians, but rather with those English officials who were glad to have him and use him before Bodyline became ostracized and then, conveniently, put him aside. He finds that impossible to forgive. He did not say so, but I gathered that he considered himself badly treated, and many who know the story of those Bodyline days will agree with him.' That's why, Fingleton reckoned, 'cricket had lost all its appeal' to him.

The talk turned to Bradman. Fingleton detected the 'old glint of battle' in Larwood's eyes whenever that name floated into the conversation. 'I always thought he was out to show me up as the worst fast bowler in the world,' said Larwood. 'Well,' he added, 'I took the view that I should try to show him up as the worst batsman. But he was a good 'un.'

After the pub closed, Larwood took Fingleton and Duckworth back to the shop. The men were pleasantly tipsy, full of the glowing companionship of the tavern. Duckworth had put on a lot of weight since giving up cricket. His stomach nearly burst through his low-buttoned waistcoat. He wedged his corpulent frame into an armchair, as if forcing a large cork back into a tight-necked bottle. Fingleton laid his trilby on the arm of the sofa and sat back, waiting as Larwood pulled out his photograph albums. He tenderly turned the pages, each of them solidly freezing a moment in time that Larwood converted into an articulate and interesting tale. The albums were a mosaic of his career, and he jigsawed them together for Fingleton. Larwood seemed to warm himself on those memories, as if the present was an inhospitably cold place and the photographs were like a door he could pass through to escape from it. As if fate decreed it so, Larwood gave Fingleton the long airmail letter he'd received that very morning from a young, would-be fast bowler from Australia who thirsted for advice from a man he'd only seen play in short clips of newsreels. 'Do you think, Mr Larwood,' the letter asked, 'that you might have been a better fast bowler if you had begun the swing of your right arm from lower down?' The letter was postmarked Bowral: Bradman's home town. As Fingleton put it so perfectly: 'As if any Australian would have wanted Larwood to be better than he was.'

Like Robinson Crusoe after the storm, there was an element of the shipwrecked mariner about Larwood in Blackpool. He was wave-tossed and had salvaged what he could from the buffeting of Bodyline. The perceptive Fingleton fastened on to it, and on to the 'sensitive' side of Larwood's nature. As he noted, there was 'something tragic' about the end of his career and Larwood had never recovered from it. A kind of paralysis had set in. He was in limbo, unable to move forward because he was anchored to his past and unable to go back because that past contained so much resentment. 'There were times,' Fingleton said, 'when Larwood thought the game not worth the candle.' Fingleton tried to persuade Larwood to accompany him to Old Trafford to watch and then meet the touring Australians. Larwood was in two minds. He did want to see Lindwall bowl. He did want to see Bill O'Reilly again. He did want to be involved with cricketers and cricket once more and end his exile. And he didn't want to stay as an outsider. But his nerve failed him. He 'never came,' said Fingleton, who thought 'the inside of an English first-class ground contained too many sad memories for him . . . '

Fingleton began waxing about Australia as a place to live: the lifestyle, the warmth of the climate and the warmth of the people too; a nation waiting to be explored and built on and grasped with large wide hands like Larwood's. Fingleton talked about Australia the way F. Scott Fitzgerald spoke about America – 'a land commensurate with our capacity to wonder'. He made it alluring, irresistible. Eventually Fingleton said, almost casually: 'If you're that fed up, Harold, why not come out to live in Australia?' There was nothing to stop him emigrating, added Fingleton. He would have the capital available from his shop if he sold it. Fingleton knew politicians who could pull appropriate strings and find him work, a home, a completely new style of living. Larwood could start over – for the third time in less than a decade – and Fingleton would be flattered to prepare the way for him. Just say the word, Fingleton said. Larwood's mind raced ahead. 'I could settle out there, and it wouldn't take me long either,' he said wistfully, thinking about the reception he'd been given in Sydney after falling just two runs short of his century in the final Bodyline Test. He thought about the heat and broad streets of the handsome city and contrasted them with the miserable wolf-grey clouds that hung over England for nine months of every year. 'When I was on tour, I saw the possibilities of going to live in Australia,' said Larwood. 'When Jack mentioned it, I thought we ought to give it a go.'

Within two days, the first newspaper reports appeared. Harold Larwood, who'd set Australia aflame with his fast bowling, was planning to return there. He wouldn't be coming back.

CHAPTER TWELVE

OUR FATE IS IN THE HANDS OF THE GODS

April 1950 – December 1950

'We're all Aussies now.' The Larwood family arrives in Australia in 1950. From left, Cyril Roper (June's fiancé), June, Enid, Mary, Freda and Lois. Harold holds his youngest daughter, Sylvia.

Tilbury: April 1950 – Brisbane: December 1950

There was no brass band or bunting, no speeches or farewell handshakes, no ceremony of any kind.

Alone with his thoughts and his family, Harold Larwood slipped away from his own country on an unseasonable, miserable-looking afternoon. The threat of rain hung in the air. The clouds were low and heavy, diluting the sun into weak, pale fingers of light. A wind looted new spring leaves from the trees and dragged the tangy taste of salt from the Essex marshes. Larwood stood unobtrusively on Tilbury's quayside, his hands in his pockets and the cold air filling his lungs. He watched uniformed men pushing trolleys stacked with leather suitcases. He gazed around him and saw the other passengers wave long goodbyes and blow extravagant kisses. He looked up at the ship, and remembered another time; a time that now seemed long ago. The 20,000-ton *Orontes* had carried Larwood on the Bodyline tour almost 18 years earlier. Now it waited to return him there, its two yellow angled funnels like a pair of stumps that a fast bowler had just knocked back. A short blast of the hooter pushed Larwood aboard; dirty oil smoke began to drift across the sky. In his new off-the-peg overcoat and horn-rimmed spectacles, a sweater beneath his jacket to warm him, Larwood was just another figure bound for a distant shore. No one bothered him, which was just as well. He was suffering from what he described as 'the worst hangover I have ever had in my life'.

Larwood had never forgotten Jack Hobbs' decency towards him in 1926 in nobly championing his Test credentials. On his final afternoon in England, Douglas Jardine hosted a lunch for Larwood. At the end of it he handed him a present that Hobbs had once given to him. It was a gold and brown pencil made to mark Hobbs' one hundredth hundred a quarter of a century earlier. The inscription read:

To D.R. Jardine. From Jack Hobbs. 1925

Larwood let the pencil roll across his palm and diffidently asked Jardine what Hobbs would think of the fact that it now belonged to him. 'Jack will be thrilled,' he said generously. Larwood slid the pencil into his pocket and set off across London to look for Hobbs. 'There was only one man I really wanted to say goodbye to . . . I knew I'd never see him again,' he said. He went into Hobbs' sporting-goods shop on Fleet Street. The

Jack Hobbs in regal pose. Even in his sixties, he still looks every inch the batting 'Master'.

sales assistant told him that Hobbs was in the Cheshire Cheese pub nearby. Larwood found him alone in a corner below its brass-coloured light fittings. 'Harold,' said Hobbs, surprised to see him. 'We'll have some champagne.' Larwood took out the pencil and laid it in his hand. Hobbs picked it up for a moment. 'It's an honour to know you have it,' he said. The two men sat on crimson velvet seats and drank 'more glasses of champagne than I can remember', according to Larwood. Their talk was all about the past.

Hobbs always maintained that Larwood was the 'fastest and most accurate bowler he had ever seen'. So fast that he explained it like this: 'I just hoped I would see the first ball and be able to move to it in time. I dreaded that he would be through me before I could get the bat down, or hit me on the toe. I knew it would be off stump or thereabouts – Harold always aimed to hit the top of the off stump.'

The afternoon wore on and turned eventually into evening before Larwood, hopelessly but blissfully drunk and disorientated, was pushed into a taxi by Hobbs, who waved him off and watched the taxi vanish into the distance. Larwood stared through the back window, waving in return. He hardly slept. He spent most of his final night in England vomiting into the toilet bowl. 'But it was worth it,' he said, 'to be with Jack Hobbs for a few more hours.'

* * *

Only one heavyweight cricket writer thought Larwood's departure to Australia was newsworthy enough to seek him out at Tilbury. John Arlott was surprised to find no other reporter on the docks. He'd expected to jostle with a tight knot of journalists gently interrogating Larwood about the history and ramifications of Bodyline and the reasons for his emigration. He'd anticipated taking his place in a long queue. With so many of them squabbling for the same quotes, and knowing Larwood's reticence about providing them, Arlott thought the story might be 'worth only a few lines'.

When Arlott reached the *Orontes*, he found Larwood in a deckchair on the tourist boat-deck with time on his hands. Arlott ran his eyes across the diminutive figure. 'Looking at him nearly twenty years after his great days,' said Arlott, 'it was as puzzling as ever to decide whence came the strength to power that terrific bowling.' The two men went for a cup of tea. Although it was already three o'clock, Larwood couldn't face the prospect of food and he refused the offer of a beer (Arlott knew nothing of his drinking session with Hobbs or his sickness as a consequence of it). Larwood was in reflective mood. He talked about the send-off Jardine's team had been given in 1932 – the newspaper bills on every corner, the photographers and Pathé news crews pushing for the best position on the quay, the MCC dignitaries crowding around to press their palms into his own for good luck, the roar of the ship's hooter, the drag of bags, the rush of people in every direction. It had been like a 'grand party', he said, with the thrill of Christmas morning about it.

Larwood told Arlott he still had the case that he'd taken on the tour. It was going back to Australia with him. He talked about his homecoming in 1933 – a far different spring day on which his name appeared in fresh, bold ink on the front page of almost every newspaper and was on everyone's lips too. He shook so many hands that the flesh became sore. Back then, as Larwood pointedly said, he was important to English cricket and a favourite son of the MCC. He talked about the Australian weather, the groundwork Jack Fingleton had done on his behalf: 'I'll never be able to repay him,' said Larwood. He didn't discuss Bodyline or his retirement from cricket and the subsequent escape to Blackpool. Arlott realized one thing. He listened and looked, and astutely picked out the sadness in Larwood's eyes, the undertow of despondency in his voice. Larwood seemed bruised and sorrowful. He tried so hard to disguise it, like a recently bereaved husband camouflaging his grief. It perturbed Arlott. He would always recall that what concerned him most – even more than the melancholia he detected in the soul – was the way in which Larwood pretended everything was fine, as if trying to convince himself of it. To hear him, Arlott said, you'd think that he had no worries about leaving England, and no reservations about going to Australia. Arlott struggled to understand why Larwood had cut himself off from cricket for so long – a decision that seemed avoidable and unnecessary to everyone but Larwood himself. He described his departure as 'sad' and observed perceptively: 'It was inescapable that he was going with courage rather than enthusiasm . . . he looked . . . a rather tragic, but brave, figure. For someone who as a boy had watched him and been excited by his great speed, he seemed a different man; fragile in a way, yet admirable in his firmness.'

Larwood and Arlott sat facing one another. 'We had finished our cups of tea and for some time had not spoken,' said Arlott. 'A little later we shook hands.' Arlott compassionately stayed on the quay until the ship pulled anchor. He felt it necessary to be there, with and for Larwood, whom he felt shouldn't be allowed to leave England without someone bidding him a proper goodbye. He deserved better than to go so anonymously, as if he was being deported like a nineteenth-century convict. It was, added Arlott, almost as though the MCC had abandoned him for the second time. Arlott looked up at Larwood. 'He waved from the rail,' remembered Arlott, watching the slim outline of his body and his raised right hand as he began to recede into the middle distance.

Almost at the very moment when the *Orontes* inched its way out of the harbour, flakes of wet snow fell. 'Have a good look at it,' Larwood told his family amid the squalls. 'We won't be seeing snow where we're going.' He remained on deck with Lois and the children until the buildings on the flat shoreline dissolved in a huddle of indistinct shapes and then disappeared behind a curtain of snow and sleet. Larwood had folded a telegram into his wallet, the last he received before boarding. 'Bon voyage,' it read. 'Take care of yourself. Good luck always. Skipper.' Jardine was solicitous to the end.

Three days later Larwood wrote an open letter to the people of Nottingham. The local newspapers published a photograph of it. Larwood's spidery handwriting and his firm signature, underlined with a flourish, were slanted across the page, as if the ship was listing across the ocean when he wrote it. 'As I, and my family are now at sea sailing to a new life, I am writing these few lines in the hope, that you will convey to the Nottingham public . . . our heartfelt thanks for the good wishes that have been showered upon us, we sincerely thank one and all . . . I would have liked to have seen everyone before leaving, but this was impossible.'

Larwood hid his anxieties about what might be waiting for him in Australia. He didn't betray – at least to his family – the nervous hand-wringing he'd gone through once the decision to emigrate became irrevocable. It was typical Larwood. No matter how much he fretted – about the ructions of Bodyline, the wilderness years of county cricket following it, the struggles in his business affairs and his own despondencies – he kept them solidly to himself, like holding in a long, deep breath. He did it not because he thought discussing them might be construed as feebleness on his own part, but to protect the feelings of his family. He didn't want to burden them. Publicly, he would say one thing. Privately, he would think the opposite. To journalists, he was upbeat about Australia: 'I am looking forward to my emigration, but I don't quite know what I'm going to do out there,' he said in one article. He reassured the newspapers that as far as Bodyline was concerned 'time has eased the heart-burning'. He explained his departure simply: 'I want to give the girls a chance,' he said. 'What I live for now is them.' He even claimed that he 'could coach', which he'd previously avoided, not wanting to become embroiled in cricket at all. 'I might be willing to give some time to it,' he lied.

But to Fingleton he was candid. Just two weeks before he sailed, Larwood trusted him enough to confess in a letter: 'Everyone is thrilled, although at times I feel a bit quaky as to what will eventually happen to us. Still we have took [sic] the plunge, and will have to see it through . . . The wife, and I, we have such responsibility for them [the children] that we shall feel happier when we have eventually settled down, which, as we know, will take time . . . I am determined to do my best out in Aussies [sic], for my kiddies sakes.' In other letters, Larwood was equally open about his sensitivity towards public opinion and his concern that it might be twisted before his arrival, or, as he put it: 'At the back of it [his mind] I am left wondering how the public will react . . . Our decision to go to Australia has certainly caused a stir, why, I don't know.' When he spoke to journalists, he promised Fingleton, he'd wrap his words in wads of cotton wool. He was afraid that anything he said, however innocent, might be misinterpreted or exploited. 'I shall try my best Jack to avoid giving the reporters anything to enlarge.' He didn't even want journalists to discover that Jardine had arranged the farewell lunch for him. 'Not a soul knows,' he wrote to Fingleton, as if eating with his 'skipper' would alienate him from the ordinary Australians with whom he wanted to forge friendships. As for cricket, Larwood was adamant: 'As regards a job, Jack, I don't mind a sports store, what I don't want is a coaching job.'

Larwood was emotionally torn. There was relief at leaving England behind him. His hard work had gone unrewarded. He was tired of coming down with a cold every bleak midwinter. He was fed up with his meagre living. After the publication of his book and his newspaper articles in 1933 and 1934, he was considered a man to be avoided as far as the MCC was concerned. What good had speaking out done him? What were the benefits of being honest? When Larwood looked back over the previous decade and a half, he came reluctantly to one gloomy conclusion: nothing had worked for him. He felt like a man who'd been rattling a key in the wrong lock. He would be more careful from now on in what he said and did. There'd been one small mercy. In 1949 – three months after Bradman knelt and then arose as Sir Donald – the MCC at last threw Larwood a conciliatory bone. He was one of 26 retired professionals awarded honorary membership. The MCC wasn't magnanimous enough to invite him to Lord's to accept it. The postman handed Larwood his membership amongst the daily delivery of bills and letters. The gesture nonetheless meant a lot to an outcast.

* * *

Until Fingleton suggested what Australia might offer, Larwood hadn't been sure what to do next. Fingleton's promise that Larwood would be sponsored and find work was instantly vindicated. As soon as the news broke, Larwood was offered both employment and accommodation. Letters were supportive, welcoming. He dealt with the practicalities of emigration. He found a buyer for the shop, and 'gradually' prepared to pack. And then the reality of what might lie ahead dawned on him. Larwood remembered the Australian view of Bodyline and the opinions he'd so bullishly expressed about it, and them, on his return home. The 'quaky' feelings he experienced – a particularly quaint expression to use – were rooted in his fears about how the man in the street might view him. Had enough time passed for the Australians to have forgotten Bodyline and forgiven him for it? Was Australia prepared to give him a chance? He began to think of specific instances of trouble during the tour.

After the last Test in 1932–33, as he crossed Australia by train, there was a stop-off at Quorn, a township and railhead in the Flinders ranges. Almost the entire town – Larwood estimated '200 to 300' people – gathered around his carriage and began to chant: 'We want Larwood.' When Larwood, who was playing bridge, didn't appear, some of them threw fruit and orange peel through the window. Others boarded the train and spat pomegranate seeds at him. As well as the spitting, he was subjected to verbal abuse. Larwood admitted afterwards that the scenes were his own fault. If he'd gone onto the platform, the ugliness 'might have been avoided,' he explained. 'The people only wanted to see me.' Larwood also recalled a night in Brisbane when he'd heard the familiar growl of 'Pommie bastards' when he, Voce, Les Ames and Tommy Mitchell went into a hotel bar. A drunken bush worker began barracking them loudly, drawing them into a fight. The man finally brandished a handgun taken from his pocket. There are conflicting stories about what happened next. Larwood claimed that the bar owner 'bundled' the barracker outside. Bill Bowes, whom Larwood didn't recall being there at all, claimed that Voce knocked the man down. A shaken-up Larwood sped out of the bar in case the shooting began.

He dwelt on the near-riot at Adelaide and the fear he had seen on the faces of Bill Voce, Les Ames, Walter Hammond and Herbert Sutcliffe at the prospect of it, realizing much later, of course, that his own expression must have betrayed the same trepidation as theirs. He saw the stark newspaper bill that described his bowling as: 'PREMEDITATED BRUTALITY'. Fingleton reassured him in letters and in the pieces he wrote for British newspapers. 'The red carpet will be out all around the Australian coast,' he wrote. 'The only ones who may worry are those Australians who played against him in the Bodyline Tests. If they sit with him in the next Tests here, they may find it difficult to look him in the eye.'

Larwood tried to convince himself that Fingleton was right. He took solace in the meeting he'd had with Keith Miller and Ray Lindwall at a lunch to honour Bradman at the Savoy in 1948. The sponsors invited Larwood and, as usual, he acted like a reluctant date and refused to go. He wasn't convinced that Bradman, or any of the other Australians, would be prepared to meet him. 'I didn't know whether Don would want me there, or how he'd respond,' he said, aware of Bradman's sensitivity about Bodyline. He thought of himself as a ghost at the feast; more so because the event had been arranged to salute the man he'd targeted and humbled during Bodyline. Wounds might be reopened, accusations made, offence taken. No, he wouldn't attend. And then George Duckworth wrote to him. Would Larwood go to the dinner with him? Under pressure from Lois, who urged her husband to accept the offer, he finally relented, albeit with trepidation in case anything went horribly wrong.

Bradman was courteous but clipped in what he said to him. Neither man spoke of Bodyline. Bradman asked after Larwood; Larwood asked after Bradman. The conversation ended, and then Larwood and Bradman parted like an estranged couple who have met unexpectedly on the street and aren't quite sure what to say to one another any more.

Apart from Bradman's polite but obviously strained greeting, which unsettled him, the other Australians embraced Larwood warmly, as if he was a member of their own tour party. The table plan was ingeniously set: Larwood sat between Miller and Lindwall, who admired him so much that he was like a pupil in awe of his teacher. Lindwall copied Larwood's action so faithfully that he turned himself into a mirror image of the Englishman. As an 11-year-old in 1932–33, Lindwall had watched Larwood from the Hill at Sydney and followed the rest of the Bodyline series in the newspapers and on the newsreels. Larwood had become the centre of his cricketing universe. Newspaper photographs capturing Larwood a split second before the point of delivery were cut out and kept, and he grew up committed to bowl like – and to be as quick as – his hero. The

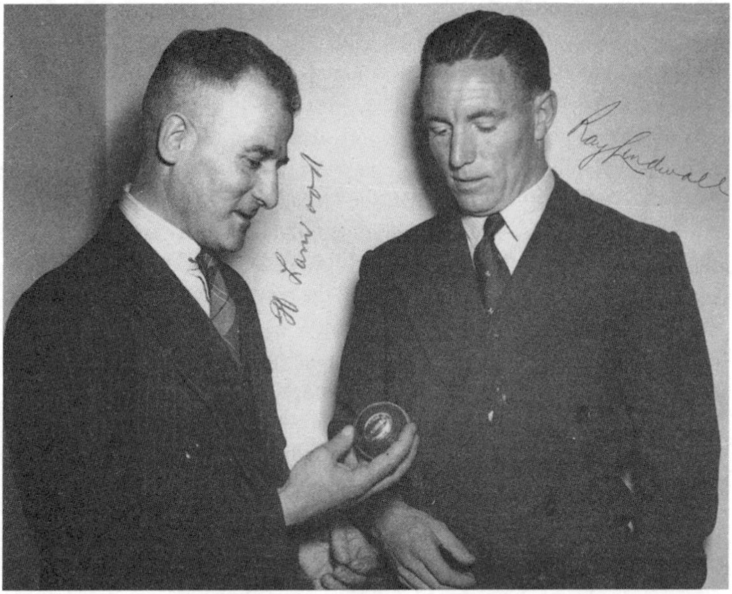

Ray Lindwall admired Harold Larwood so much that he copied his action. He met his hero for the first time during a celebratory lunch for Donald Bradman in 1948.

run to the wicket and the delivery were studiously broken down in his mind, and the information used as a template, so that Lindwall could understand and then duplicate them. He wrote about Larwood's 'smooth approach and gradual acceleration, the fire and the control in the delivery and the whipped follow-through'. He said that 'the action could not be faulted'. Watching him from the Trent Bridge pavilion on the 1948 tour, Nottinghamshire members threw accusations of plagiarism at the bowler, a charge that Lindwall gratefully accepted as a compliment. If Larwood's home crowd thought he resembled him, Lindwall knew the hours of practice had been worth it, producing a near-flawless copy. 'Why,' he asked his critics in such a definite and firm way that it guillotined the argument dead, 'shouldn't I copy the very best?'

Lindwall was anxious to meet Larwood. At a time when Larwood's confidence was low, he was glad of Lindwall's worship. Miller liked

Larwood enormously too. He approved of his gutsy, uncompromising approach to the Bodyline series – an attitude, he said, that was so inherently Australian – and he saw a man who was truthful and solidly down to earth. 'No frills,' said Miller, who would become a friend for the rest of Larwood's life. Larwood relished every minute of the long conversation. He was like a castaway who, deprived of company for a long time, can't stop talking when the rescue boat finally takes him back to the mainland. Larwood spoke so much that he 'hardly ate a thing'. The waiters took away half-eaten plates of food. Lindwall and Miller were as convincing as Fingleton had been about the benefits of life 'Down Under'. The possibilities of living there became clearer still to Larwood. But nothing Fingleton, Miller or Lindwall said about Australia entirely calmed his worries about setting foot there again.

Shortly before leaving England, he wrote to Fingleton and – in a very rare example of Larwood over-dramatizing his situation – said with candour: 'Our fate is in the hands of the Gods.'

* * *

The Gods – and the Australian people – were kind. Long after he'd established himself and his family in Australia, Larwood admitted: 'I said to my family that they'd either bless me or curse me for bringing them to Australia. I think it's been a blessing.' He also added: 'Before I left England, people said that I'd have it pretty rough out here. But it never happened that way. They still come to me and say: "I used to hate you. I used to boo you" – but that's all over now.' Larwood heard that line as soon as he moved into his new home, a bungalow in Kingsford, a suburb nearly five miles from Sydney Cricket Ground, where he could often stand in the back garden and hear the faint echo of the Hill's roar. 'Welcome to Australia,' said one of his neighbours, extending his hand. 'I just wanted you to know that 18 years ago I stood up with the rest and booed you from the Sydney Hill. Just let us know if there is anything we can do to help.' That attitude was prevalent: Australia hadn't forgotten Bodyline, or the destruction it wrought, but it had forgiven Larwood and was prepared to 'give the Pommie a go', as he put it.

Larwood was reassured as soon as he disembarked from the *Orontes*. The Larwoods had paid for their own fare – a third-class ticket. Larwood occupied one cabin with his eldest daughter June's fiancé; Lois slept in

During the Larwood family's journey to their new home in Sydney, Harold and his daughter Enid met Bill Woodfull at Melbourne Boys High School, where the former Australian captain was headmaster.

another with their five daughters. 'We didn't want to arrive in Australia on anyone else's generosity,' he said. The Australians liked his independence, the willingness to 'rough it'. Larwood wanted to melt quietly into his new country in the same way as he melted quietly out of his own. He didn't anticipate the celebrity, almost film-star treatment, that his arrival generated. He blinked at the film cameras and the photographers – this suited man in the striped shirt and tie who pulled his family around him like a blanket and then stared up and pointed in wonder at the ship which had brought them 12,000 miles. He looked astonished, as if he could barely believe – after the years of planning, the months of turning the decision over in his mind, and the weeks of travelling – that he'd finally reached his destination.

A journalist mischievously asked whether he'd come to Australia 'to retire'. He shook his head, 'My name's Larwood, not Bradman,' he replied injudiciously. Fingleton stepped in to guard Larwood from the journalists in the same way as Bill Voce had once guarded him against physical assault in Adelaide. 'If you write it, I'll skin you,' he said. The man obediently turned the page of his notebook and took another tack. In his innocent way, and in the thrill of being the centre of attention in his adopted land, Larwood had instinctively framed his answer to explain his relative poverty in contrast to Bradman's wealth. Fingleton, who knew the way an innocent sentence could be manipulated maliciously, recognized that the quote was ripe for misinterpretation and exploitation. Set in type, with a screaming headline over it, Larwood could have been accused of almost anything: jealousy at Bradman's money , disrespect for Australia's hero, resentment that he wasn't fortunate enough to be Bradman himself, or just of being unpardonably glib. Larwood would have found himself explaining and clarifying what he'd said across Australia.

He soon made stately progress around the country, as though seeing it for the first time. He was asked whether he'd like to meet Bill Woodfull in Melbourne. 'Of course,' he replied, 'if Bill Woodfull wants to meet me.' And Woodfull, the most decent and gracious of men, did want to meet him. And, of course, the series that dare not speak its name when the two of them shook hands – both now wearing suits and spectacles – was Bodyline. There was no robust arguing about it, no recollection of its great drama. There was only the appreciation of one man for another. A crowd gathered around the ship in Melbourne merely to see him. 'You'd think I'd been in films,' said Larwood. Bert Oldfield took him to dinner. He met Bill O'Reilly and Stan McCabe and Duleepsinhji, then the Indian High Commissioner in Australia. Larwood was given a tour of Adelaide, the city where possibly only police on horseback had saved him from a lynching in 1933, and the Oval, now deserted and its scoreboard blank. He stood for a while on the boundary edge, a soldier reliving a battle and hearing gunfire from long ago.

In the jostling frenzy and dense haze of those early weeks, Larwood again felt wanted and cherished by people other than his close family. He experienced the acute sensation of belonging. He had travelled a long way to find a new home – a place where he could be himself – and it enabled him to write to his parents and say with proud justification that life had at last taken an upward turn.

* * *

The Larwood family were among 120,000 migrants to Australia in 1950. They had a substantial head start over most of the rest. The mention of Larwood's name was the equivalent of 'Open Sesame' – otherwise he wouldn't have reached Australia until 1952 at earliest. When he rang the

Orient Line to book his berth, he learnt that the wait for it would be an interminable 'two years long'. As he was *the* Harold Larwood, it shrank to six weeks.

Australia's population was swelling; albeit not as quickly as the politicians and economists desired. The country required labour to build houses, lay roads and run and drive businesses that would speed its expansion. The Australian government spent considerable time and ingenious effort to promote the country. Films about it were regularly shown in church and village halls around Britain and advertising was booked in newspapers specifically to target families tired of rationing and rain, and disillusioned with rubble-strewn, bombed-out streets. The skies were bluer somewhere, and that somewhere was in New South Wales or Western Australia or in the Northern Territory. Larwood's arrival was a boon. There were no preconditions attached to his emigration, but such a recognizable figure, both the epitome of English cricket and Donald Bradman's rival, would encourage others to follow him. Larwood was famous, which made him marketable.

Australia's housing shortage meant that most migrants found themselves in basic, often very rough, temporary accommodation, which was barely tolerable. Those who went 'into the bush' frequently found no running water or electricity, and dilapidated 'homes' that were shacks. By comparison, Larwood's path from ship to home-owner was blissful and blessed. The Australians didn't exactly throw rose-petals at him, but they did make sure that he was treated with velvet care, like a dignitary. Early the following year, Larwood was shaking hands with the former Prime Minister Ben Chifley, who remained Opposition leader. Larwood spoke with a broad Nottinghamshire accent, redolent of the pits. Chifley spoke with a thick and very pure Australian accent, redolent of his upbringing. Neither man was able to decipher what the other said to him. The voices sounded to ears unaccustomed to hearing them as nothing more than a succession of grunts and muttered syllables. A clear, recognizable word broke through only occasionally. Larwood and Chifley were politely divided by a common language and communicated through smiles and gestures, like semaphore.

'I don't understand a word he said,' Chifley told Jack Fingleton, who had arranged the meeting.

'I don't understand a word he said,' Larwood told Fingleton too.

'Chifley had his pipe stuck in the corner of his mouth,' explained

Larwood; 'I couldn't understand his mumble.' With Larwood at one end of the table and Chifley at the other, the reliable Fingleton acted as interpreter. Larwood did read Chifley's thoughts about Bodyline in the newspapers. 'I think,' he said, 'that Larwood was too good for you chaps.'

Chifley was important to Larwood. On arriving in Sydney, the family was booked into a hotel until the bungalow, which would be their home for the next 45 years, became available. Larwood regarded the hotel rent of £16 as ridiculously cheap – 'there was even new furniture in the room', he said. It convinced him that Australia must be the fiscal Promised Land, where he wouldn't have to scrape together his dollars for a comfortable existence. Larwood had no idea that Chifley, who was responsible for Australia's post-war immigration boom, thought so highly of him that he'd paid for half of the cost of his lodgings; an extraordinary act of kindness for someone he hadn't yet met. Fingleton only let the secret slip after Chifley's sudden death from a heart attack – just six months after his conversation with Larwood – sadly released him from his sworn pledge to stay silent. Larwood never got the chance to say 'thank you'.

* * *

Larwood already had the guarantee of paid work as a 'guest columnist'. The *Melbourne Herald* offered £100, plus his expenses, to cover the first Test of the 1950–51 Ashes series for it and a stable of newspapers. 'I have accepted verbally,' he told Fingleton, 'and have to call in at the Heralds [sic] office before we sail, for fixing defineately [sic] . . . it will give us a good start to our Australian life.' In England, the *Sunday Express* keenly handed over the same amount and told him he could 'do what [he] liked in Australia'. The newspapers weren't bothered about Larwood's wayward spelling. His thoughts on the Test would be ghosted for him and telexed at the close of play. 'It was easier than fast bowling,' he said, 'because your muscles didn't ache at the end of it.'

Larwood was too gentle to be a convincing or acerbic critic. Kindly self-restraint meant that he didn't bring the full venom of his bowling to the printed page. He knew only too well, and too painfully, the effort it took to get through a Test match, the nervous exhaustion you experienced beforehand and the sense of failure that enveloped you after a defeat, or even after an indifferent session in the field. To condemn someone for it was to inflict further punishment. Afraid of causing too much offence, especially to the Australians, Larwood wrote in generalities. The novelty of his by-line and his technical insights nonetheless made the pieces readable. But his reserve was an obstacle to a career in journalism. He felt awkward sitting in the press box, where other reporters wanted to meet him or ask his opinions. Beside the clattering typewriters, Larwood looked on awkwardly as he jotted down the odd note on a small lined pad. Even though Jack Fingleton and Neville Cardus sat beside him, shepherding him through the rituals of the writing day, Larwood was uncomfortable.

The opening Test was in Brisbane, where Fingleton admitted 'the lot of the pressman is not easy'. In mitigation, Fingleton explained: 'He is often regarded, as he sometimes is, as a nuisance' there. Larwood soon discovered Brisbane's reluctance to lay on the hospitality for reporters. He almost didn't get into the ground at all. On the opening morning, Cardus accompanied Larwood, who carried a card which declared he was now a 'Working Journalist'. The authority of the card didn't impress the Brisbane jobsworths, as steely and implacable as traffic wardens.

Cardus and Larwood were turned away at the main entrance and sent to what Cardus called a 'more menial entrance round the corner'. The gateman there turned them away too. The two men were sent to yet another turnstile – further still from where the start of their circular and frustrating journey had begun. The clock hands nudged towards the start of play. Larwood, who liked to be punctual, began to fret. The Test might begin without him. The third gateman was just as unimpressed with the pair of flustered, bespectacled Englishmen and their official credentials. Cardus did all the negotiating while Larwood stood quietly half a pace behind him. The gateman stared suspiciously at their passes and then at both Cardus and Larwood, as if trying to recall where he'd seen their faces before. He prevaricated about letting them in; Cardus, usually as mild-mannered as Larwood, finally lost his patience. He grabbed Larwood's shoulder and pushed him forward – 'so the official could inspect him thoroughly at close quarters'.

'Look here,' said Cardus, 'this is Harold Larwood. You've heard of him? I should think so. Well, there was a time, I agree, when every precaution might have been taken to keep Harold Larwood out of all Australian cricket grounds. But, look at him now – he's quite harmless.' The gateman nodded, sheepishly waved them through, and the bewildered Larwood took his seat in the press box.

When Larwood nervously asked Douglas Jardine to leave him out of the final Test of the Bodyline series at Sydney, one of the reasons he gave was 'that I'd never watched a Test before'. Larwood claimed that he was 'curious' to experience the gladiatorial cut and thrust of it unfolding in front of him without the pressure of playing in it. The Coliseum-like spectacle of Test cricket, and specifically the baying reactions of the crowd, fascinated him. He looked forward to sitting back in a decent seat and soaking it up like an elaborate piece of theatre. 'It's strange,' he said to Fingleton in Brisbane, 'I've had to wait more than 17 years for this.'

The wait proved worthwhile. What Larwood saw was described by Fingleton as 'surely the craziest and maddest Test match of all time . . . certainly without a counterpart in living memory'. Scheduled for six days, the Test was over in only four after a deluge of rain, which landed as hard as bolts on the iron roofs and made Larwood feel as though he'd been transported back to shivery England. It saturated the uncovered pitch. The conditions became impossibly treacherous for the batsmen, who turned ashen with apprehension as the ball reared or stayed low: 20 wickets fell in one day for just 130 runs. The surface perfectly suited the 'Mystery Spinner', Jack Iverson, who took four for 43 on his debut to wreck England's second innings. Australia won by 70 runs. As the Australian wicketkeeper Don Tallon scrambled for the stumps as souvenirs at the end, Larwood was able to tell Cardus: 'If it's this good, I'll keep watching.'

CHAPTER THIRTEEN

IT'S NOT LIKE THE OLD DAYS, DON

December 1950 – February 1971

Harold Larwood was determined to pursue his new career as inconspicuously as possible.

Sydney: December 1950 – Sydney Cricket Ground: February 1971

Fiction has to avoid bizarre coincidence to be plausible; real life doesn't. In 45 years of living in Australia, Harold Larwood met Donald Bradman only four times. The first meeting was pure serendipity.

Larwood was walking through Sydney with his daughter Mary in 1950. He'd promised to buy her a watch. He turned into Martin Place – the wide thoroughfare that cuts through the main streets of the body of the city, like a connecting artery. A familiar figure began to come towards him.

Before leaving England, and then on his arrival in Australia, Larwood had steeled himself to answer predictable questions about Bradman: whether there was any residue of ill-feeling between them because of Bodyline; what Bradman made of his decision to emigrate; and what he really felt about Bradman as a batsman and as a man.

Larwood prepared his white lies. There was no ill-feeling, he insisted; in fact, there never had been. 'We were just young players back then. The series happened a long time ago and is gone and forgotten for both of us.' He had no idea how Bradman would respond to news of his emigration. Finally he made a point of stressing: 'One thing is certain. I shall definitely look up my old friend The Don.'

But Bradman wasn't an old friend and Larwood had neither the intention nor inclination to call or phone. Now, when he least expected it, here was Bradman only a few yards away. It was impossible for the two Bodyline rivals to avoid one another. Bradman had travelled to Sydney from his home in Adelaide on business, and the music of chance brought them together on a busy pavement.

'It's not like the old days,' Larwood said to Bradman, a knight of the British Empire for two years by then.

'How do you mean?' asked Bradman.

'Well,' said Larwood, gazing around him as shoppers and office workers hurried past, and the ex-cricketers stood beside one another, like a pair of inconspicuous middle-aged businessmen in suits and hats, 'thirty years ago there'd have been hundreds of people around us by now.'

Bradman agreed, and chatted for a short while before saying his mannered goodbyes, moving on after a simple tug of the brim of his hat and then vanishing around the first corner. Sir Donald Bradman was already a seriously moneyed man through his sponsorships and business interests, and also a member of the Australian Cricket Board of Control.

The first meeting for more than 15 years between Harold Larwood and Donald Bradman took place at the Savoy in 1948 at a lunch to mark Bradman's farewell tour of England.

Mr Larwood was starting afresh. 'I've never been one to worry about the material things of life and I didn't go into cricket for money,' said Larwood. 'All the same it was impossible not to think afterwards about how things had turned out for us both. Don Bradman was wealthy, and he'd been an amateur. I was the professional, and yet I was still working for a living. That was cricket back then, I suppose.' The gulf between them – personally and professionally – could not have been starker. Larwood seldom complained about Fate; usually he made best use of whatever cards it dealt him. But his reflection on the way in which good fortune and material rewards had been bestowed on Bradman in the years since Bodyline was baleful enough to suggest that the imbalance when compared with his own life briefly irked him.

Publicly, Larwood admired Bradman the batsman. 'No one can ever be as good as him – ever again,' he said and meant it sincerely. Privately, he intensely disliked Bradman as a person. 'He wasn't a very likeable fellow,' he added with self-restraint.

The irony is that Larwood and Bradman ought to have got on. There were enough common threads to have been tied into a companionable bow. Both were from families of five children; and both were obsessive about cricket and self-taught through a steely, rigid didacticism that took over their lives, and the lives of everyone who came into contact with them. Although there was an edge between them well before Bodyline – Larwood hadn't endeared himself to Bradman and vice versa – the lacerating divisions the series created made friendship or even casual acquaintance impossible.

No one at the epicentre of Bodyline came out of it without being wounded in some way. The casualty list was long: the two captains, Bill Woodfull and Douglas Jardine, and Larwood and Bradman were the most obvious and conspicuous victims. Larwood believed that Bradman had been scalded raw by the treatment he gave him. Even though in subsequent years Larwood was always willing to point out that Bradman's average in the series was higher than any other Australian batsman's and so couldn't be viewed as failure – 'we'd have given him 75 runs just to stay in the pavilion', he'd say respectfully – he felt his adversary became almost neurotic in defending each innings, his tactics to fight Bodyline and, of course, the charge that Larwood petrified him. Warwick Armstrong's view, expressed contemporaneously, that Bradman 'showed unmistakable signs of fright when facing every ball from Larwood' was a direct accusation of cowardice, and he fought to rid himself of it.

Larwood said emphatically after the series that Bradman had been frightened of him during it. The remark was the equivalent of flicking a lighted match onto dry straw. It inflamed the Australian public, who saw it as an outrageous slander and went into a rage all over again about Larwood and Bodyline. At the end of his life, Larwood withdrew the claim and replaced it with another. 'He was shaky,' said Larwood, 'when the ball moved into his ribs . . . I always tried one or two at Bradman when he came in. I thought he didn't fancy it early on.' Bradman always repudiated that suggestion as well. Even on the 50th anniversary of the series, he was stressing: 'I certainly didn't like the implication he [Larwood] made that I was frightened of this sort of bowling. That wasn't true, and I resented it very much. And I still do.' Bradman admitted that the charge had 'got under my skin'.

Larwood ought to have stood by his original claim. He spoke nothing but the truth. The proof of it lies in the fact that Bradman had a brain, for anyone capable of rational thought would have a sliver of fear running through them when Larwood came on to bowl. The Australian opener Bill Brown once confessed his relief after hearing that Larwood had been rested from a match. He said: 'Prior to that I'd been lying in bed at night worrying. I had a fairly heavy bat, you see, and I'd thought "God, I'll never get this up in time for Larwood. He'll hit me fair between the eyes and that'll be the end of me."' To want to bat against Larwood, you almost had to be half in love with easeful death.

Bradman was worried that the success of Larwood's Bodyline bowling would damage cricket. He witnessed, and also read reports about, Bodyline being replicated in lower grades of the game in Australia. By January 1933, he had already written to the MCC to discuss a change in the lbw law. He proposed extending it to the off side. The MCC did not reply. Human nature still dictates that his primary concern over Bodyline was whether Larwood's pace might damage him both physically and psychologically and significantly lower his public esteem.

Bradman had sufficient time to steel himself for the series. He realized well in advance of it that he would be specifically targeted; and he understood that the method of attack against him would be based on pace. His weaving strategies to avoid Bodyline betrayed his apprehension about coping against it, and Larwood fed on that fear. Even before the Tests began, Bradman complained to a member of the Australian Board of Control that Larwood was bowling at, rather than to, him. Bill Bowes sharply called it 'the only sign of weakness in Bradman throughout his whole career as a batsman'. He also asked to be dropped down the order from number three, which caused acute dismay among the Australian team because it reinforced the idea that he was always apart from, rather than a part of, the side. And before the fourth Brisbane Test, he confessed that he would sooner return from the Gabba 'with a pair of ducks than a pair of broken ribs', a line which again made clear how exposed and vulnerable he felt. The feeling persisted between Larwood and Bill Voce that Bradman was 'frit'; that the possibility of a serious beating from Larwood scared him to the core. In a letter to his father early in 1933, Gubby Allen also wrote that Bradman was a 'terrible little coward of fast bowling'.

Whenever Bradman discussed the most stressful experience of his career – during the series, in the months after it and well into his old age – he was really discussing Larwood's bowling. When he insisted: 'I do not know of one batsman who has played against fast Bodyline bowling who is not of the opinion that it will kill cricket' – a statement he made after his century in the second Test at Melbourne – he cited Larwood in isolation as being able to make the ball 'fly dangerously'.

Having been jarred and peppered throughout the Bodyline series, Bradman never forgot it. The writer Ray Robinson thought 'now and again a fast ball rearing at him has apparently caused in Bradman's mind an unnerving flashback to the days when he was cricket's hunted stag. Even padding down his left side has not always given him a feeling of security.' Robinson highlighted four incidents as evidence. The first was at Headingley in 1934. On his way to 304, Bradman was repeatedly bounced by Bill Bowes. 'At the end of an over he walked slowly to a point more than half-way along the pitch and patted the turf with studied care, amid a resounding yell from the Yorkshire crowd, who knew what it was all about.'

The next two incidents came in the following Test at the Oval. Bowes claimed Bradman on 244 with a short-pitched delivery, denying him successive 300s. In the second innings, Bradman backed away from him and lost his leg stump. The fourth incident was the most glaring example of the way in which Bodyline was ever-present in his thoughts. In November 1936, Victoria's Ernie McCormick gave Bradman what Robinson described as 'the most cold-sweaty half-hour he ever endured against an Australian bowler'. Bradman lowered himself in the order to number four and missed McCormick's first fiery overs. When he did bat, McCormick rattled him severely. His 'speed and menacing lift', said Robinson, 'embarrassed him almost as acutely as Larwood had done four years earlier'. Bradman accused McCormick of bowling Bodyline. The Victorian captain Hans Ebeling felt it necessary to point out the obvious. How could it be Bodyline when there were only two leg-side fielders? Also, added Ebeling, the 'umpires haven't queried the bowling'. Bradman still repeated his charge. Ebeling threw it back at him: 'You captain your side and I'll look after mine,' he told him.

As captain of Australia, Bradman had no reservations about asking his own bowlers to be just as intimidating as Larwood. In 1946, he urged Keith Miller to punish Bill Edrich on a sticky wicket at Brisbane. 'I kept hitting him . . . bang . . . bang,' said Miller, knowing that the unplayable conditions that day guaranteed an Australian win anyway. Like a boxer deliberately backing off from an injured opponent, Miller started to 'ease up . . . slow down . . . fill in time', so that he could save Edrich from serious harm. Bradman came over to him and said: 'Bowl faster.' Miller didn't want to comply. 'We'd just finished a war, and it's like walking into another war. And that really turned me completely against Test cricket as it was played then,' he said.

On the 1948 tour to England, Bradman demanded that Miller bowl short to Len Hutton and Denis Compton. Hutton got five bouncers in eight balls. One of them struck him on the shoulder. 'It isn't very pleasant, is it?' Bradman said to Hutton with bridled resentment. 'I wasn't the only one who didn't like it,' he added, the remark a straightforward reference to Bodyline, as if defending both his captaincy in that moment and protecting his honour from 15 years before. Compton caught Bradman smiling to himself at cover at Hutton's discomfort. When he walked off with him, Compton made his point: 'I saw you were enjoying yourself just now. I can't really understand why and how you were. I thought you used to say this wasn't the right way to play cricket.' Bradman snapped back: 'You've got a bat in your hand, haven't you? You should be able to get out of the way of them anyway. I used to love it when I played against bouncers. I used to hook them.' Of course, he didn't hook Larwood much.

When Larwood twice stated again, in 1980 – first during a TV interview and then in a newspaper article – that he'd claimed Bradman's wicket before he'd got off the mark at Headingley half a century earlier, it provoked a response. Bradman protested and then counter-attacked. Just as Larwood felt it necessary to make the charge, so Bradman felt obliged to dismiss it. He denied that Larwood appealed for a catch in the first place. 'If Larwood made that statement (which I doubt) it is totally untrue and its publication is objectionable to me. It . . . casts aspersions on my sportsmanship. The truth is that no such incident occurred.' Resurrecting a complaint of his own, which he'd also originally made decades earlier, Bradman insisted that he hadn't touched the ball from Larwood that got him out at the Oval in the same series. 'It swung away slightly as I played it,' he claimed. 'Noticing the swing I turned my bat at the last moment and I was amazed when Larwood appealed (he was the only one who did) and more amazed still when the umpire gave me out.'

Larwood was then nearing his 76th birthday; Bradman had just reached his 72nd. They were two elderly men picking over and disputing a dim past. Still angry, after all those years.

* * *

Ill-feeling deepened on Larwood's part when Bradman assembled a 'travelling show' in which he was the prime exhibit.

Apart from the claim that he deliberately tried to seriously hurt or injure, the most toxic charge laid against Larwood was that he threw the ball. More than 25 years after the Bodyline series was over, Bradman implied that Larwood bowled certain balls – specifically his fastest one – with a bent elbow. In 1959, Bradman became Chairman of the Select Committee on Throwing, created by the South Australian Cricket Association. The following year, he began showing a strip of black-and-white film, which he reversed. Larwood appeared on the screen bowling left-handed to disguise his identity. At the moment when the ball was about to be released, Bradman frequently stopped the film to ask his audience to name the bowler and give an opinion about the action. The few seconds of Larwood footage – he was one of several bowlers on Bradman's home movie – was shown to former and current Test umpires in May 1960 in Adelaide and then again the following month to the Imperial Cricket Conference at Lord's, where the issue of what constituted fair bowling was discussed. The film 'brought a few gasps from the assembled dignitaries', said Richie Benaud, who was working for BBC Radio as well as the *News of the World*. But Benaud added crucially: 'He then showed the same film right-handed and there was no problem at all.'

Throwing became cricket's *cause célèbre* in the late 1950s and early 1960s. In 1958–59, the pace bowler Ian Meckiff finished with match figures of nine for 107 against England in the second Test at Melbourne, where Australia won by eight wickets. Accusations against him immediately followed. Jack Fingleton called his action 'suspect'. The former England spinners Johnny Wardle and Jim Laker were more direct. Wardle said that Meckiff had thrown England out. Laker added that he had the action of a darts player. English newspapers condemned 'chucker' Meckiff. Bradman was one of the Australian selectors who continued to pick him nonetheless. He was eventually called for throwing for Victoria against Western Australia in January 1963, and then called again seven weeks later. Finally, in the first Test against South Africa in December, Meckiff was called four times in his opening over. He retired shortly afterwards. Meckiff wasn't alone. The West Indian Charlie Griffith, Derbyshire's Harold 'Dusty' Rhodes and South Africa's Geoff Griffin were also called for throwing in a period when the legality of bowling dominated the thoughts of rule-makers and enforcers.

Bradman described throwing as 'the most complex problem I have known in cricket', and added that judging it was 'not a matter of fact but of opinion and interpretation'. Fingleton's interpretation of his friend Larwood's action was the polar opposite of Bradman's. He wrote: 'All I can say is that if there was the slightest suspicion of doubt in 1932–33 about Larwood we certainly would have "thrown" that at the Englishmen. None of us ever thought there was the slightest suspicion of his delivery.' As for Bradman's evidence, Fingleton suggested it was a 'whim of the camera'. He was making the obvious point. The Australian umpires of the early 1930s weren't virginal in matters of 'chucking'. Andrew Barlow called the Western Australian fast bowler Ron Halcombe six times in one over in a friendly against Victoria in Melbourne in 1930; Barlow called Eddie Gilbert eleven times for Queensland against Victoria at the end of 1931. Larwood was studied microscopically and from every conceivable angle during Bodyline. Newspapers printed long articles about his action and a million more words were written about it and him. Not one sentence questioned its validity. On the contrary: contemporary witness statements – from almost everyone who saw him – talked about its grace and fluidity. In *Cricket Crisis,* Fingleton wrote that Larwood's run to the wicket was a 'poem of athletic grace . . . as he neared the wickets he was in very truth like the *Flying Scotsman* thundering through an east coast station . . .'

Uncomfortably aware of Bradman's accusation, Larwood was publicly mute about it. To say anything would have dragged him into an unwelcome blizzard of publicity and jeopardized the ordered calm he had carefully built around himself and his home. He had no intention of upsetting his family, and he didn't want his name appearing in the newspapers. But he drew the obvious conclusion about Bradman's motive: that it was an escape clause for his accuser. If Bradman could imply that he threw the ball in 1932–33, it would tarnish Larwood's reputation and explain why Bradman 'failed' against him. When Fingleton asked Larwood about the question of throwing in a letter in the mid-1970s, he merely replied: 'I could never throw a ball. How they do beats me.'

* * *

The gift that Harold Larwood prized above all: the ashtray from Douglas Jardine.

Even when life became chilly and desolate, and he didn't want to think about the events responsible for it, there was one Bodyline memento Larwood cherished, as though it was blessed. A silver ashtray sat, immaculately polished, on his mantelpiece. Larwood looked at it and knew that his efforts were both worthwhile and had been properly rewarded. He showed off the ashtray to guests and recited the words engraved on it to them. He carried it from Nottingham to Blackpool and then to Australia. It was his most precious cricketing possession, and he had only to look at it to remember one man: Douglas Jardine.

Jardine gave it to him in June 1933. His central purpose on a Whit Monday, which fell during Nottinghamshire's Championship match against Surrey, was to hand over a cheque from the shilling fund created for Larwood and Voce. Around 20,000 people saw the money presented to them from the pavilion balcony at Trent Bridge. It was a simple ceremony. With his hair swept back but his bald spot visible, a white handkerchief just poking from the top pocket of his grey tweed suit, Jardine smiled warmly at Larwood. Jardine made a short speech, the sentences falling out in panting gulps, like a breaststroke swimmer rising from the water to take lungfuls of air. 'I was a fortunate captain,' he said of being able to call on Larwood. 'None of you,' he added, 'can have any conception of the mental courage' he had shown in Australia. Larwood came to the microphone, hitching up his flannels with both hands before reading from a single sheet of paper, which he held close to his face, as though straining his eyes to see the text. He was nervous, like a groom reluctantly giving his wedding speech. 'I find it very difficult to express in words what I feel,' he said, describing Jardine as one of the 'finest men I have ever met . . . a magnificent captain, a great sportsman and a true friend.'

The crowds had begun to turn their backs and head for home when Douglas Jardine made his own gift: an ashtray each for Voce and Larwood. The inscription on Larwood's ashtray – every word in capital letters – was heartfelt:

TO HAROLD FOR THE ASHES – 1932–33 –
FROM A GRATEFUL 'SKIPPER'

As he looked at the ashtray, tilting it like a mirror so that it glinted in the sun, he could only mumble his thanks. The ashtray is almost four inches in diameter and feels light in the hand. The size and weight of it don't adequately reflect its importance either to the man who received it or the man who gave it to him. For Larwood, the ashtray became the symbol of the Bodyline series, the evidence that he had nothing to be ashamed of. For Jardine, it was his way of articulating his gratitude to his fast bowler, something he was unable to do with the English language alone. Jardine paid for the ashtray out of his own pocket. The altruistic act was the final confirmation for Larwood that Jardine was one of the most exemplary human beings he had ever met: decent, fair, scrupulously loyal, staunchly committed to Larwood's own cause. While others tried to make him feel like a shabby failure, Jardine was steadfast, and a true officer. Larwood would have trusted him with his life, and the lives of his children too. He knew it to be so whenever he picked up the ashtray and read those final four words again: 'From a Grateful Skipper'.

Jardine always tried to look after him; even from a distance. During the ramifications of Bodyline in the early summer of 1933, he wrote a 'private and confidential' letter to Nottinghamshire supporting Larwood. 'I should be less than human,' he said in the letter, 'if I had not developed a vast mother love, affection and pride for the side.' Jardine meant his fast bowler in particular.

In December 1954, Larwood was invited to lunch with Jardine at Sydney's Pickwick Club. His captain was attending to business in a country that, despite Bodyline, he liked enormously. Larwood and Jardine sat beside one another at a polished oval table in a discreet booth. Along with ex-Australian cricketers – including Bert Oldfield and Arthur Mailey – Larwood and Jardine went through a convivial ritual of remembrance about Bodyline. One of the other guests, Charlie Macartney, who was Larwood's first Test wicket in 1926, told him he would have 'belted the cover off Bodyline balls' if he'd played in the series. He might have done too. The 'Governor-General' of Australian cricket once hit 345 against Nottinghamshire – well before Larwood broke into the team – in less than four hours, striking 47 fours. Johnny Taylor, another Test batsman, was sure he would have played Larwood 'with a broomstick'. The host was Robert Menzies, the Australian Prime Minister. He turned to the final guest, Warren Bardsley, who had scored 53 centuries in his career, and said he'd been one of the most accomplished left-handed batsmen cricket had ever seen. 'People will talk about you after I'm dead and gone,' he said. Within a month, Bardsley had died, aged 71.

Larwood remembered his goodbye handshake with Jardine, the two of them standing on the hot pavement. 'Goodbye, Harold,' said Jardine. 'It's been lovely to see you.' Larwood took Jardine's right hand and firmly gripped his captain's forearm at the same time. 'Come back and see me again soon, Skipper,' he said, and meant it. Larwood watched Jardine walk briskly away, head up and back straight, as if going out to bat against the Australians. He neither saw nor spoke to him again.

He was nonetheless always 'Mr Jardine' or 'Skipper'. Larwood never referred to him by his Christian name. Even decades after Bodyline it was as though calling him 'Douglas' would have been a desecration or the breaking of a cross-your-heart promise. 'I was brought up to respect elderly people and gentlemen,' Larwood explained. 'I admired him as captain and still do. He was Mr then and he's Mr now, and that's the way he'll stay to me.' Asked what he thought of his captain in 1933, Larwood replied simply: 'I loved him.' The statement was strikingly unusual for the period. Grown men – especially from pit backgrounds – didn't publicly admit platonic love. It is a sign of how much Jardine meant to Larwood; how much, in fact, he would always mean to him.

Who was the greater cricketer between Bradman and Jardine? Larwood never doubted that it was Bradman. Who was the greater man? Larwood never doubted that it was Jardine.

* * *

To keep Larwood company, Jack Fingleton tried to persuade Bill Voce to emigrate to Australia too. Voce, however, couldn't wrench himself away from the green fields of Nottinghamshire and the marked change in its seasons. Even the mist and snow and spring showers held him to England. 'I'd miss it all too much,' he said of his home. Larwood missed very little. He gave up England as easily as a seat on a train.

There were essentially two reasons why, once he'd reached Australia and begun to settle in, he was able to forget England. The first was a personal tragedy. When he left his parents a few days before sailing for Australia, Larwood knew he'd never see them again. His father Robert was 73; his mother Mary 71. A telegram arrived for him exactly a month after he docked. This telegram, which still exists among the family's heirlooms, is creased and faded, the paper so worn that it feels as if it might flake away in your hand. The bleak message is still readable, the words spelt in grey capital letters:

DAD PASSED AWAY TODAY.
MOTHER

Larwood could never bring himself to throw it away. As he held the telegram in his hand, the funeral was already planned. Within weeks, his brother Joe had died of a heart condition too; he was only 40 years old. Of his four brothers, Joe was the one whom he'd tried to convince to join him in Sydney.

The second reason was the chilliness shown towards him by England touring parties in 1950–51 and 1954–55. As an ex-player and working journalist during the 1950–51 tour, he expected to be invited into the dressing room. He knew the captain, Freddie Brown, who had been the youngest member of Jardine's team. He remembered Brown, who didn't play in any of the Bodyline Tests, as an affable figure with a clean, broad smile, someone for whom the series seemed more social and recreational than sporting. He'd raised no complaints about Jardine's tactics or

Larwood's implementation of them either during the tour or after it. Larwood assumed that Brown viewed him favourably. But Brown compressed his mouth into a slit when he saw him and, apart from a surly 'hello' and the slight nod of his head in acknowledgement, Brown refused to speak to Larwood at length, ostentatiously turning his back and pointedly not shaking hands with him in front of the other players.

When Larwood tried to get into the dressing room, he said he 'wasn't allowed . . . In fact, one man [it was Brown] shut the door in my face.' Despite his membership of the MCC, despite the fact that almost a quarter of a century separated him from the Bodyline affair and despite his diffident, disarming manner – 'Harold wouldn't hurt a fly,' said Keith Miller, 'he was no trouble to anyone' – Brown was demonstrably aloof, as if Larwood was tainted by history. Larwood was mortified and embarrassed. He wasn't just another journalist nosing around for juicy gossip and a cheap headline. He was a former fast bowler who wanted to meet the team, talk cricket and catch up with the news about his friends.

His reception was antagonistic in 1954–55 also. Larwood, holding a bat to be autographed, claimed he found Trevor Bailey at the dressing-room door. He said that Bailey didn't bother with any pleasantries and told him: 'I don't want the bat,' as if italicizing the words for effect. Larwood hurled it through the open door, and watched it slide across the floor. 'I don't want it either,' he replied, walking away as Bailey gripped the frame of the door. Bailey described the claim as 'utter rubbish' and added: 'I suppose Freddie Brown was cold towards him because he didn't like Bodyline. But as a tactic, I thought it was a pretty good idea and I liked and admired Harold.'

The general hostility 'hurt me very much', said Larwood, nonetheless. He didn't broadcast how upset he was by the incidents he described. He was too genial and gentle to make a complaint about someone else's rudeness. Anyway, he said, such insensitivity was no more than an irritating gnat's bite compared with the MCC cutting him off in 1933. 'I didn't go near an England touring party unless one of them got in touch with me,' he said. There were fleeting compensations. Larwood discovered that Frank Tyson thought as highly of him as Ray Lindwall did. When Tyson asked whether he could meet him, Larwood willingly agreed. If asked, he would always decant his knowledge of fast bowling like fine wine. Tyson's first glimpse of Larwood wasn't what he had expected. 'I pictured him,' he said, 'as a not excessively tall individual, a squat,

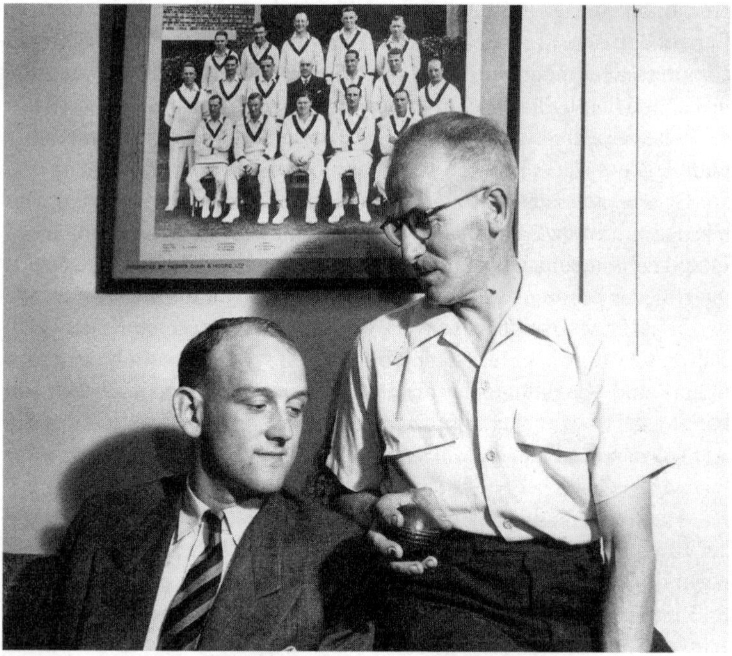

Frank Tyson asked whether he could call on Harold Larwood. Of course, said Larwood, and promptly went to the fridge for two beers after he arrived.

powerfully built man, perhaps still retaining some of his crinkly hair. I was completely wrong.' Tyson found a 'slight' and 'balding' Larwood, who immediately headed for the fridge to bring out the beer.

While England appeared to think of Larwood as damaged goods, the Australians and the West Indians took the opposite view. Frank Worrell and Richie Benaud treated him like an honoured guest. Worrell took Larwood into the dressing room and painstakingly introduced him to each player in turn. He made him feel wanted. Benaud spoke warmly and gave Larwood the respect his career statistics demanded. He was grateful for such generosity. 'Strange, isn't it?' Larwood observed. 'In the 1950s I got treated better by the countries I didn't play for. The country I did play for didn't really want to know me.' The snubs drove him closer into the arms of Australia. He set out with a primary purpose, to become a 'New

Australian', one of those migrants sailing daily into the ports who were prepared willingly to shed the past like a suit of old clothes that didn't fit them any more. There was no point, he decided, in attempting to fashion a future for himself if he clung so firmly to England.

There were plenty of men like Larwood, characters for whom life had soured or been drained of its colour, forcing them to move on and start again in Australia. Early on there was sometimes resentment and disappointment in this nomadic displacement, the sense that fortune had failed them somehow and forced them abroad. You didn't travel as far as Australia unless there was something back home that for whatever reason you could no longer face. But you still took pieces of that home with you; the memories that couldn't possibly be expunged, naturally, and also albums and framed photographs that were windows through which you could gaze at what you'd left behind and the person you'd once been. And for most of the new arrivals – Larwood among them – even the resentment at leaving England was held in check by a clear-eyed, frequently over-confident vision of what their arrival would be like. Australia made lavish promises to them. The migrants headed into the heart of it with the eager optimism of prospectors during a gold rush. Some would still experience a different kind of failure there. But not Larwood.

He carried his trophies and his cricketing ephemera with him like rusted treasure. A benefactor, whom Larwood had never met, took out a subscription to the *Football Post,* Nottingham's Saturday-night sports paper. The stranger posted it to him every week so that he wouldn't miss the scores and league tables. But he wasn't sentimental about leaving. The decision was made; there would never be a retreat back to England. As ever, he took the practical and pragmatic view about what he'd done. He'd accepted that the weight of his life had shifted from one continent to another, and he would make the very best of it. He wanted to live like an Australian, and adopt Australian attitudes and outlooks – wherever he found them. He wanted to look at Australia as if seeing it afresh, and fit into it rather than become just another Englishman forced over there with queasy apprehension. And he wanted to show his appreciation to Australia for 'taking him in', as if he'd been orphaned. In England, he'd been used to the pecking order of the class system, which he found puzzling and unjust. Larwood didn't noticeably find such divisions in Australia, where equality, he felt, was a right. Natural English reserve often made strangers appear aloof and patronizing. Not in Australia, said Larwood, where 'everyone seems to want to talk to you' – even those who had no idea about his background or circumstances.

Larwood was confident that Fingleton would fix up a job for him. He was just adamant about one thing: he didn't want to collect a wage or be given a job or title on the strength of his name alone. Larwood saw himself as an ordinary working man and he preferred to 'work like anyone else' too. He didn't see himself as a figurehead for a company; he was too shy to fulfil that sort of role. He didn't see himself as desk-bound either; he lacked a fluent command of written English. He sought 'plain, ordinary work' – something to make him pleasantly tired but satisfied with his efforts at the end of the day. He was determined not to be distant or aloof, or to trade on his reputation as a cricketer of the past. 'When it came to work people always asked whether there was anything I wanted done on my behalf,' he remembered. 'I said to them: "Well, I'll do anything but I don't want you to use my name to get it. I just want to get a job the same as any other man. I'll go out in the morning, I'll come home in the evening, I'll make enough to raise my family. That'll suit me fine."'

* * *

Work in Australia became an unassuming and unglamorous job with the anchor of routine attached to it. He'd been hired by one soft drinks company, Pepsi-Cola, where he began on the production line, and then moved on to another firm, Cottee's. He was a stock controller, making sure that distribution lorries left the warehouse carrying a full load. He preferred to be behind the scenes, where no one but his colleagues could see him. Larwood would leave home between 5 a.m. and 6 a.m. to open the factory doors. He left late at night because he had to lock them again after the last truck or van arrived back and the driver checked in. The work might have been dreary and monotonous for some. Larwood's philosophy was: 'Switch off and get stuck in.' Often on duty six days a week, he had almost no free time to establish a social life. He lived a plain, simple and uncomplicated life. Without a car, it was difficult to travel. On Sunday, family friends – also migrants from England – occasionally took Larwood and Lois for a drive. Sometimes he, Lois and the younger daughters walked to the seaside suburb of Coogee. In England, Lois washed clothes by hand and stored her food in a pantry. Now she had a

Harold Larwood indulges in a rare piece of publicity for his employers, Pepsi.

fridge and an automatic washing machine. These were the Larwoods' only luxuries until 1956 when another arrived: a television set. Larwood bought the first TV in the street to watch the Olympic Games from Melbourne. Soon the Larwoods' lounge began to resemble 'the front stalls at the picture house every night'. Neighbours' wives brought plates of home-cooked food; their husbands carried the beer. Larwood settled down each Monday evening for his favourite programme, *I Love Lucy.*

In what remained of his spare time, Larwood tended his garden, which was already well established with fruit trees and native shrubs. He cleared the peach, mulberry and plum trees to create his own *Good Life* – a vegetable garden, where he cultivated new potatoes and his own tomatoes. For Lois, he grew flowers: sweet peas, pansies and marigolds. He liked the slow, uncluttered pattern of a quiet existence that made few demands on him. This was the way he wanted to live, and he had everything he wanted. He rolled his own cigarettes and took beer from the fridge.

He'd been used to the cold, and the constant chore of wrapping up warm against it during long English winters. In Australia, he liked the iridescent blues of a sky that resembled polished glass, the ravishing colours and ferocious glare, a light as white as milk. 'We have a short winter – only three months,' he wrote to a friend in Nottingham. 'No snow, no ice, no fog.' He would often add: 'I do the garden in my shirt-sleeves most of the time.' He'd been used to cramped, almost claustrophobic English towns that seemed filthy after the destitution of the War. In Australia, he relished 'the sense of space' and the 'spic and span' streets and the wide spaces: 'vast seas of land', as he put it in a charming oxymoron. He continued, nonetheless, to think about what he termed 'The Old Country', explaining: 'One of the places I should like to see is Trent Bridge, so I keep saving and hope to win the lottery.'

Larwood preferred to stay away from cricket. He only had to leave his front gate, turn smartly right and stroll a hundred yards to find the nearest pitch. He nearly always turned left instead. He neither coached nor watched matches there in case he 'got in the way'. He didn't want a coach or player to think that he was trying to 'interfere because of my name'. In fact, Larwood never used his name for anything unless it was necessary.

If Lois bought something that needed to be delivered to the bungalow, she would order in the surname of one of her sons-in-law. Her husband did likewise. He worried that giving his name would lead to a predictable set of questions, which he didn't want to answer, and 'a lot of fuss', which he 'didn't want to get involved in'.

By 1964 he was reluctantly giving an interview in which he said: 'I'm forgotten now. When I came here, most of my work mates were immigrants from places in Europe who don't know anything about me, my name or cricket. That suits me fine. I worked my way up from the line to become a supervisor on my own initiative, not through my name. Apart from friends and the neighbours no one knows me.'

Larwood was wrong. For on that very day a letter with an English postmark lay on his dining table. The sender had written on the envelope:

Harold Larwood
Notts and England Cricketer
Somewhere near Sydney
Australia

The Australian postal service always recognized Harold Larwood, and knew where to find him.

* * *

His five daughters married, had children, took jobs and became Australians. He was soon describing the Larwoods as 'fair dinkum Aussies' and emigrating as 'the best thing I've ever done'. He said: 'We're all Aussies now. We told the girls that we'd pay for them to go home if any of them didn't like it here. But we're all still together.'

He relished the obscurity of the country, so vast he could get lost in it. And then publication of an autobiography, *The Larwood Story*, drew him into the public gaze again in 1965.

His ghost-writer, Kevin Perkins, urged Larwood to leave his own account of Bodyline for his five daughters. He argued that no one on the 'inside' of Douglas Jardine's team – players or management – had given a full or entirely detailed account of 1932–33. So much of what happened had just been whispered about, like a dark family secret that no one wanted to share. Larwood himself had been sketched only in faint outline. No book had reached into the depths of the series and pulled out his true personality, his background and motivations, or dwelt at all on what drove him on. Larwood needed to write history from his own perspective. It took five years of persuasion and almost another two before the book was finished. The hard fragments of Larwood's memory were slowly welded together with the statistical evidence from score-cards, newspaper cuttings and books. Larwood was nervous. He was not only worried about upsetting the other participants in Bodyline. He was also concerned about antagonizing the country that had given him shelter and succour, and so much else besides. He didn't want his family to face the flak for anything he wrote. He didn't want more mail lambasting him for something he'd done half a lifetime ago. And he didn't want to find himself defending his book afterwards. Always on his guard, Larwood had skimmed over or skirted around questions about Donald Bradman

Members of the 1965–66 MCC touring team visit Harold and Lois Larwood in their Sydney bungalow. From left to right: Colin Cowdrey, tour manager Billy Griffith, Jeff Jones and Ken Barrington.

or Douglas Jardine and the five Tests of the Bodyline series during the fifteen years since arriving in Australia. In committing himself to print, he was taking a risk.

The book was published in England, where it sold 20,000 copies. Reading the memoir, it is obvious that Larwood is holding himself back on the page. The reader glimpses only part of him – his shadow, perhaps. With hindsight, the observant reader learns as much about Larwood from the gaps he purposely leaves unfilled in the narrative – the scale of his desperation and dejection after Bodyline, his row with Bill Voce in 1936, his opinion of Don Bradman's personality, his financial hardships both pre- and post-war, his trepidation about leaving England for Australia and the accusations of throwing. Between the lines, you draw the conclusion that here is someone so deeply hurt that he cannot articulate it; someone so careful in what he says, and reluctant to cause offence, in case that level of hurt returns; someone so utterly bewildered about why it happened to him at all that he still can't fully grasp the reasons behind it; and someone who feels terribly wronged but is determined to retain his dignity and pride. John Arlott detected it in his review in *Wisden*. He wrote that it was 'not complete'.

The book was generally well received. Larwood's fears of being a pariah again were unfounded. He actually gained emotionally as well as financially from it. Later in the same year, England arrived in Australia for the 1965–66 Ashes series. Perkins went to the manager, Billy Griffith, and told him that Larwood was still downcast and believed no one in English cricket cared about him. Would Griffith arrange for a couple of players to call on Larwood in his Sydney bungalow? Of course, said Griffith. Colin Cowdrey and Jeff Jones visited Larwood, who was blissfully unaware that Perkins and Griffith had arranged it. From then on, Larwood's bungalow became the unwritten venue on every Ashes tour itinerary. There was always a knock at the door. Pace bowlers, such as Chris Old and Bob Willis, called. Cowdrey always visited Larwood, a boyhood hero. Larwood was so reluctant to go to the Sydney Cricket Ground that Colin Cowdrey had to take him there in a taxi in 1971 after nearly an hour of gentle arm-twisting. 'Harold didn't want to go,' said Cowdrey. 'We spent a lot of time persuading him that he'd enjoy himself.' He did enjoy himself.

'Will you pose for a photograph with Bert Oldfield?' asked a photographer. Larwood and Oldfield smiled into the lens like long-lost

Former Bodyline foes: Messrs Oldfield (second from left) and Larwood with the boots that the fast bowler wore during the 1932–33 series.

brothers reunited. When the photograph was published the following morning, Larwood began receiving calls and letters, as if people had only just realized he was still alive. He became properly reacquainted with Oldfield, and the two of them began lunching regularly together.

On the 1958–59 MCC tour, Fred Trueman, unaware of Larwood's previously chastening experiences with England, had specifically asked George Duckworth to introduce him. 'Larwood was part of my growing up,' he said. 'Everyone who was a fast bowler wanted to be as good and as quick as him.' Trueman ushered the always-reluctant Larwood into the inner sanctum. What he witnessed was a sharp example of bad feeling on Bradman's part. 'Lol', said Trueman, 'was talking to the players before Bradman walked in. He spoke to everyone else, took one look at Larwood and walked straight past him without a word.'

Now, with the 1970–71 Ashes series won under Ray Illingworth, Larwood was invited into the England dressing room again. The celebrations had begun, and Larwood spoke with the players about his own tours of Australia. And then Bradman appeared. He came in smiling and shook a few hands before his eyes began to scan the people around him. The moment Bradman saw Larwood, the smile fell away, as if someone had just handed him a telegram with bad news in it. His muscles stiffened, the set of his mouth became grim. Larwood introduced his son-in-law to Bradman and began some small talk. The atmosphere between them was 'cordial but cold'. Bradman lingered long enough not to make his departure appear blatantly rude. But very soon he swivelled his body like a gun turret and left at a brisk step.

The two men were still professionally and personally incompatible, and found it difficult to breathe the same air.

CHAPTER FOURTEEN

I LOVE A SUNBURNT COUNTRY

March 1977 – 1995

The Sydney Cricket Ground marks Larwood's 98 in the final Bodyline Test by re-creating the scoreboard of that day. The Sydney Cricket Club also honoured Larwood with membership.

Melbourne Cricket Ground: March 1977 – Kingsford: 1995

The invitation to the Centenary Test Celebration Dinner in Melbourne was elegantly laid out: an elaborate font in black ink on a square of stiff white card.

The President, Members and Committee
of the
Melbourne Cricket Club
Request the pleasure of the company of

Mr. H. LARWOOD

The recipient stared at his name, which had been typed imperfectly along a dotted line. His first instinct was promptly to reject it. So was his second instinct, and his third. It was as though he regarded the invitation as a Trojan horse, an ostensibly grand gift, but with something harmful hiding within it. Had he been asked to the dinner out of courtesy? Would anyone there want to see him? Wasn't there the probability that the celebration of Test matches between England and Australia might be spoilt or, at the very least, soiled by the mention of Bodyline? Would there be any personal hostility towards him? Those questions swarmed around Larwood, like wasps shaken from a nest.

He felt exactly as he'd done after receiving the invitation to Donald Bradman's lunch in 1948. He fretted about the consequences of accepting.

The years had gone by steadily, accumulating in the way that sand accrues at the bottom of an hourglass, but he thought of himself as young just yesterday; and he could recall Bodyline in his mind as if it had happened just yesterday too. But Harold Larwood was 72 now, and he believed the past was best left undisturbed. Bruised cricket balls sat on silver plinths in his bungalow in Sydney. Engraved on them were Larwood's distant performances: six for 24 against Yorkshire in 1928; five for 96 and five for 28 in the Sydney Test of the same year; six for 32 at Brisbane. Large black-and-white photographs in thick wood frames, attached by long string from metal hooks, hung on the walls. Here was a gallery of Test matches and faces: Stan McCabe, Douglas Jardine, Bill Woodfull, Walter Hammond and Les Ames. 'I'm young again when I look at them,' he said to visitors. 'It's the only time I get nostalgic.'

In the 27 years since his emigration to Australia, Larwood had seldom gone looking for publicity. Sometimes, however, reporters and television had come looking for him. Occasionally he was interviewed by newspapers. Documentaries and short programmes were made for TV. He and Keith Miller once reminisced together in front of a camera, both as stiffly formal as the other, as if acting from a script. He did some radio work too. On each occasion Larwood was like a man taking a bow reluctantly, always shading his eyes against the spotlight as it fell across him. Asked whether he saw many old cricketers, he would reply: 'Only when I go out – and I hardly ever go out.' Asked if he watched much cricket, he'd point out: 'Really only on TV or listening to it on radio.' Asked about cricket in general, he'd confess: 'I've lost interest in it.'

'I just want things to revolve around my family,' he explained innocently. 'I want to stay at home and be very quiet about it.'

The Centenary Test was not going to be a quiet affair. It threatened to break into his tidy domesticity like a thief, and steal his privacy again. There would be TV cameras, radio and a battalion of journalists. It also guaranteed another meeting with Bradman.

* * *

The invitation sat on the mantelpiece, where it became a burden rather than an honour. His emotions about it were contradictory. On one level he was afraid of revisiting Bodyline in case the Australians turned their backs on him again. On another, he didn't think that anyone connected with it would be interested enough to see him. As well as lacking an appetite for self-advertisement, the modest Larwood had no idea of his publicity value and didn't understand how much other cricketers wanted to reminisce with him. Another reason not to go to Melbourne was his reluctance to be seen as an old man. Always conscious of how he appeared to other people, Larwood wanted to be remembered as he had been – not as what he'd become. In 1968, on his first visit to England, he replied without pausing to a question about whether he'd make regular visits from then on. 'I'll tell you one thing,' he said. 'You'll never see me if I have to use a stick to get around or start to look really old.' Illogical as it sounds, he seemed to believe he was the only one that Time had aged. 'I much prefer to remember my friends as they were. And it would be nice if they'd remember me as I was,' he said.

Jack Fingleton urged him to go to Melbourne. His friends wouldn't care if he'd aged, said Fingleton: Bill Voce, Bill Bowes, Keith Miller and Fingleton himself wanted to share the event with him. Larwood wrote back to Fingleton offering lame excuses. His letter read like the telegram Proust used to send to hosts who asked him to dinner parties: 'Cannot Come. Lie Follows.'

'At my age,' said Larwood, 'my idea of watching cricket is on TV. How people can sit in hard seats in the hot sun day after day is beyond me.' He further dismissed the idea with another inadequate argument. 'As you know,' he told Fingleton, 'my interest in cricket these days is very low.' Fingleton didn't believe him. He knew that Larwood was wary of ghosts. He was also protecting himself against the expectation of disappointment.

At last Larwood revealed to Fingleton the real reason why he wanted to forget that the invitation had ever arrived. He was 'very, very nervous' about how he might be received in Melbourne. 'I have no wish to be embarrassed in front of the huge crowds that will be there,' he said, without explaining how such an embarrassment might occur. Larwood thought his short letter would close the argument, snapping it shut like the lid of a box. The Centenary Test would go on without him. He'd read about it in the newspapers. He might – if he cared enough about it – switch on the television. Fingleton could tell him how everything went, and pass on messages later. He would stay in his bungalow, thank you very much. 'If I say I'm not going now, then at least I can stop worrying about it,' he wrote to Fingleton, and closed with the line: 'No, we'll be staying at home and that's an end to it.'

It wasn't the end at all. His resistance towards the Centenary Test was gradually worn down in the same way that the steady drip of water eventually smooths even the hardest slab of rock. Fingleton constantly tried to coax Larwood to Melbourne. He'd be well looked after, Fingleton said. The years would soon fall away once he began talking cricket. The experience would show how tenderly others regarded him. The experience of 'catching up' would do him good. Fingleton thought his emollient approach had failed. He resolved nonetheless to ring Larwood one final time. Larwood never answered his own phone. He delegated the job to Lois. She picked up Fingleton's call and said crisply: 'I've told him he's got to go and that's the end of it.' Mrs Larwood held sway. She told him it would look 'peculiar' if he didn't attend, as if he was 'insulting Lord's' in retribution for its treatment of him. She pointed out there'd be people there who would want to talk to him. She would be beside him, anyway; there was nothing to worry about. She was sure he'd be embraced, not ignored.

Jittery and self-conscious, Larwood chain-smoked on his arrival in Melbourne in March 1977. He was unable to rid himself of the terrible notion that the decision to come might end badly for him. 'He was shy at first, and nervous,' said Joe Hardstaff junior, his former team-mate at Nottinghamshire. 'But as soon as he saw me and some of his old pals, he began to open up. He became himself again.' Around him were men who moved with crabbed slowness, men who were easily winded through walking too far, men who had bulldog folds of flesh, men who had lost weight, and men who strained to see one another clearly. 'Lol was surprised that we were as old as him,' added Hardstaff.

Larwood eventually described the Centenary Test as: 'One of the best events in my life.' The days floated by, and he would 'not have missed them for the world'. The official photograph captures Larwood on the front row beside – who else? – Bill Voce. His official pass dangles from his buttonhole like a dog tag. Further along the line is Denis Compton, his face jowly and his once-sleek black hair silver and thinning; Godfrey Evans, his mutton-chop whiskers in need of a trim; Bill Bowes, casually leaning back in his chair in a pale summer jacket, as if sitting in his own garden in the afternoon sun. Larwood met Percy Fender, his straggly moustache spread across his top lip like wings. With Voce inseparably at Larwood's shoulder again, the three comrades talked with respect of the one man who wasn't there – Douglas Jardine. Stories were swapped, beer drunk, and the gathering of what Larwood called 'friends and enemies of years ago' made him both 'sentimental' and 'grateful'. With an amalgam of surprise and relief, he said the conversations 'repaid me for making the decision to come to Melbourne'.

Far from being forgotten or shunned, Larwood became a celebrity again. Everyone, it seemed, wanted something from him – an autograph, a memory shared, a photograph or a few words. As Larwood admitted to his family, as though not quite believing his reception: 'I am treated now more as a hero than a villain.'

However difficult he found it to comprehend, his status as fêted old-time master was obvious in the letters that Lois sent to the family from Melbourne. 'Here was dad,' she said proudly, 'surrounded by children and adults all wanting his autograph . . . so bad one morning it was

Donald Bradman makes a point to Harold Larwood during the Centenary Test. Dennis Lillee looks on.

impossible to sign anything until one of the officials got the crowd to form a line. I thought he would be stuck there all day. As the line shortened, it would fill up again. It's a wonder he didn't get a sore arm.' In a letter he wrote to his daughters, Larwood's astonishment at the courtesy shown to him, and the size of the crowds, is transparent and humbling. 'Now here, mum and I have quite settled down,' he begins, 'we are being treated like "Royalty". I am very, very pleased we came.'

Larwood stood in the MCG long room 'close enough' to have 'touched' both the Queen and Prince Philip. 'It was a very, very big thrill for me,' he wrote. 'I also had a long chat with Sir Donald Bradman, and mum talked with Lady Bradman. I was very pleased that mum shared all these glory's [sic] with me . . . she enjoyed it in her quiet way, and I endeavoured to be with her as much as possible.'

Bradman and Larwood were photographed together, ostensibly swapping stories about the good old days. Larwood had a cigarette and a wine glass in his left hand; Bradman – who could hush a room through awe simply by entering it – illogically wore a large name badge on his left lapel, as if one of the most famous men in Australia needed to be identified. There were anodyne remarks about the occasion, about the number of familiar faces jammed in one place, about family matters and the weather. 'We didn't talk about cricket,' said Larwood flatly; of course, he meant Bodyline.

Bradman still upset him. During his unsatisfactory and over-long speech at the official dinner, Bradman avoided mentioning Bodyline directly, saying tersely: 'I will pass over the turbulent years.' When he finished speaking, Larwood didn't join the standing ovation. He remained in his seat, as if someone had clamped him to it. He thought the phrase 'turbulent years' was a euphemism that was unnecessary and demeaned his own skill and the efforts of others, such as Voce and Jardine. Bradman might have used the speech to heal the rift. Instead, by specifically not talking about Bodyline, he made it conspicuous again in Larwood's eyes.

Speaking of his stroll to the Melbourne wicket with Voce, Larwood explained that he had been 'pressed' into it. 'I did it only for the sakes of my daughters and all our grandchildren, so I hope you all watched it, for I was thinking of you whilst on the middle of this huge ground and huge crowd.' The confession near the end of his letter was typical Larwood: 'As usual, I was very nervous but managed to finish it off OK,' he said. Larwood's final verdict on the Test was succinct: 'It has done me a lot of good.' And so it had. The ex-cricketer who had least wanted to attend now didn't want to leave.

His stay in Melbourne was wearying – a round of official receptions and dinners and informal get-togethers. But he discovered for himself what others had been telling him all along. No one wanted to criticize him for Bodyline. Most just wanted to find out more about it. There was a compelling interest in the 1932–33 series, which the Centenary Test stirred with its remembrance of things past. The generations following Larwood's own had seen the Tests in newsreel flashes on television or read about them in books. The players, the hard facts and the circumstances of Bodyline's implementation – often even the series result – were hazy to them, like a photograph taken with a shaky hand. Anxious to hear as much as possible about 1932–33, the public queued to listen to first-hand accounts from white-haired survivors such as Larwood before it was too late. Most of the autograph-hunters, not even born when Larwood emigrated to Australia, wanted to know how such a pin-thin, kindly man had once managed to bowl so quickly and meanly. Their grandfathers were just pleased to shake the hand that had propelled the ball at more than 95 mph, and tell him shyly: 'I saw you play, you know.' Larwood smiled. 'Now there's a funny thing,' he said afterwards, 'if everyone who said they saw me play actually did see me play, you'd have needed a ground half the size of New South Wales to fit them all in.'

Larwood had experienced nothing like his frenzied reception since returning to Nottingham in 1933. One question followed another.

> 'Were you quicker than anyone else, Mr Larwood?'
>
> 'It's difficult to say,' he replied without preening. 'I never saw myself bowl.'
>
> 'Would Don Bradman survive nowadays?'
>
> 'He'd flourish. He was the greatest batman there's ever been . . . probably ever will be.' He was gently pushed on the point: 'But didn't he fail when you bowled at him in those Tests?' Eyes bright with remembering, Larwood paused before answering. 'He didn't fail. You don't fail when you average over 50.'
>
> 'What was Douglas Jardine really like?'
>
> 'He was a great man, a very good batsman and captain and I was proud – and am still proud – to have played under him.'

* * *

All rising to great places is by a twisting stair, and the path Larwood took was labyrinthine. The dark, careworn decades in England, and the years striving to make a living and a new life in Australia, had eventually led him to Melbourne and a late but glorious summer that seemed to him implausible. 'To think I nearly stayed at home,' he said to his family. Just by being himself, Larwood impressed everyone he met. He came across as neither bitter nor boastful, and self-effacing to the point of deprecation. 'Why would anyone want my signature?' he'd say. He wasn't angling for compliments. Larwood had spent so long imagining he'd be ignored that he couldn't conceive that the opposite was true.

Afterwards, letters began to pile up for him and he insisted – as he'd always done – that he should reply to each one, irrespective of whether the sender wanted to grouse, clarify a point about Bodyline or ask for a signed photograph. He'd always been ridiculously kindhearted in 'giving away' souvenirs: blazers, sweaters, pairs of boots, cricket balls on plinths, copies of photographs. He never asked for money. 'I've got so many things,' he'd say. 'At least mum has got a bit more space around the house.' More callers arrived at his bungalow, many of them journalists. He was asked his opinions on contemporary cricket. 'Well,' he said, 'I can't stand all the kissing and hugging after a wicket's been taken. It's disgusting. Even after we got Bradman out, we didn't go around embracing one another. I lay on the ground to get my breath back for the next batsman and everyone else went to their positions in the field.' He wanted batsmen to attack the bowling: 'In my day, the batsmen used to come down the track at you. Now they're stuck in the crease like startled rabbits.' He disliked helmets. 'I hate to say it, but there doesn't seem to be the same pride or even physical courage around these days. Most of the Australian batsmen I bowled against wouldn't have been seen dead in one . . . all the padding must restrict players' movements. I wouldn't have minded bowling against batsmen wrapped up in cotton wool like that.'

Within four months of returning from Melbourne, Larwood was watching the Australians at Trent Bridge. Three years later, in 1980, on his final visit to England, he saw Voce for the last time. As part of his itinerary, the friends were brought together, like old theatrical troupers, as guests of Kirkby Portland Cricket Club where Larwood had begun his bowling career half a century earlier. The two bespectacled men strolled around the outfield in highly polished shoes. In the glare of the sun, which caused them to hood their eyes with their hands, they stared at the low hills and the pasture land and the roofline of the nearby villages. Larwood jabbed his finger at distant landmarks and talked about ghosts from the past. In fact, he couldn't stop talking . . .

Even at 71, Voce looked a bear of a man. His back was perfectly straight, and his huge, bucket-like hands hung by his side. Larwood was almost miniature beside him, his tie neatly tucked into a grey V-necked sweater which he wore under his blue jacket. As Larwood reminisced, Voce nodded and added to the stories Larwood was telling. Sometimes he politely corrected his friend about a score or the bowling figures, a batsman or the weather on the day of the game. Voce reminded him that he always gave Larwood the best end from which to bowl – the breeze at his back, the slope in his favour. Larwood and Voce pieced together all their yesterdays into a whole, colourful tapestry of wickets and runs and catches. 'The mind plays tricks, Bill,' said Larwood, laughing and then playfully gripping his pal's elbow. It never mattered how long the separation between them had been. Whenever Larwood and Voce came together – even if the break had been several years – the conversation flowed naturally and seamlessly, as if the friends had just seen one another a few hours earlier and were picking up the line of a conversation that was still warm.

Larwood and Voce walked, as if joined at the hip, across to The Cricketers' Arms. They sat around a dark oak table in the corner of the bar. Their pints of beer left heavy rings on the wood. Larwood began to drain his beer and talk about his life in Australia, Nottinghamshire's Championship-winning side, the modern era. Voce sat smiling, pleased to hear his voice and remembering along with him. A gust came through the open window behind him. Voce turned to his loquacious friend and stopped him in mid-sentence. 'Harold,' he said, 'even after all these years you've still got the wind behind you.'

* * *

Back home in north Notts in 1977, Harold and Lois (centre) share memories with Bill Voce and his wife Elsie (right) and Frank Woodhead and his wife (left).

Larwood and Voce in the garden of The Cricketers' Arms, just a well-hit six from the ground where Harold began his career.

Night fell prematurely for Harold Larwood. 'As a fast bowler, I always thought my legs would go,' he said with resignation, 'but it was my eyes instead.' At first it seemed to him as if the lenses of his glasses were streaked with grime. He dismissed it as a case of feeble eyesight, the penalty of growing old. But then the world became blurry and the objects in it hard to define. Patches of light appeared around them, the way dawn breaks around the edges of a bedroom curtain. For a while he confessed the problems to no one; not even to Lois. He tried to carry on as if nothing had changed. He manoeuvred himself from memory around the house and garden and made excuses about why he couldn't play ball games with his grandchildren. He struggled through the cryptic crosswords in the morning newspaper, bringing the grid and its clues closer to his eyes. He pretended to watch a television he could barely see. On no account would he make a doctor's appointment. It was as though Larwood felt the symptoms might go away if he just ignored them.

By 1984, the deterioration in his sight had progressed to such a point that he had no option but to admit he was becoming 'practically blind'.

He was diagnosed with age-related macular degeneration. Lois wrote to her daughters. 'He says his eyes seem to be getting worse . . . they did not give him any hope of improving his sight, so that's why he thinks it is a waste of time going [again to the hospital].' By May, she was telling them: 'Dad is still able to see enough to walk about but he has had to give up peeling potatoes . . . he can still manage to wash up.' In another letter, written in the same month, she says: 'Dad has had several invitations to different functions the past two weeks, but he has had to refuse because as he says he would be too embarrassed.'

When news of his diminishing sight broke a month later, Larwood was phlegmatic about experiencing life in grey silhouette. 'I'm 80 later this year,' he said, 'but I've had a good innings. There are a lot worse off than me. I can't complain. I might not be able to get out to see my pals, but I can still have the odd beer and the occasional cigarette.' The doctors told him that his vision would deteriorate gradually. The world would begin to fade around him, like a fresco being washed away until only the dim outline of it remained. To see anything on TV, he eventually had to push his face just an inch or two from the screen, crouching to do so, the way he'd done to crawl or stoop along the low-ceilinged tunnels of the pits he'd once worked in. He lived a predominantly verbal existence. He still

Harold and Lois: remarkably stoic and sanguine after news breaks that the former fast bowler is losing his sight.

knew – and would point out to visitors – the location of his cherished photographs on the walls, his mementoes on the mantelpiece. The condition accentuated Larwood's hearing. When he heard the journalist Frank Keating stub out a cigar during an interview, he said to him: 'I think you've just put that out in my favourite ashtray.' He was right: it was the ashtray Douglas Jardine had given him in 1933.

Even when he couldn't make out the sharp contours of faces or the detail in expressions, Larwood continued to answer the door to callers, sliding his hands through the air until his fingertips finely touched the wall and he was able to guide himself safely along the passageway. On one occasion, two boys arrived to ask for his signature. He reached for pen and paper, which were kept on a nearby table for that purpose. Larwood signed and handed over the autograph. He thanked them, gently closed the door and set off down the hallway, his hand trailing along the wall once more. The bell rang again. When he opened the door, one of the boys held the piece of paper towards him and said apprehensively: 'Sorry, Mr Larwood, the page is blank.' Larwood had forgotten to depress the top of the pen. He told the story against himself, always ending it with a long laugh. Sometimes Lois talked him through the signing of an autograph. 'Your H is a bit wobbly,' she'd tell him, or: 'Careful, you might run off the end of the page.' Lois or one of his daughters answered letters on his behalf, which often included the stock apology: 'My eyesight is not too good these days and it is why I have to dictate this letter.' Even though he could see virtually nothing at all, he continued to wear his spectacles out of habit, putting them on as soon as he awoke. His life was well planned and followed a strict routine, like a benign close-order drill.

Cricketers and journalists continued to make the pilgrimage to his bungalow, and Larwood greeted them hospitably. When Graham Gooch and Darren Gough visited in 1994–95, he showed them his silver ashtray from Jardine and talked them through his 98 at Sydney, standing in front of his fireplace as if defending his stumps. Gooch asked whether the fast bowler had ever pitched the ball up during the Bodyline series. Larwood, in his dark red checked shirt and sleeveless fawn cardigan, looked at him through the thick rims of his black-framed spectacles. 'No,' he said. 'Never.'

He admitted: 'Things just seem a blur and there are times when I have to ask people who they are,' he said. 'I live in the past,' he'd add with a shake of the head. 'I've got a good memory and I like to talk cricket with anyone who can remember the older players. The trouble with people who go to see cricket now is that they only want to talk about the present day.'

Eventually, his blindness confined him to the bungalow. 'He has to be careful,' said Lois protectively, 'but he makes the best of it.' Making the best of it was the motto for his whole life.

* * *

An Australian-made mini-series, *Bodyline*, melodramatically recreated 1932–33 for the television audience of 1984, many of whom required educating about it. The broadcast was heavily slanted towards the Australian view that Douglas Jardine's tactics, and Larwood's bowling, were unfair and unsporting. Jardine was depicted as a sardonic and ruthlessly patrician figure; Larwood as a slightly cocky, naive, almost thick-headed individual who liked his beer and obeyed the orders Jardine gave him. Donald Bradman was impeccably noble, cast in a reverential light. Frequently the camera framed the actor playing him in a saintly glow, like religious iconography.

When the BBC showed the series in five parts as a prelude to the Ashes series in England in 1985, it drew ire and fire for historical inaccuracy. In one scene, Jardine visits Larwood's home, which he never

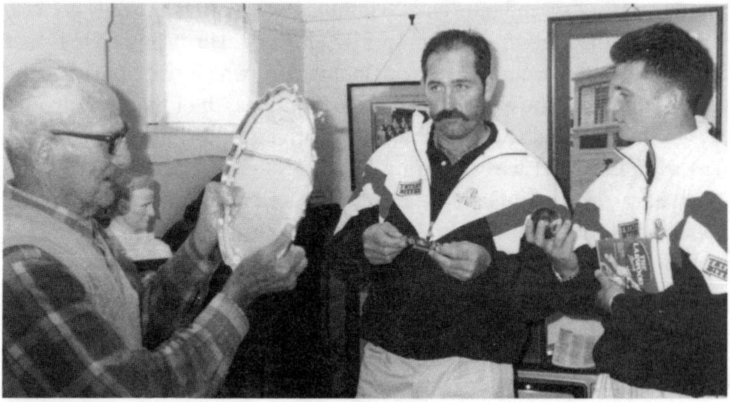

Graham Gooch and Darren Gough are talked through Harold Larwood's 98 at Sydney in 1933. Larwood holds a silver salver presented to him by Nottinghamshire.

did. In another, Les Ames is standing up to the stumps to Larwood, which for obvious reasons of self-preservation he never did either. There were countless scenes in which, for dramatic reasons, truth fell out of joint like a dislocated limb. The irregularities between what actually happened, and the way it was captured on the screen, made the Larwood family bristle with indignation.

His daughters were angry because Larwood was portrayed as a 'piss-pot and a yobbo'. Larwood was angry because he thought the programmes implied that his upbringing in a mining community made him 'inferior' and malleable. It disturbed him more than 'all the silly mistakes and bunkum . . . I came from a working-class background and was proud of it.' He claimed the 'ill feeling and swearing' in the TV version was exaggerated. Even Lois, who seldom broke cover to offer her view on cricket, was angry, and she said so because her husband was shown with visible 'hate in his eyes' when he bowled, a calumny she thought 'disgraceful'. She said: 'My husband never had hate in his eyes. It's just not in Harold's nature to be spiteful or vindictive. Anyone who's ever known him would verify that, and it's shocking and hurtful to make him appear that way when he had a fine reputation as a sportsman.'

Another Bodyline survivor, Bob Wyatt, claimed that 'most of the facts were wrong' and labelled it 'inaccurate nonsense – trash from beginning to end'. Reviewing the production, John Arlott pithily said that the running time of seven hours and 20 minutes was worthwhile only because it added to 'the longest squeal in sporting history'. He dismissed it as 'not only corny, but inaccurate – unconvincing corn which still flourishes the odd resentment'. Larwood soon found out the depth of that resentment.

In the days and weeks following the original Australian broadcast it was as if Larwood was replaying his past and experiencing the same incendiary response. Hateful, accusatory letters began arriving at his home. Larwood never had to take abusive or threatening telephone calls in 1932–33 because neither he, nor scarcely anyone else, could afford a phone. But now when his own phone rang, especially late at night or in the early hours, an anonymous barracker would be on the line to yell at Lois, who always picked up the receiver. Larwood was being denounced as a 'bastard' again. There were only three Larwoods in the telephone book; two of them were prefaced with the letter H. He wasn't difficult to track down. Some callers actually believed Larwood 'really was' the actor who played him – a man in his late twenties – rather than an old man.

Others were deranged enough to think that instead of it being an historical account, *Bodyline* was 'almost live' on Channel 10. 'If you don't stop bowling like that,' one of the callers said, 'we'll have to stop you from doing it.'

Larwood could not believe it. 'The nonsense that people have come out with,' he said. 'It still surprises me that they can still feel this way after fifty years. I put it down to the way I was shown as a baddie.' Friends complained futilely on his behalf. Joe Hardstaff junior said that Larwood never 'snarled or grimaced like the bowler in the film'. He explained: 'The most he would do is throw up his hands in anguish now and again. He was always the mildest of men temperament-wise.' Lois was incensed about the 'slum' she and Larwood had supposedly lived in – a terraced house in the worst kind of Victorian street. 'I have never seen slums like that anywhere – we always lived in a nice house . . . a lovely semi-rural area. It's just awful to think that our grandchildren will get the impression from watching that silly series that we came from a slum.'

After a month of being 'inundated with mail and phone calls from everywhere', Lois was at last able to write to her family with relief and a confession: 'Things have quietened down some . . . the pressure was beginning to get to me.' Lois admitted that she was 'getting really sick' of it. As usual, Larwood insisted that everyone who wrote must receive an acknowledgement. 'I was all for not answering most of them,' she admitted, 'but dad felt they deserved a few words in reply . . . the cost of stamps was getting rather out of hand.' Larwood turned down one invitation after another because of his failing eyesight, and because he felt it was inappropriate. Lois confirmed: 'We have had a few, which of course we have had to decline. The latest you won't believe was to a big cocktail party for all the people who took part in the Bodyline film, so you can guess what it would be like . . . it seems to me they are making a big splash and wanted to get dad there to top it off for them. He would just like them to leave him alone.'

The painter John Singer Sargent once said to a model posing for her portrait: 'I've taken the liberty of widening the brim of your hat . . . but only for compositional purposes, you understand.' For compositional purposes, hard fact in *Bodyline* sometimes wasn't allowed to interrupt the natural dramatic flow of the story. But that story was compelling. For all its manifold faults and blemishes, the mini-series was irresistibly and compulsively watchable – a high-class soap with well-defined characters that you simply couldn't ignore or turn off, and which had you agonizing about how it would end; even though, like a book you've read a dozen times before, you already know what the ending will be. Those with no desire to watch cricket would sit transfixed through *Bodyline.*

Larwood was played by a thin-faced, crop-haired Jim Holt, who the consultant coach to the series (the Australian spinner Peter Philpott) said had 'not played cricket before'. On his first attempt at bowling fast, Philpott revealed, Holt 'simply fell over' and 'as for what happened when he released the ball – well, frankly, it was anyone's guess where it might go.' In the final version, however, Holt was immaculate and convincing as a slightly coy, embarrassed and self-aware Larwood. Bradman represented the first major role for Gary Sweet, who is still told by cricket fans who recognize him: 'Put the whites on and get out there, Bradman.' The part of Jardine went to the jug-eared Hugo Weaving, another cricket novice. It is curious to think that 'Jardine' would later find fame as a drag queen in *Priscilla, Queen of the Desert*, Agent Smith in *The Matrix* and Elrond in *The Lord of the Rings*.

'Well,' said Larwood with resignation when the series ended, 'somebody must have enjoyed it.' Millions, actually. Although he didn't want it, Larwood had a new audience.

* * *

Larwood had barely been beyond his own front gate for three years when his country remembered he was still breathing. He was given an MBE for services to cricket in June 1993. As the decades had passed, without complaint he had made mental notes of cricketers who appeared in the Queen's Birthday or New Year Honours, his own name never among them. 'I don't suppose my time will come,' he had said, accepting the fact. Jack Fingleton twice – in 1977 and 1980 – vigorously lobbied politicians in person and in writing to give Larwood 'something'. In return Fingleton received polite replies and hollow promises. But when John Major became Prime Minister and carried his lifelong passion for cricket into 10 Downing Street, Larwood's turn came. He was 88 years old. 'Yourself and Jack Hobbs are my heroes,' Major told him in a telephone call which Larwood took sitting up in bed. Larwood sent him a photograph in return for the compliment: the unlikely pairing of Hobbs and Larwood walking out to bat.

Major was surprised that Larwood hardly spoke about his own achievements. 'I congratulated him,' wrote Major, 'and he thanked me for the award. And then he began to talk not of *his* exploits, but of his hero, Jack Hobbs, and innings he had played on sticky, treacherous wickets. Harold's memory was of seventy years earlier, but was as vivid as any contemporary event. This was no vainglory, just admiration for another man's skill.' When he heard later that Major's government was responsible for closing 31 pits at the cost of 30,000 jobs, Larwood said: 'I wish I knew he was planning to throw 30,000 blokes out of the pits. I'd have given him a right ear-bashing.'

Through nothing more than wishful thinking, as if he wanted to believe it, Larwood became convinced that Donald Bradman was significant in the decision to give him the award. When a TV interviewer asked him why the honour had come so late in his life, he replied: 'I think The Don had something to do with it.' The Don didn't exert any influence at all. Major was responsible for putting right what he saw as a blatant wrong. He would eventually say that Larwood had 'bowled his heart out for his country' and powerfully expressed the consensus opinion that 'his country had treated him badly' afterwards. 'I wish I could have given him a higher honour,' added Major.

Larwood admitted he had been 'embittered' over Bodyline and the treatment from his own country after it. The MBE restored his faith in England. He felt more English than at any other time since leaving the country in 1950.

In September the following year, Larwood was presented with his medal in the vice-regal chamber of Government House in Sydney, beneath a portrait of a young Queen Victoria. The night before, he'd polished his shoes and consulted Lois about which shirt to wear. A white one, she said. In the morning, he dressed himself and Lois checked his appearance. His eyes were blue, but almost completely sightless. His thinning grey hair had receded towards the crown. He wore his best dark jacket, a V-neck sweater and a tie adorned with an insignia that declared him to be a Member of the British Empire. In his playing pomp, he was like a rip of lightning. Now he moved circumspectly, gathering himself up at the ceremony and using the arm of a military adjutant like a stick. He walked with his back straight, his head steady, and listened to the pad of feet that had once galloped to the wicket. He bowed to the New South Wales Governor, Rear-Admiral Peter Sinclair, and then shook his hand. The medal, with its vivid red ribbon, was pinned high on his left lapel. The Governor told him that he'd taken a telephone call a few hours earlier: Bradman had phoned to 'offer his congratulations'. 'Who?' asked Larwood. 'Sir Donald Bradman,' repeated the Governor. 'Well, I should think that was very nice of him. Very nice indeed,' said Larwood.

Afterwards, in the gardens at Government House, as the military band played, reporters respectfully gathered around him. One journalist asked whether Larwood still defended the use of Bodyline. 'It's fast leg theory to me,' he replied. Someone else pressed the point. 'Look,' he said, 'you can talk about anything else, but not that series.' Another journalist enquired about his thoughts on the state of cricket. 'I haven't seen any cricket,' he said. 'All I can do is listen to these experts, and I can't comment on what they tell me.' A fourth asked how much he remembered of his younger days. 'I've not forgotten anything,' he said. 'There's only one thing I've lost and that's my eyesight.' What did he think of the award? 'Well, it's really nice to know that even after all these years I haven't been forgotten back in England.' And then the rarest of things occurred – when the interview was over, the reporters applauded him.

The Australian journalist Peter FitzSimons wrote: 'Mrs Larwood might well have wondered whether the press do that sort of thing often. We don't. In fact, that was the only occasion in my experience.' Larwood slipped his arm into Lois's, as if about to escort her to a dance, politely nodded his head to acknowledge the applause and moved on with dignified grace. As Larwood and his wife posed for photographs, he asked her a question she didn't hear clearly enough to answer the first time. 'What did you say, dear?' she replied. 'Are you proud of me?' asked Larwood with added softness. '*Of course* I am,' she said, and squeezed his hand. '*Of course* I am,' she said again.

FitzSimons explained the significance of the bow Larwood took in front of the Australian media. 'It was like Captain Cook had suddenly appeared,' he said. 'Larwood was a figure of great legend in Australian sport, but had never been seen . . .'

The day was long and hot and humid for a man nearing 90 who wasn't used to being outdoors. He smoked a cigarette, taking short drags, and delicately lifted a glass of champagne to his lips, his hand shaking a little. He'd neither smoked nor drunk for years, but this was a special occasion. The combination of nicotine, alcohol and heat made his head spin slowly, as if someone was gently rocking the earth beneath his feet.

Larwood felt his knees fold. He started to sink to the ground, trying to use his hands to support himself, but there was no strength in his arms or legs. He half-stumbled, and then a pair of hands caught him. Medical staff were called. Larwood was strapped onto a gurney, resting on his left side, and taken away to recover. Afterwards he typically wrote to apologize to Governor Sinclair: 'I am sorry for the inconvenience caused by my spell of giddiness,' he said. In a separate letter of thanks to John Major, he added that 'it was a day which my wife Lois and I will always cherish'. In his final paragraph, he reassured the Prime Minister: 'I am enjoying life in Australia and am in good health apart from my eyesight – so I doubt if I would be selected to play in the coming Test series as I would not be able to aim straight at a batsman's wicket.'

At home after the ceremony, he sat in his chair and his family gathered around him. To explain his fainting, he said: 'Broke my own rules . . . Only a slice of toast for breakfast, very hot day, lots of excitement and then a glass of champagne on an empty stomach . . . but I enjoyed my day. I must try to get out more often.'

And with those words, Larwood said goodbye to public life.

* * *

Larwood lived on serenely in his Sydney suburb, outliving most of the cricketers closest to him, and almost everyone involved in Bodyline.

Douglas Jardine contracted tick fever in Rhodesia in late 1957. After treatment produced no discernible change in his condition, he underwent more tests in a clinic in Switzerland. The doctors diagnosed lung cancer, which spread to his stomach and brain. He died in June 1958. His wife, swallowed by grief, destroyed his cricket things, including the Harlequin cap he had worn so defiantly in Australia. His daughter, Fianach Lawry, wondered whether her father's cancer was stress-related. 'Perhaps the pressure and strain of everything was a contributory factor to the cancer too. Cancer does tend to feed on worry, doesn't it?' she said.

Bill Woodfull collapsed on a golf course in 1965 at only 67. Woodfull had taken such a physical beating and had endured such mental torment during Bodyline that his widow Gwen blamed the series – and specifically the blow to the chest in Adelaide – for taking him from her prematurely.

Arthur Carr was shovelling snow on the driveway of his home in North Yorkshire during the winter of 1963 – one of the coldest and longest on record. He collapsed and died of a heart attack. His four-line obituary notice in the *Yorkshire Post* asked for no 'letters or flowers' and made no mention that he'd even been a cricketer, let alone captain of England. Larwood had neither seen nor spoken to Carr for nearly 25 years. He was preserved for him in the photograph of Nottinghamshire's Championship-winning team, which he hung on the wall of his bungalow in Sydney. Carr would stay in Larwood's memory exactly as he appeared in the second it took for a camera shutter to open and close. But what always came to mind was Carr's generosity of spirit, the beer each of them drank in dressing rooms and pubs and hotels. There was only one and very appropriate way that Larwood could say a proper goodbye to his skipper. On the day he heard of Carr's death, he went to the fridge and opened a bottle of beer.

Plum Warner died in 1963, with flowery tributes and the sobriquet of 'Grand Old Man of English Cricket'. His ashes were scattered in front of the Lord's stand named after him. Larwood didn't drink to his memory.

Stan McCabe fell from a cliff near his home in Sydney in 1968. Sir Len Hutton said that he possessed 'qualities that even Bradman hadn't got'. Bert Oldfield died in 1976. Larwood heard the news in an early-morning phone call, 24 hours before he was due to meet his friend for lunch. Jack Fingleton suffered a heart attack in 1981. On the way to the hospital, he asked: 'Am I going to cark it?' Bill Voce died in 1984, eight months after a local newspaper published his obituary in error. He read it while sitting in his hospital bed. Shortly afterwards Larwood looked out every day for a pigeon that on a windswept afternoon had been blown into his garden and then kept returning to it. He waited for it at his window, ready to scatter food. 'It's Bill,' he'd say of the pigeon. 'He's come back to see me.'

Each death brought back another thick slice of the past, another tidal surge of Bodyline nostalgia for Larwood, and became an excuse to show the short, familiar film clips of it. He never regretted belonging to an era which brought him such minimal financial reward. He never resented the money that others were paid as a consequence of Kerry Packer's entrepreneurial acumen. He never looked back with envy. 'Am I jealous? Not on your life,' he'd say. 'I preferred to play in my time. I've got enough money to see me and my wife through. I didn't get the financial rewards I probably deserved. But I got something else instead. The friendship of a lot of good people. Nothing else really matters, does it?'

Bill Voce is caught in his pyjamas by Harold Larwood's camera during a weekend away for the Larwood and Voce families.

Larwood grew to love his 'sunburnt country', the phrase in Dorothea Mackellar's poem 'My Country', the first draft written out of the awful stabs of homesickness she experienced in England in the early 1900s. Mackellar describes Australia's 'grey-blue distance', the 'jewel of the sea' and 'wide brown land' – all of which attracted Larwood to it in the first place.

'I'll die here,' he predicted in 1969, pausing thoughtfully as he absorbed the full impact of what he'd just said. 'Funny, isn't it?' he added, eventually. 'That's what the Australians wanted me to do in 1932, and now I'm going to do it of my own accord and in my own good time.'

Like every promise he ever made, Harold Larwood kept his word.

AFTERWORD

February 2008

Harold and Lois return to Nuncargate, 1977.

Kingsford, Sydney: February 2008

It is almost noon on a fine, early autumn day in Sydney. Anyone from England would regard it as hot enough for June. Wispy clouds, like trims of ermine, arch across a Windsor-blue sky and a zephyr disturbs the leaves in the trees, as if nudging them gently awake.

I am standing in Holy Trinity Anglican Church in Kingsford, a suburb that is a 25-minute taxi ride from Circular Quay and the Opera House. On the way I passed the deep bowl of the Sydney Cricket Ground. Now I am staring at a silver-coloured plaque fastened onto a low brick wall in the churchyard. Engraved on the plaque is the simplest of inscriptions. It is framed by a thick black border and neatly indented at each corner.

As it was in life for Harold Larwood, so it is in death too. No fuss, nothing fancy; just a few plain words:

IN LOVING MEMORY OF
OUR DEAR FATHER HAROLD LARWOOD M.B.E.
14-11-1904 – 22-7-1995
REST IN PEACE

More than 30 years after I had seen an old man lean against the pavilion gate at Trent Bridge, and was too shy even to stammer hello, I have come to Australia in search of him. I've held in the palm of my hand the ashtray that his 'grateful skipper' Douglas Jardine gave him for the Ashes; the silver cigarette case – begging to be polished – that was his frugal reward for winning the County Championship; and the MBE once pinned onto the lapel of his best jacket. I've followed a paper trail towards him: the letters he sent to his family, written lightly in blue ink; the newspaper cuttings and magazine articles which he assiduously folded and kept; the loose, random pieces of ephemera all of us save, like gathering driftwood, so that we preserve a tangible record of the small quotidian moments that make up a full life. I've seen hundreds of photographs – fastened into black-leaved albums, hung on walls, slid into frames to sit on sideboards. Photographed on the field, he looks formidably strong, the ball always gripped tightly in his hand. Photographed off it, dressed in grey civvies, he looks as delicate as a candle flame, a cigarette always between his fingers, and the tendrils of smoke curling from it like a campfire. If you put the photographs together, it's as

Harold Larwood looks back and recalls the past from his bungalow in Sydney.

if you're watching time elapse on fast forward, like thumbing the images in a child's flick book. Years, decades, generations fall away. In a few seconds the face and body change from boy to adult and then, when the last pages are turned, to old man.

I've spoken to his daughters. They've told me about a father who seldom raised his voice; who always made sure he brought home 'five of everything' so as not to show preferential treatment to one over the others; who didn't talk much about his cricket past, as though it really wasn't worth mentioning; who was still surprised that others were interested in it; who liked, and took pleasure in, the simplicity of things, and who didn't need applause or attention to make the blood run through his body.

My own father testified to it. In 1984, he sold his car and got on a plane for the only time in his life to visit three of his brothers in Sydney

– each of them £10 Poms from the 1950s. 'Is there anything you want bringing back?' he asked me. 'Harold Larwood's autograph,' I said, knowing I'd never be able to get it myself. I gave him a glossy black-and-white photograph of Larwood bowling, and my father did what countless others decided to do. He called at the bungalow. Larwood answered the door, and my father handed him the photograph, which was still in the brown envelope I'd put it in. 'It's for my son. He's a fan of yours,' he told Larwood.

'How old is he?' Larwood asked.

'He's in his twenties,' my father replied.

'Well, he can only have seen the old film,' said Larwood, smiling and signing carefully. 'Wish him the best of luck from me.'

My father shook his hand and walked back down the path, unaware that Larwood's deteriorating sight probably meant that he'd barely seen his face. He brought Larwood's photograph home pressed firmly between the pages of another gift – *Bradman: The Illustrated Biography*. When he handed over the signature to me, he said: 'You wouldn't believe he was famous, a legend even. He was such a normal bloke.' He paused for a moment, as if trying to decide what to say next. 'And so polite,' he added finally.

I've tracked Larwood through the physical landmarks of his life too. From the outside, the house he grew up in at Nuncargate has barely changed except for a plaque on the wall – a hand holding a cricket ball – which tells you that he was born there. The cricket field now has a smart pavilion, naturally named after the village's favourite son. The gap in the hedge which he once ran through to bowl grew over long ago. Electricity pylons sit on nearby hills that were once bare.

Not a brick of his shop in Blackpool survives. The corner where it once stood is now a children's playground with a modern slide and swings painted in primary colours. He'd have approved of it, his daughters tell me. The Victorian pub on the opposite corner, where he sat with Jack Fingleton and plotted his passage to Australia over several pints, has shut down and so wasn't selling beer on the lunchtime I visited it. He wouldn't have approved of *that*, his daughters say.

Even with all this evidence, he's still been hard to find, like someone cunning in a game of hide-and-seek. His bungalow in Sydney isn't a bungalow any longer. In fact, its exterior is so unrecognizable from the modest, tidy home I've seen in photographs that I assumed the taxi driver had dropped me at the wrong address. And when I went around Kingsford, asking directions to the church, passers-by gave vague or conflicting instructions, gesturing towards each point on the compass. Not one of them had heard of Larwood. When I found the church, I assumed his ashes must be interred inside it. When that search proved futile, I walked into the fresh air again and saw the rows of well-spaced plaques. My eyes scrolled across the line of names the way my finger would move down the page of a telephone book to seek out a number.

At last, he's here.

He is beside Lois, who died on Christmas Day 2001. If it were not for the addition of the letters MBE, there would be nothing to tell you that Larwood's career had gleamed and made him famous and feared, sought-after and envied. His plaque is exactly like all the others. I'm struck by the ordinariness of this memorial as well as by the anonymous corner it sits in; but I know now that this is how he would have wanted it. He always recoiled from starry glamour and distrusted anything that was meretricious or showy.

I'm struck by another thing too. His ashes lie a bowler's run-up – I slowly pace out the distance, and it is 12 strides – from an oak tree with protruding roots, which spreads its heavy shadow like a dark blanket across the plaque and makes it difficult to read in the semi-darkness. It is coincidental, but perfectly fitting, that one of the symbols of England and Englishness stands guard over him; even if the acorn from which it grew never touched English soil. I stare at the short dash on the plaque separating the two dates of birth and death, and try to absorb the fact that this inconsequential punctuation mark represents a span of almost 91 years. It is Larwood's entire life. And what a life: the hardscrabble upbringing, the filth of the pits, the break into cricket that originally led him to Australia and the miserable years in the wake of it, which improbably led him back here for good.

For six months I have been emailing one of his daughters, Enid, in preparation for my trip. Like me, she mentions the ironic twist to the 75th anniversary of Bodyline. On the back pages – and frequently on the front pages too – the past few weeks' news agenda in Australia has been dominated by the issues raised after India's threat to suspend its tour because of a three-match ban handed to spinner Harbhajan Singh for alleged racist abuse of the all-rounder Andrew Symonds. The media have called the incident 'Bollyline'. The spirits of Larwood and Jardine, and Bradman, Woodfull and Oldfield have been summoned again to explain the play on words to readers new to the story and who need to know about the long-dead. It is proof – were any needed – that Bodyline is the journey that will never end. Proof, too, that Larwood will always be remembered for it. He is drawn back to us whenever it is mentioned.

In his lifetime he accepted, but struggled fully to comprehend, the rapt and obsessive fascination with Bodyline – the shelves of books, the TV documentaries and hyperventilating dramas, the commemorative articles about old men who didn't forget written by young men who were benignly eager to interrogate them about it. He couldn't quite grasp why the periodic turning-over of such ancient earth and the minuscule scrutiny of what lay beneath it was necessary; or why the evidence was picked over by cricket and social historians and journalists with the thoroughness of a pathologist examining a bloodstain.

He became tired of answering the same questions about that bellicose series: about Jardine; about Bradman; about the development of the tactic itself; about the ball striking Oldfield; about the intense heat of the whole day in Adelaide when he needed a strong will and a stronger heart to survive the hostility of a crowd determined first to vilify and then to demonize him. He knew what he'd done, as well as what he'd witnessed, and he relayed both without embellishment. To Larwood, it was at the time just another five Tests on which the ink would quickly dry in the scorebook. But the ink has never dried . . .

Bodyline endures, almost as if it's just happened, because in the final analysis it captures the essence of George Orwell's claim about sport. At its competitive best, Orwell said, sport was 'bound up with hatred, jealousy, boastfulness, disregard of all rules and sadistic pleasure in witnessing violence'. He concluded: 'In other words, it is war minus the shooting.' For the man who did most of the shooting in 1932–33, Bodyline proved an intoxicating high, a moment of complete professional fulfilment that never returned for him. But the more I learn about Larwood, the more I am convinced that the series doesn't represent his greatest triumph. What sets him apart for me – revealing the beating heart of the man – is the manner in which he recovered from it.

All the obituaries I read chronologically recorded the detail of Larwood as a cricketer. Each matter-of-factly covered the speed of his bowling, the repercussions of it and particularly the MCC's reaction to Bodyline, dropping Larwood as if he were hazardous waste. He was drawn as the archetypal working-class hero, a noble scapegoat. Those are perfectly legitimate points to make, but both of them obscure what I believe is the main one – his inherent decency and moral courage as a human being. It is exemplified in his refusal to apologize and his natural inclination to forgive the wrongs done to him so blithely.

Even if you didn't know the course his career would take as a consequence, you might regard not saying sorry as a rash, foolhardy decision. With the benefit of knowing, you're more than likely to regard it as recklessly insane, as if he had an itch for professional suicide. But principle for Larwood always came before profit, and personal standing was more important than his livelihood. He saw it as the only moral choice he could make, an obligation to both himself and his family to do the right thing. He couldn't have lived with himself otherwise. His conviction never wavered. 'I'm glad I never apologized,' he often said. When he repeated that sentence for the last time, he was 89 years old.

He was once asked whether, like the Australian Trevor Chappell, he would have obeyed his captain's orders and bowled underarm to make sure a batsman couldn't hit a six off the last ball to win a one-day match. 'I suppose I would have done,' he said, 'but I'd have felt humiliated.' He never felt that way about Bodyline.

* * *

'What is a rebel?' asked Albert Camus, who answered his own question with the definition: 'A Man Who Says No.'

Larwood was the man who said No, though he was the most unlikely rebel who ever drew breath: sensitive, shy, diffident and always anxious not to cause offence or make a scene. Such admirable qualities offered him no protection against the intense hurt inflicted on him, and the degradation he felt, once the Bodyline tour was over. Someone incapable of committing a bad deed does not always regard it as possible in others, which is why Larwood fell into the trap of making easy presumptions about certain people he trusted and found himself badly let down. That bitterness and resentment would have calcified in the souls of lesser and less generous men. Larwood never allowed it to happen to him because he gave up his fixation on the past. He let go of it, the way a child might casually let go of a balloon. He forgave what happened and moved on; geographically as well as emotionally. He was incapable of nursing a grudge for long.

When he was a boy, one schoolteacher singled him out to be bullied and ridiculed in front of the class. The worst thing you can do is to ask

Portrait of a hero after ten years in Australia.

someone to do a job that you know is beyond them. The teacher sadistically asked questions he knew Larwood wouldn't be able to answer correctly, and then punished him with his cane. On occasions, he sent him to the head teacher for another caning, claiming that Larwood had misbehaved. Years later, already famous, Larwood met the teacher again. He not only accepted him without rancour, but also made him a friend. The vignette tells you all you need to know about Larwood's character. He handled himself with dignity; just the way his parents taught him.

In our minds we often live the lives we might have made for ourselves. But it seems to me that Larwood in the end lived the life he wanted. He lived well too, which is the best revenge. 'I've been so lucky all my life,' he regularly said. He was grateful for his home, his family, and digging around in his garden. 'You're closest to God in the garden,' he would say, the religious upbringing of his youth staying with him tangentially in old age.

The stories I heard about him emphasized his tender nature and lack of ego. There was his insistence on reading and replying to every letter he received, writing them in his own hand until blindness prevented it. There was the way he would nod and raise his trilby at any 'lady' he passed in the street in Kingsford, a common courtesy he practised long after it became unfashionable even to wear a hat, let alone tip one.

There were important friendships too. Keith Miller, who pitched his personality like a circus tent wherever he went, regularly phoned Larwood and the two of them slipped into a familiar patter that was shared like a practised comedy routine. 'Lol,' Miller would say, 'before I talk to you, put down that beer and that cigarette.' Larwood would always reply: 'How do you know I'm smoking and drinking?' Miller would then launch into whichever dirty joke he'd heard most recently. Miller's respect for Larwood ran deep. He thought that in outlook and attitude and lack of pretension, Larwood was a kindred spirit. During the war, after winning his wings with the Royal Australian Air Force, Miller flew combat missions over Europe in Mosquitoes. Just grateful to be alive, he never looked at daily life – either civilian or sporting – the same way again. When others complained of the strains and stresses of Tests, he dismissed them as irrelevant. When Miller was asked about pressure, he replied memorably: 'Pressure . . . I'll tell you what pressure is . . . Pressure is a Messerschmitt up your arse. Playing cricket is not.' Miller recognized that Larwood – because of what he went through during and after Bodyline – also knew that the game wasn't the be-all and end-all of everything. It was simply there to be enjoyed.

* * *

Larwood was a great man; and greater still because he didn't realize it. He would have been so in his quietly unassuming way even without cricket. With it, he made himself special. When *Wisden* listed its Cricketers of the Century in its 2000 edition, he was joint 17th with Ray Lindwall and Sachin Tendulkar. Of course, he'd have reacted to the accolade humbly, as if it had been the result of a clerical error. He'd have been more concerned for the feelings of the players who finished below him in the poll (including Richie Benaud, George Headley, Victor

Trumper, Malcolm Marshall, Michael Holding and Fred Trueman) rather than his own standing. 'Surely I don't deserve it,' he'd have said. We know it to be the case because that disarming phrase was his slightly embarrassed, stock reaction to everything good he was ever given. But he did deserve it. There can be no argument about Larwood's impact – however brief – on Test cricket, or the rapture his bowling inspired in anyone who saw it. He was so quick that to strap on a pair of pads against him counted as an act of bravery.

Larwood summed up his principal attitude to the art of fast bowling to Dennis Lillee. 'Never be friendly with the batsman. He is out to hit his hundreds and two hundreds against you.' For his part, Lillee was impressed with Larwood's technique and action, which he studied on film. 'It's a natural action, a very strong action, a very athletic action,' he said. 'His balance is beautiful . . . and look at the size of his forearm. He was obviously a very strong guy.' R.C. Robertson-Glasgow wrote about Larwood's shattering pace before dismissing his miles per hour as secondary to the spectacle of watching him deliver the ball: 'You didn't think of mathematics when you saw Larwood open the bowling; spectators thought of the poetry of rhythm and the panache of assault; batsmen thought of survival and, sometimes, of their wives and testamentary dispositions.' And Margaret Hughes, the first woman to report an Ashes series for a daily newspaper, became so besotted by Larwood when she saw him at Trent Bridge that her family grew 'sick' of hearing his name. 'It was as if some Greek God had journeyed from Olympus to fill the cricket field with graceful movement,' she wrote. 'I can still see him, the sun glinting on his fair hair . . . then the smoothness of his perfect action, like a modern machine, technically faultless. I wanted him to bowl throughout the day, and from both ends.'

Lois was wrong when she said that her husband never had 'hate' in his eyes. Hate, albeit in its most diluted form, is the fuel of the fast bowler. Walter Hammond saw it in Larwood, whom he said bowled with an expression of 'demonic aggression'. There was, he added, a 'tremendous upsurge of real hostility, even anger, against anyone who hit him hard'. Arthur Carr saw it too. He said that Larwood was 'scary in the way he cast a glance at a batsman'. Ron Oxenham, of Queensland, found Larwood's 'hate' almost turned him to water. When he failed to walk for a catch at short leg, during a routine tour match in 1932–33, Larwood 'went wild', dropping his fastest deliveries past Oxenham's face, the seam of the ball almost lifting the skin off his nose. Oxenham began to shiver involuntarily, as if he could feel the chill of someone walking over his grave, turning around and then walking back again. He went as white as bone china.

You can only pity the batsman, without the bubble-wrap of modern-day protection, stuck to the crease and glancing up to see Larwood steaming towards him. It must have felt like being strapped to a track and waiting for a train to run over you.

* * *

The author of a book called *The Art of Cricket* outlined his idea of the model quick bowler. 'To be a really good fast bowler one needs strong physique and stamina. The very big heavily muscled man is usually too tight and slow in his movements and the successful man is the one who is supple as well as strong.' The description fits Larwood like a bespoke suit. The writer was Sir Donald Bradman.

Larwood and Bradman didn't have a personal relationship, played against one another only briefly, never spoke on the phone, never wrote and never visited each other's homes. And yet there's a tie that binds them in a sporting embrace.

For a short but volatile period, the careers of the two men ran on parallel lines and met one another, like converging rail tracks, in Bodyline. When it was over, each went his separate way and on to quite different destinies. Bradman was the most revered man in Australia: influential, wealthy, an adroit, farsighted administrator. Larwood worked in factories and then lived on his pension. But history doesn't differentiate between what a man owns or does after his part in shaping it is over, and nor does it split apart the combatants. Larwood and Bradman are locked together, like Ali v Fraser, Borg v McEnroe and Liddell v Abrahams. They debated the controversy of Bodyline – in essence their private swordfight – without talking to one another directly. But they always monitored and often responded to what the other had to say about it. As if shut away in different rooms, their dialogue took place in newspaper and TV interviews, a 'conversation' lasting more than half a century. Like Harold Larwood, Bradman grew weary of being asked about it. Also like Larwood, he knew it was unavoidable.

For Bradman, Larwood was a dark planet that temporarily threw him out of his assured orbit. For Larwood, Bradman was the ultimate challenge, and the chance to prove himself as a fast bowler. Resentments and mistrust lingered, blighting subsequent years because of things said and left unsaid about it. But none of that mattered later on. Larwood came to regard Bradman with ever-greater respect as a batsman. He would begin a sentence with the words: 'Don was a ten times better batsman than . . . ' and then he'd add whichever contemporary name came most readily to him – Len Hutton, Colin Cowdrey, Garry Sobers, Viv Richards, Greg Chappell, Sunil Gavaskar. 'On any kind of wicket I would always have a fifty-fifty chance with Viv,' he once said of Richards. 'Bradman wouldn't give you a chance.'

For Larwood, time rather than words shaved away the enmity of Bodyline and its aftermath until nothing but calm acceptance and forgiveness was left. There was a tacit, silent reconciliation. So long after the event, it seemed trivial and petty to think, let alone care, about a few careless words. Far better to look back positively, gratefully.

When Larwood went to Lord's for the second Centenary Test in 1980, fighting off a cold that had kept him in bed for two days and left him gaunt and grey and weak, he gazed up at the paintings and photographs of Jack Hobbs, Walter Hammond, Gubby Allen and Don Bradman. He searched the walls for his own portrait. He walked around, unable to find one, and then retraced his steps, convinced he must have missed it. But there was no painting or photograph of Larwood. It was as if he'd never existed. He brushed it off as best he could. 'Perhaps I'm not good-looking enough for a picture,' he said, the faint humour disguising his dismay. And so when Larwood heard in 1990 that no picture or photograph of him was displayed in the Bradman Museum of Cricket in Bowral, he responded in the same calm way. 'I'm not worried,' he said, 'my photograph will be on the wall eventually.'

He was right. You will find more than just his photograph there now.

Always practical, Larwood made sure there was no squabbling over his possessions after his death. He divided his souvenirs among his five daughters, carefully labelling each one and dictating who would own it. Two of his daughters, Enid and Freda, decided to hand their mementoes to Bowral on permanent loan.

There are silver trophies, the case he took on the 1932–33 MCC tour, letters and scrapbooks, a newspaper bill, the articles that he read or had read to him. Larwood is ingrained in the place built to honour Bradman, and yet it strikes you as perfectly appropriate. When Douglas Jardine died,

Harold's daughters June (left) and Freda, with their parents.

Bradman responded to reporters' questions with a diplomatic: 'No comment.' When Larwood died, he made this valediction: 'His name will live in history as one of the greatest bowlers of all time.'

Eventually divided by social class and prestige as well as their opposing views, Larwood and Bradman nonetheless still share so much. Bradman stands on a plinth outside the Adelaide Oval. His statue faces the spires of St Peter's Cathedral. Larwood's statue stands in the centre of his home town, Kirkby-in-Ashfield, beside a jeweller's store, a chemist's, the Saturday market, selling all types of food and bric-a-brac, and the local branch of the Co-op. It is a strikingly beautiful piece of bronze: Larwood is in bowling pose – both muscle and sinew alive in the metal. If he ever delivers the ball, you'd better pray for the poor wretch who is coming out of the Co-op's front door at the time.

On the very day of Bradman's memorial service in March 2001 – he had died, aged 92, a few weeks earlier – Larwood's name was unveiled on the Welcome Wall of Sydney's Darling Harbour, a 100-metre-long tribute to the country's immigrants.

In a neat piece of symmetry, Australia said farewell to one of its most beloved figures and paid homage to another who chose to belong there. Harold Larwood would have liked that.

* * *

Even at his end, it was typical of Larwood that he didn't want to trouble anyone unnecessarily. For two weeks he lay in Sydney's Prince of Wales Hospital, his right arm paralyzed after a stroke. The doctors and nurses kept his condition secret. No one outside the family knew of his final illness until the news of his death was released. 'He asked us not to tell anyone. He didn't want a fuss,' said his daughter Enid.

His room had yellow walls and a small window opposite the door. At first he shared it with a talkative younger man. When there was no hope of recovery, it belonged to him alone.

In his final days, his daughters sat around his bedside, reassuring him that Lois would be cared for. They sang songs laced with messages of farewell, and which meant something to him: 'Now is the Hour', 'Wish Me Luck as you Wave me Goodbye', 'Just a Little Street Where Old Friends Meet' and 'I Still Call Australia Home':

> . . . as the world gets old and colder,
> It's good to know where your journey ends.
> And someday we'll all be together once more,
> When all the ships come back to the shore.
> Then I realize something I've always known,
> I still call Australia home.

Australia was home to Larwood. There was an opening for him to fill there, and he poured himself into it to the brim. He spent almost half of his life in his Sydney bungalow. And when he booked his passage back to England in 1968, visiting for the first time after his emigration, he discovered the country 'wasn't the same'. Larwood found it 'a bit disillusioning. Perhaps I had expected everything to be the same and so many old friends had passed on. I stopped asking about them.' The weaker light made everything paler, greyer, less vivid somehow. There'd been change for change's sake, he said. The demolition and rebuilding of structures in the flat and featureless architecture of the 1950s and 1960s

Harold Larwood's statue in Kirkby-in-Ashfield. The figure always looks poised to actually deliver the ball.

saddened him greatly because he found some places unrecognizable. Larwood was asked whether he'd contemplate returning to live in Nottingham. 'No fear,' he laughed, 'I'm a bloody Aussie now.' But he never formalized the arrangement. He remained a British citizen. 'My heart is there,' he once said of England, 'but my family is here.'

I asked each of his daughters whether he considered himself to be English or Australian. Three of them said English, the other two Australian. It doesn't really matter. The only thing that does is the way in which Larwood eventually became a man of two moons, sharing himself between two countries and two continents. He was already an integral part of Australian social history for the obvious reason that Bodyline is an integral part of it too. It was important then, and remains so now as a stage in his adopted country's progression towards maturity, and its growing together as a nation. A few games of cricket helped to do that.

Larwood played for the last time on his 90th birthday. The family – he had 13 grandchildren and six great-grandchildren – gathered for a party. A video recording of it preserves the day. He is immaculately dressed: white shirt, neat tie, dark suit. There is a cake for him – a bat and ball and nine candles, one for each decade. He holds Lois's hand; she blows out the candles and he cuts the cake with a long wooden-handled knife. And then the father, grandfather and great-grandfather takes off his jacket, goes into the yard and crouches over a bat. He waits for one of his young great-grandsons to bowl underarm to him. The wicket is a black plastic bin. The ball leaves the hand and skips low across the concrete. Larwood flicks the bat at it, misses, and the ball catches him on the outside of the right ankle. He begins to hop around. The scene is replayed – for the benefit of a photographer – and the ball strikes him on the toe of the same foot.

Sir Donald Bradman's statue outside the Adelaide Oval. Overlooking it is the majesty of St Peter's Cathedral.

As I watched the video, I thought again about the early evening when I saw him at Trent Bridge, and of the underarm ball he delivered from its pavilion gate. In that moment of remembering something else came to me: the story of an Eastern monarch who once charged his wise men to come up with a sentence which could be 'true and appropriate in all times and situations'. They gave him the words: 'And this, too, shall pass away.' Where Bodyline is concerned, I'm not so sure. Perhaps it will never pass away. We'll certainly be imagining it for a long time in its hard summer light, replaying it in film and on the page and talking about Larwood and his duel with Donald Bradman. The clocks will grow tired of ticking before we forget them – apart or together.

We live our lives forwards, but we can only understand them backwards. In that way, it dawned on Larwood how he'd be remembered, and how the early part of his cricketing life defined him.

In 1950, he sat next to Neville Cardus in the press box at Melbourne. Wickets tumbled quickly. Larwood watched the sad procession of batsmen, tramping from the pavilion and then back again. He fell silent for a while, incredulous at what he was witnessing. Eventually he said to Cardus:

> Look at them. They're getting out, one after the other. Why, when I think of my own cricket career, I seem to have spent all my time bowling to Bradman.

Harold Larwood is still bowling to Donald Bradman; he'll be bowling to Donald Bradman for evermore.

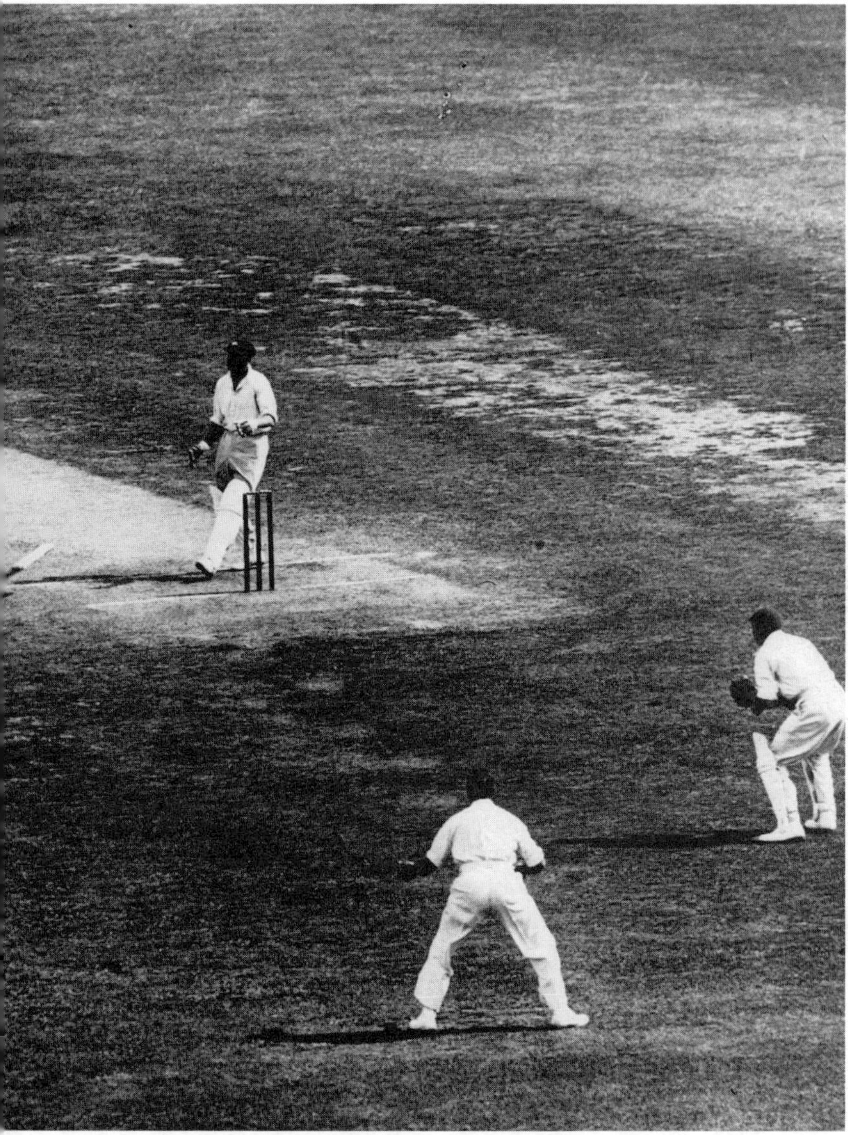

A Larwood thunderbolt sends Woodfull's bat spinning out of his hands at Adelaide, January 1933.

ACKNOWLEDGEMENTS

YOU'RE BOUND TO BE A LITTLE TAKEN ABACK when a man you don't know emails from England, says he wants to write the story of your father's life and plans to travel to Australia to do so. That's the gist of the message one of Harold Larwood's daughters, Enid, received from me almost two years ago. She was remarkably calm about it.

Enid and her husband Iain generously shared their time and hospitality, their memories and personal mementoes. They tolerated frequent emails and telephone calls from England to answer what must have seemed to them to be inconsequential or trivial questions. They were always on hand to provide a phone number or contact. They were always splendidly encouraging.

Harold was devoted to his family, and this book appears as it does because of them.

Freda asked me straightaway: 'Why do you want to write it?' When I explained my own background – Nottingham, a mining community, a passion for cricket – she grasped the reason immediately. Her husband, Roger, possesses a knowledge of cricket and cricketers that proved invaluable to me.

June and her youngest son David, Mary and her son Andrew, and Sylvia and her husband David were just as forthcoming. As Harold's eldest daughter, June talked about the late 1930s, the work Harold did on his smallholding and in his Blackpool shop, as well as outlining the family's passage to Australia. Mary and Andrew, who lived with Harold and Lois, spoke tenderly of those years and provided boxes of precious cuttings. Sylvia, the youngest daughter, recalled their early life in a new country.

Biography is like fitting together disparate pieces of a jigsaw. But without 'the girls', I couldn't have done it.

The extended members of the Larwood family were also helpful: Joyce Broughton, Margaret Broomhead and especially Sheila Abbott.

I travelled to Scotland – ironically to within a few miles of where my own father was born and raised – to meet Douglas Jardine's daughter, Fianch. I owe her a debt for lunch (she insisted on paying) as well as her time. I spoke at length to Tommy Mitchell's daughter Louise Sindall, who shared her videos, scrapbooks and letters of her father's career.

I had some cherished meetings with Molly Shentall and her husband Derek. They both spoke warmly and well of the man who was effectively Harold's sixth brother – Bill Voce. Molly and Derek, who have already kindly donated many of Bill's things to Nottinghamshire CCC, lent me cassettes and answered anything and everything I put to them.

I can't imagine what I'd have done without Peter Wynne-Thomas and the cricket library he's created at Trent Bridge. I now know that a friend of mine was right many years ago when he said: 'If Peter doesn't know something, it isn't worth knowing.'

In Bowral, The Bradman Museum of Cricket and David Wells and his staff were the Australian equivalent of Peter. So was its English representative, John Grimsley, who deserves a lot more than one good drink for his assistance and counsel.

Duncan Anderson gave me unfettered access to his remarkable collection of Nottinghamshire and Bodyline memorabilia. Bernard Whimpress pointed me in several right directions in Adelaide. Kevin Perkins, who wrote Harold's autobiography, was generous with his comments and so pleased that his friend was getting long-overdue recognition.

I spent a lot of hours in public libraries in Sydney, Nottingham and Kirkby-in-Ashfield. The National Mining Museum was indispensable too. I would like to thank the staff in each of them, and also:

Mike Abbott, Bob Appleyard, Trevor Bailey, Richie Benaud, Dickie Bird, Geoffrey Boycott, Reg Brace, Stephen Chalke, Peter Charlton, Anthony Clavane, Mark Covell, Matthew Engel, Stuart Frew, Mark Fiddian, Bill Frindall, Peter FitzSimons, Norman Giller, Cliff Gillott, Hawk-Eye (staff of), Dr Nick Harris, Lord Douglas Hurd, Frank Keating, Robin Kilburn, Jerry Lodge, Simon McGee, Sir John Major, Lisa Murray, Eric Midwinter, Geoffrey Moorhouse, Pat Murphy, Christine Nuttall, James Pickering, Matthew Richardson, David Rayvern Allen, David

Robertson, Lord David Puttnam, Andy Smart, Mark Smalley, David Smith, Rob Steen, Cliff Thomas, Chris Waters, Gwyn Watkins, Glenys Williams, Alan Whitaker, Glenys Williams, Don Wilson, Liz Wilson, Gerry Wolstenholme, John Woodcock, Kevin Wooldridge, Neil White. Apologies to anyone I've stupidly omitted.

I'd especially like to thank my agent Grainne Fox and my editors at Quercus, Jon Riley and Richard Milbank. With his interest and knowledge, Richard really ought to be writing cricket books and not just editing them.

Now, a confession:

In the book I use the word 'I' for reader accessibility. But it really ought to be 'we'. When I began writing it, Mandy was my fiancée. Halfway through it – in Australia, as it turned out – she became my wife. She accompanied me on almost every page of the journey.

Harold Larwood discovered that life frequently throws up unexpected but pleasant surprises. For him, I suppose it was the day when Jack Fingleton walked into his shop in Blackpool. For me, it was walking into a bar in Leeds one rainy evening and meeting Mandy.

I've thought about how to articulate how grateful I am to Fate for that moment. I thought about leaning on the words of some of the great writers, or the romantic poets, to explain how much she means to me. But I'll rely instead on the lyrics of those famous pop philosophers 10cc:

'If it hadn't have been for Mandy . . . well, I wouldn't be here at all.'

I don't exaggerate.

Appendix 1

WHO'S WHO

Nearly half a century after Bodyline, Harold and Bill stroll over the fields surrounding Nuncargate.

Allen, G.O.B. ('Gubby') (1902–99). Fast bowler for Cambridge University and Middlesex. Allen made 25 Test appearances and took 81 wickets at 29.37. Another 788 came in first-class matches. He was knighted in 1986. He eventually lived so close to Lord's that he had his own private gate into the ground.

Ames, Leslie (1905–90). Kent wicketkeeper-batsman, the finest of his era. Ames' 47 Tests brought 73 catches, 23 stumpings and almost 2,500 runs at 40.56, with eight centuries. His first-class career embraced 703 catches, 418 stumpings and 37,248 runs, including 102 hundreds. During the Second World War Ames served with the RAF and became a Squadron Leader.

Bardsley, Warren (1882–1954). New South Wales opening bat. Sir Jack Hobbs called him 'one of the best left-handers in the upright, classical school that I have ever seen'. In 41 Tests, Bardsley scored 2,469 runs at 40.47. In first-class matches, he made 53 centuries – 29 of them in England.

Barratt, Fred (1894–1947). Nottinghamshire all-rounder. On top of his summer work on the cricket field, Barratt spent the winters playing for Aston Villa and Sheffield Wednesday as a full-back. He made 6,101 runs for Nottinghamshire and took 1,176 wickets. He served in the First World War and was gassed.

Bowes, Bill (1908–87). Yorkshire fast bowler. Bowes spent a lifetime in cricket. He made 15 Test appearances and took 68 wickets at 22.33. His 372 first-class matches brought 1,639 wickets at 16.76. In the Second World War, he was captured at Tobruk and held prisoner for three years. After his retirement as a player, Bowes turned to journalism. He wrote his autobiography, *Express Deliveries*, covered Yorkshire and Test matches for Leeds-based newspapers and often acted as unofficial coach for several players who sought him out for advice on bowling – and how to play it.

Bradman, Donald (1908–2001). Batsman for New South Wales and South Australia. In 2000, Bradman was named as one of *Wisden*'s Five Cricketers of the Century. He is *the* greatest batsmen ever to have played the game. In 52 Test appearances, he scored 6,996 runs (highest score 334) and averaged 99.94, with 29 centuries. His first-class career statistics are equally awe-inspiring: 28,067 runs at 95.14 in 234 matches, with 117 hundreds. His highest score was 452 not out.

Brown, Freddie (1910–91). All-rounder. He took 45 wickets and scored 734 runs in 22 Tests. In a first-class career during which he represented Surrey before the Second World War and Northamptonshire (where he was captain) after it, he claimed 1,221 wickets and scored 13,335 runs. He was a popular MCC captain on the 1950–51 tour of Australia, and later President of the MCC (1971–72).

Carr, Arthur (1893–1963). Nottinghamshire batsman and county captain from 1919 until 1934. *Wisden* once described Nottinghamshire as 'Mr Carr and the professionals who support him so well'. He played in 11 Tests (237 runs at 19.75) and scored more than 21,000 first-class runs. He was an excellent fielder – usually at slip, short leg or gully – and took almost 400 catches.

Duckworth, George (1901–66). Lancashire wicketkeeper. An exceptionally fine glovesman, he claimed 753 catches and 343 stumpings in first-class cricket and 45 catches and 15 stumpings in 24 Tests. After his career ended, Duckworth was at various times farmer, hotel-owner, broadcaster, journalist and MCC chief factotum – baggage-carrier and scorer – on overseas tours.

Fender, Percy (1892–1985). All-rounder for Surrey and Sussex. Exuberant and shrewd, Fender was said to be the county captain's 'captain'. With his intuitive eye and intelligence, he was tactically superior to almost all others. His first-class career reaped

19,034 runs and 1,894 wickets. He did the double six times. Fender played in 13 Tests.

Findlay, William (1880–1953). After Eton and Oxford, Findlay played 88 times for Lancashire. He was a wicketkeeper who took 140 catches and made 27 stumpings. He became Secretary of the MCC in 1926, a post he held for ten years. He was President of his former county in 1947 and 1948.

Fingleton, Jack (1908–81). Batsman for New South Wales. As a journalist and author, he left behind writing that has not withered nor lost its relevance with age. Fingleton made 18 Test appearances and scored 1,189 runs at 42.46, with five hundreds. His highest innings was 136 against England in 1936–37. He also scored 6,816 first-class runs.

Foster, Frank (1889–1958). Warwickshire all-rounder who, with Sydney Barnes, bowled leg theory with great success on the 1911–12 MCC tour of Australia. An injury sustained on a motor-bike during the First World War left Foster lame and ended his career as a left-arm fast-medium bowler and right-hand bat. He carried Warwickshire to their first Championship in 1911 with 1,383 runs and 116 wickets. He made 11 Test appearances (330 runs, 45 wickets at 20.57). His first-class career brought 6,510 runs and 721 wickets.

Gregory, Jack (1895–1973). Fast bowling all-rounder for New South Wales. Neville Cardus described him as 'generous and likeable'. Batsmen often found him unplayable. Gregory's 85 wickets in 24 Tests came at 31.15. In 129 first-class matches he took 504 wickets. He bowled right arm, but batted left-handed – and without gloves. In Tests he scored 1,146 runs at 36.96, including two hundreds.

Gunn, George (1879–1958). His *Wisden* obituary called him 'probably the greatest' Nottinghamshire batsman. George Gunn's figures are striking: he accumulated 62 hundreds in more than 35,000 career runs and made 15 Test appearances. He was the younger brother of John Gunn and nephew of William. In 1931, both he and his son G. (George) V. (Vernon) Gunn scored a century against Warwickshire in the same innings. His son predeceased him by almost a year after a motor-bike accident.

Hammond, Walter (1903–65). Batting all-rounder for Gloucestershire. *Wisden* called him one of the 'immortals' and the statistics reinforce it. His 85 Tests brought him 7,249 runs at an average of 58.45, including 336 not out against New Zealand in Auckland in 1933 – still the highest score by an Englishman overseas. His first-class batting career was unbelievably prolific: 50,551 runs. He could also bowl with what the pros called 'nip' (he took 732 first-class wickets) and fielded brilliantly (820 career catches). Hammond was involved in a horrendous car crash in 1960 in South Africa, where he had emigrated for business reasons. It blighted his remaining years.

Hardstaff, Joe (snr) (1882–1947). Nottinghamshire batsman. The Australian crowds christened him 'Hot Stuff' during the 1907–08 Ashes tour on which he made 1,384 first-class runs (including three centuries) and averaged more than 51. His scoring in first-class cricket totalled 17,146 runs. After his playing career ended, Hardstaff became an umpire and stood in 21 Tests.

Hardstaff, Joe (jnr) (1911–90). Nottinghamshire batsman. As with so many players, the Second World War disrupted what could well have been Hardstaff's most prolific period. He nonetheless went on two Ashes tours (in a total of 23 Test appearances) and finished top of the averages in 1949 with 2,251 runs at 72.61. He made his debut at 19, scoring a fifty in only his second Championship match for Nottinghamshire, and finished with 31,847 runs at 44.35.

Hawke, Martin Bladen (Lord Hawke) (1860–1938). Always remembered for his most famous remark, uttered in 1925 – 'Pray

God, no professional shall ever captain England' – and the Spy image of him as a young man in striped cap and blazer. He was a towering influence on English cricket and actually enhanced rather than hindered the lot of the pro by introducing winter pay. He captained Yorkshire for 28 years (eight Championships) and was the club's President for four decades. He made five Test appearances (four as captain) and scored almost 17,000 first-class runs. At various times, he was MCC President, treasurer, trustee and selector.

Heane, George (1904–69). He shared the Nottinghamshire captaincy with Stuart Rhodes in 1935, but took the job alone the following summer. He held it until 1946. Heane scored 6,183 first-class runs – including nine centuries – at 25.34.

Hobbs, John Berry ('Jack') (1882–1963). Surrey opening batsman, dubbed 'the Master' by Douglas Jardine. With Herbert Sutcliffe, Hobbs formed England's greatest opening partnership. In 61 Tests Hobbs made 5,410 runs at 56.94 with 15 centuries (including 3,636 runs at 54.27 in 41 Ashes Tests), and in all first-class cricket more than 61,000 runs at 50.65. He scored more than half of his first-class hundreds after his 40th birthday. On his retirement Hobbs had made 197 centuries. The Association of Cricket Statisticians subsequently declared two hundreds made on a private tour of Ceylon (Sri Lanka) to be first class, taking his total to 199.

Iremonger, James (1876–1956). Iremonger was a renaissance man as far as sport was concerned. As a cricketer he scored more than 16,500 runs (at 35.06) and took 619 wickets (at 22.97). From 1901 to 1909, he scored 1,000 runs for Nottinghamshire every summer. As a footballer, he was a left-back for Nottingham Forest and, briefly, England. He also played one match for Notts County – as goalkeeper. Iremonger also showed considerable skill at bowls and his county described him as 'one of those truly gentlemen professionals'.

Jackson, F.S. (1870–1947). He led what cliché demands to be called a 'Boy's Own Life' – but, in his case, it happened to be true. As well as his cricketing prowess – he played 20 Tests for England and scored almost 16,000 first-class runs for Yorkshire – Jackson served in the Second Boer War, became a Lieutenant Colonel in 1914, an MP in 1915 and a cabinet minister in 1922. In 1927 he became Governor of Bengal, where he survived an assassination attempt from close range.

Jardine, Douglas (1900–1958). Batsman for Oxford University and Surrey. Over the span of his eventful career, essentially from 1920 to 1934, Jardine scored 14,848 runs (average 46.83), including 35 centuries. For England he played 22 Tests and made 1,296 runs (average 48.00). Jardine was more than a courageous cricketer. He was a courageous man, too. In the Second World War, he served with distinction in France and India after persuading the Royal Berkshire Regiment to commission him.

Lilley, Ben (1894–1950). He took 657 catches in his Nottinghamshire career, which began in 1921 but did not bring him a regular place until 1925. He promptly became the first of the county's wicket-keepers to score 1,000 runs in a season. He did it again three summers later. Having retired with a thumb injury in 1937, Lilley took on a pub but began to suffer ill-health, which led to his premature death.

McCabe, Stan (1910–68). Batsman for New South Wales. Don Bradman described McCabe's 232 against England at Trent Bridge in 1938 as the greatest innings he ever saw. He beckoned his team onto the balcony to watch it. McCabe played in 39 Test matches and scored 2,748 runs, including six centuries, at 48.21. His first-class career for New South Wales brought 11,951 runs at 49.39.

Macartney, Charles (1886–1958). Batsman for New South Wales, nicknamed the 'Governor-General'. In 35 Tests, Macartney hit 2,132 runs – including seven centuries – at 41.80. His first class-career brought him a highest score of 345 and more than 15,000 runs at 45.78.

Miller, Keith (1919–2004). All-rounder for Victoria and New South Wales. With his Hollywood looks and exuberant spirit, Miller was called the 'the golden boy' and consequently given the nickname 'Nugget'. One of ten inaugural members of Australian cricket's Hall of Fame, Miller is regarded as its greatest all-rounder – taking 170 wickets and scoring almost 3,000 runs in 55 Tests.

Mitchell, Tommy (1902–96). Derbyshire leg-break bowler. He played in five Tests and took eight wickets. For Derbyshire – with whom he won the County Championship in 1936 – he took a further 1,483 wickets at 20.59.

Oldfield, Bert (1894–1976). Wicketkeeper for New South Wales. Serving as a corporal in the 15th Field Ambulance, 15th Brigade, during the Great War, Oldfield was buried for 'several hours' during the 1918 bombardment at Polygon Wood. Somehow he survived. He made 54 Test appearances for Australia – 38 of them against England – and took 78 catches and 52 stumpings.

O'Reilly, Bill ('Tiger') (1905–92). Leg-break and googly bowler for New South Wales. Bradman considered him the greatest bowler he ever saw. In 27 Tests he took 144 wickets at 22.59 apiece, and in all first-class cricket 774 wickets at the exceptionally low average of 16.60.

Paynter, Eddie (1901–79). Lancashire batsman who scored more than 20,000 first-class runs. His 20 Tests (1,540 runs) are dominated by one fact: his Test average in seven appearances against Australia was 84.42. He once kept wicket for an entire second innings of an Ashes Test, taking a catch and conceding only five byes.

Pataudi, Nawab of (1910–52). Batsman for Oxford University and Worcestershire, and the only man to play Test cricket for both England and India. Pataudi's first-class career brought him 8,750 runs, but only six Test appearances. He died while playing polo on his son's 11th birthday.

Rhodes, Wilfred (1877–1973). Yorkshire all-rounder who bowled left-arm spin and batted right-handed. Rhodes' first-class career stretched for 32 years. It began in 1898, and he played his final Test, against the West Indies, in 1930, shortly before his retirement, when he was 52 years and 165 days old. No one older has played Test cricket. In 58 Tests, he made 2,325 runs and took 127 wickets. In his first-class career, his figures are astonishing: 39,969 runs and 4,204 wickets.

Richardson, Vic (1894–1969). Batsman for South Australia. The archetypical Australian sportsman: tough, competitive and versatile. There was almost nothing Richardson couldn't do. As well as playing cricket, he captained South Australia in Australian Rules and represented the state in baseball. He was also a good lacrosse player and an excellent swimmer. He made 19 Test appearances and scored 706 runs. He bequeathed his combative spirit to three cricketing grandsons: the Chappell brothers Ian, Greg and Trevor, all of whom represented Australia.

Richmond, Thomas Leonard ('Titch') (1890–1957). A leg-spin and googly bowler for Nottinghamshire, Richmond finished with 1,148 wickets at 21.06 and took 10 wickets in a match 19 times. He couldn't bat – only 1,532 runs at an average of 9.82. His fielding was so poor that he frequently found himself at deep third man, where *The Cricketer* described him as 'not likely to have a catch'.

Staples, Arthur (1899–1965). As well as playing first-class cricket, Staples kept goal for Mansfield Town and Bournemouth. He broke into Nottinghamshire's team in 1924 and took four summers to establish himself properly. He was a stock bowler – medium pace – and a batsman who scored 12,457 runs with a highest score of 153 not out. He took 632 wickets at 29.62.

Staples, Sam (1892–1950). Elder brother of Arthur, Sam's career was delayed, like so many others, by the Great War. Aged 27, he made his debut for Nottinghamshire in 1920 and played for them 385 times. He was a superb slip fielder, taking 329 catches – 39 of them in the 1926 season. He scored 6,248 runs and his slow bowling brought him 1,268 wickets (including 9 for 141 against Kent in 1927) at 22.77.

Sutcliffe, Herbert (1894–1978). Yorkshire opening bat. The Great War meant that Sutcliffe didn't make his county debut until he was already 24. In a career lasting twenty years – 1919 to 1939 – Sutcliffe scored 50,670 first-class runs at an average of 52.02. In Test matches he made 4,555 runs at an average of 60.73, with 16 hundreds. (Among batsmen who have played 20 Tests or more, only Headley, Pollock and Bradman have a higher Test average than Sutcliffe.) J.M. Kilburn wrote that Sutcliffe was 'immaculate, alert, brisk of movement, serene in respose . . . his off-drive wore a silk hat'.

Voce, Bill (1909–84). Left-arm fast bowler for Nottinghamshire. Voce took 98 Test wickets in 27 appearances at 27.88, and 1,558 in first-class matches at 23.08. He was still playing for Nottinghamshire 'in a crisis' up until 1952. He coached successfully, first at Trent Bridge and then at the MCC.

Walker, Willis (1892–1991). Nottinghamshire batsman. On his death, Walker was the oldest surviving first-class cricketer. He played for Nottinghamshire before the Great War and rejoined them in the early 1920s. He made 18,242 runs at 32.45, including his highest score of 165 not out against Middlesex at Lord's in 1930. He took two wickets – both in the same match against Worcester at Trent Bridge in 1926. He later coached at Charterhouse.

Warner, P.F. ('Plum') (1873–1963). Batsman for Oxford University and Middlesex. Warner scored 622 runs in 15 Test matches at an average of 23.92, with one century. He captained the MCC on the 1903–04 and 1911–12 tours of Australia, and was manager on the 1932–33 tour. Warner later became President of the MCC, and was knighted for services to cricket in 1937. The 1921 *Wisden* observed: 'There have been many greater cricketers than Pelham Warner but none more devoted to the game.'

Whysall, William ('Dodge') (1887–1930). Only 43 when he died of blood poisoning, Whysall was described by *Wisden* as possessing 'unlimited patience and a defence most difficult to penetrate'. He scored runs, too – 2,717 in Nottinghamshire's Championship-winning side of 1929. With George Gunn he shared in 40 century opening partnerships. He made 51 centuries himself and toured Australia in 1924–25.

Woodfull, Bill (1897–1965). Opening bat for Victoria, and Australian captain against Jardine's 1932–33 MCC side. Woodfull's life was centred on much more than cricket. His other passion was teaching. As headmaster of Melbourne High School, he was given an OBE for services to education. Referred to as 'The Rock', Woodfull scored 2,300 runs at 46.00 in his 35 Tests.

Appendix 2

HAROLD LARWOOD: FIRST-CLASS RECORD

ALL FIRST-CLASS MATCHES

Bowling

1924	**M**	**O**	**Mds**	**R**	**W**	**Avge**
	1	26	5	71	1	71.00

1925	**M**	**O**	**Mds**	**R**	**W**	**Avge**
	20	477.1	98	1315	73	18.01

1926	**M**	**O**	**Mds**	**R**	**W**	**Avge**
Championship	23	693.2	164	1755	96	18.28
Tests	2	95	19	252	9	28.00
Other Notts Matches	2	35	10	90	7	12.86
Other Matches	5	151	24	412	25	16.48
Total	32	974.2	217	2509	137	18.31

1927	**M**	**O**	**Mds**	**R**	**W**	**Avge**
Championship	17	543.2	126	1500	91	16.48
Other Notts Matches	2	38	10	87	5	17.4
Other Matches	3	48	11	108	4	27.00
Total	22	629.2	147	1695	100	16.95

1928	**M**	**O**	**Mds**	**R**	**W**	**Avge**
Championship	25	669.5	163	1636	116	14.10
Tests	2	50	13	114	6	19.00
Other Notts Matches	2	24	5	61	4	15.25
Other Matches	2	91	23	192	12	16.00
Total	31	834.5	204	2003	138	14.51

1928–29: MCC in Australia	**M**	**O**	**Mds**	**R**	**W**	**Avge**
Tests (6-ball overs)	5	259.1	41	724	18	40.22
Other matches (8-ball overs)	8	152.3	20	530	22	24.09
Total	13	462.2*	61	1254	40	31.35

**Calculated on 6-ball overs*

1929	**M**	**O**	**Mds**	**R**	**W**	**Avge**
Championship	20	496.3	101	1475	80	18.43
Tests	3	102.4	34	186	8	23.25
Other Notts Matches	5	148	23	457	24	19.04
Other Matches	4	124	24	417	5	83.40
Total	32	871.1	182	2535	117	21.66

1930	**M**	**O**	**Mds**	**R**	**W**	**Avge**
Championship	18	444	90	1125	89	12.64
Tests	3	101	18	292	4	73.00
Other Notts Matches	1	28	2	94	4	23.50
Other Matches	3	48	14	111	2	55.50
Total	25	621	124	1622	99	16.38

1931	**M**	**O**	**Mds**	**R**	**W**	**Avge**
Championship	20	535.3	111	1294	105	12.32
Tests	1	DNB				
Other Notts Matches	4	99	31	212	23	9.21
Other Matches	2	17	0	47	1	47.00
Total	27	651.3	142	1553	129	12.03

1932	**M**	**O**	**Mds**	**R**	**W**	**Avge**
Championship	24	684.4	162	1639	141	11.62
Other Notts Matches	2	41	17	63	8	7.87
Other Matches	6	141	24	382	13	29.38
Total	32	866.4	203	2084	162	12.86

1932–33: MCC in Australia	M	O	Mds	R	W	Avge
Tests (6-ball overs)	5	220.2	42	644	33	19.51
Other Matches (8-ball overs)	5	45.7	3	173	16	10.81
Total	10	281.3*	45	817	49	16.67

*Calculated on 6-ball overs

1933	M	O	Mds	R	W	Avge
Championship	12	10	3	18	1	18.00
Other Notts Matches	1	DNB				
Total	13	10	3	18	1	18.00

1934	M	O	Mds	R	W	Avge
Championship	22	485.2	101	1316	78	16.85
Other Notts Matches	1	27	2	99	4	24.75
Total	23	512.2	103	1415	82	17.25

1935	M	O	Mds	R	W	Avge
Championship	26	874.1	201	2202	98	22.46
Other Notts Matches	2	44.2	13	114	4	28.50
Total	28	918.3	214	2316	102	22.70

1936	M	O	Mds	R	W	Avge
Championship	20	656.1	159	1499	116	12.92
Other Notts Matches	2	23	6	45	3	15.00
Total	22	679.1	165	1544	119	12.97

1936: India	M	O	Mds	R	W	Avge
	2	44	10	157	2	78.50

1937	M	O	Mds	R	W	Avge
Championship	18	672.2	148	1671	68	24.57
Other Notts Matches	2	20.2	5	49	2	24.50
Total	20	692.4	153	1720	70	24.57

1938	M	O	Mds	R	W	Avge
Championship	8	103	16	339	4	84.75
Other Notts Matches	1	15	7	27	2	13.50
Total	9	119	23	366	6	61.00

TOTALS:	M	O	Mds	R	W	Avge
	361	9406.5 198.2*	2092	24,994	1427	17.51

*8-ball overs

Harold Larwood took 234 catches.

Batting

1924	M	I	NO	HS	R	Avge
Championship	1	0	0	0	0	0

1925	M	I	NO	HS	R	Avge
Championship	20	27	12	70	361	24.06

1926	M	I	NO	HS	R	Avge
Championship	23	30	4	44	364	14.00
Tests	2	2	0	5	5	2.50
Other Notts Matches	2	3	0	17	27	9.00
Other Matches	5	5	1	31	55	13.75
Total	32	40	5	44	451	12.88

1927	M	I	NO	HS	R	Avge
Championship	17	17	5	67*	309	25.75
Other Notts Matches	2	2	1	4	8	8.00
Other Matches	3	DNB	0	0	0	0
Total	22	19	6	67*	317	24.38

1928	M	I	NO	HS	R	Avge
Championship	25	29	8	101*	560	26.66
Tests	2	2	1	32	49	49.00
Other Notts Matches	2	3	1	10*	17	8.50
Other Matches	2	DNB	0	0	0	0
Total	31	34	10	101*	626	26.08

1928–29: MCC in Australia	M	I	NO	HS	R	Avge
Tests	5	8	0	70	173	21.62
Other Matches	8	6	0	79	194	32.33
Total	13	14	0	79	367	26.21

1929	M	I	NO	HS	R	Avge
Championship	20	20	3	53*	233	13.70
Tests	3	4	0	35	50	12.50
Other Notts Matches	5	7	1	59*	118	19.96
Other Matches	4	5	1	27*	53	13.25
Total	32	36	5	59*	454	14.64

1930	M	I	NO	HS	R	Avge
Championship	18	21	6	101*	414	26.60
Tests	3	5	1	19	63	15.75
Other Notts Matches	1	1	0	25	25	25.00
Other Matches	3	4	0	47	70	17.50
Total	25	31	7	101*	572	23.83

1931	M	I	NO	HS	R	Avge
Championship	20	30	2	68	508	18.14
Tests	1	DNB	0	0	0	0
Other Notts Matches	4	5	1	102*	306	76.50
Other Matches	2	1	0	11	11	11.00
Total	26	36	3	102*	825	25.00

1932	M	I	NO	HS	R	Avge
Championship	24	28	4	56	433	18.04
Other Notts Matches	2	8	0	45	56	7.00
Other Matches	6	2	0	67	154	77.00
Total	32	38	4	67	643	18.91

1932–33: MCC in Australia	M	I	NO	HS	R	Avge
Tests	5	7	1	98	145	24.16
Other Matches	5	6	1	81	113	22.6
Total	10	13	2	98	258	23.45

1933	M	I	NO	HS	R	Avge
Championship	12	18	2	62*	392	24.50
Other Notts Matches	1	1	0	10	10	10.00
Total	13	19	2	62*	402	23.64

1934	M	I	NO	HS	R	Avge
Championship	22	30	5	80	391	15.64
Other Notts Matches	1	1	0	0	0	0
Total	23	31	5	80	391	15.03

1935	M	I	NO	HS	R	Avge
Championship	26	34	2	61	704	22.00
Other Notts Matches	2	4	0	31	58	14.50
Total	28	38	2	61	762	21.16

1936	M	I	NO	HS	R	Avge
Championship	20	24	4	41*	274	13.70
Other Notts Matches	2	1	0	20	20	20.00
Total	22	25	4	41*	294	14.00

1936: India	M	I	NO	HS	R	Avge
	2	3	0	9	17	5.66

1937	M	I	NO	HS	R	Avge
Championship	18	19	3	34	217	13.56
Other Notts Matches	2	1	0	34	34	34.00
Total	20	20	3	34	251	14.76

1938	M	I	NO	HS	R	Avge
Championship	8	13	1	59	212	17.66
Other Notts Matches	1	1	1	87*	87	0
Total	9	14	2	87*	299	24.91

TOTALS:	M	I	NO	HS	R	Avge
	361	438	72	102*	7290	19.91

Harold Larwood made 3 hundreds and 25 fifties.

TEST MATCHES

1926 v AUSTRALIA

Lord's

Bowling:	O	M	R	W
	32	2	99	2
	15	3	37	1
	47	5	136	3

Batting: DNB
Catches: 0
Scores: Australia 383 (Bardsley 193*) and 194–5 (Woodfull 133)
England 475 for 3 declared (Hobbs 119, Hendren 127)
Result: Match Drawn

The Oval

Bowling:	O	M	R	W
	34	11	82	3
	14	3	34	3
	48	14	116	6

Batting: 0, 5
Catches: 1
Scores: England 280 (Sutcliffe 76; Mailey 6–138) and 436 (Hobbs 100, Sutcliffe 161)
Australia 302 (Collins 61, Gregory 73) and 125 (Rhodes 4–44)
Result: England won by 289 runs

1928 v WEST INDIES

Lord's

Bowling:	O	M	R	W
	15	4	27	1

Batting: 17*
Catches: 1
Scores: England 401 (Tyldesley 122, Chapman 50)
West Indies 177 and 166
Result: England won by an innings and 58 runs

The Oval

Bowling:	O	M	R	W
	21	6	46	2
	14	3	41	3
	35	9	87	5

Batting: 32
Catches: 2
Scores: West Indies 238 (Roach 53) and 129
England 439 (Hobbs 159, Sutcliffe 63, Tyldesley 73; Griffith 6–103)
Result: England won by an innings and 71 runs

1928–29 v AUSTRALIA

Brisbane

Bowling:	O	M	R	W
	14.4	4	32	6
	7	0	30	2
	21.4	4	62	8

Batting: 70, 37
Catches: 4
Scores: England 521 (Hendren 169) and 342 for 8 declared (Mead 73, Jardine 65*; Grimmett 6–131)
Australia 122 and 66
Result: England won by 675 runs

Sydney

Bowling:	O	M	R	W
	26.2	4	77	3
	35	5	105	1
	56.2	9	192	4

Batting: 43
Catches: 0
Scores: Australia 253 (Woodfull 68; Geary 5–35) and 397 (Woodfull 111, Hendry 112, Ryder 79)
England 636 (Hammond 251, Hendren 74, Geary 66) and 12 for 2.
Result: England won by 8 wickets

Melbourne

Bowling:	O	M	R	W
	37	3	127	3
	16	3	37	1
	53	6	164	4

Batting: 0
Catches: 0
Scores: Australia 397 (Kippax 100, Ryder 112, Bradman 79) and 351 (Woodfull 107, Bradman 112; White 5–107)
England 417 (Hammond 200, Jardine 62, Sutcliffe 58; Blackie 6–94) and 332 for 7 (Sutcliffe 132).
Result: England won by 3 wickets

Adelaide

Bowling:	O	M	R	W
	37	6	92	1
	20	4	60	0
	57	10	152	1

Batting: 3, 5
Catches: 2
Scores: England 334 (Hammond 119, Hobbs 74; Grimmett 5–102) and 383 (Hammond 177, Jardine 98)
Australia 369 (Jackson 164, Ryder 63) and 336 (Ryder 87, Bradman 58, Kippax 51; White 8–126)
Result: England won by 12 runs

Melbourne

Bowling:	O	M	R	W
	34	7	83	1
	32.1	5	81	0
	66.1	12	164	1

Batting: 4, 11
Catches: 0
Scores: England 519 (Hobbs 142, Leyland 137, Hendren 95) and 257 (Hobbs 65, Leyland 53 not out)
Australia 491 (Bradman 123, Woodfull 102, Fairfax 65; Geary 5–105) and 287 for 5 (Ryder 57 not out)
Result: Australia won by 5 wickets

1929 v SOUTH AFRICA

Edgbaston

Bowling:	O	M	R	W
	42.4	17	57	5
	11	6	12	0
	53.4	23	69	5

Batting: 6
Catches: 0
Scores: England 245 (Hendren 70) and 308 for 4 declared (Sutcliffe 114, Hammond 138)
South Africa 250 (Mitchell 88, Catterall 67) and 171 for 1 (Catterall 98, Mitchell 61*)
Result: Match drawn

Lords

Bowling:	O	M	R	W
	20	4	65	1
	12	3	17	1
	32	7	82	2

Batting: 35, 9
Catches: 0
Scores: England 322 (Sutcliffe 100, Hendren 73; Bell 6–99) and 312 (Leyland 102, Tate 100*)
South Africa 322 (Morkel 88, Christy 70) and 90 for 5.
Result: Match drawn

Headingley

Bowling:	O	M	R	W
	14	4	35	1
	DNB			

Batting: 0
Catches: 0
Scores: South Africa 236 (Catterall 74, Vincent 60; Freeman 7–115) and 275 (Owen-Smith 129)
England 328 (Hammond 65, Woolley 83; Quinn 6–92) and 186 for 5 (Woolley 95*)
Result: England won by 5 wickets

1930 v AUSTRALIA

Trent Bridge

Bowling:	O	M	R	W
	15	8	12	1
	5	1	9	1
	20	9	21	2

Batting: 18, 7
Catches: 0
Scores: England 270 (Hobbs 78, Robins 50 not out; Grimmett 5–107) and 302 (Hobbs 74, Hendren 72, Sutcliffe 58 retired hurt; Grimmett 5–94)
Australia 144 (Kippax 64*) and 335 (Bradman 131)
Result: England won by 93 runs

Headingley

Bowling:	O	M	R	W
	33	3	139	1

Batting: 10*
Catches: 2
Scores: Australia 566 (Bradman 334, Kippax 77, Woodfull 50; Tate 5–124)
England 391 (Hammond 113; Grimmett 5–135) and 95 for 3.
Result: Match drawn

The Oval

Bowling:	O	M	R	W
	48	6	132	1

Batting: 19, 9
Catches: 1
Scores: England 405 (Sutcliffe 161, Wyatt 64, Duleepsinhji 50) and 251 (Hammond 60, Sutcliffe 54; Hornibrook 7–92)
Australia 695 (Bradman 232, Ponsford 110, Jackson 73, McCabe 54, Fairfax 53*)
Result: Australia won by an innings and 39 runs

1931 v NEW ZEALAND

Old Trafford

Bowling: DNB
Batting: DNB
Catches: 0
Scores: England 224 for 3 (Sutcliffe 109*, Duleepsinhji 63)
Result: Match drawn

1932–33 v AUSTRALIA

Sydney

Bowling:	O	M	R	W
	31	5	96	5
	18	4	28	5
	49	9	124	10

Batting: 1
Catches: 0
Scores: Australia 360 (McCabe 187*) and 164
England 524 (Sutcliffe 194, Hammond 112, Nawab of Pataudi 102)
Result: England won by 10 wickets

Melbourne

Bowling:	O	M	R	W
	20.3	2	52	2
	15	2	50	2
	35.3	4	102	4

Batting: 9, 4
Catches: 0
Scores: Australia 228 (Fingleton 83) and 191 (Bradman 103)
England 169 (Sutcliffe 52; O'Reilly 4–52) and 139 (O'Reilly 5–66)
Result: Australia won by 111 runs

Adelaide

Bowling:	O	M	R	W
	25	6	55	3
	19	3	71	4
	44	9	126	7

Batting: 3*, 8
Catches: 0
Scores: England 341 (Leyland 83, Wyatt 78, Paynter 77; Wall 5–72) and 412 (Hammond 85, Ames 69, Jardine 56)
Australia 222 (Ponsford 85) and 193 (Woodfull 73, Bradman 66)
Result: England won by 338 runs

Brisbane

Bowling:	O	M	R	W
	31	7	101	4
	17.3	3	49	3
	38.3	10	150	7

Batting: 23
Catches: 1
Scores: Australia 340 (Richardson 83, Bradman 76, Woodfull 67) and 175
England 356 (Sutcliffe 86, Paynter 83) and 162 for 4 (Leyland 86)
Result: England won by 6 wickets

Sydney

Bowling:	O	M	R	W
	32.2	10	98	4
	11	0	44	1
	43.2	10	142	5

Batting: 98
Catches: 1
Scores: Australia 435 (Darling 85, McCabe 73, O'Brien 61, Oldfield 52) and 182 (Bradman 71, Woodfull 67; Verity 5–33)
England 454 (Hammond 101, Sutcliffe 56) and 168 (Hammond 65*)
Result: England won by 8 wickets

OVERALL TEST RECORD

Bowling:	Mat	O	M	R	W	Ave
	21	828.1	167	2212	78	28.35

Batting:	Mat	I	R	NO	HS	Ave
	21	28	485	3	98	19.40

Catches: 15

Appendix 3

AUSTRALIA v ENGLAND 1932–33

The photograph of Harold Larwood, signed by the fast bowler himself, that the author's father brought back for him from Australia.

1st Test – Sydney Cricket Ground

2nd December 1932

Toss – Australia, who chose to bat first

Australia 1st Innings		R	M	B	4s	6s	SR
W.M. Woodfull	c Ames b Voce	**7**	38	34	0	0	20.58
W.H. Ponsford	b Larwood	**32**	93	79	0	0	40.50
J.H.W. Fingleton	c Allen b Larwood	**26**	72	77	3	0	33.76
A.F. Kippax	lbw b Larwood	**8**	28	27	0	0	29.62
S.J. McCabe	not out	**187**	242	233	25	0	80.25
V.Y. Richardson	b Hammond b Voce	**49**	120	108	5	0	45.37
W.A.S. Oldfield	c Ames b Larwood	**4**	8	4	0	0	100.00
C.V. Grimmett	c Ames b Voce	**19**	53	37	2	0	51.35
L.E. Nagel	b Larwood	**0**	1	1	0	0	0.00
W.J. O'Reilly	b Voce	**4**	6	8	1	0	50.00
T.W. Wall	c Allen b Hammond	**4**	33	18	1	0	22.22
Extras	(b 12, lb 4, nb 4)	**20**					
Total	all out (102.2 overs)	**360** (3.51 runs per over)					

Fall of wickets: 1-22 (Woodfull), 2-65 (Ponsford), 3-82 (Fingleton), 4-87 (Kippax), 5-216 (Richardson), 6-231 (Oldfield), 7-299 (Grimmett), 8-300 (Nagel), 9-305 (O'Reilly) 10-360 (Wall)

Bowling	O	M	R	W	Econ
H. Larwood	31	5	96	5	3.09
W. Voce	29	4	110	4	3.7
G.O.B. Allen	15	1	65	0	4.33
W.R. Hammond	14.2	0	34	1	2.37
H. Verity	13	4	35	0	2.69

England 1st Innings		R	M	B	4s	6s	SR
H. Sutcliffe	lbw b Wall	**194**	436	496	13	0	39.11
R.E.S. Wyatt	lbw b Grimmett	**38**	96	91	3	0	41.75
W.R. Hammond	c Grimmett b Nagel	**112**	192	242	16	0	46.28
Nawab of Pataudi	b Nagel	**102**	327	380	6	0	26.84
M. Leyland	c Oldfield b Wall	**0**	1	1	0	0	0.00
D.R. Jardine	c Oldfield b McCabe	**27**	68	82	2	0	32.92
H. Verity	lbw b Wall	**2**	14	15	0	0	13.33
G.O.B. Allen	c & b O'Reilly	**19**	65	66	2	0	28.78
L.E.G. Ames	c McCabe b O'Reilly	**0**	5	8	0	0	0.00
H. Larwood	lbw b O'Reilly	**0**	6	7	0	0	0.00
W. Voce	not out	**0**	3	1	0	0	0.00
Extras	(b 7, lb 17, nb 6)						
Total	all out (229.4 overs)	**524** (2.28 runs per over)					

Fall of wickets: 1-112 (Wyatt), 2-300 (Hammond), 3-423 (Sutcliffe), 4-423 (Leyland), 5-470 (Jardine), 6-479 (Verity), 7-519 (Allen), 8-522 (Ames), 9-522 (Larwood), 10-524 (Pataudi)

Bowling	O	M	R	W	Econ
T.W. Wall	38	4	104	3	2.73
L.E. Nagel	43.3	9	110	2	2.51
W.J. O'Reilly	67	32	117	3	1.74
C.V. Grimmett	64	22	118	1	1.84
S.J. McCabe	15	2	42	1	2.80
A.F. Kippax	2	1	3	0	1.50

Australia 2nd Innings		R	M	B	4s	6s	SR
W.M. Woodfull	b Larwood	**0**	23	19	0	0	0.00
W.H. Ponsford	b Voce	**2**	11	9	0	0	22.22
J.H.W. Fingleton	c Voce b Larwood	**40**	144	120	5	0	33.33
S.J. McCabe	lbw b Hammond	**32**	65	69	3	1	46.37
V.Y. Richardson	c Voce b Hammond	**0**	1	1	0	0	0.00
A.F. Kippax	b Larwood	**19**	37	35	1	0	54.28
W.A.S. Oldfield	c Leyland b Larwood	**1**	14	21	0	0	4.76
C.V. Grimmett	c Allen b Larwood	**5**	17	15	1	0	33.33
L.E. Nagel	not out	**21**	51	59	4	0	35.59
T.W. Wall	c Ames b Allen	**20**	4	29	3	0	68.96
W.J. O'Reilly	b Voce	**7**	5	9	1	0	77.77
Extras	(b 12, lb 2, w 1, nb 2)	**17**					

Total all out (63.3 overs) **164** (2.58 runs per over)

Fall of wickets: 1-2 (Ponsford), 2-10 (Woodfull), 3-61 (McCabe), 4-61 (Richardson), 5-100 (Kippax), 6-104 (Oldfield), 7-105 (Fingleton), 8-113 (Grimmett), 9-151 (Wall), 10-164 (O'Reilly)

Bowling	O	M	R	W	Econ
H. Larwood	18	4	28	5	1.55
W. Voce	17.3	5	54	2	3.08
G.O.B. Allen	9	5	13	1	1.44
W.R. Hammond	15	6	37	2	2.46
H. Verity	4	1	15	0	3.75

England 2nd Innings		R	M	B	4s	6s	SR
H. Sutcliffe	not out	**1**	1	1	0	0	100.00
R.E.S. Wyatt	not out	**0**	1	0	0	0	0.00
Extras		**0**					

Total 0 wickets (0.1 overs) **1** (6.00 runs per over)

Bowling	O	M	R	W	Econ
S.J. McCabe	0.1	0	1	0	6.00

England won by 10 wickets

2nd Test – Melbourne Cricket Ground

30th December 1932

Toss – Australia, who chose to bat first

Australia 1st Innings		R	M	B	4s	6s	SR
J.H.W. Fingleton	b Allen	**83**	234	227	3	0	36.56
W.M. Woodfull	b Allen	**10**	53	33	0	0	30.30
L.P.J. O'Brien	run out	**10**	65	47	0	0	21.27
D.G. Bradman	b Bowes	**0**	1	1	0	0	0.00
S.J. McCabe	c Jardine b Voce	**32**	76	58	1	0	55.17
V.Y. Richardson	c Hammond b Voce	**34**	74	66	5	0	51.51
W.A.S. Oldfield	not out	**27**	84	66	1	0	40.90
C.V. Grimmett	c Sutcliffe b Voce	**2**	7	6	0	0	33.33
T.W. Wall	run out	**1**	10	3	0	0	33.33
W.J. O'Reilly	b Larwood	**15**	15	13	1	0	115.38
H. Ironmonger	b Larwood	**4**	5	4	1	0	100.00
Extras	(b 5, lb 1, w 2, nb 2)	**10**					
Total	all out (86.3 overs)	**228** (2.63 runs per over)					

Fall of wickets: 1-29 (Woodfull), 2-67 (O'Brien), 3-67 (Bradman), 4-131 (McCabe), 5-156 (Fingleton), 6-188 (Richardson), 7-194 (Grimmett), 8-200 (Wall), 9-222 (O'Reilly), 10-228 (Ironmonger)

Bowling	O	M	R	W	Econ
H. Larwood	20.3	2	52	2	2.53
W. Voce	20	3	54	3	2.70
G.O.B. Allen	17	3	41	2	2.41
W.R. Hammond	10	3	21	0	2.10
W.E. Bowes	19	2	50	1	2.63

England 1st Innings		R	M	B	4s	6s	SR
H. Sutcliffe	c Richardson b Wall	**52**	156	182	5	0	28.57
R.E.S. Wyatt	lbw b O'Reilly	**13**	56	51	0	1	25.49
W.R. Hammond	b Wall	**8**	9	7	1	0	114.28
Nawab of Pataudi	b O'Reilly	**15**	60	78	0	0	19.23
M. Leyland	b O'Reilly	**22**	68	62	2	0	35.48
D.R. Jardine	c Oldfield b Wall	**1**	11	7	0	0	14.28
L.E.G. Ames	b Wall	**4**	9	10	0	0	40.00
G.O.B. Allen	c Richardson b O'Reilly	**30**	68	74	3	0	40.54
H. Larwood	b O'Reilly	**9**	11	11	1	0	81.81
W. Voce	c McCabe b Grimmett	**6**	29	30	0	0	20.00
W.E. Bowes	not out	**4**	6	9	0	0	44.44
Extras	(b 1, lb 2, nb 2)	**5**					
Total	all out (85.3 overs)	**169** (1.97 runs per over)					

Fall of wickets:1-30 (Wyatt), 2-43 (Hammond), 3-83 (Pataudi), 4-98 (Sutcliffe), 5-104 (Jardine), 6-110 (Ames), 7-122 (Leyland), 8-138 (Larwood), 9-161 (Voce), 10-169 (Allen)

Bowling	O	M	R	W	Econ
T.W. Wall	21	4	52	4	2.47
W.J. O'Reilly	34.3	17	63	5	1.82
C.V. Grimmett	16	4	21	1	1.31
H. Ironmonger	14	4	28	0	2.00

Australia 2nd Innings		R	M	B	4s	6s	SR
J.H.W. Fingleton	c Ames b Allen	**1**	6	9	0	0	11.11
W.M. Woodfull	c Allen b Larwood	**26**	85	71	0	0	36.61
L.P.J. O'Brien	b Larwood	**11**	21	13	0	0	84.61
D.G. Bradman	not out	**103**	185	146	7	0	70.54
S.J. McCabe	b Allen	**0**	4	5	0	0	0.00
V.Y. Richardson	lbw b Hammond	**32**	44	48	3	0	66.66
W.A.S. Oldfield	b Voce	**6**	15	15	1	0	40.00
C.V. Grimmett	b Voce	**0**	6	5	0	0	0.00
T.W. Wall	lbw b Hammond	**3**	34	22	0	0	13.63
W.J. O'Reilly	c Ames b Hammond	**0**	7	8	0	0	0.00
H. Ironmonger	run out	**0**	6	2	0	0	0.00
Extras	(b 3, lb 1, w 4, nb 1)	**9**					
Total	all out (56.5 overs)	**191** (3.36 runs per over)					

Fall of wickets: 1-1 (Fingleton), 2-27 (O'Brien), 3-78 (Woodfull), 4-81 (McCabe), 5-135 (Richardson), 6-150 (Oldfield), 7-156 (Grimmett), 8-184 (Wall), 9-186 (O'Reilly), 10-191 (Ironmonger)

Bowling	O	M	R	W	Econ
H. Larwood	15	2	50	2	3.33
W. Voce	15	2	47	2	3.13
G.O.B. Allen	12	1	44	2	3.66
W.R. Hammond	10.5	2	21	3	1.93
W.E. Bowes	4	0	20	0	5.00

England 2nd Innings		R	M	B	4s	6s	SR
H. Sutcliffe	b O'Reilly	**33**	53	63	4	0	52.38
M. Leyland	b Wall	**19**	58	51	2	0	37.25
Nawab of Pataudi	c Fingleton b I'monger	**5**	34	36	0	0	13.88
W.R. Hammond	c O'Brien b O'Reilly	**23**	51	43	2	0	53.48
D.R. Jardine	c McCabe b I'monger	**0**	2	3	0	0	0.00
L.E.G. Ames	c Fingleton b O'Reilly	**2**	8	10	0	0	20.00
R.E.S. Wyatt	lbw b O'Reilly	**25**	54	50	3	0	50.00
G.O.B. Allen	st Oldfield b I'monger	**23**	51	63	1	0	36.50
H. Larwood	c Wall b I'monger	**4**	11	7	0	0	57.14
W. Voce	c O'Brien b O'Reilly	**0**	3	5	0	0	0.00
W.E. Bowes	not out	**0**	2	2	0	0	0.00
Extras	(lb 4, nb 1)	**5**					
Total	all out (55.1 overs)	**139** (2.51 runs per over)					

Fall of wickets: 1-53 (Sutcliffe), 2-53 (Leyland), 3-70 (Pataudi), 4-70 (Jardine), 5-77 (Ames), 6-85 (Hammond), 7-135 (Wyatt), 8-137 (Allen), 9-138 (Voce), 10-139 (Larwood)

Bowling	O	M	R	W	Econ
T.W. Wall	8	2	23	1	2.87
W.J. O'Reilly	24	5	66	5	2.75
C.V. Grimmett	4	0	19	0	4.75
H. Ironmonger	19.1	8	26	4	1.35

Australia won by 111 runs

3rd Test – Adelaide Oval

13th January 1933

Toss – England, who chose to bat first

England 1st Innings		R	M	B	4s	6s	SR
H. Sutcliffe	c Wall b O'Reilly	**9**	46	182	0	0	20.93
D.R. Jardine	b Wall	**3**	20	7	0	0	16.66
W.R. Hammond	c Oldfield b Wall	**2**	15	7	0	0	13.33
L.E.G. Ames	b Ironmonger	**3**	39	10	0	0	7.89
M. Leyland	b O'Reilly	**83**	180	62	13	0	43.68
R.E.S. Wyatt	c Richardson b G'mett	**78**	164	51	3	3	44.31
E. Paynter	c Fingleton b Wall	**77**	185	78	9	0	35.64
G.O.B. Allen	lbw b Grimmett	**15**	37	74	2	0	50.00
H. Verity	c Richardson b Wall	**45**	154	9	2	0	30.61
W. Voce	b Wall	**8**	14	30	1	0	61.53
H. Larwood	not out	**3**	3	11	0	0	75.00
Extras	(b 1, lb 7, nb 7)	**15**					
Total	all out (146.1 overs)	**341**	(2.33 runs per over)				

Fall of wickets: 1-4 (Jardine), 2-16 (Hammond), 3-16 (Sutcliffe), 4-30 (Ames), 5-186 (Leyland), 6-196 (Wyatt), 7-228 (Allen), 8-324 (Paynter), 9-336 (Voce), 10-341 (Verity)

Bowling	O	M	R	W	Econ
T.W. Wall	34.1	10	72	5	2.10
W.J. O'Reilly	50	19	82	2	1.64
H. Ironmonger	20	6	50	1	2.50
C.V. Grimmett	28	6	94	2	3.35
S.J. McCabe	14	3	28	0	2.00

Australia 1st Innings		R	M	B	4s	6s	SR
J.H.W. Fingleton	c Ames b Allen	**0**	5	8	0	0	0.00
W.M. Woodfull	b Allen	**22**	89	65	0	0	33.84
D.G. Bradman	c Allen b Larwood	**8**	18	17	1	0	47.05
S.J. McCabe	c Jardine b Larwood	**8**	21	25	1	0	32.00
W.H. Ponsford	b Voce	**85**	216	213	8	0	39.90
V.Y. Richardson	b Allen	**28**	95	81	1	0	34.56
W.A.S. Oldfield	retired hurt	**41**	123	114	4	0	35.96
C.V. Grimmett	c Voce b Allen	**10**	29	24	1	0	41.66
T.W. Wall	b Hammond	**6**	22	19	0	0	31.57
W.J. O'Reilly	b Larwood	**0**	8	9	0	0	0.00
H. Ironmonger	not out	**0**	1	0	0	0	-
Extras	(b 2, lb 11, nb 1)	**14**					
Total	all out (95.4 overs)	**222** (2.32 runs per over)					

Fall of wickets: 1-1 (Fingleton), 2-18 (Bradman), 3-34 (McCabe), 4-51 (Woodfull), 5-131 (Richardson), 6-194 (Ponsford), 7-212 (Grimmett), 7-222* (Oldfield, retired not out), 8-222 (O'Reilly), 9-222 (Wall)

Bowling	O	M	R	W	Econ
H. Larwood	25	6	55	3	2.20
G.O.B. Allen	23	4	71	4	3.08
W.R. Hammond	17.4	4	30	1	1.69
W. Voce	14	5	21	1	1.50
H. Verity	16	7	31	0	1.93

England 2nd Innings		R	M	B	4s	6s	SR
H. Sutcliffe	c sub (O'Brien) b Wall	**7**	13	11	1	0	63.63
D.R. Jardine	lbw b Ironmonger	**56**	254	266	2	0	21.05
R.E.S. Wyatt	c Wall b O'Reilly	**49**	133	138	4	3	35.50
G.O.B. Allen	lbw b Grimmett	**15**	52	59	2	0	25.42
W.R. Hammond	b Bradman	**85**	221	247	8	0	34.41
M. Leyland	c Wall b Ironmonger	**42**	108	93	5	0	45.16
L.E.G. Ames	b O'Reilly	**69**	169	173	6	0	39.88
H. Verity	lbw b O'Reilly	**40**	115	131	2	0	30.53
H. Larwood	c Bradman b I'monger	**8**	14	12	1	0	66.66
E. Paynter	not out	**1**	17	15	0	0	6.66
W. Voce	b O'Reilly	**8**	7	10	0	0	80.00
Extras	(b 17, lb 11, nb 4)	**32**					
Total	all out (191.3 overs)	**412** (2.15 runs per over)					

Fall of wickets: 1-7 (Sutcliffe), 2-91 (Wyatt), 3-123 (Allen), 4-154 (Jardine), 5-245 (Leyland), 6-296 (Hammond), 7-394 (Ames), 8-395 (Verity), 9-403 (Larwood), 10-412 (Voce)

Bowling	O	M	R	W	Econ
T.W. Wall	29	6	75	1	2.58
W.J. O'Reilly	50.3	21	79	4	1.56
H. Ironmonger	57	21	87	3	1.52
C.V. Grimmett	35	9	74	1	2.11
S.J. McCabe	16	0	42	0	2.62
D.G. Bradman	4	0	23	1	5.75

Australia 2nd Innings		R	M	B	4s	6s	SR
J.H.W. Fingleton	b Larwood	**0**	8	14	0	0	0.00
W.M. Woodfull	not out	**73**	235	208	2	0	35.09
W.H. Ponsford	c Jardine b Larwood	**3**	13	11	0	0	27.27
D.G. Bradman	c & b Verity	**66**	73	71	10	1	92.95
S.J. McCabe	c Leyland b Allen	**7**	21	19	1	0	36.84
V.Y. Richardson	c Allen b Larwood	**21**	83	76	3	0	27.63
C.V. Grimmett	b Allen	**6**	10	8	1	0	75.00
T.W. Wall	b Allen	**0**	1	4	0	0	0.00
W.J. O'Reilly	b Larwood	**5**	3	10	1	0	50.00
H. Ironmonger	b Allen	**0**	2	1	0	0	0.00
W.A.S. Oldfield	absent hurt						
Extras	(b 4, lb 2, w 1, nb 5)	**12**					
Total	all out (69.2 overs)	**193** (2.78 runs per over)					

Fall of wickets: 1-3 (Fingleton), 2-12 (Ponsford), 3-100 (Bradman), 4-116 (McCabe), 5-171 (Richardson), 6-183 (Grimmett), 7-183 (Wall), 8-192 (O'Reilly), 9-193 (Ironmonger)

Bowling	O	M	R	W	Econ
H. Larwood	19	3	71	4	3.73
G.O.B. Allen	17.2	5	50	4	2.88
W.R. Hammond	9	3	27	0	3.00
W. Voce	4	1	7	0	1.75
H. Verity	20	12	26	1	1.30

England won by 338 runs

4th Test – Brisbane Cricket Ground

10th February 1933

Toss – Australia, who chose to bat first

Australia 1st Innings		R	M	B	4s	6s	SR
V.Y. Richardson	st Ames b Hammond	**83**	159	146	6	0	56.84
W.M. Woodfull	b Mitchell	**67**	244	232	7	0	28.87
D.G. Bradman	b Larwood	**76**	156	138	11	0	55.07
S.J. McCabe	c Jardine b Allen	**20**	28	28	4	0	71.42
W.H. Ponsford	b Larwood	**19**	48	40	2	0	47.50
L.S. Darling	c Ames b Allen	**17**	29	21	2	0	80.95
E.H. Bromley	c Verity b Larwood	**26**	65	52	2	0	50.00
H.S.B. Love	lbw b Mitchell	**5**	31	24	0	0	20.83
T.W. Wall	not out	**6**	32	25	0	0	24.00
W.J. O'Reilly	c Hammond b L'wood	**6**	7	11	1	0	54.54
H. Ironmonger	st Ames b Hammond	**8**	11	13	1	0	61.53
Extras	(b 5, lb 1, nb 1)	**7**					
Total	all out (121 overs)	**340** (2.80 runs per over)					

Fall of wickets: 1-133 (Richardson), 2-200 (Woodfull), 3-233 (McCabe), 4-264 (Bradman), 5-267 (Ponsford), 6-292 (Darling), 7-315 (Bromley), 8-317 (Love), 9-329 (O'Reilly), 10-340 (Ironmonger)

Bowling	O	M	R	W	Econ
H. Larwood	31	7	101	4	3.25
G.O.B. Allen	24	4	83	2	3.45
W.R. Hammond	23	5	61	2	2.65
T.B. Mitchell	16	5	49	2	3.06
H. Verity	27	12	39	0	1.44

England 1st Innings		R	M	B	4s	6s	SR
D.R. Jardine	c Love b O'Reilly	**46**	190	191	3	0	24.08
H. Sutcliffe	lbw b O'Reilly	**86**	266	244	10	0	35.24
W.R. Hammond	b McCabe	**20**	90	93	1	0	21.50
R.E.S. Wyatt	c Love b Ironmonger	**12**	47	44	1	0	27.27
M. Leyland	c Bradman b O'Reilly	**12**	45	48	1	0	25.00
L.E.G. Ames	c Darling b I'monger	**17**	82	65	1	0	26.15
G.O.B. Allen	c Love b Wall	**13**	26	31	2	0	41.93
E. Paynter	c Richardson b I'monger	**83**	238	218	10	0	38.07
H. Larwood	b McCabe	**23**	33	27	3	0	85.18
H. Verity	not out	**23**	162	157	1	0	14.64
T.B. Mitchell	lbw b O'Reilly	**0**	1	4	0	0	0.00
Extras	(b 6, lb 12, nb 3)	**21**					
Total	all out (185.4 overs)	**356** (1.91 runs per over)					

Fall of wickets: 1-114 (Jardine), 2-157 (Sutcliffe), 3-165 (Hammond), 4-188 (Wyatt), 5-198 (Leyland), 6-216 (Allen), 7-225 (Ames), 8-264 (Larwood), 9-356 (Paynter), 10-356 (Mitchell)

Bowling	O	M	R	W	Econ
T.W. Wall	33	6	66	1	2.00
W.J. O'Reilly	67.4	27	120	4	1.77
H. Ironmonger	43	19	69	3	1.60
S.J. McCabe	23	7	40	2	1.73
E.H. Bromley	10	4	19	0	1.90
D.G. Bradman	7	1	17	0	2.42
L.S. Darling	2	0	4	0	2.00

Australia 2nd Innings		R	M	B	4s	6s	SR
V.Y. Richardson	c Jardine b Verity	**32**	64	64	2	0	50.00
W.M. Woodfull	c Hammond b M'chell	**19**	124	105	1	0	18.09
D.G. Bradman	c Mitchell b L'wood	**24**	32	31	3	0	77.41
W.H. Ponsford	c Larwood b Allen	**0**	4	4	0	0	0.00
S.J. McCabe	b Verity	**22**	82	75	1	0	29.33
L.S. Darling	run out	**39**	109	80	3	0	48.75
E.H. Bromley	c Hammond b Allen	**7**	34	30	0	0	23.33
H.S.B. Love	lbw b Larwood	**3**	12	14	0	0	21.42
T.W. Wall	c Jardine b Allen	**2**	5	4	0	0	50.00
W.J. O'Reilly	b Larwood	**4**	8	4	1	0	100.00
H. Ironmonger	not out	**0**	3	2	0	0	0.00
Extras	(b 13, lb 9, nb 1)	**23**					

Total all out (68.3 overs) **175** (2.55 runs per over)

Fall of wickets: 1-46 (Richardson), 2-79 (Bradman), 3-81 (Ponsford), 4-91 (Woodfull), 5-136 (McCabe), 6-163 (Bromley), 7-169 (Darling), 8-169 (Love), 9-171 (Wall), 10-175 (O'Reilly)

Bowling	O	M	R	W	Econ
H. Larwood	17.3	3	49	3	2.80
G.O.B. Allen	17	3	44	3	2.58
W.R. Hammond	10	4	18	0	1.80
T.B. Mitchell	5	0	11	1	2.20
H. Verity	19	6	30	2	1.57

England 2nd Innings		R	M	B	4s	6s	SR
D.R. Jardine	lbw b Ironmonger	**24**	132	112	2	0	21.42
H. Sutcliffe	c Darling b Wall	**2**	9	11	0	0	18.18
M. Leyland	c McCabe b O'Reilly	**86**	222	235	10	0	36.59
W.R. Hammond	c Bromley b I'monger	**14**	71	75	0	0	18.66
L.E.G. Ames	not out	**14**	40	36	0	1	38.88
E. Paynter	not out	**14**	12	11	2	1	127.27
Extras	(b 2, lb 4, nb 2)	**8**					

Total 4 wickets(79.4 overs) **162** (2.03 runs per over)

Fall of wickets: 1-5 (Sutcliffe), 2-78 (Jardine), 3-118 (Hammond), 4-138 (Leyland)

Bowling	O	M	R	W	Econ
T.W. Wall	7	1	17	1	2.42
W.J. O'Reilly	30	11	65	1	2.16
H. Ironmonger	35	13	47	2	1.34
S.J. McCabe	7.4	2	25	0	3.26

England won by 6 wickets

5th Test – Sydney Cricket Ground

23rd February 1933

Toss – Australia, who chose to bat first

Australia 1st Innings		**R**	**M**	**B**	**4s**	**6s**	**SR**
V.Y. Richardson	c Jardine b Larwood	**0**	4	5	0	0	0.00
W.M. Woodfull	b Larwood	**14**	69	59	0	0	23.72
D.G. Bradman	b Larwood	**48**	71	56	7	0	85.71
L.P.J. O'Brien	c Larwood b Voce	**61**	107	88	7	0	69.31
S.J. McCabe	c Hammond b Verity	**73**	172	129	11	0	56.58
L.S. Darling	b Verity	**85**	148	129	8	0	65.89
W.A.S. Oldfield	run out	**52**	138	96	4	0	54.16
P.K. Lee	c Jardine b Verity	**42**	35	44	7	0	95.45
W.J. O'Reilly	b Allen	**19**	37	27	1	0	70.37
H.H. Alexander	not out	**17**	17	17	2	0	100.00
H. Ironmonger	b Larwood	**1**	4	4	0	0	25.00
Extras	(b 13, lb 9, w 1)	**23**					
Total	all out (108.2 overs)	**435** (4.01 runs per over)					

Fall of wickets: 1-0 (Richardson), 2-59 (Woodfull), 3-64 (Bradman), 4-163 (O'Brien), 5-244 (McCabe), 6-328 (Darling), 7-385 (Lee), 8-414 (Oldfield), 9-430 (O'Reilly), 10-435 (Ironmonger)

Bowling	**O**	**M**	**R**	**W**	**Econ**
H. Larwood	32.2	10	98	4	3.03
W. Voce	24	4	80	1	3.33
G.O.B. Allen	25	1	128	1	5.12
W.R. Hammond	8	0	32	0	4.00
H. Verity	17	3	62	3	3.64
R.E.S. Wyatt	2	0	12	0	6.00

England 1st Innings		**R**	**M**	**B**	**4s**	**6s**	**SR**
D.R. Jardine	c Oldfield b O'Reilly	**18**	33	50	1	0	36.00
H. Sutcliffe	c Rich'son b O'Reilly	**56**	155	137	4	0	40.87
W.R. Hammond	lbw b Lee	**101**	207	205	12	0	49.26
H. Larwood	c I'monger b Lee	**98**	138	148	10	1	66.21
M. Leyland	run out	**42**	77	87	6	0	48.27
R.E.S. Wyatt	c I'monger b O'Reilly	**51**	161	196	5	0	26.02
L.E.G. Ames	run out	**4**	32	27	0	0	14.81
E. Paynter	b Lee	**9**	39	29	1	0	31.03
G.O.B. Allen	c Bradman b Lee	**48**	102	104	6	0	46.15
H. Verity	c Oldfield b Alex'r	**4**	14	14	0	0	28.57
W. Voce	not out	**7**	29	35	0	0	20.00
Extras	(b 7, lb 7, nb 2)		16				
Total	all out (171.2 overs)	**454** (2.64 runs per over)					

Fall of wickets: 1-31 (Jardine), 2-153 (Sutcliffe), 3-245 (Hammond), 4-310 (Larwood), 5-330 (Leyland), 6-349 (Ames), 7-374 (Paynter), 8-418 (Wyatt), 9-434 (Verity), 10-454 (Allen)

Bowling	**O**	**M**	**R**	**W**	**Econ**
H.H. Alexander	35	1	129	1	3.68
S.J. McCabe	12	1	27	0	2.25
W.J. O'Reilly	45	7	100	3	2.22
H. Ironmonger	31	13	64	0	2.06
P.K. Lee	40.2	11	111	4	2.75
L.S. Darling	7	5	3	0	0.42
D.G. Bradman	1	0	4	0	4.00

Australia 2nd Innings

Australia 2nd Innings		R	M	B	4s	6s	SR
V.Y. Richardson	c Allen b Larwood	**0**	1	2	0	0	0.00
W.M. Woodfull	b Allen	**67**	185	168	5	0	39.88
D.G. Bradman	b Verity	**71**	97	69	9	0	102.89
L.P.J. O'Brien	c Verity b Voce	**5**	22	20	0	0	25.00
S.J. McCabe	c Jardine b Voce	**4**	6	6	1	0	66.66
L.S. Darling	c Wyatt b Verity	**7**	10	13	1	0	53.84
W.A.S. Oldfield	c Wyatt b Verity	**5**	22	25	0	0	20.00
P.K. Lee	b Allen	**15**	30	21	2	0	71.42
W.J. O'Reilly	b Verity	**1**	2	3	0	0	33.33
H.H. Alexander	lbw b Verity	**0**	1	1	0	0	0.00
H. Ironmonger	not out	**0**	2	3	0	0	0.00
Extras	(b 4, nb 3)	**7**					
Total	all out (54.4 overs)	**182** (3.32 runs per over)					

Fall of wickets: 1-0 (Richardson), 2-115 (Bradman), 3-135 (O'Brien), 4-139 (McCabe), 5-148 (Darling), 6-161 (Oldfield), 7-177 (Woodfull), 8-178 (O'Reilly), 9-178 (Alexander), 10-182 (Lee)

Bowling	O	M	R	W	Econ
H. Larwood	11	0	44	1	4.00
W. Voce	10	0	34	2	3.40
G.O.B. Allen	11.4	2	54	2	4.62
W.R. Hammond	3	0	10	0	3.33
H. Verity	19	9	33	5	1.73

England 2nd Innings

England 2nd Innings		R	M	B	4s	6s	SR
D.R. Jardine	c Rich'son b I'monger	**24**	58	57	2	0	42.10
R.E.S. Wyatt	not out	**61**	195	215	4	0	28.37
M. Leyland	b Ironmonger	**0**	12	16	0	0	0.00
W.R. Hammond	not out	**75**	123	140	6	2	53.57
Extras	(b 6, lb 1, nb 1)	**8**					
Total	2 wickets (71.2 overs)	**168** (2.35 runs per over)					

Fall of wickets: 1-43 (Jardine), 2-43 (Leyland)

Bowling	O	M	R	W	Econ
H.H. Alexander	11	2	25	0	2.27
S.J. McCabe	5	2	10	0	2.00
W.J. O'Reilly	15	5	32	0	2.13
H. Ironmonger	26	12	34	2	1.30
P.K. Lee	12.2	3	52	0	4.21
L.S. Darling	2	0	7	0	3.50

England won by 8 wickets

TEST MATCH AVERAGES: ENGLAND

Batting

Player	Mat	Inns	NO	Runs	HS	Ave	SR	100	50
E. Paynter	3	5	2	184	83	61.33	37.62	0	2
W.R. Hammond	5	9	1	440	112	55.00	41.23	2	2
H. Sutcliffe	5	9	1	440	194	55.00	37.03	1	3
R.E.S. Wyatt	5	9	2	327	78	46.71	34.02	0	3
Nawab of Pataudi	2	3	0	122	102	40.66	24.69	1	0
M. Leyland	5	9	0	306	86	34.00	39.08	0	2
H. Verity	4	5	1	114	45	28.50	24.56	0	0
H. Larwood	5	7	1	145	98	24.16	67.12	0	1
G.O.B. Allen	5	7	0	163	48	23.28	38.17	0	0
D.R. Jardine	5	9	0	199	56	22.11	25.31	0	1
L.E.G. Ames	5	8	1	113	69	16.14	30.79	0	1
W. Voce	4	6	2	29	8	7.25	30.85	0	0
W.E. Bowes	1	2	2	4	4*	-	36.36	0	0
T.B. Mitchell	1	1	0	0	0	0.00	0.00	0	0

Bowling

Player	Mat	Overs	Mdns	Runs	Wkts	BB	Ave	Econ	SR
H. Larwood	5	220.2	42	644	33	5/28	19.51	2.92	40.0
T.B. Mitchell	1	21.0	5	60	3	2/49	20.00	2.85	42.0
H. Verity	4	135.0	54	271	11	5/33	24.63	2.00	73.6
W. Voce	4	133.3	24	407	15	4/110	27.13	3.04	53.4
G.O.B. Allen	5	171.0	29	593	21	4/50	28.23	3.46	48.8
W.R. Hammond	5	120.5	27	291	9	3/21	32.33	2.40	80.5
W.E. Bowes	1	23.0	2	70	1	1/50	70.00	3.04	138.0
R.E.S. Wyatt	5	2.0	0	12	0	-	-	6.00	-

TEST MATCH AVERAGES: AUSTRALIA

Batting

Player	Mat	Inns	NO	Runs	HS	Ave	SR	100	50
D.G. Bradman	4	8	1	396	103*	56.57	74.85	1	3
S.J. McCabe	5	10	1	385	187*	42.77	59.50	1	1
L.S. Darling	2	4	0	148	85	37.00	60.90	0	1
W.M. Woodfull	5	10	1	305	73*	33.88	30.68	0	3
P.K. Lee	1	2	0	57	42	28.50	87.69	0	0
V.Y. Richardson	5	10	0	279	83	27.90	46.73	0	1
W.A.S. Oldfield	4	7	2	136	52	27.20	39.88	0	1
J.H.W. Fingleton	3	6	0	150	83	25.00	32.96	0	1
W.H. Ponsford	3	6	0	141	85	23.50	39.60	0	1
L.P.J. O'Brien	2	4	0	87	61	21.75	51.78	0	1
L.E. Nagel	1	2	1	21	21*	21.00	35.00	0	0
H.H. Alexander	1	2	1	17	17*	17.00	94.44	0	0
E.H. Bromley	1	2	0	33	26	16.50	40.24	0	0
A.F. Kippax	1	2	0	27	19	13.50	43.54	0	0
C.V. Grimmett	3	6	0	42	19	7.00	44.21	0	0
W.J. O'Reilly	5	10	0	61	19	6.10	59.80	0	0
T.W. Wall	4	8	1	42	20	6.00	33.87	0	0
H.S.B. Love	1	2	0	8	5	4.00	21.05	0	0
H. Ironmonger	4	8	3	13	8	2.60	44.82	0	0

Bowling

Player	Mat	Overs	Mdns	Runs	Wkts	BB	Ave	Econ	SR
T.W. Wall	4	170.1	33	409	16	5/72	25.56	2.40	63.8
W.J. O'Reilly	5	383.4	144	724	27	5/63	26.81	1.88	85.2
H. Ironmonger	4	245.1	96	405	15	4/26	27.00	1.65	98.0
P.K. Lee	1	52.4	14	163	4	4/111	40.75	3.09	79.0
D.G. Bradman	4	12.0	1	44	1	1/23	44.00	3.66	72.0
L.E. Nagel	1	43.4	9	110	2	2/110	55.00	2.51	131.0
C.V. Grimmett	3	147.0	41	326	5	2/94	65.20	2.21	176.4
S.J. McCabe	5	92.5	17	215	3	2/40	71.66	2.31	185.6
H.H. Alexander	1	46.0	3	154	1	1/129	154.00	3.34	276.0
E.H. Bromley	1	10.0	4	19	0	-	-	1.90	
-L.S. Darling	2	11.0	5	14	0	-	-	1.27	-
A.F. Kippax	1	2.0	1	3	0	-	-	1.50	-

BIBLIOGRAPHY

Ames, L., *Close of Play*, 1953
Andrews, B., *The Hand that Bowled Bradman*, 1973
Arlott, J., *The Great Ones*, (ed.), 1967
The Great Bowlers, 1968
Fred: Portrait of a Fast Bowler, 1978
Jack Hobbs, 1981
A Word from Arlott, (selected by David Rayvern Allen), 1983
Arlott on Cricket, (selected by David Rayvern Allen), 1984
Another Word from Arlott, (selected by David Rayvern Allen), 1985
Arlott in Conversation with Mike Brearley, 1986
The Essential John Arlott, 1989
Basingstoke Boy, 1990
Arnold, P., *The Illustrated Encyclopaedia of World Cricket*, 1987/1990
Bailey, T., and Trueman, F., *From Larwood to Lillee*, 1983
Batchelor, D., *The Match I Remember*, 1950
Bearshaw, B., *From the Stretford End: The Official History of Lancashire CCC*, 1990
Birley, D., *The Willow Wand*, 1982
A Social History of English Cricket, 1999
Blaxland, G., *J.H. Thomas: A Life for Unity*, 1965
Blunden, E., *Cricket Country*, 1944
Bradman, D., *My Cricketing Life*, 1938
Farewell to Cricket, 1950/1988
The Art of Cricket, 1958
The Bradman Albums, 2 vols, 1987
Brendon, P., *The Dark Valley: A Panorama of the 1930s*, 2000
Briggs, S., *Stiff Upper Lips and Baggy Green Caps: A Sledger's History of the Ashes*, 2006
Bose, M., *Keith Miller*, 1979
A History of Indian Cricket, 1990
Browne, F., *Some of it was Cricket*, 1979
Bromby, R. (ed.), *A Century of Ashes*, 1982
Buchanan, H. (ed.), *Great Cricket Matches*, 1962
Boycott, G., *The Best XI*, 2008
Bowes, B., *Express Deliveries*, 1958
Brodribb, G., *Maurice Tate*, 1976
Next Man In: A Survey of Cricket Laws and Customs, 1985
Cannadine, D., *Class in Britain*, 1998
Cardus, N., *Days in the Sun*, 1924
The Summer Game, 1929
Good Days, 1934
Close of Play, 1956
The Playfair Cardus, 1963
Play Resumed with Cardus, 1979
Cardus on the Ashes, 1989
The Wisden Papers (ed. Green, B.), 1989
Carew, D., *To the Wicket*, 1946
Cary, C., *Cricket Controversy*, 1948
Carr, A.W., *Cricket with the Lid Off*, 1935
Cockburn, C., *The Devil's Decade*, 1973
Constantine, L., *Cricket and I*, 1931
Cricket in the Sun, 1946
Corbett, T., and King, J., *The Wisden Book of Test Captains*, 1990
Crook, F., *Talking Cricket*, 1989
Derriman, P., *Bodyline (illustrated)*, 1984
Bodyline: The Cricket 'War' between England and Australia, 1986
Our Don Bradman, 1987
Docker, E.W., *Bradman and the Bodyline*, 1978
Douglas, C., *Douglas Jardine, Spartan Cricketer*, 1984/2003
Downer, S., *100 Not Out: A Century of Cricket on the Adelaide Oval*, 1972
Eagar, P., and Arlott, J., *An Eye for Cricket*, 1979
Engel, M. *The Guardian Book of Cricket*, (ed.), 1986
Tickle the Public: One Hundred Years of the

BIBLIOGRAPHY

Popular Press, 1996
Fahey, M., and Coward, M., *The Baggy Green: The Pride, Passion and History of Australia's Sporting Icon*, 2008
Ferguson, W.H., *Mr Cricket*, 1960
Fiddian, M., *Ponsford and Woodfull*, 1988
Fingleton, J., *Cricket Crisis: Bodyline and Other Lines*, 1946
Brightly Fades the Don, 1949
Brown and Company: The Tour in Australia, 1951
Masters of Cricket, 1958
Fingleton on Cricket, 1972
The Immortal Victor Trumper, 1978
Batting from Memory, 1981
FitzSimons, P., *Everyone and Phar Lap*, 1999
Foot, D., *Wally Hammond: The Reasons Why*, 1998
Forsyth, C., *Pitched Battles: The History of the Australia–England Cricket Wars*, 1977
Frindall, B., *The Wisden Book of Test Cricket*, 1876/77–1977/78
Frith, D., *The Fast Men*, 1975/1982
Australia versus England: An Illustrated History of every Test Match since 1877, 1981/2007
Archie Jackson: The Keats of Cricket, 1987
Bodyline Autopsy, 2002
Inside Story: Unlocking Australian Cricket's Archives, with Gideon Haigh, 2008
Geddes, M., *Remembering Bradman*, 2002
Gibson, A., *The Cricket Captains of England*, 1979
Glynn, I., and Glynn, J., *The Life and Death of Smallpox*, 2004
Green, B., *The Lord's Companion*, 1987
The Wisden Papers, 1989
Gregory, K. *In Celebration of Cricket*, (ed.), 1978
From Grace to Botham: Fifty Master Cricketers from The Times, (ed.), 1989
Gordon, Sir H., *Background of Cricket*, 1938
Griffin, A.R., *The Nottinghamshire Coalfield 1881–1981*, 1981
Growden, G., *Jack Fingleton: The Man who Stood Up to Bradman*, 2008
Harte, C., *The History of Australian Cricket*, 1993
Haigh, G., *Australian Cricket Anecdotes*, (ed.), 1996
The Summer Game: Australia in Test Cricket 1949–71, 1997
Mystery Spinner: The Story of Jack Iverson, 1999
Endless Summer: 140 Years of Australian Cricket in Wisden, (ed.), 2002
Inside Story: Unlocking Australian Cricket's Archives, with David Frith, 2008
Hammond, W., *Cricket My Destiny*, 1946
Cricket My World, 1947
Cricketers' School, 1950
Harris, B., *Jardine Justified*, 1933
Haynes, B., and Lucas, J., *The Trent Bridge Battery: The Story of the Sporting Gunns*, 1985
Hayter, P., *Great Tests Recalled*, 1990
Hayter, R. (ed.), *The Best of the Cricketer 1921–1981*, 1981
Hele, G., and Whitington, R., *Bodyline Umpire*, 1974
Hobbs, J., *The Fight for the Ashes, 1932–33*, 1933
Holmes, B., and Marks V., *My Greatest Game*, 1987
Holmes, E.R.T., *Flannelled Foolishness*, 1957
Hoult, N. (ed.), *The Daily Telegraph Book of Cricket*, 2007
Howat, G., *Plum Warner*, 1987
Cricket's Second Golden Age: The Hammond–Bradman Years, 1989
Hughes, M., *All on a Summer's Day*, 1953
Hutchins, B., *Don Bradman: Challenging the Myth*, 2002
Hutton, L., *Cricket is My Life*, 1956
James, C.L.R., *Beyond a Boundary*, 1963
Cricket, 1986
Jardine, D.R., *In Quest of the Ashes*, 1933
Cricket, 1936
Keneally, T., Adam-Smith, P., and Davidson, R., *Australia: Beyond the Dreamtime*, 1987
Kilburn, J.M., *Yorkshire*, 1950
Kippax, A., *Anti-Bodyline*, 1933
Knightly, P., *Australia: Biography of a Nation*, 2000

Larwood, H., *Bodyline?*, 1933
Larwood, H., and Perkins, K., *The Larwood Story*, 1965/1995
Le Quesne, L., *The Bodyline Controversy*, 1983
Ledbetter, J., 100 *Nottinghamshire County Cricket Club Greats*, 2003
Lee, F., *Cricket, Lovely Cricket*, 1960
Lemmon, D., *The Great Wicketkeepers*, 1984
Percy Chapman, 1985
For the Love of the Game, 1993
Lewis, T., *Double Century: The Story of MCC and Cricket*, 1987
Lillee, D., *The Art of Fast Bowling*, 1978
Lindsay, P., *Cricketing Lives: Don Bradman*, 1951
Lindwall, R., *Flying Stumps*, 1954
Lucas, E.V., *100 Years of Trent Bridge*, 1938
McDevitt, P.F., *May the Best Man Win: Sport, Masculinity and Nationalism in Great Britain and Empire 1880–1935*, 2004
McGilvray, A., *The Game is Not the Same*, 1985
The Game Goes On, 1987

Magee, B., and Milligan, M., *On Blindness*, 1995
Marshall, M., *Gentlemen and Players: Conversations with Cricketers*, 1987
Mason, R., *Jack Hobbs*, 1960
Walter Hammond, 1962
Plum Warner's Last Season, 1970
Warwick Armstrong's Australians, 1971
Ashes in the Mouth: The Story of the Bodyline Tour 1932–33, 1982
Mailey, A., *And Then Came Larwood*, 1933
10 for 66 and All That, 1959
Major, J., *The Autobiography*, 1999
Martin-Jenkins, C., *Cricket – A Way of Life: The Cricketer Illustrated History of Cricket*, 1984
Mant, G., *A Cuckoo in the Bodyline Nest*, 1992
Marchant, J., *The Greatest Test Match*, 1953
Maxwell, J. (ed.), *The ABC Cricket Book: The First 60 Years*, 1994
Medlicott, W.N., *British Foreign Policy Since Versailles*, 1952
Melford, M., *Pick of the Cricketer*, (ed.), 1967
Fresh Pick of the Cricketer, (ed.), 1969
Menzies, R., *Afternoon Light*, 1967
The Measure of the Years, 1970
Midwinter, E., *The Illustrated History of County Cricket*, 1992
Lives in Cricket: George Duckworth, 2007
Miller, K., *Cricket Caravan*, 1950
Cricket Crossfire, 1956
Moorhouse, G., *Lord's*, 1983
Morgan, A., *J. Ramsay MacDonald*, 1987
Moyes, A.G., *Bradman*, 1948
Mullins, P., and Derriman, P., (eds.), *Bat and Pad: Writings on Australian Cricket 1804–1984*, 1984
Murphy, P., *Tiger Smith*, 1981
Nandy, A., *The Tao of Cricket*, 2007
O'Reilly, B. and Egan, J., *The Bradman Era*, 1984
Tiger O'Reilly, 1984
Oldfield, B., *Behind the Stumps*, 1938
The Rattle of the Stumps, 1954
Page, M., *Bradman: The Illustrated Biography*, 1983
Parkinson, M., *On Cricket*, 2002
Parky, 2008
Paynter, E., *Cricket All the Way*, 1962
Peebles, I., *Talking of Cricket*, 1953
Batter's Castle, 1958
Straight from the Shoulder, 1969
Spinner's Yarn, 1977
Peel, M., *The Last Roman: Colin Cowdrey*, 1999
Peskett, R., *The Best of Cricket*, 1982
Perry, R., *Bradman's Best*, 2001
Bradman's Best Ashes Teams, 2002
Keith Miller, 2005
Philpott, P., *A Spinner's Yarn*, 1990
Pollard, J. (ed.), *Six and Out: The Legends of Australian and New Zealand Cricket*, 1967
Pugh, M., *We Danced All Night: A Social History of Britain between the Wars*, 2008
Rae, S., *It's Not Cricket: A History of Skulduggery, Sharp Practice and Downright Cheating in the Noble Game*, 2001
Rayvern Allen, D., *Arlott*, 1994
Reddick, T., *Never a Cross Bat*, 1979
Reynolds, P.A. *British Foreign Policy in the Inter-War Years*, 1954
Rice, J., *The Presidents of the MCC*, 2006
Richardson, V.Y., *The Vic Richardson Story*, 1967
Rijks, M., *The Eccentric Entrepreneur: Sir Julien Cahn*, 2008
Roberts, E.L., *Cricket in England: 1894–1939*, 1946
Robertson-Glasgow, R.C., *The Brighter Side of Cricket*, 1933
Cricket Prints, 1943
More Cricket Prints, 1948
46 Not Out, 1948
Robinson, R., *Between Wickets*, 1948
From the Boundary, 1951
The Wildest Tests, 1972
On Top Down Under, 1975
After Stumps Were Drawn (selected by Jack Pollard), 1985
Root, F., *A Cricket Pro's Lot*, 1937
Rosenwater, I., *Sir Donald Bradman*, 1978
Ross, A., *The Cricketer Companion*, (ed.), 1960
Green Fading into Blue, 1999
Ryder, R., *Cricket Calling*, 1995
Shawcroft, J., *Local Heroes: The Story of the Derbyshire Team which Won the County Championship*, 2006
Shillinglaw, A. L., *Bradman Revisited: The Legacy of Sir Donald Bradman*, 2003
Sissons, R., *The Players*, 1988
Sissons, R., and Stoddart, B., *Cricket and Empire: The 1932–33 Bodyline Tour of Australia*, 1984
Smith, R.L., *Harold Larwood*, 2006
Steen, R., *The New Ball, Vol. One: England v Australia*, (ed.), 1998
This Sporting Life, 1999
Streeton, R., *P.G.H. Fender*, 1981
Sutcliffe, H., *For England and Yorkshire*, 1935
Swanton, E.W., *Best Cricket Stories*, 1963
Barclay's World of Cricket, with John Woodcock and various authors, 1966/1986
Gubby Allen: Man of Cricket, 1985
Symons, J., *The General Strike*, 1957
Synge, A., *Sins of Omission: The Story of the Test Selectors 1899–1990*, 1990

BIBLIOGRAPHY

Taylor, A.J.P., *English History 1914–1945*, 1965
Tebbutt, G., *With the 1930 Australians*, 1931
Thomas, J.H., *My Story*, 1938
Todd, E., *Harold Larwood: A Brief Biography*, 2008
Travers, B., *94 Declared: Cricket Reminiscences*, 1981
Tyson, F., *A Typhoon Called Tyson*, 1961
The Century-Makers: The Men Behind the Ashes 1877–1977, 1980
The Test Within, 1987
Valentine, B., *Cricket's Dawn that Died: The Australians in England 1938*, 1991
Various authors, *The Daily Worker Cricket Handbook*, 1949
County Champions, 1981
200 Years of Australian Cricket 1804–2004, 2004
Warner, Sir Pelham., *The Fight for the Ashes in 1930*, 1930
The Book of Cricket, 1911–1945
Cricket Between Two Wars, 1942/1946
Long Innings, 1951
Gentlemen v Players, 1953
Wheeler, P., *Bodyline: The Novel*, 1983
Whimpress, B., and Hart, N., *Adelaide Oval: Test cricket 1884–1984*, 1984
Whitington, R.S., *Keith Miller: The Golden Nugget*, 1981
Williams, C., *Bradman*, 1997
Williams, M. (ed.), *Double Century: 200 Years of Cricket in The Times*, 1985
Wilde, S., *Letting Rip*, 1994
Wilmot, R.E., *Defending the Ashes 1932–33*, 1933
Wisden Cricketers' Almanack, various editions, 1911–2002
Wisden Book of Cricketers' Lives, 1989
Woodcock, J., *The Times One Hundred Great Cricketers*, 1998
Wooldridge, I., and Dexter, E., (eds.), *International Cavaliers' World of Cricket*, 1970
Wright, G., *Wisden on Bradman*, 1998
Wyatt, R.E.S., *Three Straight Sticks*, 1951
Wynne-Thomas, P., *Trent Bridge: A History of the Ground to Commemorate the 150th Anniversary (1838–1988)*, 1987
Who's Who of Cricketers, with Philip Bailey and Philip Thorn, 1985
Harold Larwood: His Record Innings-by-Innings, 1989
The History of Nottinghamshire CCC, 1992
Zurbrzycki, J., *Immigrants in Australia. A Demographic Survey Based on the 1954 Census*, 1955

Print media

Nottingham Evening Post, Nottingham Evening News, Nottingham Guardian, Nottingham Football Post, Notts Free Press, Nottingham Topic, Nottingham Sport, The Newark Advertiser, The Mansfield Chronicle and Echo, The Times, The (Manchester) Guardian, The Daily Telegraph, The Daily Express, The Independent, The London Evening Standard, The London Evening News, The Sunday Times, The Observer, The Independent on Sunday, The Sunday Telegraph, The Sunday Express, The Sun, The Daily Mirror, The Sunday Dispatch, The Daily Herald, Reynold's News, The News of the World, The Sunday Mirror, The Daily Worker, The Daily Mail, The Mail on Sunday, The Daily Star, The Weekly News, The Derby Evening Telegraph, The Yorkshire Post, The Yorkshire Evening Post, The Derbyshire Times, The Manchester Evening News, The Blackpool Gazette, The Northampton Chronicle and Echo, The Cricketer, The Wisden Cricketer, Playfair Cricket Monthly, Australian Women's Weekly, Brisbane Courier Mail, The Sydney Morning Herald, Sydney Referee, The Melbourne Age, The Melbourne Argus, The Melbourne Herald, The Australian, The Australasian, Smith's Weekly, Adelaide Advertiser.

Television, film and radio

Bodyline: The Documentary (BBC); *Bodyline, It's Just Not Cricket* (ABC); *The Australian Cricket Archives 1905–1961* (ABC); *Bradman: Reflections on a Legend* (ABC); *Fast and Furious (Yorkshire Television)*; *Memorial Service for Harold Larwood* (family DVD); *90th Birthday Party for Harold Larwood* (family DVD); *Packer and Poms* (BBC); *Larwood 1957* (BBC); *Golden Greats of Cricket* (Benson and Hedges); *20th Century Cricket* (Classic Pictures); *News programmes 1977 to 1980* (BBC, ITN, ABC); *News programmes 1994 to 1995* (Central TV, BBC, ITN, ABC, Channel 9); *Nottinghamshire* (Pathé News); *Larwood 1930 and 1934* (BBC); *The Poms Down Under 1932–33* (BBC); *Don Bradman Recalls (ABC)*; *The Bradman Tapes* (ABC); *Cricket, the Golden Age* (BBC); *Interviews with Harold Larwood and Bill Voce* (BBC Radio Nottingham – various years); *Talking Cricket – Sydney and Trent Bridge* (BBC World Service); *Bodyline* (ABC).

INDEX

Numbers in **bold** refer to pages with illustrations.

INDEX

INDEX

INDEX

PICTURE ACKNOWLEDGEMENTS

The publishers are grateful to the following sources for permission to reproduce images:

The Larwood family/The Bradman Museum of Cricket, Bowral*: 1, 4, 19, 20, 25, 28, 35, 40, 45, 50, 51, 52, 55, 61, 65, 73, 76, 83, 85, 86, 89, 94, 100, 101 (top left), 101 (top right), 102, 103, 104, 105 (bottom left), 105 (bottom right), 106, 107 (bottom left), 107 (bottom right), 112, 117, 119, 121, 133, 135, 137, 139, 143, 145, 147, 150, 153, 159, 168, 171, 173, 175, 190, 203, 228 (top left), 228 (top right), 243, 247, 249, 257, 261, 271, 273, 279, 282, 289, 294, 300, 301, 303, 313, 314, 315, 317, 325, 327, 330, 335, 340, 342, 349, 355, 388

Patrick Eagar: 11, 309

David Frith: 163

Duncan Hamilton: 363

Getty Images: iv, viii–ix, 7, 54, 68, 74, 111, 125, 136, 155, 169, 177, 183, 198, 199, 217, 220, 225, 234, 264, 297, 344–5

Nottinghamshire County Cricket Club: 30, 211

* These images come from Harold Larwood's private collection. After his death in 1995, the Larwood family passed them to the Bradman Museum of Cricket, Bowral, on permanent loan.

ROOT
HOBBS
PARKER
SUTCLIFFE
HENDREN
KILNER
WOOLLEY
MACAULAY
TATE
ENGLAND
V
AUSTRALIA
THIRD TEST MATCH
LEEDS.
July 10. 12 & 13. 1926.
STRUDWICK
LARWOOD
J Webb Douglas Studio, Nottm.